IMPERIAL ECLIPSE

Studies of the Weatherhead East Asian Institute, Columbia University

The Studies of the Weatherhead East Asian Institute of Columbia University were inaugurated in 1962 to bring to a wider public the results of significant new research on modern and contemporary East Asia.

IMPERIAL ECLIPSE

Japan's Strategic Thinking about Continental Asia before August 1945

Yukiko Koshiro

CORNELL UNIVERSITY PRESS ITHACA AND LONDON

First published 2013 by Cornell University Press
Printed in the United States of America

Library of Congress Cataloging-in-Publication Data

Koshiro, Yukiko.
Imperial eclipse : Japan's strategic thinking about continental Asia before August 1945 / Yukiko Koshiro.
p. cm.
Includes bibliographical references and index.
ISBN 978-0-8014-5180-5 (cloth : alk. paper)
1. Japan—Foreign relations—Asia. 2. Asia—Foreign relations—Japan. 3. Japan—Foreign relations—1912–1945. 4. World War, 1939–1945—Japan. I. Title.
DS33.4.J3K67 2013
327.520509'041—dc23 2012039751

Cornell University Press strives to use environmentally responsible suppliers and materials to the fullest extent possible in the publishing of its books. Such materials include vegetable-based, low-VOC inks and acid-free papers that are recycled, totally chlorine-free, or partly composed of nonwood fibers. For further information, visit our website at www.cornellpress.cornell.edu.

Cloth printing 10 9 8 7 6 5 4 3 2 1

Contents

Maps and Tables

Maps

Tables

Acknowledgments

The suburbs of Yokohoma in the 1960s betrayed hardly any trace of Japan's Eurasian-Pacific War. Just two decades after surrender, the war was already a distant event of the past, and we children had little desire to feel any connection. Japanese society did not encourage us to do so either, other than imparting the rather powerful moral lesson that war, a very general and abstract concept lacking historical specificity, meant only killing and destruction and as such was inherently wrong. None of the adults around me who lived through the war—my immediate family, relatives, neighbors, and even teachers—talked about Japan's war at all, much less recounted their opinions and memories of it.

The rare exceptions proved the rule. Every year at our New Year's family reunion, my grandmother would reminisce about the massive Yokohama air raid of May 29, 1945, that claimed ten thousand lives. As her house began burning, she fled with her small children and barely cheated death. She grabbed only an *ohitsu* (a wooden container for cooked rice) and a pair of hair clippers. Feeding the children was her top priority during the war and so the ohitsu was a precious item. And the clippers? When the air raid began, she happened to be trimming the hair of one of her sons. At this point in the story, she giggled wryly. Her adult children, my aunts and uncles, laughed at her blunder, too. How many times I heard this episode I can't recall: it was one of the rare occasions my grandmother or anyone else in the family talked about their experiences in Japan's war. Only much later, when my uncles and aunts were in their sixties and seventies, did they begin sharing small episodes of the war, still selectively. Along the way I learned that some maternal and paternal relatives had lived and worked in Korea and Manchuria. No one has ever been forthcoming with details.

In the last phase of the war my father was a young signal corps engineer stationed in southern Taiwan. The only thing he used to tell my sister and me about his wartime experience was that he ate bananas as often as he wanted, because no fighting ever occurred on the island. He portrayed his time in Taiwan as ridiculously carefree. We believed it. Long after his passing I learned that his unit had to remain in Taiwan for more than a year after August 1945. Things were not as simple as he had conveyed. As for my mother, she began working as a teenage substitute teacher in April 1945, and she lived with her students, who had been compulsorily evacuated to a remote mountain area. She never told us about her life there or anything whatsoever about her wartime experience. Only recently, six decades later, did she begin telling us bits and pieces of stories. We learned that in 1940 as her school's student representative, she attended the emperor's 2,600th Anniversary Ceremony held at the Kashihara Shrine in Nara. Unable to muster any enthusiasm, she lip-synched all the recitations and songs in the ceremony, she explained with a small guilty grin. Even today she does not tell us how or what she taught to her wartime students. My older relatives' stories were so limited and fragmented that I could never get a sense of the war they lived through.

In my own research, I avoided tackling Japan's war. Once I began teaching in the United States, students, American and international alike, asked me with such vehemence about Japan's Pacific War and Japanese colonialism that I realized I could no longer avoid formal study of the war. When the Enola Gay controversy in 1995 broke out, my American students wanted me to explain what the Japanese people thought of the exhibit, to relate the Japanese side of story surrounding the atomic bombs, and to confirm whether the Japanese were really fanatics prepared to fight to the last man, woman, and child. Having always emphasized that every episode in Japanese history has some logical explanation, I found myself unable to provide these students one convincing enough, due to the sheer paucity of evidence in either English or Japanese. I promised my students that I would remedy this absence and so this study began.

Serious research began in 1999 during a year at Waseda University on the Nihon Gakujutsu Shinkōkai (The Social Science Research Council) fellowship, under the sponsorship of Hirano Ken'ichirō. When Anders Stephanson of Columbia University provided the opportunity of publishing a historiographical study of Japan's war, I combed Waseda library's basements for materials for the article completed under his guidance.

A year later I returned to the United States to resume teaching. Williams College, Bates College, Colgate University, and American University all generously offered me time, space, and resources to continue this research, while allowing me to engage in fascinating discussions with not only their faculty members but also students in courses on modern Japan, US–East Asian relations, and World War II. Without the support and encouragement of Sam Crane of Williams College and Dennis Grafflin of Bates College, the early stages of this project would never have taken off. Sam Crane helped me renew my career path in the United States and accommodated my status as a resident-researcher during the second year at Williams. Offering me invaluable moral support, Dennis Grafflin went out of his way to help edit an early draft of the book-length manuscript.

Given how challenging this project proved to be, I have been fortunate to receive numerous forms of professional support and assistance. Grants from the Association for Asian Studies and the Japan Foundation allowed me to return to Japan for archival research in the summers in 2001 and 2002. Many people have offered me venues for presenting my research to audiences of different backgrounds. Bob Immerman of Columbia University hosted my talk at the East Asian Institute Brown Bag Lunch Talk and Ray Moore of Amherst College invited me to talk about my research in his class on modern Japanese history. Ronald Richardson of Boston University also invited me to present my research about Japan's wartime perceptions of white people in the lecture series sponsored by the African American studies program. Sugita Yoneyuki of Osaka University invited me to his panel at the Second International Convention of Asian Scholars (ICAS2), held in Berlin, Germany, where I benefited from interacting with European scholars and their accounts of Japan's war.

In 2006, I returned to Japan for a permanent teaching position, the first of my career. Colleagues and students at Nihon University College of International Relations, made this enormous transition a surprisingly smooth and pleasant one. I am particularly indebted to the late Konami Takashi, honorary professor of the Tokyo University of Foreign Studies, and also Watanabe Akio, honorary professor of the University of Tokyo, for making my return to the Japanese academic circle possible. Through the arrangement of Watanabe Akio, I began to test out my research by presenting my work to my new Japanese colleagues of different disciplines. My appreciation goes to Itō Takashi, organizer of Kindai Nihon Shiryō Kenkyūkai (Japanese Modern Historical Manuscripts Association), Akutsu Hiroyasu, now at Bōei Kenkyūjo (the National Institute for Defense Studies), and Fuji Kazuhiko, counselor of the Cabinet Intelligence and Research Office, Government of Japan.

In addition to research funding, Nihon University College of International Relations provided me with a travel grant in 2008 that allowed me to visit Stony Brook University and discuss the project with Michael Barnhart and his graduate students. Annual field trips to Saipan with my seminar students, partially funded by the university, have widened my perspective of the Pacific War. I thank Mr. and Mrs. Willie and Ayako Matsumoto, the tour coordinators in Saipan, for introducing us to the island's battlegrounds and for making vivid what happened there.

Writing a book is quite a different matter from conducting research. Only a dependable network of people and institutions rendering support and encouragement makes it possible. *American Historical Review* and *Diplomatic History* published preliminary versions of my research. I benefited greatly from working with their reviewers in improving the manuscripts, particularly Bruce Cumings of the University of Chicago, who gave me a new way to look at World War II in Asia. I thank the *American Historical Review* and the publisher, the University of Chicago Press, for permission to adapt my article, "Eurasian Eclipse: Japan's End Game in World War II" (109, no. 2 [April 2004]), © 2004 by the American Historical Association (all rights reserved). And I thank *Diplomatic History* and the publisher, Wiley-Blackwell, for permission to draw on my article, "Japan's World and World War II" from *Diplomatic History* 25, no. 3 (summer 2001).

Madge Huntington of Columbia University's Weatherhead East Asian Institute, whom I owe so much for fostering my first book, *Trans-Pacific Racisms*, again opened the door for me in the long path toward book publication. After Madge's retirement, Daniel Rivero took care of my manuscript for the Studies of the Weatherhead East Asian Institute. Roger Haydon of Cornell University Press saw to it, with thorough attention, that the manuscript could become a book. I sincerely thank all three of them for their unceasing support and warm enthusiasm for this project. A gracious anonymous reader for Cornell University Press pushed me with invaluable suggestions to improve the manuscript at a late stage. In particular, I humbly thank the Weatherhead East Asian Institute's anonymous reader, who read the manuscript twice and who inspired me with incisive comments to transform the manuscript into the foundation of this book. All such arrangements, I have to add, were possible thanks to the enduring support of my mentor Carol Gluck of Columbia University. Countless e-mail exchanges with her gave me new ideas and strength to move the manuscript forward. I cannot thank her enough for her support since my first days in Columbia graduate school. Finally I would like to mention Elizabeth (Liz) H. Lee, special editor and friend. I am so grateful she remained patient working with me on this very difficult project all these years, even when she must have hoped to spend more quality time with Sophie, her beloved daughter.

Writing and teaching international history for the global community is an essential task for scholars in this century. In both the United States and Japan, I had opportunities to teach courses on Japan's war not only to American and Japanese students but also to international students from more than twenty countries, from Bulgaria, China, France, Germany, India, Indonesia, Kenya, Korea, Malaysia, the Philippines, and Spain to El Salvador and Haiti. These students offered the perspectives of their countries and generations about World War II and Japan's Eurasian-Pacific War. They are a treasured source of inspiration for this book. These students make me hopeful that a new generation of people can discuss the Eurasian-Pacific War in a global language.

"Write for forty years from now. Don't write for now," I've been advised. I hope I have. And I also want to tell my family that, now, I probably understand.

A Note on Japanese, Chinese, and Korean Names

In this book, Japanese, Chinese, and Korean names are given in traditional forms—that is, the family name precedes the given name. Where a cited person has published in English or is well-known in the West, the name is given in Western order, family name last.

Archives and Manuscripts

For original Japanese titles, call numbers and, other information about specific files and documents in these series, please see notes.

DRO Diplomatic Record Office, Japanese Ministry of Foreign Affairs, Tokyo
"Miscellaneous data on the Japanese Communist Party" series
"Miscellaneous statistical data on foreign residents in Japan" series
"Miscellaneous data on Soviet politics" series
"The Greater East Asia War: intelligence gatherings" series
"The Greater East Asia War: peace operations in Sweden, Switzerland, Vatican, etc." series
"The Second European Great War: postwar management" series

LOC Library of Congress, Washington, DC
"Japanese Army and Navy Archives, 1868–1945," microfilm collection
"Japanese Rarities," microfilm collection

MAL Military Archival Library, National Institute for Defense Studies, Tokyo
Military Police Headquarters, *The Public Response to the Potsdam Proclamation, August 1945 (Top Secret)*
Rear Admiral Takagi Sokichi Papers (1945)
The Imperial General Headquarters, *Studies of Estimated Conditions in the Spring of 1946* (July 1, 1945)
The Seventeenth Area Army Staff Operations Plans Division, *The Top Secret Strategic Planning Journal (series B)* (1945)
The Seventeenth Area Army, *History of Operation Planning (the first draft)* (n.d.)

NARA National Archives and Records Administration, Washington, DC and College Park, MD
"Records of the Office of Strategic Services"

NDL National Diet Library, Tokyo
"The Pacific Association" series
"The South Manchuria Railway Company Research Department" series

Primary Sources

CCCO

Morishima Toshio, ed., *Daihon'ei Riku-gun bu, Tairiku-Mei Tairiku-Shi sōshūsei* (The Imperial General Headquarters, the Division of the Army, a comprehensive collection of the Continental Orders and the Continental Instructions), 10 vols. (Tokyo: MT Shuppan, 1994).

DCJ

Fujiwara Akira, ed., *Shiryō Nihon gendai-shi* (Documents of contemporary Japanese history), vol. 1, "Guntai-nai no hansen undō" (Antiwar movement within the Imperial Japanese Army) (Tokyo: Ōtsuki Shoten, 1980).

IDS

Chōsen Sōtoku-fu, *Dai-85-kai Teikoku Gikai setsumei shiryō* (August 1944) (The governor-general of Korea, Documents submitted to the 85th Imperial Diet Session), reprinted in Kondō Kin'ichi, ed., *Taiheiyō Senka shūmatsu-ki Chōsen no chisei* (*Chōsen kindai shiryō—Chōsen Sōtoku-fu kankei jyūyō bunsho senshū* [2]) (Politics of Korea in the last period of the Pacific War [Modern Korean documents—selected documents of the Governor-General of Korea (2)]) (Tokyo: Gannandō Shoten, 1961).

JC

Gaimu-shō, *Nihon no sentaku: Dai-Niji Sekai Taisen shūsen shiroku* (The Ministry of Foreign Affairs, ed., Japan's Choice—Historical records on the conclusion of World War II), 3 vols. (Tokyo: Yamate Shobō, 1990).

NRPP

Awaya Kentarō and Kawashima Takane, eds., *Haisen-ji zenkoku chian jōhō* (National reports on peace preservation at the time of defeat), 7 vols. (Tokyo: Nihon Tosho Center, 1994).

RJD

Sanbō Honbu, *Haisen no kiroku* (The General Staff Office, A record of Japan's defeat) (Tokyo: Hara Shobō, 1967).

SHKA

Miyata Setsuko, ed., *Chōsen-gun gaiyō-shi* (A survey history of the Chōsen Army) in *15-nen Sensō gokuhi shiryō shū*, [The collection of top secret documents on the Fifteen Years War]), vol. 15 (Tokyo: Fuji Shuppan, 1989).

SKTM

Miyata Setsuko, ed., *Chōsen shisō undō gaikyō* (A survey of the Korean thought movement) in *15-nen Sensō gokuhi shiryō shū* [The collection of top secret documents on the Fifteen Years War]), vol. 28 (Tokyo: Fuji Shuppan, 1991).

TSWJ

Daihon'ei Rikugun-bu Sensō Shidō han, *Kimitsu sensō nisshi* (The Imperial General Headquarters Army War Operations Plan Division, Top secret war journal), 2 vols. (Tokyo: Kinsei Sha, 1998).

WHS–KA

Bōei-chō Bōei-Kenkyūjo Senshi-shitsu, ed., *Senshi sōsho—Kantō-gun* (The Defense Agency, The Defense Research Institute, Military History Department, ed., War history series—the Kwantung Army), vol. 2 (Tokyo: Asagumo Shinbun Sha, 1974).

WHS–PMB, vol. 1

Bōei-chō Bōei-Kenkyūjo Senshi-shitsu, ed., *Senshi sōsho—Hondo kessen junbi*, vol. 1, *Kantō no bōei* (The Defense Agency, Defense Research Institute, Military

History Department, ed., War history series—Preparation for mainland battle, vol. 1 [Defense of Kanto]) (Tokyo: Asagumo Shinbun Sha, 1971).

WHS–PMB, vol. 2

Bōei-chō Bōei-Kenkyūjo Senshi-shitsu, ed., *Senshi sōsho—Hondo kessen junbi*, vol. 2, *Kyūshū no bōei* (The Defense Agency, Defense Research Institute, Military History Department, ed., War history series—Preparation for mainland battle, vol. 2 [Defense of Kyūshū]) (Tokyo: Asagumo Shinbun Sha, 1972).

WHS–PPW

Bōei-chō Bōei-Kenkyūjo Senshi-shitsu, ed., *Senshi sōsho—Hoku-Shi no chian sen*, vol. 2 (The Defense Agency, Defense Research Institute, Military History Department, ed., War history series—Peace Preservation War in North China), vol. 2 (Tokyo: Asagumo Shinbun Sha, 1971).

WIC

Awaya Kentarō and Chadani Sei'ichi, eds., *NiCchū Sensō tai-Chūgoku jōhō sen shiryō* (The collection of documents on the war of intelligence on China during the Sino-Japanese War), 11 vols. (Tokyo: Gendai Shiryō Shuppan, 2000).

Introduction

THE WORLD OF JAPAN'S EURASIAN-PACIFIC WAR

This book is about Japanese thinking before, during, and especially at the end of World War II, based on Japanese documents, many of which have not previously been used or explored for that purpose. All history is written backward. Since the US military occupation, Japan's defeat has been told almost entirely from the framework known as the "Pacific War" narrative, as if everyone at the end of the war knew how Japan's military losses to the United States alone would lead to its postwar recovery and reentry into the American-centered world order. This US-fostered public memory elides Japan's war in China and the fall of Japan's colonial empire, and many of the lessons of these events have been neglected in the nation's "regeneration" since August 1945. To restore the comprehensive landscape of Japan's war, which was continental before becoming Pacific, this study returns the Soviet Union to the scene and renames the conflict the Eurasian-Pacific War. It investigates the world the Japanese once possessed, fought for, and relinquished.

In envisioning its empire, prewar Japan had an intense awareness of and focus on Eurasia and reckoned with the formidable presence of Russia and then the Soviet Union as intermediaries of Western culture and communist ideology. Only toward the war's end, in seeking to secure the nation's survival, did Japanese planners begin including the United States as a factor in the changing geopolitics of the Eurasian and Pacific convergence. Under the US military occupation, the Pacific War narrative eclipsed Japan's Eurasian worldview and produced Japan's postwar amnesia about its colonial empire.

In spite of the extensive study of World War II and the Pacific War, our knowledge of the geopolitical thinking and strategy of Japan's leaders, especially in the last stage of the war, remains murky. Little has been written about how, by the fall of 1944, various members of the Japanese government and the Imperial General Headquarters had concluded that the Soviet Union would eventually enter the war against Japan. Japanese leaders knew that Moscow needed neutrality with Japan in order to devote its resources to the European front; once Germany was defeated, neutrality with Japan would become immaterial. During diplomatic negotiations with Moscow for possible peace mediation with the United States, Japanese leaders closely watched Soviet preparations for launching a war against Japan. Monitoring political factions within China and Korea and their networks with the United States and the Soviet Union, Japanese war planners concluded that the Soviet Union had significant connections with regional nationalists that could help check US hegemonic ambitions in East Asia. They hoped that Soviet presence in the region would achieve a desirable balance of power in the power vacuum created by the fall of Japan's empire.

The timing for such a strategic shift coincides with a fundamental restructuring of the command system within Japan's wartime government that took place when Japan's defeat by the United States in the Pacific seemed unavoidable. In July 1944, following the fall of Saipan, Koiso Kuniaki, then governor-general of Korea, was chosen to serve as prime minister of Japan to replace the Tōjō cabinet, which for most of World War II had governed Japan under Prime Minister Hideki Tōjō. Koiso was not a favorite choice of the Imperial Army. Neither did Emperor Hirohito, nor Kido Kōichi, lord keeper of the privy seal, prefer him due to his connection to the March Incident of 1931, the abortive coup d'état attempt by members of the Sakura-kai (Cherry Society) within the Imperial Army. With no consensus on a more suitable alternative, however, Koiso assumed the position. A token prime minister, Koiso nonetheless succeeded in establishing on August 4, 1944, the Supreme Council for the Direction of the War (Saikō Sensō Shidō Kaigi) and in securing a unified command system for facilitating decision making about war operations and strategies, allowing both the prime minister and the foreign minister to participate in deliberations by the supreme command.[1]

This was a breakthrough in wartime decision making, since previously the Imperial General Headquarters (Daihon'ei) alone had coordinated wartime efforts between the army and navy. The Imperial General Headquarters' wide scope of command prerogatives excluded the prime minister and his government from

1. In the English literature, the "Supreme Council for the Direction of the War (Saikō Sensō Shidō Kaigi)" has often been abbreviated simply as the "Supreme War Council." This is confusing since the English name "Supreme War Council" also refers to the Liaison Conference and this convention blurs significant changes in decision making. In this book, therefore, the Supreme Council for the Direction of the War appears without abbreviation.

operational and strategic planning. By November 1937, a few months after the outbreak of the Sino-Japanese War, the Imperial General Headquarters and Government Liaison Conference (Daihon'ei Seifu Renraku Kaigi) had been established within a newly structured Imperial General Headquarters with an aim of bringing the chiefs of army and navy General Staff into closer consultation with the government. Not only did facilitating agreement on strategic planning between army and navy prove difficult, the Liaison Conference also found it hard to affect military autonomy and to coordinate decisions and needs of the army and navy with the resources and policies of other government branches.

Koiso's term in office began on July 22, 1944, and coincided with multiple defeats and predicaments faced by the Japanese on all fronts. With a sense of urgency, the military leaders endorsed Koiso's proposal for the new command system and agreed to share power with representatives from the civilian branches.[2] The core members of the Supreme Council for the Direction of the War included the chief of army staff (sanbō sōchō), the chief of naval staff (gunrei-bu sōchō), the prime minister, the minister of foreign affairs, the minister of war (riku-gun daijin), and the minister of the navy (kai-gun daijin)—Japan's "Big Six," as they were known to the Allied nations. Other high-ranking officers were invited to attend as necessary. Unlike the Liaison Conference, the new council, sitting together with the emperor, would have ultimate power and as such could aim to better orchestrate political and military strategies when it set war policies. Because of this wider involvement of members of the government and the Imperial General Headquarters, Japan's new leaders began to give increasing weight to the Soviet Union as they considered how to dissolve Japan's empire.

After the war, the United States, the sole occupier of Japan, chose to diminish the significance of Eurasia in Japan's world by fostering a US-centric vision of Japan's war among the Japanese people through media and education. This process reduced Japanese war planners and their thinking to traces in the historical record. The complexity of the geopolitical, ideological, racial, and cultural dimensions of Japan's war gave way to a simplistic image of Japan's "irrational and reckless" defiance of the United States in the Pacific. Japan's capitulations to the Allied Forces in China, Manchuria, Korea, and other parts of Asia were funneled into a vision of surrender to the United States alone. The Soviet Union faded from occupied Japan's war memory. Under the US-Japanese security alliance, a myth emerged that the United States since the time of Commodore Perry had inspired and supported the Japanese people; Japan's aggression against the United States was consequently a senseless betrayal. This nurtured another postwar myth

2. Akira Iriye, *Power and Culture: The Japanese-American War, 1941–1945* (Cambridge, MA: Harvard University Press, 1981), 178.

that the Japanese were grateful that the United States had protected the nation from the Soviet Union, now understood only as a threat and not as a potential countervailing force to American hegemony.

The Tokyo War Crimes Tribunal (1946–48) reinforced the perception that Japanese wartime leaders, in chaotic disarray, were incapable of devising and pursuing coherent war goals. The characterization of these leaders as disoriented and powerless has led scholars to read Japanese actions almost exclusively in the non-Japanese context of President Truman's decision to use the atomic bombs. Their premise is that only a form of "shock therapy," either the two atomic bombs, the Soviet entry into the war against Japan, or both, could have compelled the leaders in Tokyo to surrender. In the debates over the orthodox theory (that the United States deployed the atomic bombs to end the war without invading the mainland) and the revisionist theory (that the United States used the atomic bombs to intimidate the Soviet Union and to secure advantage in leadership in postwar world), Japanese strategic thinking has been largely left out of the scholarly purview.[3] However much external forces—the shock of the atomic bombs, the Soviet entry into the war—contributed to the end of the war, they alone cannot account for Japan's ability to adapt to, or even to prosper in, the postwar world. In forming exit strategies, Japan's war planners had an eye on reorienting the country after the war.

Japanese wartime leaders erased their deliberations by destroying many wartime records. Shortly after the Japanese government decided to accept the Potsdam Proclamation, cabinet members incinerated large numbers of official documents in expectation of an impending war crimes trial, in which the United States was expected to play a leading role. On August 7, 1945, only one day after Hiroshima and one day before the Soviet entry in the war against Japan, the Japanese Ministry of Foreign Affairs decided on the expeditious destruction of classified documents related to wartime diplomacy. Coming earlier and much more swiftly than the Imperial General Headquarters' similar decision about military documents, this course of action slated for destruction a range of documents more extensive than that of the military. Diplomatic documents concerning China were the first to be destroyed; next, the Soviet papers; and finally, Axis diplomacy papers. The documents—especially diplomatic ones—that survived destruction and became widely known were those wartime leaders deemed safe and appropriate to a presumed yardstick of postwar American justice.[4] These surviving documents

---

3. For overviews of the current state of the discussion, see Tsuyoshi Hasegawa, ed., *The End of the Pacific War—Reappraisals* (Stanford, CA: Stanford University Press, 2007), and Samuel Walker, "Recent Literature on Truman's Atomic Bomb Decision," *Diplomatic History* 29, no. 2 (April 2005): 311–34.

4. Yoshida Yutaka, *Gendai rekishigaku to sensō sekinin* (Contemporary history studies and Japan's war responsibilities) (Tokyo: Aoki Shoten, 1997): 127–34; Usui Katsumi, Yoshimura Michio, and

validated "correct" narratives of the war by affirming that Japanese leaders were uninformed, disorganized, and even irrational in their resolve to fight until the last soldier.

While there is no knowing how many wartime documents on strategic planning for postdefeat survival were destroyed, considerable evidence of such planning remains preserved in little-known documents of the government, the military, the Ministry of Foreign Affairs, and a number of colonial agents, long excluded from the standard list of official sources on Japan's war. Geopolitical analyses conducted in the effort to chart a survival strategy can be found in archival documents marked "Top secret" or "Confidential." They have also been catalogued under innocuous subjects such as "communism," "intelligence," the "war in Europe," and the "Chōsen Army (Chōsen-gun)" at the archives of the Japanese Ministry of Foreign Affairs and the National Institute for Defense Studies, Tokyo. These documents quietly but firmly show that the Japanese government and military harbored no hope that Moscow would remain neutral. Unlike postwar retrospective accounts that vilify the Soviet Union for its "surprise attack" on August 8, 1945, the documents reveal that the Japanese not only anticipated that attack but calculated its probable impact on East Asia.

The records of the Supreme Council for the Direction of the War reveal regular discussions about the Soviet entry into the war. The Supreme Council for the Direction of the War, otherwise known as the "inner cabinet," met at the Imperial Palace and played a distinctive role in unifying military strategy and diplomacy. It consistently evaluated the significance of the Soviet factor in Japan's war. Meetings usually involved reviewing drafts of diplomatic and military strategies as well as comprehensive reports evaluating and predicting war conditions.[5] When discussing crucial issues, the Supreme Council for the Direction of the War requested Emperor Hirohito's attendance and, in his presence, it met as the Imperial Conference (Gozen Kaigi). The council's records indicate that by June 1945 even Emperor Hirohito had learned that the Soviet Union would most likely soon enter the war against Japan, because Japan had no means to prevent it.[6]

The strategic assumption that the Soviets would enter the war permeated the Continental Orders (Tairiku-Mei), a series of highest-level military orders issued in the name of the emperor directly to the Imperial Army, as well as the Continental

---

Hosoya Chihiro, *Gaikō Shiryō-kan no nijū-nen to shōrai (zadankai)* ([Roundtable] The past and future of the Diplomatic Record Office of the Ministry of Foreign Affairs), in *Gaikō Shiryō Kanpō* (the Diplomatic Record Office Newsletter), vol. 5 (Tokyo: 1992): 43–45.

5. Robert Butow, *Japan's Decision to Surrender* (Stanford, CA: Stanford University Press, 1954), 16 and 81–82.

6. "Kongo torubeki sensō shidō no kihon taikō ni kanshi Gozen Kaigi keika gaiyō" (Summary report of the Imperial Conference concerning the basic instruction on the war), in RJD, 263 and 272–273.

Instructions (Tairiku-Shi), specific instructions issued by the chief of army staff regarding the execution of Continental Orders.[7] From 1937 through the war's end in August 1945, the Imperial General Headquarters (and after August 1944 the Supreme Council for the Direction of the War, to be specific) issued 1,392 such orders. Top leaders including Umezu Yoshijirō, Itagaki Seishirō, Prince Higashikuni, Doihara Kenji, Yamada Otomi (of the Kwantung Army), Hata Shunroku, and Sugiyama Gen cosigned these imperial orders. Soviet-related orders reveal that military plans covering battlefields from Korea and China to Manchuria anticipated the eventual Soviet entry into the war in Asia.[8] More significantly these orders instructed the Japanese military not to launch all-out counteroffensives but rather to take up passive defenses against Soviet assaults.

Some of the same strategic principles were also manifest in *Kimitsu sensō nisshi* (Top secret war journal), one of the most comprehensive classified documents produced at the Imperial General Headquarters. The Army War Operations Plans Division of the Imperial General Headquarters recorded its day-to-day activities and planning in a handwritten journal, which had long been hidden by its keepers in obscure locations. This allowed it to escape confiscation by the US occupation government. Today it offers insight into how staff officers viewed the Soviet Union vis-à-vis the United States in the period between June 1940 and July 1945.[9] This journal sometimes has been deemed insignificant because its keepers arbitrarily injected their personal opinions and also because the Army War Operations Plans Division allegedly had limited access to critical information on the war's progress.[10] Such criticism needs to be reevaluated since the Army War Operations Plans Division's strategies are congruent with the Continental Orders and the Continental Instructions in establishing the Soviet entry into the war against Japan as a trigger for further action. Evidence of Japan's Soviet strategy lies in these top-level military documents.

---

7. The original minutes of the Supreme Council for the Direction of the War have been available in print in Japanese since 1967 and should be investigated for what they might reveal about Japan's war planning. For this record, see RJD.

8. For this ten-volume compilation of all orders in print, see CCCO.

9. The entire document is now available in published form: TSWJ.

10. TSWJ, vol. 1, vii–xiv. This two-volume record should not be confused with *Daihon'ei kinitsu nisshi* (The Imperial General Headquarters secret journal), published in 1952 by Colonel Tanemura Sakō, a central member of the Army War Operations Plans Division since December 1939. Based on his own personal diary he kept during the war, Tanemura brought to light daily activities within the Imperial General Headquarters on the eve of a birth of independent Japan, a decision hailed by Shigemitsu Mamoru, wartime foreign minister (1–4). In contrast to Tanemura's book, or memoir, which is imbued with his opinions and also marred by his postwar hindsight, this two-volume record is the official business log of the Army War Operations Plans Division. Tanemura Sakō, *Daihon'ei kinitsu nisshi* (The Imperial General Headquarters secret journal) (Tokyo: Daiyamondo Sha, 1952).

Wartime popular journals and newspapers reveal that government censorship did not necessarily quell open discussions of how Japan should best cope with the progress of various aspects of the Eurasian-Pacific War in rapidly changing international conditions. Memoirs published after the war and collections of handpicked documents from Japan's war require careful scrutiny about whether they exclude, re-create, or invent the facts. During the war the Japanese public was better informed of the intricacies of world politics than conventionally believed. They read daily newspaper coverage of China's civil war as well as of discord among the Allies, particularly between Washington and Moscow, and mulled over the manner of Japan's survival in the reconstruction of a postwar world flanked by the United States and the Soviet Union. For the Japanese people, the "conclusion" of Japan's war was never about a resolution as simple as "ichioku gyokusai" (honorary deaths of 100 million imperial subjects)—a fanatic slogan soliciting national suicide in the event of an American invasion of Japanese mainland. Herein lies one of the core arguments of the book: war cannot only be understood exclusively as a phenomenon of elites who are responsible for policymaking. The opinions and experiences of ordinary Japanese people as well as elites during this war demonstrate the excising of considerations about how the war would be concluded from the orthodox accounts of the Pacific conflict between the United States and Japan.

Japan's war must be placed in the context of the rise and fall of the Japanese colonial empire. Initially, Western powers endorsed and celebrated Japan's rise to imperial power. After entering the Western-centered world order in the late nineteenth century bound by the unequal treaty system, Japan had to prove that it had the aptitude to be an imperialist power, a prerequisite for a modern and industrialized state. The United States and Britain, two leading Western powers with stakes in the Pacific and China respectively, interpreted Japan's victories in the Sino-Japanese War of 1894–95 and the Russo-Japanese War of 1904–5 as proof of Japan's successful modernization, not as the beginning of Japan's overseas aggression. They moved to abolish the unequal treaties with Japan and recognized Japan as the first and only Westernized (modernized) nation in Asia. Japan subsequently acquired Taiwan in the Treaty of Shimonoseki and the southern half of Sakhalin in the Treaty of Portsmouth, the latter mediated by US president Theodore Roosevelt. Following the tenets of international law, China, Russia, and the United States recognized Japan's acquisition of Korea as its colony. After World War I, the League of Nations awarded Japan the mandate to administer German colonies in the southern Pacific—the Caroline, Mariana, and Marshall islands.

Japan's territorial expansion did not bring equal status with the Anglo-American powers. Conflicts with the United States over immigration laws and the failure to incorporate a racial equality clause in the preamble to the Covenant of the League of Nations led Japan's leaders to realize that because of racism it could not fit into the legal and cultural norms of the Anglo-American-centered world. Japan's unilateralism and military aggression were attempts to defy Anglo-American supremacy. This misguided pride led Japan to force on other Asian peoples Japanese-style modernization and rule. Japan's ostensible goal was cultural and racial: to remove the Anglo-American influence from Asia and to restore Asia for the Asians. Japan, like its Western rivals, had no intention of recognizing the sovereignty and self-rule of other Asians. Japan found itself increasingly isolated from both the West and Asia.

The road to ruin began with the Manchurian Incident in 1931, which alienated Japan from the League of Nations. The state of Manchukuo was meant to secure for Japan "Lebensraum": additional territory to protect and further Japanese interests in China, to buffer against the military and communist threat of the Soviet Union, and to procure sufficient resources for the Japanese military in the event of war against the United States. After a brief cease-fire following the Tanggu Truce with Chiang Kai-shek's Guomindang (GMD) regime in 1933, full-scale war eventually broke out in July 1937. Japan's attack on the Nationalists expanded into a separate campaign against guerrilla forces led by Mao Zedong's Chinese Communist Party (CCP). Meanwhile Japan's withdrawal from the League of Nations drew the nation into a new alliance with Germany. The Tripartite Pact of September 1940 effectively integrated Japan's efforts to build a Greater East Asia Coprosperity Sphere with World War II in Europe. When Japan eyed European colonies in Southeast Asia as a source of more natural resources to invest in the war dragging on in China, German aggression in France facilitated Japan's military advance into the French colony of Indochina. Upon Britain's request, the United States demanded that Japan withdraw from French Indochina as well as China, which in turn led Japan to open another front against the United States and Britain.

Once the Pacific War began, the United States and Britain resolved to dismantle the Japanese empire. Although Japan's possession of the colonies (except for Manchukuo) was not illegal under contemporary international law, the Allied Powers now regarded Japan's rise as a colonial power as integral to Japan's war crimes against its neighbors as well as the Western nations. In the Cairo Declaration of November 1943, the United States and Britain, along with China, located the beginning of Japan's imperialist war against China in the Sino-Japanese War, between 1894 and 1895, and accordingly demanded the restoration of Taiwan and the Pescadores to Chiang Kai-shek's China. By the summer of 1944, US forces had taken all the former Japanese territories of the South Sea Mandate. In the Yalta Agreement of February 1945, the United States, Britain, and the Soviet Union agreed that the Soviet Union would recover Japan's spoils from the Russo-Japanese

War of 1904–5. The Allies did not necessarily aim to accord independence to those people whom they intended to "liberate" from Japan. After occupying Saipan and Tinian, the jewels of Japan's South Sea Mandate, the United States did not "return" the islands to the native Chamorros and Carolinians but quickly set up a military administration on the islands. Likewise the Allies considered the Koreans too politically immature for self-rule, so they pondered the next "guardian" of Korea.

The Japanese government and the Imperial General Headquarters monitored the plans of the Allies for the disposition of Japan's colonies, began to anticipate insightfully how postcolonial East Asia would emerge, and built exit strategies around them. Japanese observers studied China's civil war and the competing Korean nationalist movements, with particular attention to US and Soviet interference, and Chinese and Korean responses to them. Extensive intelligence activities began with Japan's North China Area Army, which was created after the Marco Polo Bridge Incident of 1937 from units of the Kwantung Army and soon became a law unto itself, and after December 1941 controlled Japanese Army units in north China. The North China Area Army predicted that the CCP's greater popular appeal over the GMD would lead it to emerge as the victor in this civil conflict and ultimately to unify China. They also noted Mao's growing resolve to secure China's independence from both Washington and Moscow. Japanese authorities caught early signs of a split between Chinese communists and the Soviet Union and considered their delicate rivalry conducive to creating a desirable postwar balance of power.

The Governor-General's Office in Korea had studied the various Korean nationalist movements and noticed that communists, while dominant, were still weak and manipulated by the Soviets. This assessment was shared by the Chōsen Army, a garrison force of the Imperial Japanese Army in Korea whose primary tasks were to guard the peninsula against the Soviet threats and also to suppress anti-Japanese uprisings within Korea itself. Since its commander in chief possessed power equal to that of the governor-general, the army's parallel investigation produced a penetrating analysis of political inclinations among Koreans and their links to foreign powers. In particular, the Japanese authority suspected the Soviet Union's growing ambitions for the peninsula and predicted that the peninsula would become a contested stage for US-Soviet struggle for power even before the war's end.

While they did not necessarily prefer the Soviets to the Americans as Japan's successor as the "leader of Asia," Japanese war planners understood that the Soviet Union could influence the regional settlement. Ideologically and geopolitically Japan's relationship with the Soviet Union was replete with ironies and contradictions. As a communist state, the Soviet Union's open opposition to imperialism and colonialism appealed to nationalists all over East Asia, especially those engaged in anti-Japanese and anticolonial activities. Less well known is that culturally and racially the Soviet Union was understood to possess "Asian" qualities absent in Anglo-American allies. The Eurasian Soviet Union shared borders with China and Korea and had native Asian populations. Anti-Bolshevik refugees pouring into Japan and Manchukuo brought Russian culture. In Manchukuo the government granted Russian residents the right to coexist with Japanese, Chinese, Manchu, Koreans, and Mongols under the state slogan of racial harmony.

Burdened with ambiguous goals, missions, and self-identities, Japan's war grew to be a loosely interwoven sequence of battles fought with disparate opponents and alliances in diverse geographical, ideological, and cultural landscapes. The various facets of Japanese military action in Asia and the Pacific bear diverse names, each charged with often incommensurable meaning: the "Greater East Asia War," the "Sino-Japanese War," the "Pacific War," the "Fifteen Years War," "World War II," the "US-Japanese War," the "Far Eastern War," the "Anglo-American-Japanese War," the "Soviet-Japanese War," and the latest, the "Asian-Pacific War," invented in the 1990s. The absence of a commonly agreed-on name for the war points to the nation's torn memories and allegiances and to the difficulties of achieving a comprehensive world-historical narrative of Japan's war.

The "Fifteen Years War" focuses on the long-term nature of Japan's aggression in Asia and emphasizes its tragic scale. "World War II" focuses on Japan's relations with the Axis powers and posits Japan's war in a European context. The "Pacific War" zeroes in on Japan's focus on the United States as a foe during the war and as an ally afterward. The "Sino-Japanese War" criticizes the criminality of Japan's militarism against Asian peoples and calls for Japanese reconciliation with Asia and Asianness. "Asian-Pacific War" was coined in the 1990s to reflect the multiplicity of Japan's war.[11] Yet this name still omits Japan's European front and, more importantly, fails to include the Soviet Union in such a way as to reflect its wartime diplomatic and military engagements with Japan. A better denomination for Japan's war would be the "Eurasian-Pacific War."

With the exception of the "Soviet-Japanese War" narrative that emerged in Japan only after the demise of the Soviet Union in 1991, the Soviet Union is not a key figure in most of these narratives. The elision of the Soviet Union from the memory and narrative of Japan's war conveniently facilitated the simplification of Japan's war into a one-dimensional narrative focused on a single enemy and war goal. Precisely because the Soviet Union had provided a critical nexus to the wars in Asia and the Pacific, its erasure helped sever the comprehensive whole of

11. Kisaka Jun'ichirō, "Ajia-Taiheiyō Sensō no koshō to seikaku" (The name and the character of the Asian-Pacific War), *Ryūkoku Hōgaku* (Ryukoku Law Review) 25 (March 1993): 28–76.

Japan's war into two separate pieces, each unrelated to the other. Its erasure thus obscured the geopolitical and ideological factors that sustained Japan's colonial empire.

Under the US military occupation, these dimensions of Japan's war vanished from the official history and the Japanese began living in *sengo*, a state of postwar reflection on the nation's "humbling" defeat by the United States alone. Although the Japanese government announced the end of sengo in 1956, the state of reflection continues. Even the death of Emperor Hirohito in 1989 did not end sengo. Japan's exclusive surrender to the United States never brought closure to the history of Japan's colonial empire. On the contrary, the incompleteness of the history of Japan's war has impeded this closure. The Japanese people still live with the aftermath of their war precisely because contemporary East Asia—the two Chinas and the two Koreas, for example—reflects remnants of their wartime strategic thinking. The constraint of the Pacific War narrative has led Japan to avoid reckoning with its colonial past. To move on, Japan needs first to unearth the legacy of its wartime strategic thinking and planning in the comprehensive landscapes of Eurasia and the Pacific.

Part I

THE PLACE OF RUSSIA IN PREWAR JAPAN

1

COMMUNIST IDEOLOGY AND ALLIANCE WITH THE SOVIET UNION

The Japanese government claims today that in "the history of the world it would be difficult to find two other nations who once engaged in war and have so rapidly established such a strong partnership as Japan and the United States."[1] The US government agrees, saying that after World War II Japan became an anchor of US security in East Asia and also one of its most important economic partners.[2] So strong and self-evident do these bonds appear that other strategic configurations for postwar Japan seem implausible. This chapter recovers the plausibility, among Japanese government planners and the educated public alike during the Eurasian-Pacific War, of a postwar Japan oriented toward, even allied with, its closest geographic neighbor, the Soviet Union, America's cold-war nemesis.

A handful of observers late in World War II insisted that a defeated Japan would decisively turn away from Asia and the Soviet Union toward the United States. John Emmerson, a member of the Dixie Mission (the US Army Observer Group) that met with Mao Zedong at Yan'an in 1944, asserted with no elaboration, "The Japanese fundamentally like us [Americans] more than they do the Russians."[3] With years of experience as a political attaché at the Tokyo Embassy,

1. See "Overview of Japan-U.S. Relationship (February 2009)" on the Embassy of Japan in the United States of America's homepage, available online at http://www.us.emb-japan.go.jp/english/html/japanus/japanusoverview2009.htm, accessed June 2012.

2. "Summary" in Congressional Research Service's "Japan-U.S. Relations: Issues for Congress" (September 23, 2011), RL33436, available online at http://www.fas.org/sgp/crs/row/RL33436.pdf.

3. "Secret: the Japanese Communist Party, a Memorandum from John K. Emmerson, Chungking, China, January 5, 1945," RG 226, M1642, Roll 62, Frames 46–54 [Microfilm Collection], NARA.

he was confident that Japan, once defeated, would never side with Russia again. If by "the Japanese" Emmerson meant a small exclusive group of Japanese businessmen, bankers, financiers, and traders who had had high stakes in the American market, he might have been right. In his famous memorandum of February 14, 1945, Prince Konoe Fumimaro signaled the danger of Japan's reliance on the Soviet Union to Emperor Hirohito: Moscow's ultimate interest was to turn Japan communist. The prospect of communist revolution, Konoe claimed, was ubiquitous across East Asia, from Yan'an, Manchuria, Korea, and Taiwan to Japan, and even within the Japanese Army. Emperor Hirohito should make peace with the United States before the Soviet Union joined the war against Japan in order to preclude a communist takeover of East Asia.

Emmerson and Konoe were no clairvoyants. During the war, their contentious observations represented two of many possible envisioned strategic organizations for postwar Japan. After the war, their observations became self-evident truths within the historical narrative fostered during the US occupation of Japan. The manufactured historical memory of the postwar period radically simplifies wartime Japan's complex, diverse, and nuanced relations with, and visions of, the wider world. Through the war, Japanese leadership and the broader population alike viewed Russian and the Soviet Union with respect, and even though the relationship between the two countries was well know for competition and animosity, many Japanese also hoped to cultivate cooperation with the Soviets. Failing to recognize this complexity precludes understanding the nature of Japan's Eurasian-Pacific War.

Japan and Russia first clashed over Korea and Manchuria in the Russo-Japanese War of 1904–5. In 1907 the Kwantung Army, a one-division force, was assigned to guard the South Manchuria Railway and the Liaotung Peninsula. After receiving independent status in 1920, the Kwantung Army increasingly assumed a politicized role in determining policy in Manchuria. From that point on the Kwantung Army monitored Russian and then Soviet forces across the Manchurian border.

When the Bolshevik Revolution challenged the ideological legitimacy of Japan's capitalist and colonial pursuits within the imperial system, the Japanese government joined the anti-Bolshevik war at the invitation of President Woodrow Wilson and fought in Siberia from 1918 to 1920. By the early 1930s, the Japanese government had extirpated the Japanese Communist Party and battled communists across the colonial empire while denouncing the Moscow-based Comintern for aiding and instructing them.

In realpolitik terms the Soviet Union posed a double menace of military force and ideology to the Japanese empire. Despite all this, the two neighboring countries shared a pragmatism that facilitated coexistence. In establishing diplomatic relations with the Soviet Union in 1925, Japan declared that its domestic crackdown on communism and its friendship with the Soviet Union were two separate matters. The Soviet government concurred that its amity with Japan rested on mutual respect for their respective sociopolitical systems and the principle of nonintervention in each other's domestic politics. In this spirit the Soviet embassy in Tokyo expressed uneasiness about Japanese media coverage of alleged financial ties between the Japanese Communist Party and the Soviet government, which the Japanese government identified closely with the Comintern, or the Third International.[4]

The establishment in 1932 of Manchukuo, whose northern border was set directly against Soviet territory, forced further compromises in Japan's strategy concerning the Soviet Union. After two large-scale military confrontations at Changkufeng (at the convergence of the Soviet, Korean, and Manchukuo borders) in July 1938 and Nomonhan (on the Manchukuo-Outer Mongolian border) in May 1939, in both of which the Kwantung Army suffered devastating losses, the Japanese government chose not to provoke the Soviets any further and adopted a policy of "keeping peace and status quo" (*seihitsu hoji*). Backed up by the neutrality pact, this policy remained Japan's strategic stance with the Soviet Union until the last stage of World War II.[5]

Eliminating communist influence in East Asia was Japan's self-imposed task, as manifest in the Anti-Comintern Pact with Germany that Japan concluded in November 1936. The Japanese government situated itself as a third political force that was both anticommunist and anticapitalist. It aimed to create a self-sufficient colonial empire independent of both Soviet and Anglo-American influences. Japan's parallel battles in China against both Chiang Kai-shek's nationalist regime and Mao Zedong's Chinese Communist Party (CCP) testified to its dual push against communism and capitalism. Strategically Japan could not wage a two-front war against the United States and the Soviet Union and, therefore, concluded in April 1941 the Soviet-Japanese Neutrality Pact, which became a critical precondition for the war against the United States. Amid the quagmire of war in

4. "Gokuhi: Zai-Ro Tanaka Tokichi Taishi hatsu Shidehara Gaimu Daijin ate" (Top secret: a telegram from Tanaka Tokichi, Ambassador to Russia, to Foreign Minister Shidehara) (February 1, 1930); "Nihon Kyōsan-tō jiken happyō ni taisuru Sobieto gawa no taido ni kansuru ken" (Soviet reactions to the revelation of the Japanese Communist Party incident) (November 9, 1929); all in "Nihon Kyōsan-tō kankei zakken: Kyōsan-tō to Sorenpō to no kankei" (Miscellaneous data on the Japanese Communist Party: relationship between the JCP and the Soviet Union) [I-4-5-2-3-3], DRO.

5. "Tai-Bei–Ei-Ran-Shou sensō shūmatsu sokushin ni kansuru fuku-an" (A draft proposal for expediting the end of the war against the United States, Britain, Netherlands, and Chiang's China) (November 15, 1941), in Sanbō Honbu (The Imperial General Headquarters), ed., *Sugiyama memo* (Tokyo: Hara Shobō, 1967), vol. 1, 523–24, quoted in Nakayama Takashi, "Nihon no sensō sakusen shidō ni okeru Soren yōin, 1941–45" (The Soviet factor on Japan's conduct of war and military operations in 1941–45), *Seiji Keizai Shigaku* (Journal of historical studies), no. 333 (March 1994), 43.

China, Japan allied itself with the Soviet Union. While maintaining peace and the status quo, Japanese leaders constantly evaluated probable Soviet influence on the revolutionary future of East Asia.

Within the Japanese government, differences about the Soviet-Japanese Neutrality Pact existed. Not merely an exclusive product of military and geopolitical calculations, the neutrality pact also reflected Japan's strategic goal of creating a revolutionary East Asian bloc. This inclination had its roots in wide-ranging discussions that occurred before the 1930s about Japan and communist ideas. With the outbreak of the Sino-Japanese War, a number of political and intellectual leaders sought a link between communist ideology and Japan's revolution under its East Asian new order. The Shōwa Kenkyūkai (Shōwa Research Association), an informal organization of intellectuals engaged in discussing reforms of political and economic structures in the 1930s, envisioned a new world order that included the Soviet Union as a challenge to the Anglo-American political and economic systems. Foreign Minister Matsuoka Yōsuke shared this view when he signed the neutrality pact. By tracing the historical process of how the Japanese turned to the Soviet Union as a model and ally, this chapter demonstrates how the years 1938–40 became a watershed in Japan's relations with the Soviet Union that led to the 1941 Neutrality Pact.

Allures of Utopia

Like their leaders, everyday Japanese had a spectrum of nuanced views about the Soviet Union and the Russians. Many people, especially those in radical antigovernment, anti-imperialistic movements, long had been inspired by their Eurasian neighbor. Some even engaged directly with Moscow. Their activities made Japan's relationship with the Soviet Union all the more multifaceted and protean.

The Japanese people's modern search for a utopian society began when the Meiji government launched an oppressive national project of industrialization and imperialism in the late nineteenth century. Members of antigovernment movements looked to model societies outside Japan. The Japanese looked to the revolutionary experiences of both America and Russia (and later the Soviet Union). To ask whether Japanese people had historically preferred the United States over Russia (or the Soviet Union) or vice versa is misleading. In envisioning changes suited to Japanese society, Japanese freely synthesized the two nations' traditions as they saw fit. In this process, Japan became the junction of trans-Siberian and trans-Pacific routes on a global circuit of radical thoughts and movements.

The "opening" of Japan has been celebrated as the achievement of American Commodore Matthew Perry.[6] As George Samson argues, however, "American and English historians sometime overlook the important part played by Russia in bringing about the opening of Japan."[7] Japan and Russia's history of interactions dates back to the seventeenth century.[8] The Eurasian empire situated across the Sea of Okhotsk and the Sea of Japan, Russia was long the closest geographic and cultural Western nation to Japan. After the Russian empire reached the Pacific Ocean in 1638, Russian explorers and maritime hunters in the Sea of Okhotsk crossed paths with Japanese castaways, shipwrecked merchants, fishermen, and tourists. They were rescued and taken to St. Petersburg because the Russian tsarist government, interested in opening trade with Japan, wanted to learn about their country, customs, and practices, and language. The first written record of such a case documents a Japanese trader from Osaka named Denbei, who was shipwrecked in 1695, rescued in 1697 in Kamchatka by a troop of Cossacks, and taken to meet with Peter I in 1702. Denbei spent the rest of his life in St. Petersburg as an expert on Japan. The first Japanese language school opened in 1735 as part of the Academy of Sciences and another opened in 1786 in Irkutsk, both with Japanese castaways as language instructors. The most celebrated Japanese castaway, Daikokuya Kōdayū, returned to Japan in 1793 ten years after his shipwreck and provided the Edo Bakufu, Japan's samurai regime, with comprehensive knowledge about Russia.

Tsarist Russia continued to expand its sphere of influence beyond central Asia. In 1689 it established diplomatic contact with Qing China through the Treaty of Nerchinsk, which established a border between the two nations. Some limited trade, primarily by caravan followed. By the early nineteenth century, Russia, with growing ambitions for the Pacific Ocean, was competing against the

---

6. The Bakufu leaders knew the schedule of Perry's squadron. Shortly after the Perry's squadron left Norfolk, Virginia, the friendly Dutch king had advised the Bakufu not to resist but to comply with American demands so as to avoid repeating the recent tragedy of China in the Opium War of 1840–42. The Japanese leaders got the message.

7. George Sansom, *The Western World and Japan: A Study in the Interaction of European and Asiatic Cultures* (1949; reprinted Tokyo: Charles Tuttle, 1950), 245.

8. Japan's relations with the West began before the Edo period. In 1543 shipwrecked Portuguese en route to Canton accidentally reached a small island off the southern tip of Kyūshū and subsequently opened trade relations with the islanders. Spanish, Italian, British, and Dutch traders and missionaries followed. On two separate occasions, in 1585 and 1615, Japanese Catholic converts traveled to Rome and had papal audiences. A group of Japanese merchants crossed the Pacific Ocean to reach Mexico for trade negotiations in 1610. Even after the Tokugawa Shogunate prohibited in 1641 any contact with the Christian West, the Dutch were given special dispensation and continued to trade with Japan for almost two centuries; they thus provided considerable influence on Japan's scientific and technological developments.

United States and Britain to be the first nation to use Japanese ports for trade. The Russian mission occurred almost simultaneously with Perry's expedition, but with fewer weapons. Merely a month after Commodore Perry arrived at Uraga with his gunboat tactics, Admiral Efimii Putiatin entered the port of Nagasaki in August 1853 for diplomatic negotiations. Refusing to negotiate with the Bakufu, Perry issued an ultimatum that Japan sign an agreement to open several Japanese ports for American use one year later. In contrast, Putiatin's mission anchored at the port of Nagasaki, the only port formally open for limited foreign trade, and began full diplomatic negotiations with the Bakufu in December 1853. After the negotiation deadlocked over a territorial dispute over the Sakhalin and Kurile islands, Putiatin temporarily left Nagasaki in early January 1854 on the condition that Russia would be given the same rights should Japan conclude a commercial treaty with another nation in Russia's absence. In February Perry returned to Kanagawa with a more threatening force of nine ships and pressed the Bakufu to sign a treaty on March 31, 1854. In December 1854 Putiatin secured a treaty of friendship similar to the one Perry had concluded.

Russia and the United States thus provided Japanese intellectuals with two portals through which they could study the outside world and think about Japan's future. Yoshida Shōin (1830–59), a samurai revolutionary who attempted to stow away in a ship of Perry's squadron, embodied an early Japanese desire to learn about America. Robert Louis Stevenson commemorated his heroic action in an essay about Yoshida under his popular name, Torajiro.[9] His apparent preference for America over Russia was, however, in part an accident. Yoshida had originally planned to go to Russia by similar means. Only after he missed the Russian squadron at Nagasaki did Yoshida seek to capitalize on Perry's return to the Bay of Edo in 1854.

Given Yoshida's familiarity with both the United States and Russia, he may well have known Mitsukuri Shōgo's 1845 work, *Kon'yo zushiki* (Annotated maps of the world), which depicted George Washington as the hero who expelled the British and led the American colonies to independence.[10] Meanwhile his samurai mentor Sakuma Shōzan was impressed by how Russia's Peter I had turned an "obstinately backward country" into an honorable nation in a short period of time by importing technology from Europe.[11] Even though Yoshida saw the United

---

9. Robert Louis Stevenson, *Familiar Studies of Men and Books* (New York: Scribner, 1896).

10. The first Japanese reports about America were provided by Mitsukuri Shōgo, geographer in the school of Dutch Studies, in his 18475 *Kon'yo zushiki* (Annotated maps of the world) in three volumes. For the English text, see Peter Duus, *Japanese Discovery of America: A Brief Biography with Documents* (Boston: Bedford/St. Martin, 1997).

11. Shinobu Seizaburō, *Shōzan to Shōin: kaikoku to jōi no ronri* (Shozan and Shoin: arguments concerning ending the seclusion and expelling foreigners) (Tokyo: Kawade Shobō, 1975), 101–2.

States and Russia as imperialist threats to Japan, he and Sakuma agreed that Russia's rapid growth into a modern and powerful nation provided the better model for Japan. This judgment had led Yoshida to his initial attempt to gain passage on the Russian ship.[12]

Japan carried out the Meiji Restoration of 1868—an abolition of the samurai regime—and began rapidly building a modern (Westernized and industrialized) nation-state with the immediate purpose of revising the unequal treaty system with the West and defending itself from further encroachments of Western imperialism. By then the United States was preoccupied with the Civil War and Britain was Japan's most dominant trading partner. As the new Japanese government and people learned of the desolate poverty in Russia under tsarist corruption, largely from the British accounts, the reputation of tsarist Russia declined quickly. When the Japanese government dispatched students and officials to study abroad in the various Western nations, only 9 students headed for Russia while 149 students went to the United States, 126 to Britain, 66 to Germany, and 42 to France.[13] The United States assisted Japan's modernization in the fields of primary education, agricultural science, and even colonial enterprise. American general Charles LeGendre served as an adviser to the Japanese government and instructed military operations against Taiwan in the early 1870s. From Russia the Japanese government anticipated learning the Russian language, for diplomatic and commercial negotiations, but little else.[14]

Some renowned Japanese intellectuals preferred the American system to the Russian system. Fukuzawa Yukichi, an intellectual, educator, and a champion of the popular rights movement in the 1880s, admired Anglo-American republicanism and disdained Imperial Russia's constitutional absolutism (*rikken dokusai*). Fukuzawa viewed poverty in Russia as a seed for antiauthoritarian insurrections that would in turn invite more repression.[15] In contrast Fukuzawa highly regarded Americans for the "advanced" standard of living he observed during inspection tours in the 1860s. He admired well-to-do American families on the East Coast for their independent spirit and he even claimed that these "enlightened" citizens kept the nation moving forward in accordance with its founding

---

12. Terao Gorō, *Kakumeika Yoshida Shōin* (Yoshida Shoin: a revolutionary life) (Tokyo: Tokuma Shoten, 1973), 213–20; Shinobu Seizaburō, *Shōzan to Shōin*, 9–10, 98–101, 150–53.

13. Togawa Tsuguo, "Meiji Ishin zengo no Nihonjin no Roshia-kan" (Japanese views of Russia around the time of the Meiji Restoration), in Nakamura Yoshikazu and Thomas Rimer, eds., *Roshia bunka to Nihon* (Russian culture and Japan) (Tokyo: Sairyū Sha, 1995), 44.

14. Miyanaga Takashi, *Bakumatsu Oroshiya ryūgakusei* (Japanese students in Russia in the last phase of the Edo period) (Tokyo: Chikuma Shobō, 1991), 6–10, 223–31.

15. Togawa Tsuguo, "Meiji Ishin zengo no Nihonjin no Roshia-kan," in Nakamura and Rimer, eds., *Roshia bunka to Nihon*, 48–50.

principles. Fukuzawa respected the stabilizing effect of America's abundant wealth on the nation's democracy.[16]

Antiestablishment intellectuals also found inspiration in American democracy. By the 1880s the new Westernized government in Tokyo had already prioritized building infrastructure and military strength over improving people's welfare. Japanese dissidents began the "liberty and popular rights" movement and called for popular sovereignty and freedom of speech. The introduction of Alexis de Tocqueville's *Democracy in America* (in two different translations published in 1873 and 1881–82), as well as Francis Lieber's *On Civil Liberty and Self-Government* (in two different translations published in 1876 and 1880), energized Japanese dissidents in their fight against the oppressive Japanese government. They also regarded the United States as an ideal place for political exile. A student of Fukuzawa's, Baba Tatsui (1850–88) founded the Liberal Party (Jiyū-tō) in 1881, went to the United States in 1886, and eventually died in Philadelphia. On January 7, 1888, about thirty Japanese political exiles, mostly student-laborers, established the Patriotic League in San Francisco to promote their antigovernment movement abroad.[17] Ueki Emori (1857–92), cofounder of the Liberal Party, praised the United States and France as places where the people had heroically fought for and won rights. He wrote a version of the Bill of Rights in 1881 with an emphasis on the right to bear arms and to rebel.[18]

Komuro Shigehiro, a journalist and classical poet, thematized the American political struggle for freedom in a poem of 1882. The poem celebrated those who left Europe for the unknown land of America in the quest to be free, who fought for seven years against British oppression for independence, and who ultimately built a prosperous nation.[19] Similar romantic notions appeared in a vernacular political novella, *Kajin no kigū* (Chance encounters with Western belles), published in 1885. In Philadelphia, the Japanese protagonist learns from two Western belles about the American War of Independence. As he learns of other recent revolutionary movements around the world, the protagonist becomes deeply sympathetic to the universal fight for justice.

Meanwhile the intensifying radical intellectual discourse against the tsarist government attracted Japanese interest. Unlike the American War of Independence of a century earlier, the Russian movement was a contemporary process,

---

16. For the English translation of Fukuzawa's views of America, see Peter Duus, *Japanese Discovery of America: A Brief Biography with Documents*, 145–50 and 185–90.

17. Yuji Ichioka, *The Issei: The World of the First Generation Japanese Immigrants, 1885–1924* (New York: Free Press, 1988), 14–16.

18. Matsunaga Shōzō, *Jiyū byōdō o mezashite—Nakae Chōmin to Ueki Emori* (Toward freedom and equality: Nakae Chomin and Ueki Emori) (Tokyo: Shimizu Shoin, 1984), 92–95.

19. Komuro Shigehiro, "Jiyū no uta" (Song of liberty), in Sangū Makoto, ed., *Nihon gendai-shi taikei* (Anthology of modern Japanese poems) (Tokyo: Kawade Shobō, 1974), vol. 1, 60–61.

unfolding before the eyes of Japanese activists. In 1861, merely eight years after Perry and Putiatin first reached Japan, Russian anarchist leader Mikhail Aleksandrovich Bakunin, an opponent of Marx's theory of centralization, showed up in Yokohama after escaping from a Siberian prison. From there Bakunin set sail to the United States, crossed the Atlantic Ocean, and eventually met with Karl Marx in London.

Japanese dissidents in the Popular Rights Movement of the 1880s did not share Fukuzawa's assessment of Russian unrest. They learned of revolutionary concepts through people like Russian anarchist and journalist Lev Mechnikov, who began teaching Russian at the Tokyo School of Foreign Languages (Tokyo Gaikokugo Gakkō) in its founding year 1873. To them Russia's *Narodniki* movement embodied the voice of an oppressed people yearning for freedom.[20] These Japanese learned of the latest political developments in Russia often through English language newspapers published in Japan.[21] They read Sergei Stepniak's *Underground Russia* and other accounts of terrorist activities, political assassinations, and treason trials.[22] Their fascination with Russia's revolutionary movement found expression in the political novella *Kyomu-tō jitsuden-ki kishūshū* (A true story of the Nihilist Party, 1885), which tells the story of Sophia Perovskaya and her struggles against the tsarist government officials.[23] Uchida Ryōhei, a "patriotic" politician with imperialistic ambitions, published *Roshia bōkoku-ron* (Doomed Russia) in 1901 and predicted, based on his observations during his trip to Russia in 1898, that a revolution to abolish the tsarist system and remedy social injustices was inevitable.

During the Russo-Japanese War, Russian political exiles tried to mobilize Russian prisoners of war in Japan through antitsarist propaganda. George Kennan, an American war correspondent stationed in Japan, believed in the antitsarist revolution and attempted to aid the exiles. Kennan arranged to invite Nikolai Sudzilovsky (alias Nicholas Russel), a Russian exile who had become a politician in Hawaii, to Japan. With approval from the Japanese Army general Terauchi Masatake, Sudzilovsky visited camps for Russian prisoners of war and disseminated

---

20. For the latest English language study of Mechnikov and his contribution to the contemporary Japanese intellectual and cultural life, see Sho Konishi, "Reopening the 'Opening of Japan': A Russian-Japanese Revolutionary Encounter and the Vision of Anarchist Progress," *American Historical Review* 112, no. 1 (February 2007): 101–30.

21. Wada Haruki, "Nichi-Ro kankei to Amerika" (Japanese-Russian relations and America), in Nakamura and Rimer, eds., *Roshia bunka to Nihon*, 20–21.

22. George Sansom, *The Western World and Japan: A Study in the Interaction of European and Asiatic Cultures* (New York: Vintage, 1973), 401.

23. Wada Haruki, "Nichi-Ro Kankei to America," 21–22. The Russian struggle for freedom and liberty was often symbolized by an attractive female for romantic effect, just as the American struggle was in *Kajin no kigū*.

revolutionary ideas. The first Red Flag came to fly on Japanese soil thanks to this peculiar Russo-American collaboration. Toward the end of the war, the tsarist government suspected that some forty-six thousand Russian prisoners of war held by Japanese authorities had become a formidable revolutionary force, and it requested that the Japanese government not send them back en masse to Vladivostok.[24]

A confluence of global intellectual currents led Japanese socialists, communists, and anarchists to develop under American influence. Dwight Whitney Learned, an American economist, was the first university professor to lecture on communism and socialism in Japan. A protégé of Theodore Woolsey—president of Yale University from 1846 to 1871 and author of *Communism and Socialism in Their History and Theory*—Learned came to Kyoto in 1878 by arrangement with the American Board of Commissioners for Foreign Missions. He encouraged his Japanese students at Doshisha University, the elite Protestant institution, to translate his mentor's work. Although the work was poorly translated, the Japanese preface praised Learned's ambition, hoping that these new ideas on communism and socialism, which were spreading rapidly across Western Europe though not in America, had a better chance at taking root in Japan.[25]

Japan's early labor movement, which progressed into socialist and communist movements, developed with an American flair. In 1886 Takano Fusatarō (1869–1904), a young Japanese entrepreneur, arrived in San Francisco determined to create a successful business career. His encounter with George McNeill's works awoke him to the issue of the welfare of laborers. In 1891 along with several other Japanese immigrants, Takano organized Shokkō Giyū-kai (The Fraternal Society of Laborers and Artisans), primarily in order to conduct research on American labor unions for possible adoption in Japanese society. He returned to Japan in 1896 and the following year, along with Katayama Sen, started organizing iron workers and railway employees in much the same spirit as the American Federation of Labor (AFL).[26] Kōtoku Shūsui (1871–1911) participated in Japan's early socialist movement and, in search of the shortest path toward socialism, became increasingly attracted to Russian anarchist Peter Kropotkin as well as American syndicalism. Kōtoku corresponded with Albert Johnson, a veteran anarchist in

24. Kimura Takeshi, "Nichi-Bei shakai undō kōryū-shi" (History of interactions of Japanese and American social movements), in Kaikoku Hyakunen Kinen Bunka Jigyō-Kai, ed., *Nichi-Bei bunka kōshō shi* (History of US-Japanese cultural relations) (Tokyo: Yōyō Sha, 1955), vol. 4, 551–60. Also see Wada Haruki, "Nichi-Ro kankei to America," 22–23.

25. Kimura Takeshi, "Nichi-Bei shakai undō kōryū-shi," 487–92.

26. Takano Fusatarō, *Meiji Nihon Rōdō Tsūshin* (Reports of Meiji Japanese laborers), reprint, with introduction by Ōshima Kiyoshi and Nimura Kazuo (Tokyo: Iwanami Bunko, 1997). Also see Kimura, "Nichi-Bei shakai undō kōryū-shi," 501.

California, to whom he confided his desire to attack the Japanese government from overseas. In June 1906 Kōtoku established the Social Revolutionary Party, which attracted some forty Japanese members from the Berkeley area. The party also called for international brotherhood with Chinese immigrant workers through the elimination of national and racial prejudices. He made San Francisco a logistical base for Japanese socialism, much as the Russian revolutionaries did with Switzerland.[27]

Katayama Sen (1860–1933) exemplifies some of the linkages Japanese communists developed with both Russia and America. Born to a farming family in Japan, Katayama from 1884 to 1896 studied at Grinnell College, Andover Theological Seminary, and Yale Divinity School. Upon his return to Japan he became a leader of the labor union movement as a Christian socialist. In 1901 Katayama—along with Kōtoku, Abe Isoo, and Kawakami Kiyoshi, and two others—founded the Social Democratic Party (Shakai Minshu-tō). The party's eight fundamental principles were the abolition of racial discrimination, demilitarization for world peace, abolition of the class system, public ownership of land and capital, public ownership of the transportation system, equal distribution of wealth, equal participation in politics, and full state subsidies for education.[28] In 1904 during the Russo-Japanese War, Katayama attended the Sixth Congress of the Second International held in Amsterdam as the Japanese representative. He shook hands with the Russian delegate, and they affirmed a mutual antiwar standpoint. In 1906 he cofounded the short-lived Japan Socialist Party (Nippon Shakai-tō).

After a series of imprisonments by the Japanese government, he returned to San Francisco in 1914. In the fall of 1916, S. J. Rutgers, one of the earliest American Marxist-Leninists, offered to finance his relocation to New York City and Katayama subsequently moved to the East Coast. Making the acquaintance of Trotsky, Bukharin, Madame Kollontai, and exiled Russian revolutionaries, he became a Marxist-Leninist. His small apartment on West 56th Street became a salon for young Japanese radicals. In July 1919 Katayama published a small English book, *The Labor Movement in Japan,* and the following year he joined the newly formed independent Communist Party of America and established the Association of Japanese Socialists in America, a forerunner of Japan's Communist Party. Until 1921 when he departed for Moscow to serve as chairman of the Far Eastern People's Congress, Katayama helped unify the American Communist Party and even went to Mexico to help organize communist activities. In

27. Yuji Ichioka, *The Issei,* 105; Germaine A. Hoston, *Marxism and the Crisis of Development in Prewar Japan* (Princeton, NJ: Princeton University Press, 1986), 22.

28. Sumiya Mikio, *Nihon no rekishi: Dai Nihon Teikoku no shiren* (A history of Japan: challenges of Imperial Japan) (Tokyo: Chūkō Bunko, 1974).

1922 the Japanese Communist Party (Nihon Kyōsan-tō) was founded by Comintern directive, on which Katayama had worked considerably. Katayama was the only Asian in his lifetime to be appointed to the presidium of the Third International.[29]

With the birth of the Soviet Union, the Japanese and US governments both affirmed their official anticommunist position. In August 1918 at Washington's invitation, the Japanese government sent troops to Siberia in a joint military action with the United States, Britain, France, and Canada to foil the revolution. The Japanese government endorsed aspects of Wilsonianism as a desirable approach to world order, specifically its emphasis on a world market and capitalist-industrialist activities.

As Japan's economic and financial systems became more integrated into the global market, Japanese business leaders praised the American (Puritan) emphasis on hard work, frugality, competition, and meritocracy. They took an interest in the generation of harmony between capitalists and society through charitable works, and an interest in scientific management, and they attempted to introduce these concepts to Japan. Like Fukuzawa Yukichi, Japanese with experience studying business and management at elite American institutions celebrated American wealth because it allowed for an upward social mobility that made American society classless.[30] Yet proponents of the American economic system did not necessarily endorse the American political system. Yoshino Sakuzō, a champion of Japan's liberalism in the 1920s, denounced democracy as mobocracy: democracy was synonymous with anarchism and socialism, preludes to chaos and the collapse of the Japanese empire.

Having already experienced an early split in the Japan Socialist Party between "moderates," who supported parliamentarianism, and "radicals," who demanded direct action, some Japanese socialists continued to value ties with the United States. After the massive arrest of socialists and subsequent execution of twelve anarchists in January 1911, Japan's Yūai-kai (Friendly Society), a Christian-based social reform organization, adopted a moderate-conservative tactic of compromising with businesses and grew rapidly under the slogan of harmony between business owners and labor. The organization also helped female workers to unionize. In 1915 two representatives of the Japan Friendly Society headed for

29. Robert Scalapino, *The Japanese Communist Movement, 1920–1966* (Berkeley: University of California Press, 1967), 6–7.

30. Kimura Masato, "Senzen no jitsugyō-kai" (Prewar business community in Japan), in National Institute for Research Advancement (NIRA), ed., *Amerika kenkoku no rinen to Nichi-Bei kankei* (The founding of the United States and US-Japan relations) NIRA Report no. 940051 (Tokyo: NIRA, 1995), 103–8.

the United States to meet with representatives of the AFL and the California State Federation of Labor, including Samuel Gompers. The AFL's policy of Asian racial exclusion did not discourage them from learning from American labor unions.[31]

Around World War I, Japanese in search of an ideal society looked worldwide—not just to the American or Russian context—for leaders who were attempting to put the concepts of emancipation, liberty, and equality into practice. In 1918 students at Tokyo Imperial University organized Shinjin-Kai (New Men's Association) to promote a democracy of cultural and civilized people. They also sought pragmatic reform for Japan. Their journal *Demokurashī* (Democracy) discussed thinkers from Jean-Jacques Rousseau, Emma Goldman, Karl Liebknecht, Leo Tolstoy (commonly known as "the father of emancipation"), Peter Kropotkin, Karl Marx, Abraham Lincoln, and Vladimir Lenin. Japanese feminists also looked all over the world for inspiration. From the 1880s on, upper- and working-class women explored the ideas of Swede Ellen Key, Brits Olive Schreiner and M. G. Fawcett, and American Charlotte Perkins Gilman, among others. Although some sympathized with the Western feminist movement in the Christian context, others identified with proletarian, socialist, and communist goals and claimed liberation from capitalist oppression. Japanese liberals and radicals freely synthesized American and Russian political ideas.

A proletarian cultural movement was in full bloom in the late 1920s. In the academic and literary realm, Soviet and Russian studies enjoyed a rich and vibrant following of Japanese students. Historians, economists, and other social scientists engaged with the Japanese Communist Party and its Trotskyist opponents in a historic controversy over the nature of Japanese society, modernization, capitalism, and the mechanism of a projected revolution. Out of this debate emerged *Tanemaku Hito* (The sowers of seeds), a journal founded in 1921 dedicated to proletarian literature, which shared thematic overlaps with the earlier naturalist movement.

Some Japanese Marxists and leftists believed that American society, in its fight for liberty and equality, was primed for a proletarian revolution. A number of Japanese Marxists also imagined and defined an alliance with black Americans in their anti-imperialist and anticolonialist fight. Like some American socialists and communists, they saw oppressed black people as the vanguard of the world's proletarian movement. In 1923 critic Akamatsu Katsumaro predicted in *Kaizō* (Reconstruction)—a highly regarded monthly journal founded in 1919 that became a forum on all aspects of national and world affairs—that black Americans would eventually help overthrow Japan's imperialism as part of their

31. Yuji Ichioka, *The Issei*, 128–45.

racial-proletarian movement.[32] When *Amerika Sentan Bungaku Sōsho* (Collection of avant-garde American literature) was published in 1930, its editors imbued the work with a Marxist mission by including several selections by black American writers, introducing them as a beacon of the American struggle for the liberation of the oppressed.[33]

The political activities of a subset of Japanese émigrés in America underlined the global fight against Japanese imperialism on American turf. Katayama Sen helped the American Communist Party recruit and organize a network of Japanese laborers in Los Angeles, San Francisco, and Seattle. One of their early anti-imperialist, antifascist, and antiwar campaigns targeted elite cadets of the Japanese Naval Academy who were annually dispatched by the Japanese Navy on goodwill squadrons to the United States, Europe, and Australia. Japanese communists in America distributed leaflets to the young Japanese cadets, reminding them of the Battleship Potemkin uprising, the 1905 mutiny of Russian crew members recognized as the beginning of the Russian Revolution of 1917.[34] They also shipped periodicals, news sheets, and pamphlets to Japan and obtained crucial collaboration from sailors and other people engaged in trans-Pacific traffic. Up until the outbreak of the Pacific War, more than a hundred different communist periodicals, newsletters, and pamphlets disguised as mundane publications were smuggled into Japan from the United States and circulated in Japanese towns. These publications called on Japanese workers to collaborate with American workers on strikes and other actions in an effort to improve their working and living conditions. Sometimes Japanese readers would write letters to the editor that would appear in American communist publications.[35]

The Japanese émigré community on the West Coast was led by people like Nishiuji Tsunejirō, Joe Koide, and Karl Yoneda who developed ties with Nosaka Sanzō, a founder of the Japanese Communist Party and a member of the executive committee of the Comintern. Karl Yoneda, born in California in 1906, went to Japan to study between 1913 and 1926 and after returning to the United States joined the American Communist Party. Yoneda edited the *Rōdō Shinbun* (Japanese labor news), a publication of the American Communist Party, while also serving in the Congress of Industrial Organization (CIO) and the International Longshoremen's and Warehousemen's Union. Miyagi Yotoku, born in Okinawa

---

32. Akamatsu Katsumaro, "Kokujin kaihō undō no gensei to sono keikō—jinshu tōsō to kaikyū tōsō" (The current status and trend of the black liberation movement—a race struggle and a class struggle), *Kaizō* 5, no. 8 (August 1923): 76–85.

33. Yukiko Koshiro, "Beyond an Alliance of Color: The African American Impact on Modern Japan," *positions: east asia cultures critique* 11, no. 1 (spring 2003): 192–95.

34. DCJ, vol. 1, 315–20.

35. Rodger Swearingen and Paul Langer, *Red Flag in Japan: International Communism in Action, 1919–1951* (Cambridge, MA: Harvard University Press, 1952), 64.

in 1905, joined his father on the West Coast in 1919 to pursue a career in painting. The racism Miyagi encountered led him to turn to Marxist studies and to become a member of the Japanese branch of the American Communist Party. In 1933 on a Comintern directive, he departed for Japan to play a role in the Sorge spy ring.[36]

This particular political movement of Japanese émigrés was not unchallenged by the American and Japanese governments. Between 1931 and 1934 seventeen Japanese communists were expelled from America under the Criminal Syndicalism Act. In January 1932 the so-called Long Beach Incident led to the mass arrest by the Los Angeles Police Red Squad of more than a hundred communists, nine of whom were Japanese.[37] Facing deportation, which would result in their arrest by the Japanese authorities, they opted to go to Moscow with the help of the American Communist Party. The Japanese government by then had discovered that trans-Pacific communist networks, with a wide range of bases across the United States, were smuggling antigovernment, antiwar pamphlets and publications into Japan. By the summer of 1938, Japanese Ministry of Foreign Affairs agents in the United States had identified at least four hundred suspected Japanese (and a few Chinese and Korean) communists.[38] In southern California alone, there were approximately two hundred Japanese communists.

Many Japanese émigrés on the East Coast developed an idiosyncratic love for both communism and America. After the passage of the Japanese Exclusion Act of 1924, some two thousand Japanese remained in America, most without US citizenship. Half were diplomats, military attachés, bankers, businessmen, and journalists; the rest were students, artists, restaurant cooks, waiters, servants, and other menial workers. In 1929 members of the latter group organized the Japanese Workers Club and joined the Japanese section of the American Communist Party. Encouraged by the New Deal culture of the 1930s, they developed distinct views of peace, democracy, and freedom by blending American and Soviet ideals. Most of them cultivated close ties with the John Reed Club of New York City and were dubbed by other Japanese as "daun taun aka" (downtown reds).

---

36. Chalmers Johnson, *An Instance of Treason: Ozaki Hotsumi and the Sorge Spy Ring*, expanded ed. (Stanford, CA: Stanford University Press, 1990), 92–94.

37. Yuji Ichioka, "Beyond National Boundaries: The Complexity of Japanese-American History," *Amerasia Journal* 23, no. 3 (winter 1997–98): vii. Instead of being deported back to Japan, they chose to be sent to the Soviet Union. They were all executed during Stalin's Purification Campaign. The number of Japanese arrests is from Katō Tetsurō, "Rongu Bīchi jiken (the Long Beach incident)," May 2000, http://homepage3.nifty.com/katote/longbeech.html.

38. Swearingen and Langer, *Red Flag in Japan*, 61–65.

The Soviet Union as Radical Hope

Setting differences in state ideology aside, the Japanese and Soviet governments actively engaged in strengthening ties between the two peoples. Yet the Soviet Union did not forsake its revolutionary goals. Without the legal consent of the Japanese government, the Soviet Union solicited working-class Japanese to study at the Communist University of the Toilers of the East (KUTV). In 1928 the Japanese Foreign Ministry estimated some 1,000 foreign students, ranging in age from twenty to thirty-two, studied at KUTV: 400 Chinese students comprised the majority, followed by 350 ethnic minorities within the Soviet Union. Between 30 and 40 were Japanese, 21 of whom were identifiable. They lived in a dormitory and studied under Japanese communists Takahashi Sadaki and Yamamoto Keizō and several Russian instructors. Vasilii Erochenko, the blind poet who sojourned in Japan between 1916 and 1921 while attending a school for the blind, taught Russian. These Japanese students also studied economics, the history of world revolution, Leninism, philosophy, labor union theory, and Japanese studies. Except for two farmers, all of the Japanese students had been factory workers: metalworkers, lathe machinists, printers, seamen, celluloid workers, and shoemakers.[39] Japanese Communist Party member Tokuda Kyūichi was instrumental in recruiting and sending these Japanese workers to KUTV via Shanghai and Vladivostok.[40]

In the wake of Lenin's death in 1924, the controversy between Stalin and Trotsky signaled that the Soviet Union after Lenin was divided over the interpretation of world revolution. Stalin's victory legitimized his theory of "socialism in one country" and ended Trotsky's call for the Communist International to adopt a more global revolutionary agenda. Japanese observers understood that Stalin prioritized domestic economic and industrial development over world communist revolution.

Supporting evidence for this development came from Moscow even amid the Japanese government's mass arrests of communists between 1928 and 1930.

39. "Tokyo Chihō Saibansho Kenji-kyoku Kūtobe ni tsuite" (The Tokyo District Public Prosecutors Office Report on the KUTV) (September 1928)," in *Nihon Kyōsan-tō kankei zakken—Honpōjin shugisha no zai-Ro Tōhō Kinrō-sha Kyōsan Daigaku ryūgaku kankei* (Miscellaneous data on the Japanese Communist Party—on Japanese communists studying at the Communist University of the Toilers of the East [KUTV] in the Soviet Union) [I-4-5-2-3-7], DRO.

40. "Ōsaka Chihō Saibansho Kenji-kyoku Shisō-bu Nakagawa Seizō chōshū-sho" (The Osaka District Public Prosecutors Office Thought Department report on the case of Nakagawa Seizo) in *Nihon Kyōsan-tō kankei zakken—Honpōjin shugisha no zai-Ro Tōhō Kinrō-sha Kyōsan Daigaku ryūgaku kankei* (Miscellaneous data on the Japanese Communist Party—on Japanese communists studying at the Communist University of the Toilers of the East [KUTV] in the Soviet Union) [I-4-5-2-3-7], DRO.

Responding to the Japanese government's suspicions that it channeled financial aid to the Japanese Communist Party, the Soviet Embassy in Tokyo called these claims unsubstantiated. The Soviet Embassy in Tokyo declared that the Soviet government had dutifully observed the agreement between Moscow and Tokyo to respect each other's political and social systems so it could not possibly financially aid a political organization such as the Japanese Communist Party that would challenge Japan's status quo. In a written statement, the Soviet Embassy argued that the Third International had learned a hard lesson in Shanghai, where it had wasted a substantial sum of money on those who looked like communist comrades but proved to be alien vagabonds with no sense of commitment or skill. A Russian-language newspaper published in Harbin quipped that since Moscow would not confess to its ties with the Japanese Communist Party, Japan might as well accept Moscow's story just for the sake of better diplomacy.[41] The Japanese government did just that and chose pragmatic diplomacy.

As soon as Japan recognized the sovereignty of the Soviet Union in 1925, the Japanese government helped found the Russo-Japanese Association (Nichi-Ro Kyōkai), with enthusiastic support from Japanese businessmen who hoped to improve the interactions of Russians and Japanese and to help boost trade. Only a year before, the United States had antagonized the Japanese by passing legislation banning Japanese immigration. With headquarters in Tokyo and several branches across Japan, the Russo-Japanese Association began promoting the two nations' understanding through high-profile members. The inaugural president was Prince Kan'in-no-miya Kotohito (later chief of the General Staff), and council members included prominent figures such as Viscount Ishii Kikujirō (former foreign minister and a member of the Privy Council), Viscount Shibusawa Eiichi (international businessman and philanthropist), Viscount Takahashi Korekiyo (minister of agriculture and commerce), Yasuda Zenzaburō (head of the Yasuda *zaibatsu*), Asano Sōichirō (the "cement king"), and Matsuoka Yōsuke (then director of the South Manchuria Railway).

The association's most important achievement was the establishment of the Institute of the Russo-Japanese Association (Nichi-Ro Kyōkai Gakkō), later known as the Harbin Institute in Manchuria, which aimed to promote Russian and Soviet area studies. Very similar in concept, organization, and operation to the TōA Dōbun Shoin (East Asia Common Culture Academy) in Shanghai, this institute trained Japanese to be experts on the Soviet Union through a three-year curriculum of Russian language, Soviet business and commercial practices,

---

41. "Nihon Kyōsan-tō jiken happyō ni taisuru Sobieto gawa no taido ni kansuru ken" (November 9, 1929), in *Nihon Kyōsan-tō kankei zakken—Kyōsan-tō to Sorenpō to no kankei* (Miscellaneous data on the Japanese Communist Party—on the relationship between the Japanese Communist Party and the Soviet Union) [I-4-5-2-(3-3)], DRO.

Russian history, geography, customs, and culture. As of 1929, ninety-one students were enrolled, all but two of them government fellowship recipients. Nine Japanese, one Chinese, and eight Russian instructors offered courses, while one Russian and three Japanese staff members assisted the institute's administration. Sugihara Chiune, a Japanese diplomat later known as a savior of Lithuanian Jews escaping Nazi persecution, taught Russian at this institute.[42]

While some Japanese feared Moscow's intentions, others had a more optimistic outlook. One Japanese analyst later argued that behind Moscow's early pacifist stance with Japan lay two factors: continuing reliance on capitalist nations for trade and technological transfer, and the domestic political instability that culminated in the Great Purge. He pointed to improving relations between the United States and the Soviet Union as another indicator of the Soviet Union's desire for coexistence with capitalism (and imperialism) for the sake of economic growth.[43] In the aftermath of the Nomonhan Incident, the *Hōchi* newspaper's editorial argued on October 28, 1939: "Even when Japan and the Soviet Union differ in the *professed intention for the state* [*kokka-teki tatemae*], we have to keep in mind that we have to observe our mutual interests as neighbors" (emphasis added). *Tatemae* (professed intention) in the Japanese language often cynically implies the total opposite of *hon'ne* (real intention). The editorial was suggesting that calls for a worldwide communist revolution could only be a façade of the Soviet state and that its pursuit of national interest could not be much different from Japan's own.

The Soviet Union captured popular Japanese interest with its state-sponsored cultures just as imperial Russia had. The closest exemplar of Western civilization to Japan, Russia had since the late nineteenth century offered Japan romantic visions of cultural modernity very different from those inspired by the United States. Russian Orthodox missionaries taught villagers in impoverished northern regions of Japan, whereas American Protestant missionaries focused on urban, educated, upper-class Japanese. After the success of the Japanese translation of Ivan Turgenev's *Hunter's Sketches* in 1888–89, Russian literature became perhaps the most loved and revered foreign literature for Japanese people of all backgrounds, male and female, urban and rural, intellectual and working class. In the 1920s and 1930s the Soviet Union became a lodestar for Japanese writers, artists, critics, and intellectuals. These Japanese keenly followed the avant-garde art, music, poetry, literature, and theater emerging from the transition to the Soviet

---

42. "Nichi-Ro Kyōkai kiyaku (revised in October 1925)" and "Nichi-Ro Kyōkai gakkō kisoku" in "Honpō ni okeru kyōkai oyobi bunka dantai kankei—Nichi-Ro Kyōkai kankei," vol. 2 [I-1-10-0-2-1], DRO.

43. Sonobe Shirō, "Soren taigai seisaku no kihon-teki kōsatsu" (Basic observations of Soviet foreign policy), *Kaizō* 20, no. 9 (September 1938): 173–81.

system. Futuristic arts, illustration, and architectural designs in Japan in the 1920s reveal considerable influence from Soviet artists.[44] Sergei Eisenstein's cinematography had a lasting, visible impact on Japan's cinematography bolstered by his explanation that traditional expressions of Japanese art, such as haiku, resembled his montage theory.[45]

Japanese readers seeking information about the Soviet Union, its society, culture, and people, fueled a demand for publications concerning the topic. Bookstores in Japan as well as Manchuria, Korea, Taiwan, and China sold a popular monthly journal *Gekkan Roshiya* (Russia monthly), first published in 1935 by Nisso Tsūshin Sha (Japanese-Soviet Communications Company).[46] The *Asahi* newspaper carried advertisements for this journal on its front page until the last phase of World War II, which suggests both the popularity of this journal and the acceptability of its vision in wartime Japan.

The Soviet Union portrayed and analyzed in *Gekkan Roshiya* was both a culturally attractive neighbor and a major diplomatic and military concern. The journal carried scholarly analyses of contemporary issues such as Soviet wartime economic planning, its military strength, its strategies toward Asia (including the CCP), and even the delicate matter of the Soviet-Japanese Neutrality Pact. The arts and entertainment section projected a vibrant and affable society through its coverage of Soviet lifestyles of society, women, factory workers, and peasants, and its reportage of the differences between city and country living. It also reported on theatrical arts, music, cuisine, and travel. The journal's publication of translations of Russian poetry, short stories, drama, and excerpts from novels underscored the range of its readership.

In contrast the Japanese only had a vague and fragmented sense of the United States. On one hand America symbolized a stern and aloof American Protestantism embodied in the small, influential community of missionaries and their prominent Japanese converts. They led social reform movements such as temperance, abolition of prostitution, and special education for orphans and disabled children. Though they championed worthy causes, Japanese converts hardly seemed eager to tackle the larger problem of the nation's poverty. On the other hand, America represented flamboyance and hedonism, manifested in Hollywood films and jazz music. In the Japanese imagination, ordinary American men and

---

44. Okumura Katsuzō, "Shinkō geijutsu undō to Roshia-Soren" (Russian and Soviet influences on Japan's avant-garde arts) in Okumura Katsuzō and Sakon Takeshi, eds., *Roshia bunka to kindai Nihon* (Russian culture and modern Japan) (Tokyo: Sekai Shisō Sha, 1998), 134–37. For detailed analysis of Russian-Japanese cultural interactions, see chapter 2.

45. Ōhira Yōichi, "Nihon eiga-kai ni ataeta Roshia eiga (riron) no eikyō" (The impact of Russian cinematographic theory on Japanese film making) in *Roshia bunka to kindai Nihon*.

46. After April 1943 the journals were available only through subscription, due to governmental restrictions on paper supply.

women owned automobiles, enjoyed going to the movies, danced, drank, smoked, and indulged in sensual adventures. Ordinary Japanese must have had a hard time understanding how these activities could symbolize individual and societal freedom and embody American progress and democracy.

A dictionary of US-Japanese cultural exchange published in 1983 required little space to list elements of American culture that penetrated and affected Japanese society before 1945: flour, potatoes, Ford motor cars, household electric appliances, ballroom dance, radio broadcasts, tennis, baseball, and the "flappers" of the 1920s.[47] The United States and Japan had been important trade partners since even before World War II; however, business was in the hands of a few affluent Japanese, and contacts with American and other Western cultures were limited for most Japanese. In the prewar period, more than 80 percent of Japanese lived away from westernized cities. Peasants, who constituted more than 40 percent of the population, barely subsisted and had no exposure to Western luxuries.[48]

Wartime Japanese studies of the United States maintained that the generation of American wealth motivated US policy toward Japan and East Asia. In May 1941 the South Manchuria Railway Company (SMR) Research Department (Mantetsu Chōsa-bu) published a ninety-one page confidential report on US Far Eastern policy, the first in a series on geopolitics. The report repeatedly emphasized that America's highly developed monopolistic capitalism and unprecedented accumulation of wealth had enabled it to influence world politics to the benefit of American capitalism. United States foreign policy had traditionally justified capitalist expansion on the basis of ideological rationality rather than economic necessity. America's self-righteousness had led its own people to believe that the Anglo-Saxons (the core American population) were the chosen people and that their democracy and humanism should be the ideal for the entire human race. On the basis of that exceptionalism, they aimed to secure American hegemony by establishing an international political and economic system most favorable to US interests. The United States had increased its interference in the Far East with the conviction that the American people were obliged to supervise the backward and barbaric people of the Far East. Since the United States had occupied and annexed Hawaii, the Philippines, and Guam primarily for military reasons, the report suggested, the purpose of American intervention in the Far East,

---

47. Kamei Shunsuke et al., eds., *Nichi-Bei bunka no kōryū shō-jiten* (A mini-dictionary of US-Japanese cultural exchange) (Tokyo: Esso Sekiyu Kōhō-bu, 1983).

48. Yukiko Koshiro, "Japan's World and World War II," *Diplomatic History* 25, no. 3 (summer 2001): 439.

the very reason for the current conflict with Japan, was to ensure the expansion of the American system in the region.[49]

As an alternative to the image of an avaricious United States, Soviet communism became alluring to Japanese, even to disillusioned soldiers. Prince Konoe Fumimaro had concerns that military officers might be tempted to lead a communist insurrection because most of them came from lower-middle-class families with considerable exposure to hunger and poverty and thus were susceptible to communist ideology.[50] In fact significant numbers of officers and enlisted personnel felt betrayed by the perpetual policy of expansion that had originally promised to save their families from poverty. The tide of revolutionary sentiment among soldiers began to surge in November 1929, when a group of communists within the Imperial Army organized a Japanese branch of the Anti-Imperialist Alliance (Hantei Dōmei Nihon Shibu) and attempted to overthrow the military. Although most leaders had been arrested by 1933, new draftees secretly promoted sabotage and propaganda among fellow soldiers. In one legend of March 1933, unsubstantiated by military records, Japanese Communist Party member and Kwantung Army soldier Ida Sukeo donated 100,000 bullets to the Chinese Liberation Army and then committed suicide.[51] Between 1931 and 1942, ninety-nine Japanese soldiers escaped and joined either the Soviet Army or the CCP Army. In the same period Japan's secret police subverted at least sixteen communist plots led by officers in the Imperial Army.[52] The most sensational arrest of a communist with a military background was that of Kodai Yoshinobu, member of the Sorge international spy ring. After graduating from Meiji University's Department of Law in 1935, he joined the army and did garrison duty in Manchuria and Korea. From his army discharge in 1939 until his arrest in 1942, he supplied information on the Japanese Army to Richard Sorge.

Japanese citizens in cities and villages swapped rumors of Soviet victory in World War II. Secret police investigation records reveal that Japanese from peasants and working-class people to intellectuals espoused Marxist interpretations of the war in criticizing the Japanese government. In 1937 a social science teacher at a primary school in Osaka was imprisoned for teaching his fourth- and fifth-grade students communist values: "In a communist nation, the state controls all the means of production and takes charge of equal distribution of goods. There

49. Mantetsu Chōsa-bu Sekai Jōsei Chōsa-kai, *Hi: Amerika no sekai seisaku ni okeru Kyokutō seisaku no jijō* (Confidential: the place of Far Eastern policy in the US world strategy) (May 1941), NDL.

50. See "Konoe-kō no jōsō bun" (Konoe Memorandum), reprinted in JC, vol. 1: 259–63.

51. For the collection of records of antimilitary and antiwar movements within the Japanese Army, see DCJ.

52. DCJ, vol. 1, chapters 3–4.

are no rich or poor. Laborers and peasants are not oppressed. On the contrary, they govern the nation. When citizens fall sick or become aged, the state takes care of them free of charge."[53]

A shoemaker was arrested for commenting to neighbors that Japan should emulate the Soviet-style planned economy to feed everyone in the country. In the event of Japan's final defeat, he continued, his senior comrade (*aniki*) would come from the north and make him and others happy. An accountant at a Buddhist temple told priests that Japan's surrender to the United States would not much improve the status of laborers anyway.[54] A tinker was interrogated by the military when he was caught telling his neighbor about the invincibility of the Soviet Union: "Japan can in no way beat the Soviets—as they are firmly upheld by the Communist Party, which takes care of laborers and the poor, something our government never does." A shopkeeper told his fellow villagers that the current war was a war of aggression, a war to defend only Japanese capitalists' concessions and to benefit military-industrial conglomerates. In another part of Japan, a bus driver told his co-workers how the war exploited the working-class people and only benefited the capitalist class. In a village of northern Japan, military police picked up a soldier's cap along a railway track and discovered a handwritten statement inside: "I am an Internationalist. . . . Long Live Communism. . . . I am not afraid of death. . . . A true peace is possible only with the International." The military tracked down the cap's owner, who had just been drafted and sent to the war front in northern China.[55]

On the war fronts, student draftees from elite universities were allowed to read works by Dostoevsky, Gorky, Marx, and Lenin. An economics major at Tokyo Imperial University, who eventually died a kamikaze pilot in Okinawa, wrote, "My stomach turns over when I see the lifestyles of the very rich, as I did in Karuizawa [Japan's premier resort community], just like the conduct of soldiers—as if they owned the world!—which I have recently witnessed, and even the way in which bureaucrats and capitalists carry out their existence. In the long run, however, I guess that things will take their own course."[56] Another student from the university wrote, "After all, most students at the Imperial Universities are conservative, caring only for their success by catering to the capitalist class." A physics student wrote that, amid the war's chaos, he discovered the contradictions of class

53. Inagaki Masami, *Mou hitotsu no hansen fu—senchū no rakugaki kaeuta ni miru* (*Different kinds of anti-war music—graffiti and parodied songs*) (Tokyo: Nihon Tosho Center, 1994), 104.

54. "Sankō tsuzuri, Keiho-kyoku Hoan-ka, 1943–1944," MJ-144 "Japanese Rarities," Reel 8, 3.15 thru 3.25 [Microfilm Collection], LOC.

55. Inagaki, *Mou hitotsu no hansen fu*, 17–23.

56. Karuizawa is Japan's exclusive resort community originally developed by and for Westerners in the late nineteenth century and inhabited by upper-class Japanese sojourners. See chapter 2 for Karuizawa's place in Japan's sociocultural history.

society, sympathizing with the proletarian class that could afford neither the luxury of culture nor the philosophy of suffering.[57] One soldier wrote to his friend that he was reading Nikolay Bukharin, the Russian communist leader and theoretician, out of intellectual hunger. Disgusted by a killing rampage by Japanese soldiers in the past four months, he hoped to work for the have-not class when he returned home.[58]

Graffiti praising communism appeared on walls at public lavatories, shrines and temples, on blackboards at schools, and even bulletin boards at train stations. Sometimes letters in support of communism were delivered to high-ranking military officials and even the military police. "Have faith in communism," "Make friends with the Soviet Union for our own happiness," "Join the Soviet Union for international communist revolution," "Down with Japanese imperialism, defend our Soviet," chanted these graffiti. "Refuse the draft paper in the name of Lenin," "Rise, all the Proletarians," "Give up arms, return home, and start the revolution," "Turn this war into the communist revolution!" One young technician at a film theater was arrested for a writing on a lavatory wall: "Give us freedom / Emancipate means of production / Abolish capitalism and establish Republican communism / New society and new culture / Where women participate in building socialism / And receive the same wage / Without taking away men's jobs / Men and women side by side / Work to build socialism."[59]

Pro-American Japanese intellectuals had failed to persuade Japanese society. Kiyosawa Kiyoshi, a journalist who went to America at the age of seventeen and worked his way through Whitworth College, was an expert on US affairs and US-Japanese relations and was posthumously celebrated for his liberal views even during the war. His wartime diary *Ankoku nikki* (Diary of darkness), kept between 1942 and 1945, expressed his resolve to support neither capitalism nor Marxism, but instead advocated absolute freedom to occupy a middle ground as a matter of individual conscience. For this kind of "free and independent thinking," he credited the American educational system. This was, however, the extent of his praise for the American way. He wrote only two diary entries celebrating the virtue of American education: once when an acquaintance, a Harvard-educated Japanese youth, tended his garden at his cottage in Karuizawa; and, on another occasion, when this same youth fixed his waffle maker, refrigerator, and other

---

57. Nihon Senbotsu Gakusei Kinen-kai, ed., *Kike wadatsumi no koe* (Tokyo: Iwanami Bunko, 1982), 17, 139, 157, and 164. For the English translation, see Midori Yamanouchi and Joseph Quinn, trans., *Listen to the Voices from the Sea—Writings of the Fallen Japanese Students* (Scranton, PA: University of Scranton Press, 2000). The selections cited above can be found in pages 95, 99, and 123 of the English translation. The English version is not a full translation of the original. The criticism of Tokyo Imperial students, for example, is truncated in the English translation.

58. Inagaki, *Mou hitotsu no hansen fu*, 24.

59. Inagaki, *Mou hitotsu no hansen fu*, 41–48, 65–82.

home appliances. Kiyosawa asserted that only recipients of an American-style education were pragmatic, sincere, courteous, and dutiful. Otherwise, his affinity for the American way remained limited.

In spite of his background as a labor migrant in America, Kiyosawa disparaged lower-class Japanese. He despised crass menial laborers in Karuizawa, pitied intellectuals without servants, derided military officers for their lack of sophistication arising from their lower-middle-class background, and despised the ignorant masses who failed to see golf as an important activity of rest and relaxation for intellectuals even during wartime. Kiyosawa worried about a "feudalistic" communist revolution—a "theft" from the "haves"—should these uneducated peasants and blue-collar workers continue to defy authorities and speak up against the government.[60] When he expressed such spiteful class consciousness, his "American-inspired liberalism" exhibited the arrogance of the materially affluent and morally superior Japanese elites.

Japan's wartime government was as concerned about plots by pro-US elites as it was about possible communist plots, but the authorities did not consider a pro-American grassroots revolt likely. American freedom and democracy were not propagated in prewar Japan as solutions to poverty and hunger. The appeal of American values as expressed by elites like Kiyosawa most likely escaped ordinary Japanese.

Alliance with the Soviet Union

The vision of allying with the Soviet Union as a buffer against Anglo-America's advance into Asia had roots in Japan's continental policy. Shortly after the Russo-Japanese War, Itō Hirobumi and Gotō Shinpei, the patriarchs of Japan's colonialism in Korea, put forward a plan for a Eurasian continental alliance including Russia to prevent the United States from interfering with Japan's pan-Asianism.[61] Tracing the evolution of the idea of an alignment with the Soviet Union shows that the neutrality pact Japan concluded with the Soviets in 1941 was not necessarily an aberration from Japan's diplomacy but its understandable outcome. Particularly important was the Japanese expectation that the revolutionary ambitions of the Soviet Union, however harmful in the domestic context, would

---

60. Kiyosawa Kiyoshi, *Ankoku nikki* (Diary in darkness) (Tokyo: Iwanami shoten, 1960), 55, 59, 77–78, 113–14, 164–65. For the English translation, see Eugene Soviak, ed., *A Diary of Darkness: The Wartime Diary of Darkness* (Princeton, NJ: Princeton University Press, 1998), 48, 51, 63, 112, and 169–70. The English translation omits portions of the entries at the translators' discretion.

61. Saitō Yoshie, *Azamukareta rekishi* (Betrayed history) (Tokyo: Yomiuri Shinbun Sha, 1955), 89; quoted in Minowa Kimitada, *Matsuoka Yōsuke* (Tokyo: Chūkō Shinsho, 1971), 49.

check the Anglo-American establishment and allow Japan room in a new world order.

Matsuoka Yōsuke, signatory to the Tripartite Pact of September 1940, and who concluded the Soviet-Japanese Neutrality Pact in April 1941, promoted the Soviet Union as a potential buffer. Matsuoka, who experienced American racism as a young immigrant on the West Coast, resided in St. Petersburg from late 1912 to late 1913, during which time he found the Russian people to be friendly and welcoming even as he predicted the demise of the Romanov dynasty.[62]

From the beginning of his career, Matsuoka showed interest in the potential of leveraging Russia as a force that could protect Japan's continental interests. In 1894, only a year after his arrival in the United States as a young student-labor immigrant, the Sino-Japanese War broke out. He observed the Triple Intervention and hoped the Anglo-Japanese alliance would check the threat of Russia. A decade later when Japan won the Russo-Japanese War and obtained the Kwantung region (southern Manchuria) among its spoils of war, the young diplomat Matsuoka envisioned alliance with Russia as a measure to thwart the United States' continental ambitions and to safeguard Japan's interests. In the fall of 1907, Matsuoka is said to have discussed with Yamagata Aritomo, president of the Privy Council, a scheme for forming an alliance with Russia in the manner of the aforementioned Gotō Shinpei's plan. By that time, the United States had shown a growing interest in purchasing the South Manchurian Railway and "neutralizing" Manchuria through an open door policy for "equal" trade and commercial opportunities in Manchuria. Matsuoka advocated the alliance for Great Asianism (*dai Ajia shugi*) consisting of Britain, Japan, Russia, France, and Germany as a way to ward off the United States on the Asian continent.[63]

Matsuoka kept this vision alive as Russia was reborn as the Soviet Union and he became a director and then vice president of the South Manchurian Railway Company with a greater responsibility in defending Japan's continental interests. In early November 1932, as he headed Japan's delegation to the League of Nations following the issuance of the Lytton Report, Matsuoka stopped in Moscow and met with Maxim Litvinov, people's commissar for foreign affairs, and Lev Karahan, the deputy people's commissar for foreign affairs. According to Matsuoka's memoir, during a five-day stay in Moscow, Matsuoka, Litvinof, and Karahan discussed a possible Soviet-Japanese nonaggression pact. From Matsuoka's perspective, the Soviet Union was an outsider in the world led by the League of Nations and thus could tolerate Japan's Manchukuo as the challenge to such a world order.

62. Toyoda Jō, *Matsuoka Yōsuke: higeki no gaikōkan* (Matsuoka Yosuke: a tragic diplomat) (Tokyo: Shinchō Sha, 1979), vol. 1, 105–10.

63. Toyoda, *Matsuoka Yōsuke*, vol. 1, 87–92.

While never affirming the tenets of communism, Matsuoka praised the Soviet Union for "conducting a great experiment for human beings, whereas western civilization is in decline."[64]

In March 1933 Japan withdrew from the League of Nations in protest of the league's condemnation of Japan's illegal occupation of Manchuria. Merely eight months later the Soviet Union received Washington's diplomatic recognition and in September 1934 it joined the league. Having observed how quickly Japan and the Soviet Union switched positions on the world stage, Japanese officials doubted that the Soviet Union's "assimilation" into the "family of nations" was real and were skeptical about Anglo-American sincerity in accepting the communist state into their circle. In spite of its military might, the Soviet Union, much like Japan previously, had a peripheral existence in the Anglo-American world and this marginality continued to draw Japanese attention.

The year 1939 was a turning point for Japanese-Soviet relations. Once World War II broke out in Europe in September, Japanese analysts predicted that the Soviets would shift their focus to the European front and attempt to avoid confrontation with Japan. An agreement in April resolved the heated Russo-Japanese dispute over fishing rights. The Nomonhan Incident of May–August ended in September with a Soviet-Japanese armistice. On December 31 of that year, the Russo-Japanese Fishing Accord formally renewed fishing rights in adjacent territorial waters and settled Soviet debt claims in Manchukuo.

Tokyo began pondering a "radical" alliance with the Soviet Union. The Shōwa Research Association supported such an alliance. After the outbreak of Sino-Japanese War in 1937 the association shifted its focus to Japan's foreign policy and influenced Prime Minister Konoe Fumimaro's November 1938 "New Order in East Asia" declaration. Konoe believed a New Order in East Asia would insure permanent stability of the region built on a relationship of mutual political, economic, and cultural aid and cooperation between Japan, Manchukuo, and China. Japan had failed to win Anglo-American recognition as military, politico-economic, and racial equals. To the Japanese, this rejection added "moral" legitimacy to its pan-Asianism, which sought to rid Asia of Anglo-American imperialism and to redefine Asian modernity under its leadership.

To achieve regional stability, the association devised a plan of multiple tactics against the powers. Their plan notably did not conceive of the Soviet Union as a force to be kept out of East Asia. The plan first called for expelling Britain and neutralizing the United States and France in Asia. Then while strengthening ties with Germany, Japan should try its best to avoid war with the Soviet Union. Rōyama Masamichi, a leading proponent of democratic socialism, welcomed the

64. Toyoda, *Matsuoka Yōsuke*, vol. 1, 266–68; vol. 2, 106–13.

German-Soviet Nonaggression Pact, because he regarded it as a step toward the creation of regional blocs. Not only did Nazi Germany and the Soviet Union share radically new political and economic orders, they also despised the Wilsonian world order created after World War I. Given these shared interests, Rōyama anticipated that Germany and the Soviet Union could together form the "new imperialism" against the "old imperialism," which hopefully could coexist with Japan's pan-Asianism.[65]

The plan to invite the Soviets to join the "New Order" of the Axis powers emerged from the belief that the Soviets would support, rather than oppose, Japan's "revolutionary" challenge to Anglo-American world dominance. On the eve of signing the Tripartite Pact with Germany, Matsuoka confessed that the accord was a prelude to shaking hands with the Soviet Union.[66] Matsuoka proposed to establish a Eurasian bloc of Japan, Germany, Italy, and the Soviet Union as a deterrent against the Anglo-American alliance. Its Asian component would curb the US intervention in China.[67]

By July 1939 a wider spectrum of Japanese leaders had endorsed this idea. Former prime minister Prince Konoe Fumimaro, ambassador to Italy Shiratori Toshio, and ambassador to Germany Ōshima Hiroshi all supported a Japanese-German-Italian-Soviet alliance.[68] Takagi Sōkichi, the Imperial Navy's leading planner, inspired by the signing of the German-Soviet Nonaggression Pact, examined several options for multilateral diplomacy and recommended this particular four-nation alliance as the most beneficial to Japan's interests.[69] In November 1940, the monthly journal *Kaizō* echoed this sentiment in an article that predicted a Soviet-Japanese nonaggression pact as the natural sequel to the Tripartite Pact. The May 1941 issue of *Kaizō* featured four articles on the neutrality pact with the Soviet Union, two of which stressed its linkage to the Tripartite

---

65. William Miles Fletcher III, *The Search for a New Order: Intellectuals and Fascism in Prewar Japan* (Chapel Hill: University of North Carolina Press, 1982), 109, 139.

66. Minowa Kimitada, *Matsuoka Yōsuke—sono ningen to gaikō* (Matsuoka Yosuke—personality and diplomacy) (Tokyo: Chūkō Shinsho, 1971), 173; Matsuoka Yōsuke Denki Kankō-kai (Matsuoka Yosuke Biography Editing Committee), ed., *Matsuoka Yōsuke—sono hito to shōgai* (Matsuoka Yosuke—his Life and Personality) (Tokyo: Kōdansha, 1974), 783, 799.

67. Hosoya Chihiro, "The Japanese-Soviet Neutrality Pact," in James Morley, ed., *The Fateful Choice: Japan's Advance into Southeast Asia, 1939–1941* (New York: Columbia University Press, 1980), 47 and 50; Miyazaki Yoshiyuki, "Saikō Matsuoka gaikō—sono kokunai seiji-teki yōin" (Matsuoka diplomacy reconsidered—a remedy for national consensus), *Gunji Shigaku* (The journal of military history) 27, nos. 2 & 3 (December 1991): 34; Minowa Kimitada, *Matsuoka Yōsuke* (Tokyo: Chūō Kōron Sha, 1989), 173.

68. Torii Tami, *Shōwa 20-nen* (1945), vol. 1, no. 1 (Tokyo: Sōshi Sha, 1985), 335–39.

69. Nomura Minoru, "Nichi-Doku-I-So rengō shisō no hōga to hōkai" (Rise and decline of the concept of Japanese-German-Italian-Soviet alliance), *Gunji shigaku* (The journal of military history) 11, no. 4 (March 1976): 2–14, especially 6–9.

Pact.[70] Because of the *Kaizō* articles and other news sources, the public knew there were ambitions to use the Soviet Union to contain Anglo-American global domination.

Stalin seemed to take an interest in neutrality with Japan. Matsuoka visited Moscow in late March 1941 on his way to Berlin and Rome to reaffirm the Axis alliance. Stalin is said to have been amused by Matsuoka's invitation to join the Tripartite Pact as an effort to challenge Anglo-American capitalism. Stalin first tested Matsuoka, directing him to tell the German foreign minister Joachim von Ribbentrop that "the Anglo-Saxons had never been Russia's 'friends.'" After visiting Germany and Italy, Matsuoka stopped in Moscow on his way home via the Trans-Siberian Railway. He detailed how Russia would be integrated into the tripartite arrangement through a Soviet-Japanese nonaggression pact regarding sovereign territories, including Outer Mongolia (for the Soviets) and Manchukuo (for Japan). Supplementing the German-Soviet Nonaggression Pact with a similar treaty with Japan would avoid war on the Soviet European and Asian fronts. Stalin decided to sign the neutrality pact.[71]

After the outbreak of the Soviet-German war, the Japanese government abided by the Soviet-Japanese Neutrality Pact and declined Germany's request to attack the Soviet Union. Instead the Japanese Army advanced southward into French Indochina, a decision that led to direct confrontation with the United States. In the course of the Nomura-Hull talks that began informally in the spring of 1941 between Japanese ambassador Nomura Kichisaburō and United States secretary of state Cordell Hull, the prospect of American intervention in East Asian affairs became real when the US government, using the threat of an oil embargo, demanded Japan's withdrawal from not only French Indochina, but China as well. Matsuoka had hoped to pressure the United States with the four-nation alliance, in addition to the Axis alliance, so that it would agree to sit at the negotiation table with Japan.

Though Matsuoka is said to have been devastated by the news of Pearl Harbor, because it destroyed any hope for rapprochement with the United States, the plan for a German-Japanese-Soviet alliance stayed afloat for some time through the support of the Imperial Army and the Foreign Ministry. From Japan's perspective the neutrality pact with the Soviet Union dampened the antifascist spirit

---

70. Gushima Kenesaburō, "Sangoku Dōmei to NiSso kankei" (The Tripartite Pact and Japanese-Soviet relations), *Kaizō* 22, no. 20 (November 1940): 288–95. The two articles that appeared in the May 1941 issue of *Kaizō* (23, no. 9) were Baba Hideo, "NiSso Chūritsu Jōyaku no seiritsu to igi" (Conclusion and significance of the Japanese-Soviet Neutrality Treaty), 102–4; and Ōkubo Tetsuo, "Sangoku Dōmei yori NiSso Chūritsu Jyōyaku e" (From the Tripartite Alliance to the Japanese-Soviet neutrality treaty), 105–9.

71. Gabriel Gorodetsky, *Grand Delusion: Stalin and the German Invasion of Russia* (New Haven, CT: Yale University Press, 1999), 8, 193, and 197.

of the Grand Alliance. At a more subtle level, rapprochement between Japanese fascism and Soviet communism undermined the ideological legitimacy of Asian communist movements against the Japanese empire.

Evidence suggests that the Japanese public believed throughout the Pacific War that Moscow and Washington shared little under the Grand Alliance. Nakano Gorō, a communist and a former immigrant to the United States who had been deported as an enemy national in the summer of 1942, explained his skepticism about the Grand Alliance in a June 1944 journal article about the enigma of wartime American-Russian cultural relations. Americans saw Russians as filthy workers and peasant revolutionaries. When Germany attacked Russia, Russians became transformed in American eyes to the harmless and pitiful prey of Nazism. Their popularity soared. Yet this newfound embrace of Russians still revealed underlying divisions. Nakano cited the Warner Brothers film *Mission to Moscow* (1943), which portrayed real political figures such as Stalin and Churchill. *Life* magazine acknowledged that the Russians looked so Americanized that they might be living in Kansas City. Producing a commercial film out of the somber business of American-Russian diplomacy was itself so American in taste and style; reproducing Russia in the American image demonstrated typical American vanity and self-satisfaction. The American public would never accept any narrative but one that showed the American way of life triumphant over the Soviet. Nakano thus contended that the many cultural and ideological differences between the United States and the Soviet Union would make it difficult to cement an alliance.[72]

Even after the Pacific War began, the Japanese press, especially the progressive monthly journal *Kaizō*, discussed the Soviet Union and communism in a positive light. The relative freedom of public debate on communism was possible due to a lack of any unified regulation of the media. Different agencies such as the Home Ministry, the Japanese Cabinet Information Bureau (Naikaku Jōhō-bu), and the Information Department of the War Ministry adopted different codes of censorship. An article that received approval from the Home Ministry and went into print might still receive postpublication censorship by the War Ministry.[73] In this way Japanese readers had opportunities to learn about current world conditions of "imperialism" (*teikoku-shugi*) and "communism" (*kyōsan-shugi*).

---

72. Nakano Gorō, "Bei-So kankei no bunka-teki kōsatsu" (Cultural observations of American-Russian relations), *Gekkan Roshiya* (Russia monthly) 10, no. 6 (June, 1944): 2–10.

73. Hōsei Daigaku Ōhara Shakai-mondai Kenkyū-jo, "Nihon rōdō nenkan tokubetsu-ban: Taiheiyō Sensō-ka no rōdō undō," dai-5-hen "Genron tōsei to bunka undō," dai-6-shō "Shuppan katsudō" (Ohara Institute for Social Research, Hosei University, "The labor year book of Japan, special edition," Section 5, "Speech control and cultural movement," chapter 6, "Publication activities") (October 1965), available online at http://oohara.mt.tama.hosei.ac.jp/rn/senji2/rnsenji2-223.html.

A crackdown on the procommunist press went into effect with the Yokohama Incident, in which dozens of journalists and researchers were arrested and tortured by the Special Higher Police of Yokohama. In September 1942 *Kaizō* published, with permission from both the Interior Ministry and the Japanese Cabinet Information Bureau, "Sekaishi no dōkō to Nihonshi" (Japanese history and a trend in world history). Its author, Hosokawa Karoku, called on Japan to learn from the Soviet Union and to endorse the principles of freedom and independence for all people in order to make the East Asian new order a true success. The Army Press Section openly questioned the discretion of the *Kaizō* editorial board in printing such a procommunist article. The subsequent arrest and investigation of Hosokawa converged with a completely separate investigation of the SMR Research Department; together the two investigations suggested that communist sympathizers, including Hosokawa, were plotting to rebuild the Japanese Communist Party.

Stalin openly renounced any ties with Japanese communists. Confronting an acute need to reaffirm his alliance with Roosevelt and Churchill, Stalin declared in May 1943 that the Soviet Union was focusing on the anti-Hitler coalition and not fomenting world revolution. Acknowledging that each country had particular societal contradictions that could complicate how it addressed labor movements, Stalin said the Soviet Union could not possibly coordinate all communists around the world. He dissolved the Comintern because it would only hinder the further strengthening of national workers' parties. This gave the Japanese government, after the Yokohama Incident, room to continue the policy of neutrality with the Soviet Union. Communist ideology, as Japan's multifaceted wartime interactions with the Soviet Union illustrated, did not impede their relationship.

The Soviet Union was more than a double-edged sword for Japan. While the Japanese government considered communist ideology harmful to Japan's national polity (kokutai), the Japanese also found its revolutionary vision of progress appealing. If Japan could harness the power of its potential enemy across the border, they could perhaps work together as gatekeepers of Asia. To regard prewar Japan simply as anticommunist and anti-Soviet obfuscates the nature of Japan's Eurasian-Pacific War.

2

CULTURE AND RACE

Russians in the Japanese Empire

Before the war, many Japanese people had a sense of belonging to Eurasia, physically, psychologically, and culturally. Moscow and Berlin were closer to Japan than New York and Washington, DC. The intricate railway networks built across Korea and Manchuria under Japan's colonial rule connected with trans-Siberian rail routes so Japanese could travel to Europe by train, which was three times faster than a voyage by sea. Trans-Siberian railway tickets had been sold in Japan since 1911. Starting in 1927 Japanese travelers could purchase international train tickets to European cities at major train stations within the colonial empire, including Tokyo, Yokohama, Osaka, Pusan, Pyongyang, and Dalian. For prewar Japanese, Moscow served as a gateway to Europe. In 1937, a Japanese tourist could travel from Tokyo to Moscow in ten to eleven days, and via Moscow, Berlin in thirteen days, and Paris in fourteen days.[1] A voyage from Yokohama to major port cities of the West Coast of the United States via Honolulu took about two weeks; a transcontinental train ride from the West Coast to the East Coast via Chicago took another two days or more.

---

1. Sōda Hideo, Maboroshi no jikoku-hyō (Short-lived train timetables) (Tokyo: Kōbun Sha, 2005), chapter 1. According to Sōda (pp. 20–76), the trans-Eurasian train travel in 1937 took place as follows. Depart Tokyo on super express train Fuji at 15:00, arrive at Shimonoseki at 9:30 the following day and take a ferry departing there at 10:30 and reach Pusan at 18:00. Depart Pusan on express train Hikari at 18:55 and arrive at Hsinking (Changchun), the capital of Manchukuo, at 23:06 on the following (third) day, and Harbin at 7:20 on the fourth day. After twenty-six hour ride from Harbin, reach Manzhouli on the sixth day and transfer to the trans-Siberian railway. Arrive at Moscow at 11:30 on the eleventh day, Berlin at 10:23 on the thirteenth day and Paris at 6:43 on the fourteenth day.

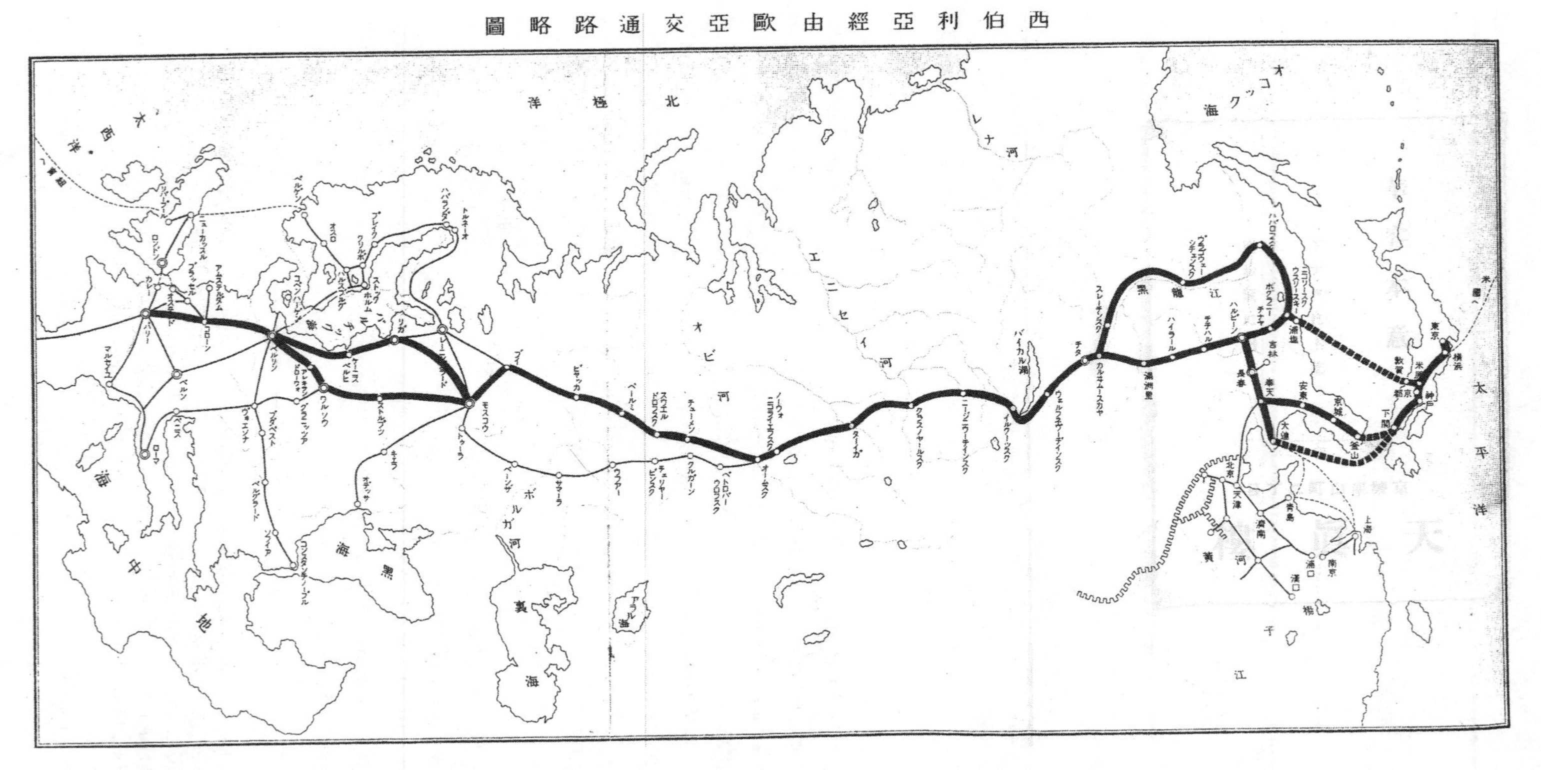

MAP 2.1 The Trans-Eurasian Continental Railway Network via Western Siberia, 1927. Three broken lines indicate ferry routes that connected Japan to the Eurasian continent at the ports of Dalian, Pusan, and Vladivostok, respectively. From Moscow, one could continue by train to Paris, Berlin, and Rome, as well as Stockholm, Vienna, London (via ferry ride from Calais, France), and even to Constantinople.

Source: Uemura Tomokiyo, *Ōshū ryokō an'nai* (Guide to Travel to Europe) (Tokyo: Shinkō Sha, 1927; reprint Yumani Shobō, 2000).

At both popular and governmental levels, the sense of cultural proximity to Russia further enhanced the vision of Russia as a member of the East Asian order. The paucity of Japanese-American cultural and social contacts made it difficult for the Japanese to envision a trans-Pacific alliance that could enrich Japan's colonial empire. In contrast the Japanese celebrated compatibility of Japanese and Russian cultures even during the war and never attempted to rid Russian culture from their empire in the name of pan-Asianism.

Popular perceptions as well as scholarly studies defined Russia's demographic and cultural character as multiethnic and multiracial, which helped the Japanese to develop a sense of affinity with the Russians and to celebrate the two peoples as members of Eurasia. In contrast to Japan's postwar image, the Japanese empire was fairly tolerant of racial and ethnic diversity, including intermarriage between Japanese masters and colonial subjects, most of which took place between Japanese women and colonial men.[2] The Soviet-Japanese Neutrality Pact, signed on April 13, 1941, was much more than a military pact: to the Japanese it was also a means to cosmopolitanism in Japan's colonial empire. After signing the neutrality pact, Stalin is said to have embraced Foreign Minister Matsuoka Yōsuke in celebration of their common Asian roots. Stalin's reference to his Georgian background emphasized the notion of Russians as "Asians" to the Japanese public. Some Japanese leaders, notably Prince Higashikuni Naruhiko, repeatedly reiterated the Asian unity of Russians and Japanese against the Anglo-American invasion of China.[3] This racial view had an ironic manifestation in Nazi propaganda that condemned Russians as "Asiatics" and "Mongols" whose "innate barbarism" augmented their fanaticism for communism, just like another group of "subhumans," the Jews.[4] The lesser "whiteness" of the Russians facilitated their inclusion in Japan's Pan-Asian rhetoric.

Under the neutrality pact, the Japanese government praised the Soviet Union as a nation of diverse racial, ethnic, and national groups that did not sanction discriminatory racism against outsiders. In contrast, even when experimenting with multiethnic and multiracial state building in Manchuria, Tokyo never appreciated the United States as a nation of immigrants. Ordinary Japanese people saw blacks, Jews, American Indians, and above all Asians as permanent outcasts

2. Yukiko Koshiro, "East Asia's 'Melting-Pot': Reevaluating Race Relations in Japan's Colonial Empire," in Walter Demel and Rotem Kowner, eds., *Race and Racism in Modern East Asia: Western and Eastern Constructions* (Leiden: Brill, 2012).

3. Higashikuni Naruhiko, *Ichi kōzoku no sensō nikki* (A war diary of one member of the Imperial Family) (Tokyo: Nihon Shūhō Sha, 1957).

4. Omer Bartov, "Germany's Unforgettable War: The Twisted Road from Berlin to Moscow and Back," *Diplomatic History* 25, no. 3 (summer 2001): 413. The four-nation alliance of Japan, Germany, Italy, and the Soviet Union existed briefly, from the conclusion of the Soviet-Japanese Neutrality Pact on April 13, 1941, until the outbreak of the German-Russian war in June that year.

of American society and believed this racial and ethnic schism weakened America.[5] The perception of Russia's historical connections to Asian peoples, and America's lack of one, drove these divergent characterizations. The Intelligence Bureau (Jōhō-kyoku) of the Japanese Ministry of Foreign Affairs positively reported on the Asian flavor of Moscow in its monthly analysis of international relations.[6] After the outbreak of the Pacific War, the journal *Gekkan Roshiya* (Russia monthly) occasionally covered issues of ethnic diversity within the Soviet Union. With a strong emphasis on Russia's historical interactions with Asia, these articles described how Russia, a Mongol tributary in the thirteenth century, defeated and absorbed the Khanate of the Golden Horde in the fourteenth century and began the great thrust across Siberia in the sixteenth century. They asserted that Turkic peoples—Turkmen, Uzbeks, Tajiks, Kazakhs, and Kirghiz—constituted the historical, ethnic, and emotional foundation of the Soviet Union. The racial and ethnic amalgamation of nation building, these articles claimed, meant that Soviet citizens possessed certain Asian characteristics.[7]

Ono Nobuzō, a professor at Chūō University argued that the Soviets were tolerant of non-Western peoples and less chauvinistic compared to other Europeans because the Slavs had long lived in a conglomerate Eurasia. This tradition of emotional and cultural egalitarianism among races (*minzoku*) was further reinforced under the communist system.[8] Imaoka Jūichirō, a linguist specializing in Hungarian and Finnish, acknowledged that the Soviet Union had internal nationalist and ethnic conflicts. Persecution of and discrimination against Asian minorities existed because the Russian empire and the Soviet Union had developed side by side with Asian (non-Slavic and non-Russian) peoples. An expert also on Pan-Turanism, Imaoka claimed that the Soviets' dealings with Asian demands to preserve their own languages, culture, customs, and lifestyles had let it, more than any other European government, to be cognizant of Asian aspira-

---

5. On wartime Japanese understanding of Americans and their society, see John Dower, *War without Mercy: Race and Power in the Pacific War* (New York: Pantheon, 1986), which focuses on the slogan "Kichiku BeiEi (Demonic and beasty Anglo-America)." The difficulty of finding Japanese records on America may be attributed to the censorship that prohibited any reference to the enemy. In *Trans-Pacific Racisms and the U.S. Occupation of Japan* (New York: Columbia University Press, 1999), I discuss popular Japanese understandings of American racism immediately after the war, which allows a glimpse into their wartime mindset. See pp. 63–64, for example.

6. Jyōhō-kyoku, *Kokusai Jijō* (23) "Mosukuwa no hanashi" (The Bureau of Information, International Affairs [23] "A story of Moscow"), May 25, 1942.

7. Hasegawa Shun, "Roshiyajin kishitsu" (The Russian characteristics), *Gekkan Roshiya* 9, no. 5 (May 1943): 34–38; Chiba Ryō, "Surabu minzoku-shi kan to Sekai Taisen" (The historic view of the Slavs and World War II), *Gekkan Roshiya* 9, no. 9 (September 1943): 4–12.

8. Ono Nobuzō, "Sobietto Renpō no sensō shidō hōshin (2)" (The Soviet Union and its war planning and principle [2]), *Gaikō Jihō*, no. 953 (January 1, 1945): 27.

tions for liberation and self-rule. This history, Imaoka concluded, inspired hope that the Soviet Union would understand Japan's pan-Asianism.[9]

Prince Higashikuni Naruhiko, along with Ishiwara Kanji, Koiso Kuniaki, Kuahara Fusanosuke, and Gotō Ryūnosuke, set a goal of sensitizing Russians to their Asian identity.[10] Expressing enthusiasm for this proposal throughout the war, Prince Higashikuni wrote in his private journal, "Japan has to give the Soviet Union a keen awareness of being a member of Asia so that it will never stand on the side of the whites" (April 14, 1942); "Stalin is aware of and proud of being Asian, so it's necessary to have the Soviet people feel the same way" (September 27, 1944); and "We have to try to help Soviet people develop an Asian identity so we can stand together against Anglo-America" (May 15, 1945).[11]

An anonymous essay in *Gaikō Jihō* (Diplomatic review) in May 1944 argued that the Soviet Union was a dualistic nation (*ryōmen-teki kokka*) that embodied the geographical and racial essences of Europe and Asia. Since modern Japan had also acquired a dualistic national character by assimilating Western civilization while retaining its distinctive Asianness, this would allow the two nations' diplomacy to move along the progression of equality and mutuality.[12]

Positive perceptions of Russian tolerance of Asians had been confirmed by increasing contact between Japanese and Russians during Japan's continental expansion in the early twentieth century. After the Bolshevik Revolution, thousands of Russian political refugees settled in Japan and across the Japanese empire. Whereas Japanese immigrants to the United States triggered diplomatic tension, Russian émigrés in Japan, though far fewer in number than Japanese in America, rarely created cultural friction, even in wartime. In the shift from cosmopolitanism in the Taishō period to isolationism in the 1930s, Russian cultural imports continued to be appreciated. After the creation of Manchukuo, the presence of Russians in the Japanese empire was regarded as a precious link to the West. Under the state slogan of racial harmony, the government even granted the Russian residents full legitimacy to coexist with the Japanese, Chinese, Manchu, Koreans and Mongols.

Comparative surveys of personal interactions Japanese had with Americans and Russians in Japan imply that Americans in general did not attempt to break

9. Imaoka Jūichirō, "Sorenpō no minzoku mondai" (The ethnic and national problems within the Soviet Union), *Gekkan Roshiya* 8, no. 9 (September 1942): 20–24.

10. Higashikuni Naruhiko, *Ichi kōzoku no sensō nikki* (A war diary of one member of the Imperial Family) (Tokyo: Nihon Shūhō Sha, 1957), 103, 107, 138–39, 147, 184.

11. Higashikuni, *Ichi kōzoku no sensō nikki*, 103, 107, 147, 184.

12. Jiron—"NiSso kankei yurugazu" (My opinion—Soviet-Japanese relations will not change), *Gaikō Jihō*, no. 945 (May 1, 1944): 4.

racial barriers. In contrast, various records from the prewar period affirm that Russia was a far closer neighbor to Japan than America. Wartime Japan had reasons to retain its Eurasian neighbor to the north as an ally and to regard its presence in East Asia as a natural consequence, not as an invasion by an outsider.

Americans in Japan: The Most Isolated

Sergei G. Elisseeff (1889–1975), son of a wealthy businessman in St. Petersburg, Russia, was the first Western (white) student ever enrolled full-time in Tokyo Imperial University and later became a founder of Japanese studies in the United States. Majoring in classical Japanese literature, Elisseeff completed his bachelor's degree with honors in 1912, and his master's degree in 1914, before returning to Russia. Soon afterward in 1921 he fled the Bolshevik Revolution to France, where he taught Japanese literature at the Sorbonne. In 1932 he was invited to teach at Harvard University. From then until 1955, when he returned to Paris, he was a driving force behind the development of Japanese studies in the United States.

Although Elisseeff served as an agent of rich and flourishing cultural exchanges between Japan, Russia, and America, distinctive differences marked the cultural and racial relationship between Russians and Japanese and that between Americans and Japanese, which provided a nuanced psychological backbone of Japan's Eurasian-Pacific War. Elisseeff immersed himself in Japanese culture; he studied and played with Japanese classmates; he lived in a traditional Japanese-style house; and he mingled with members of a literary circle. Like him, thousands of Russian émigrés lived among the Japanese, even as Japanese immigrants on the West Coast faced discrimination. Worse, Americans in Japan did not assimilate but lived in an upscale community isolated from ordinary Japanese people. The aloof lifestyle of Americans in Japan only affirmed the Japanese conception of white racism or racism by white people against others.

The enactment in the United States of a series of anti-Oriental immigration and naturalization laws—originally aimed at Chinese laborers but quickly expanded to target other Asians at the turn of the twentieth century—severely hurt Japanese pride by conveying that the Japanese, too, were inferior. The Japanese became intensely aware of how Americans distinguished between them on the basis of America's "whiteness" and Japan's "nonwhiteness."[13]

As a rising imperial power, Japan found it inappropriate and humiliating to be treated by Western nations as just another Asian nation. The particular circum-

---

13. Yukiko Koshiro, *Trans-Pacific Racisms and the U.S. Occupation of Japan* (New York: Columbia University Press, 1999), 3.

TABLE 2.1 Alien population in Japan by nationality, 1876–1937

	NATIONALITY						
YEAR	CHINA	US	UK	GERMANY	RUSSIA	FRANCE	TOTAL
1876	2449	274	1279	231	51	260	4972
1895	3642	1022	1878	493	222	391	8246
1905	10388	1612	2114	616	58	531	16558
1911	8145	1762	2633	815	112	530	14970
1924	16902	1870	1848	930	818	398	24122
1932	17819	2015	1969	1040	1537	462	26885
1937	15526	2347	2360	1959	1590	583	30838

Source: Nihon Tōkei Kyōkai (Japan Statistical Association), *Nihon chōki tōkei sōran*, vol. 1 (Historical statistics of Japan) (Tokyo: Japan Statistics Bureau, 1987), 52–53.

stances of Japanese immigration to the United States and the political stature of the United States in the world community forced the Americans to confront the dual racial identity Japan had created for itself.[14] Japan felt the US government should, and did, treat the Japanese nation as a symbolic "honorary white" race in the international community. Treating individual Japanese immigrants as honorary whites, however, proved impossible in American society where human interactions across color lines were controlled by rigidly constructed antimiscegenation, immigration, and naturalization laws. The US government ultimately chose to brand Japanese immigrants undesirable members of a nonwhite race—a designation the Japanese government had attempted to avoid at all cost since the late nineteenth century. The anti-Japanese Immigration Act of 1924 was America's final refusal to address the disjunction between how it dealt with Japan as a nation diplomatically (as an honorary white nation) and how it dealt with Japanese as individuals (as nonwhites). This action prompted Japanese nationalists to justify severing any psychological affinity with the United States and, in turn, to promote Japan's road to pan-Asianism.[15]

American sojourners in prewar Japan had steadily grown in number since the late nineteenth century and had always outnumbered German residents, even after Germany became Japan's ally through the Anti-Comintern Pact in 1936. Nonetheless, these Americans alienated ordinary Japanese people from America. With a self-important sense of mission and superior wealth, these American residents kept themselves apart from ordinary Japanese as no other Westerners

14. In *Trans-Pacific Racisms and the U.S. Occupation of Japan*, I explain that modern Japan developed a contradictory self-identity that fused a demand for the diplomatic status of an honorary white with an insistence on the fact that the Japanese were an oppressed colored race. I call this complex racial awareness Japan's "dual racial identity."

15. Koshiro, *Trans-Pacific Racisms*, 9–12.

TABLE 2.2 Occupations of US, British, German, and French residents in Japan, 1924

US RESIDENTS (TOTAL POP: 1870/POP WITH JOBS: 922)		BRITISH RESIDENTS (TOTAL POP: 1848/POP WITH JOBS: 810)	
Christian missionaries	359 (38.9%)	Traders and businessmen	432 (53.3%)
Teachers and professors	243 (26.3%)	Christian missionaries	150 (18.5%)
Traders and businessmen	220 (23.9%)	Teachers and professors	124 (15.3%)
Engineers	47 (5.1%)	Engineers	60 (7.4%)
US government officials	33 (3.6%)	British government officials	33 (4.1%)
Journalists	14 (1.5%)	Journalists	8 (1%)
Medical doctors	6 (0.6%)	Medical doctors	3 (0.4%)
GERMAN RESIDENTS (TOTAL POP: 930/POP WITH JOBS: 434)		**FRENCH RESIDENTS (TOTAL POP: 398/POP WITH JOBS: 269)**	
Traders and businessmen	230 (53%)	Christian missionaries	118 (43.9 %)
Teachers and professors	74 (17.1%)	Teachers and professors	101 (37.5%)
Engineers	66 (15.2%)	Traders and businessmen	34 (12.6%)
Christian missionaries	49 (11.3%)	French government officials	11 (4.1%)
German government officials	11 (2.5%)	Engineers	5 (1.9%)
Journalists	2 (0.5%)	Journalists	0 (0%)
Medical doctors	2 (0.5%)	Medical doctors	0 (0%)

Source: "Naichi zairyū gaikokujin shokugyō betsu jin'in hyō" (Statistical chart of foreign residents and their occupations in Japan proper) (December 1924), in "Zai Honpō gaikokujin ni kansuru tōkei chōsa zakken" (Miscellaneous statistical data on foreign residents in Japan), vol. 1 [K-3-7-0-15], DRO.

did. American whiteness was a peculiar racial and cultural phenomenon even in Japan. Demographically, American residents were the most "isolated" of Westerners in Japan.[16] American residents in Japan had a very narrow range of occupations. The American population was characterized by extremely high percentages of missionaries and teachers. In contrast businessmen formed the largest occupational group among British residents. Although French residents had even higher concentrations of missionaries and teachers, Americans exceeded the French in number.

In 1924, 775 Christian missionaries worked in Japan: 359 of them Americans (46.3 percent), followed by 150 British (19.3 percent) and 118 French (15.2 percent). The overall presence of the American missionaries in Japan was amplified because they mostly lived with spouses and children, whereas most of the French missionaries were Catholic priests. In the same year, there were 661 foreign

16. Naimu-shō Keiho-kyoku, "Zairyū gaikokujin gaikyō" (Summary reports of foreign residents in Japan) (December 1921), in Ogino Fujio, ed. *Tokkō keisatsu kankei shiryō shūsei* (Anthology of documents concerning the Japanese Special Higher Police) (Tokyo: Fuji Shuppan, 1992), vol. 15, 29.

TABLE 2.3 Foreign residents in various occupations, 1924

CHRISTIAN MISSIONARIES (TOT. 775)		EDUCATORS (TOT. 661)		TRADERS AND BUSINESSMEN (TOT. 3399)	
United States	359	United States	243	China	2060
Britain	150	Britain	124	Britain	432
France	118	France	101	Germany	230
Canada	49	Germany	74	United States	220
Germany	49	China	38	India	114
		Russia	26	Switzerland	46
				Portugal	37
				France	34

Source: "Naichi zairyū gaikokujin shokugyō betsu jin'in hyō" (Statistical chart of foreign residents and their occupations in Japan proper) (December, 1924), in "Zai Honpō gaikokujin ni kansuru tōkei chōsa zakken" (Miscellaneous statistical data on foreign residents in Japan), vol. 1 [K-3-7-0-15], DRO.

teachers and professors: 243 were Americans (36.8 percent), followed by 124 British (18.8 percent), and 101 French (15.3 percent). The same occupational trends by nationality continued into the 1930s. In 1932 out of 2,015 American residents, 734 had jobs and 1,281 were family members. Of those with occupations, 246 (33.5 percent) were missionaries and 255 (34.7 percent) were educators, while 171 (23.3 percent) were traders and businessmen and 39 (5.3 percent) were engineers. That year American missionaries comprised 27.9 percent of all foreign missionaries residing in Japan (881), followed by British (163, or 18.5 percent) and Canadian (117, or 13.3 percent) missionaries. American educators also comprised 33.6 percent of all foreign teachers in Japan (759), followed by British (149, or 19.6 percent) and French (112, or 14.8 percent).[17]

The autobiography of Edwin Reischauer (1910–90), a distinguished scholar of Japanese studies at Harvard University and later US ambassador to Japan in the early 1960s, illustrates the segregated lifestyle of American missionaries and their families. Born in Japan in 1910 to missionary parents, Reischauer grew up close to two Japanese maids, both daughters of Christian families. The Japanese maids had a habit of calling him "little master" (*kodan'na sama*) and his older brother "young master" (*waka dan'na sama*). He claimed that his family treated these Japanese girls with respect and as equals—or perhaps "with an excess of American egalitarianism" in his own words. He admitted that these two Japanese maids were the most influential Japanese presence in his life, because he had few

17. Naimu-shō Keiho-kyoku, "Naichi kyojyū gaikokujin shoku-betsu jin'in hyō" (July 1932), in "Zai Honpō gaikokujin ni kansuru tōkei chōsa zakken" (Miscellaneous statistical data on foreign residents in Japan), vol. 1 [K-3-7-0-15], DRO.

to no contacts with ordinary Japanese people. During his commute to an international school, he and his Western classmates enjoyed playing pranks on train conductors. He wrote that Western children enjoyed immunity from official reprimand without speculating why the Japanese officials did not, or could not, punish them. Reischauer did not play with Japanese children. He wrote in his autobiography that it was because the Japanese people tended to discriminate against whites, but he also confessed his parents were class-conscious and did not want their children to mingle with unsophisticated Japanese children from a lower echelon of society. As a result Reischauer had limited contact only with the children of Japanese colleagues of his parents, Japanese students who attended his English-speaking school, and children of the upper-class Japanese families whom he met on the tennis court in the exclusive summer resort of Karuizawa. He once agreed to teach English to one such boy when he was twelve, but with his ability to teach understandably limited he confessed that no genuine friendship emerged out of these unexciting lessons.[18]

Japanese Protestants also contributed to Japanese perceptions of America as distant and aloof. In the late nineteenth century, Japanese Protestant converts enjoyed privileged contact with the American establishment through American missionaries in Japan and formed a small but influential community bridging the Pacific. Japanese Protestants acquired a degree of American patriotism enshrined with religious fervor and adopted the American missionary sentiment toward heathen Japanese. They were trained to envision that remaking Japan in the image of Protestant America would make Japan a superior land of democracy and freedom.

In his early years, the Protestant Uchimura Kanzō (1861–1930) believed that America was blessed with unprecedented levels of freedom and humanism and that America's republicanism nurtured great arts and literatures.[19] Nitobe Inazō (1862–1933) saw Perry's expedition to Japan as a manifestation of God's will that the spirit of the United States should spread across the world. Nitobe believed Japan should be the first Asian nation to embrace the American mission and to help realize the American dream in Asia.[20] Takagi Yasaka, a protégé of Nitobe, strongly believed that the American Protestant tradition, especially manifest in conscientious individualism, provided the fundamental pillar of American

---

18. Edwin Reischauer, *My Life between Japan and America* (New York: Harper & Row, 1986), 9–11, 20–21. See also the Japanese version, Tokuoka Takao, trans., *Raishawā jiden* (Autobiography of Reischauer) (Tokyo: Bungei Shunjū Sha, 1987), 29–33, 46.

19. Kamei Shunsuke, *Uchimura Kanzō* (Tokyo: Chūkō Shinsho, 1977), 53.

20. Furuya Jun, "Amerika kenkoku no rinen zou no hen'you," in National Institute for Research Advancement (NIRA), ed., *Amerika kenkoku no rinen to Nichi-Bei kankei* (The founding of the United States and US-Japan relations) NIRA Report no. 940051 (Tokyo: NIRA, 1995), 89.

democracy. In order for Japan to develop liberal democracy, he felt the Japanese first had to adopt the Puritan spirit. This was a problematic thesis, because it assigned a moral precondition to the adoption of American democracy: the Japanese were not "good" enough to understand American democracy unless they accepted Protestantism. By adhering to this line of thinking, the leading Japanese Protestants separated themselves from their fellow Japanese and further contributed to the image of America's exclusivity.

The sense of oneness with the United States cultivated by Japanese Protestants was shattered when the American government moved to prohibit all Japanese immigrants based on their racial inability to assimilate into American civilization. Japanese Protestant leaders realized that under American racism all Japanese were alike, regardless of whether they were Protestant (civilized) or not (heathen). Nitobe was determined never to visit the United States again until the Immigration Act of 1924, known in Japan as the Japanese Exclusion Act of 1924, was abolished. He argued that the corrupt America of his day had no redemptive Lincoln figure and insisted from this point forward that Japan alone should provide Asia, and the world, with spiritual guidance. Uchimura declared that racism was a sign of moral decline among American people, who were no longer the true scions of Puritans who built America on a belief in God, justice, and humanity for all. Uchimura stated that it was time for Japanese Christians to sever ties with corrupt American Christians and to become independent in their faith in God. Toward that goal Uchimura suggested five anti-American actions: do not migrate to the United States, do not use American-made products, do not receive American aid, do not read works published by Americans, and do not attend American churches.[21] Such extreme proposals suggest how Uchimura's early commitment to the American ideal had a fragile foundation in his vain desire to be "equal" with the "superior" Americans.

Efforts to salvage a trans-Pacific friendship were made by Christians such as Sydney Gulick, Kagawa Toyohiko, and even Nitobe Inazō, but the limit of such attempts is embodied in the figure of Takagi Yasaka, a student of Uchimura and the founding father of American studies in Japan during this critical moment in US-Japanese relations. As a child Takagi learned about the United States from his father, a former samurai-scholar who studied at Amherst College and who became a professor of English at Gakushūin University, the exclusive institution for aristocratic and wealthy students. Takagi believed in the American Protestant tradition, especially its privileging of the individual consciousness, which provided the spiritual basis for American democracy.

---

21. Furuya Jun, "Amerika kenkoku no rinen zou no hen'you," 93–95.

In 1916, on graduating from Tokyo Imperial University with a law degree, Takagi started a career at the Ministry of Finance. When A. Barton Hepburn, the American legislator and banker, offered donations in 1918 to create a professorship of American studies at Tokyo Imperial University, the school recruited Takagi to inaugurate the Hepburn professorship. The university sent him to Harvard University to earn a master's degree in American history. At Harvard he studied topics from Thomas Jefferson and Turner's frontier thesis to American economic history. Upon returning to Tokyo Imperial University in 1924 at the age of thirty-five, Takagi began teaching courses on the US constitution, history, and foreign relations. In the 1930s he wrote on the Japanese exclusion law as well as American progressivism and also became a member of the Institute of Pacific Relations, serving as an ambassador of goodwill between the two nations. Impressive and expansive as his friendships with leading scholars, politicians, and businessmen in both Japan and the United States were, his scholarly works were never consistent in theme and theory and his focus on America was too diffuse to give a clear indication of his views on American-Japanese relations. Should the trans-Pacific relationship only belong to people with power and prestige? Who would define and shape the nature of such a relationship? Should it belong to Japanese Protestant converts like him? In spite of his commitment to US-Japanese friendship, Takagi's scholarly works did not answer any of these questions.

After the passage of the Japanese Exclusion Act in 1924, American-Japanese friendship ironically turned into a fashionable topic for high society, both old and new money, interested in promoting good business relationships in spite of America's anti-Japanese immigration policy. Capitalist interests (which also embraced the imperialist venture) replaced Protestant missionary zeal in the pursuit of trans-Pacific friendship. As John Dower has argued, Joseph Grew, the US ambassador to Japan from 1932 to 1942, aimed to improve friendship with Japan, but he did so by equating high society with "real" Japan and gourmet dining with democracy. Grew, with his clubbish propensity, particularly favored a circle of aristocratic, moderate, and westernized Japanese, which included the emperor, the old court, "old liberals," and "pacifists." Their upper-class tastes allowed them to bond well with their American friends.[22] United States-Japanese friendship seemed to be the domain of increasingly selective groups.

The American residents' association with powerful and wealthy Japanese was most apparent in Karuizawa, Japan's premier resort town. In the late nineteenth century, American and Canadian missionaries built their own village in this serene mountain region and turned Karuizawa into their summer camp. By the

22. John Dower, *Empire and Aftermath: Yoshida Shigeru and the Japanese Experience, 1878–1954* (Cambridge, MA: Harvard University Press, 1979), 111.

1890s Karuizawa, now a small replica of an immaculate Western community, began attracting a select group of wealthy Japanese, who hoped to emulate the Western lifestyle available there and who also enjoyed socializing with the Western residents. By the early twentieth century, Karuizawa was the Mecca of an exclusive circle of upper-class Japanese, including aristocrats and even members of the Imperial family and high-ranking government officials.

American sojourners dominated the community of Karuizawa. In 1932 foreigners owned a total of 1,096 vacation houses there: Americans owned the most (525, or 47.9 percent), followed by the British (236, or 21.5 percent) and Germans (116, or 10.6 percent). Of 217 houses in Karuizawa owned by foreigners, 116 (53.5 percent) belonged to Americans, while 51 (23.5 percent) belonged to British and 25 (11.5 percent) to Germans. Of the 525 American residents in Karuizawa, 101 were missionaries who comprised 56.1 percent of the total population of Western missionaries in Karuizawa. Sixty-one of these Americans were educators, representing 54.5 percent of the population of foreign educators in Karuizawa.[23] In Karuizawa American spirituality was juxtaposed with American wealth.

American alienation from the Japanese public is further witnessed in the life of William Merrell Vories (1881–1964), the foremost pro-Japanese American living in prewar Japanese society. A Christian missionary who came to Japan in 1905 as an English teacher at a public high school in Shiga Prefecture, Vories married a daughter of a Japanese viscount and became a naturalized Japanese citizen in January 1941. Yet he never settled into a typical Japanese life. After being fired by the school for what it called his Christian propaganda during his two-year teaching stint, Vories launched a missionary-commercial enterprise. Called "the Yankee of all Yankees" by his Christian missionary friend Kagawa Toyohiko, Vories founded the Ōmi Mission (later renamed as the Ōmi Brotherhood, Inc.), a self-sufficient community in the American colonial style on Lake Biwa, on the outskirts of the ancient capital city of Kyoto. The community contained an office for his architectural firm, a trading office to import and sell American goods, a pharmaceutical plant, a sanatorium, a hospital, schools, and a YMCA hall, among other institutions. The mission had no visible social or cultural integration with surrounding Japanese communities. Even more so than Karuizawa, the community was a transplant of America onto Japanese soil.

Vories designed such prominent buildings as the Yama-no-ue Hotel, Karuizawa Tennis Court Club House, Tōyō Eiwa Girls' High School, Meiji Gakuin, and Doshisha University (both schools founded by American Protestant missionaries

---

23. Tokkō-hi (Confidential: the Japanese Special Higher Police), "Karuizawa hisho gaikokujin ni kansuru ken" (Reports of foreign residents vacationing in Karuizawa) (August 16, 1932), in "Zai Honpō gaikokujin ni kansuru tōkei chōsa zakken" (Miscellaneous statistical data on foreign residents in Japan), vol. 4 [K-3-7-0-15], DRO.

and that catered to upper-middle-class Japanese). He also designed more than four hundred Western-style houses—mansions, summer cottages, and ultramodern residences—for his Japanese clientele. His prominent clients included the Mitsui family (one of the *zaibatsu*); Marquis Tokugawa Yorisada, one of the great patrons of Western music in Japan; and Asabuki Tsunekichi, president of Imperial Life Insurance, the first president of the Tennis Association of Japan, and a charter member of the Tokyo Rotary Club.

As the most pro-Japanese American in the prewar period, Vories was celebrated for teaching "humanism" through his architectural styles. His humanism, blended with American pragmatism, emphasized family and individualism, sunlight and ventilation, and above all modesty in design.[24] All these values were meant for Japan's high society; Vories did not preach his American gospel to Japanese families who did not have the luxury of owning a mansion.

American attitudes to and practice of intermarriage made their racial isolation stand out further among the foreign Westerners. A 1927 survey conducted among 400 American and other European missionaries in Japan disclosed racial prejudice. Although 20 percent of them stated that "categorically the white race is superior to all others," a large number of them expressed opposition to interracial marriage because it resulted in biological degeneration.[25] Commensurate with rigid miscegenation laws in the United States, American intermarriage with Japanese citizens occurred at a much lower rate compared to other Westerners. In 1938 there were 7,577 alien residents in the Prefecture of Hyōgo, which contained the international port city of Kobe. The largest group was Chinese, (3,384 or 44.7 percent), trailed by the British (843, or 11.1 percent), German (620, or 8.2 percent), Russians/Soviet (425, or 5.6 percent), American (420, or 5.5 percent), French (137, or 1.8 percent), Canadian (90, or 1.2 percent), and Italian (69, or 0.9 percent).[26] According to the 1935 census of intermarriage, 16.5 percent of French (16), 13.3 percent of Swiss (13), and 11.6 percent of British (93) residents married Japanese. In contrast only 3.4 percent (13) of all American residents had Japanese spouses, only slightly higher than Chinese (2.4 percent [132]), but much

---

24. Yamagata Masaaki, *Bōrizu no jūtaku—dendō sareta Amerikan sutairu* (Houses Vories built—the gospel of American style) (Tokyo: Sumai no Toshokan, 1988); Yamagata Masaaki, *Bōrizu no kenchiku—Yūtopia to toshi no hana* (The architectural style of Vories—utopia and urban flowers) (Tokyo: Sōgen Sha, 1989).

25. A. Jorgensen, "Missionary Opinion on Race," *Japan Christian Quarterly* (January 1927), quoted in Carlo Caldarola, *Christianity: The Japanese Way* (Leiden: E. J. Brill, 1979), 39. Also see Yukiko Koshiro, "Introduction—Bridging an Ocean: American Missionaries and Asian Converts Reexamined," *Journal of American-East Asian Relations* 5, nos. 3–4 (fall–winter 1996): 221–22.

26. "Kyojū gaikokujin kokuseki betsu jin'in hyō," in "Zai Honpō gaikokujin ni kansuru tōkei chōsa zakken" (Miscellaneous statistical data on foreign residents in Japan), vol. 1 [K-3-7-0-15], DRO.

TABLE 2.4 Percentage of intermarriages with Japanese citizens in Hyōgo Prefecture, 1935

NATIONALITY	TOTAL POPULATION	POPULATION WITH JAPANESE SPOUSES	PERCENTAGE OF INTERNATIONAL MARRIAGE
Philippines	36	9	25
France	97	16	16.5
Switzerland	98	13	13.3
Britain	805	93	11.6
Germany	508	41	8.1
India	328	15	4.6
Netherlands	177	8	4.5
US	381	13	3.4
China	5443	132	2.4
Russia/USSR	406	8	2.0

Sources: "Kyojū gaikokujin kokuseki betsu jin'in hyō," in "Zai Honpō gaikokujin ni kansuru tōkei chōsa zakken" (Miscellaneous statistical data on foreign residents in Japan), vol. 1 [K-3-7-0-15], DRO; "Gaikokujin to kekkon seru Honpōjin narabi ni konketsuji chōsa ni kansuru ken" (Reports on Japanese nationals with foreign spouses and their mixed-blood offspring) (July 22, 1935), in "Zai Honpō gaikokujin ni kansuru tōkei chōsa zakken" (Miscellaneous statistical data on foreign residents in Japan), vol. 4 [K-3-7-0-15], DRO.

lower than Germans (8.1 percent [41]). There were no marriages between American women and Japanese men, whereas 37.5 percent of French and 17 percent of German intermarriages occurred with Japanese men. There were 626 mixed-race children at the time of this census: 342 of them had Chinese, 75 British, 61 German, 20 American, 18 French, 14 Swiss, 12 Dutch, and 2 Italian heritages. No further details about their living conditions were recorded.[27]

Robert Crowder, an English teacher from Illinois who taught at an elite Japanese high school in Kyūshū until the day of Pearl Harbor, wrote about the American tendency to establish isolated communities abroad. In Pyongyang, Korea, where he first taught English before he moved to Japan, he observed:

> [In] a quiet, beautiful little city where I performed my educational duties, [t]he school buildings and staff were complete American transplants. Even the students, for the most part, were Americans—the children of missionaries and businessmen. Life within the school compound was quite pleasant, with everyone's energies concentrated on teaching the children and converting the natives. There seemed to be no interest in,

27. "Gaikokujin to kekkon seru Honpōjin narabi ni konketsuji chōsa ni kansuru ken" (Reports on Japanese nationals with foreign spouses and their mixed-blood offspring) (July 22, 1935), in "Zai Honpō gaikokujin ni kansuru tōkei chōsa zakken" (Miscellaneous statistical data on foreign residents in Japan), vol. 4 [K-3-7-0-15], DRO.

> or recognition of, the art and culture of Korea. At times, I felt as though I might just as well have been living back in Bethany, Illinois, my small home town.[28]

According to his autobiography, Crowder had good rapport with Japanese colleagues, students, and neighbors in Kyūshū. On the day of the attack on Pearl Harbor, as police officers escorted him down the street, shopkeepers stood at their entrances bowing and saying good-bye. A few months later when he was interned in a defunct leprosarium, a Japanese colleague from the high school passed to him through the fence a box containing his cherished gold cuff links. He shared but a few examples of his friendship with Japanese. After he returned to the United States in 1943, he never visited Japan again.

Prewar Japan did not establish its own American studies. During the Pacific War a limited readership had access to publications on American studies, but the works were neither cohesive as a field, nor were they generally of high quality.[29] One book that appears to have had appeal to lay readers was *Amerika seishin to Amerika Kirisuto-kyō* (The American spirit and American Christianity) by the Christian philosopher Abe Kōzō. He expressed that America's self-identification as the chosen ones drove its global expansion. While every people possess exceptionalist awareness, Abe argued, the American case had a Messianic message. Americans had a Puritan concept of themselves as the chosen people saved by God's grace and they regarded all others as sinners destined to perish, unless saved by the Americans. In other words, the Americans saw themselves as saviors of the world. Americans rationalized interactions with other peoples in politics, diplomacy, and culture as a part of a mission to rescue the sinful and to achieve God's

---

28. Robert Crowder, "An American's Life in Japan before and after Pearl Harbor," *Journal of American-East Asian Relations* 3, no. 3 (fall 1994): 260.

29. *Amerika no sekai seiha-shugi kaibō* (Dissection of the American principle of global conquest) is a collection of four scholarly essays. "Amerika ryōdo kakuchō no rinen to teikoku-shugi no dōkō" (Trends in the American principle of territorial expansionism and imperialism) by Hosoiri Fujitarō, a professor at Rikkyo University, introduces three leading historians Samuel F. Bemis, Charles A. Beard, and Fred A. Shannon and their critical views of American expansionism. See Taiheiyō Kyōkai (The Pacific Association), ed., *Amerika no sekai seiha-shugi kaibō* (Dissection of the American principle of global conquest) (Tokyo: Taiheiyō Kyōkai Shuppan, 1944), 236–38, NDL. Also see the five-volume series on the contemporary American affairs published by Taiheiyō Kyōkai Amerika Kenkyū-shitsu (The Pacific Association, Division of American Studies) between January and June 1944. The topics covered in the series were the profiles of leading American newspaper columnists and broadcasting journalists; Wendell Willkie and his worldview reflected in his highly popular 1943 book *One World*; Field Marshal Jan Christiaan Smuts, prominent South African military leader, his worldview, and its comparison with that of the United States; the summary of *Journey among Warriors*, the book of war reportage by Ève Denise Curie, the French-American journalist and also the younger daughter of Marie Curie; and the book review of Nicholas Spykman's *America's Strategy in World Politics*. See Taiheiyō Kyōkai Amerika kenkyū-shitsu, "Beikoku jikyoku chōsa shiryō (Documents related to research on the US current state of affairs), in five volumes, NDL.

will. Abe claimed that this sense of "chosenness" had long since lost its religious purity and had degenerated into the Anglo-Saxon supremacist ideology that justified America's materialistic global expansion.[30]

The Americans' exclusive and isolated lifestyle reinforced such views. American sojourners showed that they were incapable of living with the Japanese, a situation already the case on the West Coast of the United States. The popularity of Hollywood movies, musicals, jazz, and baseball among urban Japanese failed to narrow the distance between the two peoples.

Russians in Japan: The Blue-eyed Neighbors

Tanizaki Jun'ichirō, a leading writer of modern Japanese literature known for his sensual aestheticism, saw the Russians as a white people distinct from the Americans. In his early works he depicted the figure of a white Westerner as a sensual poison for Japanese culture and civilization. By the time of his *Makioka Sisters* series in 1943, he no longer characterized the friendships of Japanese protagonists with Russian residents of Kōbe in this way. These Russians were no longer deviant seducers who charmed Japanese into unconditional capitulation and worship. The Japanese protagonists freely interacted with the Russians as equals.[31] Russian whiteness did not impose psychological and physical distance on the Japanese. Russian whiteness did not preclude moral imperfection, which made Russians more accessible to Japanese.

Russians were not free of anti-Japanese racism: the concept of the Yellow Peril originated in communications between the German kaiser Wilhelm II and the Russian tsar Nicholas II in the late nineteenth century. Russian literature written around the Russo-Japanese War portrayed Japanese as simian cowards with slanted eyes and buckteeth. These portrayals, however, coincided with more complex images of Japanese people being aesthetic, spiritual, hardworking, and above all, "just like Russians."[32]

---

30. Abe Yukizō, "Amerika seishin to Amerika Kirisuto-kyō" (The American spirit and American protestantism), in Taiheiyō Kyōkai, ed., *Amerika kokuminsei no kenkyū* (Studies on American national characters) (Tokyo: Taiheiyō Kyōkai Shuppan, 1944), 53–109, NDL.

31. Nakamura Yoshikazu, "Mottomo mijika na Seiyōjin" (The most intimate Westerners) in Naganawa Mitsuo and Sawada Kazuhiko, eds., *Ikyō ni ikiru—raiNichi Roshiajin no sokuseki* (Living in the strange land: stories of Russians in Japan) (Yokohama: Seibun Sha, 2001), vol. 1, 8–11.

32. Barbara Heldt, "Roshia bungaku ni egakareta Nihonjin—hen'yō suru aidentiti" (Images of Japanese in Russian literature: ever-changing identities) in Nakamura Yoshikazu and Thomas Rimer, eds., *Roshia bunka to Nihon* (Russian culture and Japan) (Tokyo: Sairyū Sha, 1995), 202–22. The English version of her work appeared in Kin'ya Tsuruta, ed., *The Walls Within* (Vancouver: Institute of Asian Research, University of British Columbia, 1989).

The Japanese derogatory term *Rosuke* evoked an image of the cowardly Russians beaten in the Russo-Japanese War. Yet race never became an issue in the Russo-Japanese relationship as it did in US-Japanese relations. Russian émigrés, with no residential segregations imposed on them, integrated into Japanese society with relative ease; they freely practiced Christianity and their children attended Japanese schools with local children.

Japan's continental expansion into Manchuria in the early twentieth century increased direct contacts between Japanese and Russian settlers. Between 1917 and 1921 when approximately 2 million Russians left the country due to the Bolshevik Revolution (600,000 to Germany; 400,000 to France; and the rest to the Baltic nations, the Balkans, the United States, Canada, and Australia), thousands of Russians chose to settle in the Japanese empire. The first recorded asylum seekers in Japan were five naval cadets who in December 1917 escaped from a cruiser anchored at the port of Nagasaki and in disguise took a train to Tokyo.[33] In 1922 when the League of Nations issued the Nansen Passport, an internationally recognized identity card given as emergency relief for Russian refugees unable to get ordinary passports, the Japanese government, along with thirty other governments in the world, moved to honor the cards.

By 1924 there were 1,167 "white" (anti-Bolshevik) Russian settlers in Japan proper, according to Foreign Ministry records. At the Russian immigration peak in 1930, 1,666 Russian refugees resided in Japan proper. Since there were probably more Russians than indicated by the official figure, some 2,000 Russians were thought to have been living in Japan before World War II.[34] Another 1,500 Russians, including those of Slavic, Ukrainian, Belarus, Tatar, Serbian, Polish, Romanian, and Jewish descents, spread across the Japanese empire, from Korea and southern Sakhalin to Manchuria. In addition to these political refugees, approximately 200 Russians chose to remain in the southern half of Sakhalin when that part of the island became a Japanese colony after the Russo-Japanese War.

Russian émigrés arrived in Japan amid the high tide of Taishō culture. It was a fortunate coincidence that by then the Japanese people had cultivated a positive image of Russia from a successful theatrical adoption of Tolstoy's play *Resurrection* and its theme song "Kachūsha no uta" (Song of Katyusha), which became a national hit.[35] The Russian émigrés brought a medley of Western culture and

---

33. Petr E. Podalko, "Roshiyajin wa ikani shite rai-Nichi shitaka" (How the Russians came to live in Japan), in Nakamura Yoshikazu, Naganawa Mitsuo and Nagayo Susumu, eds., *Ikyō ni ikiru—raiNichi Roshiajin no sokuseki* (Yokohama: Seibun Sha, 2003), vol. 2, 38–39.

34. Sawada Kazuhiko, "Nihon ni okeru Hakkei Roshiajin no bunka-teki eikyō" (Cultural influence of the White Russians in Japan), *Ikyō ni ikiru*, vol. 1, 31.

35. Okumura Katsuzō, "Nichi-Ro no bunka kōryū" (Russo-Japanese cultural interactions), in *Roshia bunka to kindai Nihon* (Russian culture and modern Japan) (Tokyo: Sekai Shisō Sha, 1998),

quickly won for themselves the affectionate phrase "*aoi me no*" (blue-eyed), establishing their unique place in Japan. The early wave of Russian refugees (1917–23) came largely from a bourgeois background in Imperial Russia, some even from aristocratic families. The second wave of the refugees (1923–45) consisted largely of commoners—peasants, retail store owners, peddlers—who subsequently took up similar occupations in Japan. These heterogeneous groups of emigrants brought to Japan two different, yet commensurable, worlds of Russia: the dazzling aristocratic cultures of Saint Petersburg and Moscow, best represented in ballet, opera, and classical music and, at the opposite end of the spectrum, the humble ethos of hard-working Russian laborers and peasants. Compared with the relatively homogenous community of American residents in Japan, these Russians presented far wider and richer aspects of the West through their interactions with Japanese from different social and economic strata.

In Japan Russians became renowned artists and entertainers. Russian pianists and violinists performed for Japanese audiences, and trained future Japanese artists. Emmanuel Metter became conductor of the Osaka Philharmonic Orchestra and trained future conductors and composers such as Asahina Takashi and Hattori Ryōichi. The Takarazuka Revue Company (Takarazuka Kagekidan), an all-female musical theater troupe founded in 1914, hired Russian émigré musicians and dancers as both performers and instructors.

Not all Russians in Japan were refugees. Anna Slavina and her daughters Ekaterina and Nina, all with theatrical backgrounds in Tsarist Russia, contributed to the birth of modern theater and film in Japan. Anna Slavina was originally discovered and recruited in Pusan, Korea, in 1917 by Shōkyokusai Tenkatsu, the celebrated Japanese magician, during her international tour. Arriving in Japan as new members of Tenkatsu's troupe, she and her daughter Ekaterina (Kitty) subsequently founded the Slavina Theatrical Company (Slavina Gekidan) and traveled across Japan, performing Western dramas and dances.

Ekaterina Slavina began a career as a white (Western) film star in the pioneering era of Japanese cinema. Ekaterina's lead performance as a Westerner was epoch-making in an age when Japanese actors and actresses played Westerners by using false big noses and light-colored wigs. A fluent Japanese speaker, Ekaterina played leads in films that celebrated international (and interracial) friendship and romance. *Hikari ni tatsu on'na* (A woman standing in light, 1920) is a melodrama about a refugee actress from Russia; *Kōzan no himitsu* (Secret of a mining mountain, 1920) is an action film about a labor dispute in the vicinity of Tokyo; and *Kyokkō no kanata e* (Beyond the aurora, 1921) is a romance between a young

---

10–12. Note this song, composed by a Japanese musician, is unrelated to "Katyusha," a famous Russian wartime song composed in 1938.

Japanese pioneer and a Western woman in snow-buried Kamchatka. The third film ends with Ekaterina and her Japanese lover (played by Moroguchi Tsuzuya, Japan's most popular actor of the time) kissing and celebrating their love and future together. Though this closing scene featured only silhouettes on snow, this film was among the first Japanese films to have a kissing scene. According to post-1945 mythology, the US military occupation introduced kissing scenes to Japanese films to emancipate the Japanese people from oppressive social mores.[36] This Russian actress took a step in that direction long before World War II. In 1923 Ekaterina and her sister Nina played leads in *Otenba musume* (Tomboys), a comedy about the clash between wild Japanese sisters who always play pranks and Western sisters who behave like traditional upper-class Japanese ladies. The film critics praised the Slavina sisters for perfectly performing the role of *yamato nadeshiko* (quintessential Japanese ladies, both spiritually and in appearance).

In 1926 after receiving legal permission to live in Japan, Ekaterina learned traditional Japanese dance and eventually became the first Westerner to receive an official license to teach Japanese apprentices.[37] Meanwhile, when the Shōchiku Kinema, Japan's leading motion-picture studio, opened an acting school in 1920, Anna, mother of Ekaterina, was invited to be the school director and to teach Japanese actors and actresses how to act with more sophisticated-looking Western mannerisms, from walking and eating to moving around in Western clothes. In 1921 and 1922 she produced, directed, and performed *Salome* at the prestigious Meiji Theater, inspiring the team of Shimamura Hōgetsu and Matsui Sumako, who later revised the work and performed it to national acclaim at the Teikoku Theater in 1931.

Russian émigrés also introduced Western foods. Nakamura-Ya, a high-profile bakery in Shinjuku, the bustling commercial district in Tokyo whose owners were known for their patronage of writers and artists and even political refugees from abroad, hired Russian émigré bakers, including one pâtissier who had once served at the tsarist court. They introduced Russian cakes, bread, and piroshki to urban Japanese families. Fuji-Ya, a nationwide chain of Western confectionery stores and restaurants founded in 1910, also flourished thanks to the skill of a Russian pâtissier it hired. A pâtissier who had once served the Romanovs, Makarov

36. Kyoko Hirano, *Mr. Smith Goes to Tokyo: Japanese Cinema under the American Occupation, 1945–1952* (Washington, DC: Smithsonian Institution, 1992), 154–65. Also see John W. Dower, *Embracing Defeat: Japan in the Wake of World War II* (New York: W.W. Norton, 1999), 149–50.

37. Sawada Kazuhiko, "Nihon ni okeru Hakkei Roshiajin no bunka-teki eikyō," *Ikyō ni ikiru*, vol. 1, 37–38. Sawada Kazuhiko, "Joyū Surabina oyako no tabiji—rai-Nichi Hakkei Roshiajin kenkyū" (Journey of the Slavinas—a study of the White Russians in Japan), *Saitama Daigaku Kiyō* (Saitama University Review) 32, no. 1 (1996): 77–95.

Goncharoff, fled the Bolshevik Revolution, settled in Japan, and opened his sweets shop in Kobe in 1923. He eventually expanded his business to the Tokyo area. After a failed attempt to relocate to Seattle, the Morozoff family also arrived in Kobe in 1925. Valentine Morozoff popularized chocolates, candies, and other Western-style confections as part of Japan's new urban culture. Their "baby bars," a chocolate with a concocted filling of peanuts, honey, egg whites, millet jelly and sugar, remained popular with Japanese consumers through the 1930s.[38] The Goncharoff and the Cosmopolitan (of Valentine Morozoff) Confectionaries remain highly regarded establishments in Japan today.

In sports the most famous blue-eyed professional athlete in prewar Japan was Victor Starffin (1918–57), a pitcher for Japan's top baseball team the Tokyo Giants. He arrived in Japan with his family in 1925 and attended Japanese schools from elementary to high school. In spite of the strong desire of his school and local fans to see him play for elite Waseda University, Starffin joined the Tokyo Giants and turned professional. He became one of the best and most popular professional baseball players of the time. In 1935 he went to the United States as a member of the Tokyo Giants and played a total of 110 games against AA, AAA teams, and even amateur teams, with a result of 75 wins, 34 losses, and 1 tie. Starffin, a tall blond who spoke native Japanese with Japanese mannerisms, drew attention from the American media and curious spectators alike. The San Francisco Missions of the Pacific Coast League unsuccessfully tried to recruit Starffin as a potential star pitcher in the major leagues. In 1939 and 1940 he received consecutive MVPs of the year and kept playing baseball until 1944.[39] Another son of Russian refugees in Hokkaidō, A. Vorobyov became a star wrestler at Waseda University and eventually won Japan's middleweight championship in 1936.[40]

The socioeconomic status of Russians in Japan contrasted starkly with that of other Westerners. The majority of Russian émigrés were of modest to low socioeconomic status, some even held menial jobs, an unlikely phenomenon among other Westerners, especially Americans. Only twenty-five Russians regularly summered in Karuizawa in three shared cottages. If the Russians could afford summer

---

38. Kawamata Kazuhide, *Kosumoporitan monogatari: since 1926* (A story of the cosmopolitan: since 1926) (Hyōgo: Cosmopolitan Seika, 1990).

39. After World War II, he temporarily worked for the office of the Supreme Commander for the Allied Powers (SCAP) but returned to professional baseball in 1947. In 1955 he won 300 games as a pitcher, setting the all-time record in Japan's baseball history. Today in Asahikawa, Hokkaidō a baseball stadium is named "Starffin Stadium," the first one in Japan named after an individual player. Natasha Starffin, *Roshia kara kita ēsu* (An ace pitcher from Russia) (Tokyo: PHP Kenkyūjo, 1986); Ushijima Hidehiko, *Fūsetsu Nihon yakyū—V. Starffin* (V. Starffin—stormy years of Japanese baseball) (Tokyo: Mainichi Shinbun, 1978).

40. Sawada Kazuhiko, "Nihon ni okeru Hakkei Roshiajin no bunka-teki eikyō,"40–41.

houses at all, they tended to be in Japanese residential areas near Tokyo such as Kamakura, Miura, Hayama, Odawara, and Ashigara, affordable excursions for ordinary Japanese.[41]

This modest image dovetailed with the activities of the Russian Orthodox Church. Since the first Russian missionary arrived in Japan in 1861, the Russian Orthodox Church and the missionaries had been especially active in impoverished villages in northern Japan. They recruited about 30,000 Japanese converts, another sharp contrast to the association of American Protestant churches with upper-middle-class Japanese in large cities. As of 1907 the ratio of financial contributions made by individual Japanese members of the American Methodist Church and the Russian Orthodox Church was approximately nine to one.[42] While schools run by American churches emphasized English education, the first Russian Orthodox theological school in Japan, founded by Nicholas (1836–1912), offered courses on Japanese history and classical Chinese, demonstrating sensitivity to its Japanese surroundings.[43]

A statistical look at Russians living in Japan confirms their diverse and relatively humble lifestyles. In 1924, 818 Russians legally worked in Japan, most as heads of families. Only 26 of them (3.2 percent) were educators, followed by 8 engineers, and 14 traders and businessmen. The rest, scattered across Japan, worked in low-paying jobs as bakers, peddlers, dressmakers, shopkeepers, ranchers, fishermen, entertainers, musicians, and servants. A typical occupation for Russian émigrés was peddling. Carrying on their backs textiles, including kimono, they went door to door in towns and villages, even in Tokyo. They most commonly carried *rasha*, a woolen fabric used for winter clothes such as jackets, coats, shawls, and throws. The Russian peddlers were good at charming Japanese clients with their exotic appearance and their spoken Japanese. They looked like connoisseurs, even when they were not, especially when they sold modern (Western) items such as fabrics, watches, and cosmetics.[44] In southern Sakhalin writers and journalists were drawn to the Russians because they made the otherwise indifferent environment cosmopolitan. Renowned literary figures such as Kitahara Hakushū and Iwano Hōmei

41. "Gai-hi dai-1366-gō, Shōwa 7-nen 8-gatsu 15-nichi Kanagawa-Ken-Chiji Yokoyama Sukenari, 'Hisho gaikokujin jōkyō (dai-3-pō),'" (Confidential foreign affairs report, no. 1366, August 15, 1932, Yokoyama Sukenari, the Governor of Kanagawa Prefecture, "A survey of foreign residents on summer vacations [the 3rd Report]") in "Zai Honpō gaikokujin ni kansuru tōkei chōsa zakken" (Miscellaneous statistical data on foreign residents in Japan), vol. 4 [K-3-7-0-15], DRO.

42. Naganawa Mitsuo, "Meiji no Seikyōkai" (The Russian Orthodox Church in Meiji Japan) in Nakamura and Rimer, eds., *Roshia bunka to Nihon*, 257.

43. Douglas Weiner, "Sōgo Imēji no henka" (Changes in mutual images) in Nakamura and Rimer, eds., *Roshia bunka to Nihon*, 287.

44. Petr E. Podalko, "Roshiyajin wa ikani shite raiNichi shitaka," in Nakamura, Naganawa and Nagayo, eds., *Ikyō ni ikiru* vol. 2, 42.

wrote about Russian children peddling sweet breads in baskets at train stations as if these were scenes from Hans Christian Andersen's tales, which were very popular among Japanese, young and old.[45]

The Russians' predominantly working-class employment pattern continued during the Pacific War. Statistics of the foreign population of Tokyo in 1942 and 1943 listed some fifty-seven Russian tailors, beauticians, fur traders, factory workers, bakers at the Imperial Hotel, a janitor at the TōA Kenkyūjo, and their families. Four Russians attended Tokyo Imperial University, the Nippon Dental University (Nihon Shika Daigaku), Waseda University, and the Jikei University School of Medicine (Tokyo Jikei Kai Ika Daigaku).[46]

The rich diversity of their lifestyles could be seen in Hakodate, Hokkaidō, one of the earliest ports opened to Western trade in the mid-nineteenth century. In 1917 only 10 or so Russians resided in this port city; by 1925 the official figure had increased to 157. Hakodate served as a port of entry for asylum seekers who smuggled themselves on board fishing and cannery ships. At the peak approximately 300 Russians lived in and around Hakodate. Most Russians who settled in Hakodate were engaged in the fishing industry. Some Russian women became spouses of Japanese traders and fishermen. In the nearby villages of Yugawa and Zenigamezawa settled the Russian Old Believers, who followed the rituals predating the reform of the Russian Orthodox Church in the seventeenth century. Harshly persecuted under the tsars, many fled into the Far East in the eighteenth century and lived in isolation for centuries. Some of them eventually reached Hakodate. They settled there as self-sufficient farmers and apiculturists and sold homemade bread and raspberry jam to Japanese locals.[47]

Russian residents were not free from Japanese government surveillance. A governor of Gifu Prefecture sent the Special Higher Police (Tokkō) a report of a thirty-seven-year-old white Russian émigré, a peddler of pots and pans, who had on November 29, 1934, arrived in Nakatsugawa, a post town and an important local market and retail center during the Edo period. The official record introduced his detailed background as follows: born in Kazan, the capital city of Tatarstan, this Russian émigré had once served in the tsar's army. Losing his family in the Bolshevik Revolution, he had escaped to Manchuria where he began peddling pots and pans. After he arrived in Japan in 1927, he made his living traveling

45. Shimizu Megumi, "Saharin kara Nihon e no bōmeisha" (Exiles from Sakhalin to Japan), in Naganawa and Sawada, eds., *Ikyō ni ikiru*, vol. 1, 79.

46. "Zairyū gaikokujin meibo (1942 and 1943)," in "Zai Honpō gaikokujin ni kansuru tōkei chōsa zakken" (Miscellaneous statistical data on foreign residents in Japan), vol. 4 [K-3-7-0-15], DRO.

47. Shimizu Megumi, "Roshia Kakumei-go Hakodate ni kita Roshiajin," in Shimizu Megumi, *Hakodate Roshia sono kōryū no kiseki* (History of interactions between Hakodate and Russia) (Hakodate: Hakodate Nichi-Ro Kōryū-shi Kenkyū-kai, 2005), 323.

TABLE 2.5 Employment patterns of Russian émigrés in Japan proper, 1924–38*

1924 TOTAL POP: 818		1932 TOTAL POP: 1,167		1937–38 TOTAL POP: 1,385			
Educators	26	Missionaries	17	Missionaries	2	Nurse	1
Students	4	Educators	17	Educators	8	Entertainers	4
Engineers	8	Traders/bankers	50	Students	11	Dressmaker	1
Merchants	50	Engineers	4	Journalists	3	Tanner	1
Traders/bankers	14	Musicians	15	Sculptor	1	Fur trader	1
Kimono peddlers	32	Dress peddlers	133	Writer	1	Dress shop clerks	8
Textile peddlers	209	Kimono peddlers	55	Company employees	9	Grocery store clerks	3
Ranchers	10	Textile peddlers	81	Salesman	1	Bakers	2
Fishermen	5	Dress makers	29	Clerk	1	Cosmetics clerks	2
Entertainers	5	Bakers	5	Typists	2	Jewelry store clerk	1
Dancers	3			Baseball player	1	Dress peddlers	79
Musicians	15			Musicians	2	Cosmetics peddlers	12
Servants	17			Masseurs	2	Textile peddlers	6
				Blanket peddlers	2	Food peddler	1
				Dressmakers	5	Servants	2

Sources: "Naichi zairyū gaikokujin shokugyō betsu jin'in hyō" (Statistical chart of foreign residents and their occupations in Japan proper) (1924) (1932), both in "Zai Honpō gaikokujin ni kansuru tōkei chōsa zakken" (Miscellaneous statistical data on foreign residents in Japan), vol. 1 [K-3-7-0-15], DRO; "Zairyū gaikokujin kokuseki betsu shokugyō-hyō no ken" (Chart of foreign residents sorted by nationality and occupation) (April 1937), in "Zai Honpō gaikokujin ni kansuru tōkei chōsa zakken" (Statistical data on foreign residents in Japan), vol. 2 [K-3-7-0-15-1], DRO.

* Job categories are not comprehensive; figures exclude the employees' families and dependents.

around the nation. On this particular tour he had left Tokyo two months before, peddled in Nagano, and come to Gifu via Kiso, a region he had visited twice the previous year as well. The report concluded that there was nothing particularly suspicious about his identity and activities.[48]

Even other Westerners thought the Russian émigrés were different. Edwin Reischauer reminisced about his childhood days in Tokyo: "I remember at the age of five looking down from the deck of our ship docking in San Francisco and being astounded at the sight of white men working as stevedores and black men mixed among them. At that time almost the only Westerners in Japan were missionaries, teachers, diplomats, businessmen, and occasional tourists. I had never seen a white man doing manual labor, unless one counts the occasional forlorn Russian refugee who would trudge the streets of Tokyo selling cloth from a large pack on his shoulder."[49]

The contrast between the Russians and other Westerners also existed in Japan's colonies. Korea as of 1936 had 698 Western residents with jobs, the largest group being the Americans (322), the second the British (122), both far more than the white Russians and Soviet citizens combined (112). Of these Americans in Korea, 166 (51.6 percent) were Christian missionaries, accounting for 47.7 percent of all the Western Christian missionaries combined. The remaining Americans in Korea were teachers (66), businessmen (44), medical doctors (22) and nurses (12), engineers (11), and a government official (1). The British residents shared a similar pattern of occupations.[50] In Taiwan as of 1936 there were 203 aliens (excluding the Chinese) with jobs, 108 of them British, 16 Americans, and 12 Russians.[51] All British and American residents in Taiwan were missionaries, teachers, bankers, traders and businessmen, doctors and nurses, or government officials. None was a menial laborer.

Russian settlers, male and female, held a diverse array of jobs across the Japanese colonies. In 1937 the Kwantung leased territory (Kantō-shū) had a total of 1,808 foreigners. 1,197 of them were white Russians and 136 Soviets, together comprising 73.7 percent of all foreigners. Of white-collar workers, there were Russian Orthodox Church missionaries (17), bankers and businessmen (65), engineers (18), and employees of the Manchurian Railway (22). Beyond these

---

48. "Tokkō hi hatsu dai-1850-gō" (The Special Higher Police, undisclosed origin, no. 1850) (December 6, 1934), in "Sorenpō naisei kankei zassan—Hakkei Rokokujin no seiji katsudō" (Miscellaneous data on Soviet politics—political activities of White Russians), vol. 3 [A-6-5-0-1-2], DRO.

49. Reischauer, *My Life between Japan and America*, 3–4. See also the Japanese version, Tokuoka Takao, trans., *Raishawā jiden*, 22.

50. The Chinese population was 12,510 (86.4 percent), comprising the majority of foreigners in Korea.

51. "Zai Honpō gaikokujin ni kansuru tōkei chōsa zakken" (Miscellaneous statistical data on foreign residents in Japan), vol. 1 [K-3-7-0-15]. Also see vol. 2 [K-3-7-0-15-1], DRO.

categories, there were music and language teachers (17), musicians (6), dancers (18), shop clerks (84), waiters and waitresses (24), security guards (41), barber (1) and manicurists (5), touts and barkers (*kyakuhiki*) (24), confectioners (9), food dealers (7), restaurant owners (6), cooks (3), landlords and innkeepers (40), peddlers (5), poultry farmers (6), milk farmers (5), tailors and seamstresses (29), rasha traders (3) and leather traders (24).[52] Of the 58 American citizens living in the Kwantung leased territory, 31 were white-collar workers, 8 Christian missionaries, and 4 government officials. In the southern part of Sakhalin in 1937, 167 out of 327 foreigners were Russians, 50 were peasants, 9 merchants, 7 day laborers, 6 fox farmers, 5 clothing retailers, and the rest peddlers, shoemakers, bakers, students and unemployed.[53] Even in Saipan, a Japanese mandate since 1919, several Russian émigrés peddled razors, hair clippers, cosmetics, and clothes. One of them was a former police chief in Tsarist Russia who had come to Kobe with his family after the Bolshevik Revolution but moved to Saipan alone. He sublet a room from the local Chamorro family, frequented a Japanese owned café and bakery, and enjoyed chatting with the locals.[54]

In Manchukuo, the Russian population was on the rise. In 1933, out of 85,044 Westerners living in Manchukuo including the Kwantung region, 43,050 were Russians. After the Soviet Union recognized Manchukuo in 1935 and pledged nonintervention, Japanese officials in Manchukuo welcomed more Russian émigrés, some stateless and some with Chinese citizenship, to enrich the social and cultural life of Manchukuo with Western flair. In 1936, while the number of Western residents dropped to 67,355, the Russian population increased to 53,603. Soviet citizens resided alongside Russian émigrés: in 1933 there were 38,396 and in 1936 there were 10,168.[55]

American visitors to Manchukuo were both shocked and impressed by such Japanese-Russian interactions, which upset their concepts of race relations. In Manchukuo white men worked for less than yellow men. In Harbin hotels white Russian boys worked as elevator boys and courteously greeted Japanese guests.[56] In the 1930s a growing number of Japanese-Americans in the mainland United

---

52. "Zairyū gaikokujin kokuseki betsu shokugyō hyō (Showa 12-nen 12-gatsu matsu genzai)" (A table of a number of foreign residents in Japan in various occupations, tabulated by nationality [December 1937]), vol. 2 [K-3-7-0-15-1], DRO.

53. "Zai Honpō gaikokujin ni kansuru tōkei chōsa zakken" (Miscellaneous statistical data on foreign residents in Japan), vol. 1 [K-3-7-0-15], DRO.

54. Nomura Shin, *Nihon-ryō Saipan no ichiman-nichi* (Ten thousand days in the Japanese mandated Island of Saipan) (Tokyo: Iwanami Shoten, 2005), 136–37.

55. Kajii Yoshihiro, "Igirisu kara mita Nihon no Manshū shihai: senkan-ki gaikō hōkoku o chūshin ni (1)" (Japan's control of Manchukuo observed by Britain, with an analytical focus on the interwar annual reports), *Ritsumeikan Hōgaku* (Ritsumeikan Law Review) 290 (2003): 48–49.

56. John Stephan, "Hijacked by Utopia: American Nikkei in Manchuria," *Amerasia Journal* 23, no. 3 (winter 1997–98): 9.

States and Hawaii regarded emigration to Manchukuo as providing better career prospects. There they could live not just free from white domination but also as the master race.

In Manchuria sexual liaisons between Japanese males and Russian females were not taboo. The city of Harbin was known for "hospitable" blond and blue-eyed Russian girls who welcomed Japanese clients in fluent Japanese.[57] In *Modan Gāru* (Modern girl), a collection of essays published in 1926, American-educated journalist Kiyosawa Kiyoshi in one essay portrayed the lifestyle of American women with due deference to feminism. In another he wrote of accompanying his male Japanese friends to a Harbin club where fair-skinned Russian dancers, hostesses, and café waitresses—as well as Jewish, Japanese, and Chinese women—entertained guests. While reiterating his opposition to prostitution (Kiyosawa had gone to the United States under the influence of Uchimura Kanzō, Japan's pioneering Protestant), Kiyosawa nonetheless admitted that he felt an inexplicable freedom in Harbin, where there was no stifling Anglo-Saxon morality, but only easy interactions among Russians, Japanese, and Chinese.[58]

Russian intermarriage with Japanese was not forbidden, but in Japan proper almost no Russians married Japanese citizens, because most Russian émigrés came to Japan as families. According to the 1935 statistics of Hyōgo Prefecture, only 8 of 406 Russian residents were married to Japanese.[59] In Manchukuo interracial marriage existed between Japanese (and Japanese-Americans) and white Russians, at the time prohibited in California and many other states.[60] The author of a 1942 Japanese travelogue on northern Manchuria speculated that the more distinctly Russian character of these interracial households could be attributed to the Japanese command of Russian language and culture, which he called a sure sign of Japanese continental expansion. The author also explained that Russian families welcomed interracial marriages because of the prospect of social and economic security. Although the author raised concerns about the hybridization of Japanese race and culture, he affectionately portrayed Russian-Japanese children playing with Manchu children, wishing them a better future.[61]

---

57. Bungei Shunjū, ed., *Saredo waga "Manshū"* (My Manchuria nonetheless) (Tokyo: Bungei Shunjū Sha, 1984). See, for example, "Harubin no on'na" (Women of Harbin), 45–46.

58. Kiyosawa Kiyoshi, "Modan gāru" (Modern girl) reprinted in Yamamoto Yoshihiko, ed., *Kiyosawa Kiyoshi senshū* (Tokyo: Nihon Tosho Center, 1998), vol. 1.

59. "Gaikokujin to kekkon seru Honpōjin narabi ni konketsuji chōsa ni kansuru ken" (Reports on Japanese nationals with foreign spouses and their mixed-blood offspring) (July 22, 1935), in "Zai Honpō gaikokujin ni kansuru tōkei chōsa zakken" (Miscellaneous statistical data on foreign residents in Japan), vol. 4 [K-3-7-0-15]; "Zai Honpō gaikokujin ni kansuru tōkei chōsa zakken zairyū gaikokujin kokuseki betsu jin'in hyō," vol. 1 [K-3-7-0-15-1], DRO.

60. John Stephan, "Hijacked by Utopia," 22.

61. Fukuda Shinsei, *Hoku-Man no Roshia buraku* (The Russian village in northern Manchuria) (Tokyo: Tama Shobō, 1942), 208–17.

Russians in Japan's Pan-Asianism

Japan's anti-Americanism, epitomized in the surprise attack on Pearl Harbor and the suicidal kamikaze attacks, has been mistaken for Japan's absolute anti-Western and antiwhite stance in the war. Japan's Greater East Asia War was waged against Anglo-America as a racial and cultural clash (*jinshu-teki shōtotsu*), a nationalistic competition (*minzoku taikō*) between the Yamato and Anglo-American races (*minzoku*). Only in 1944 did the Japanese government ban steel guitars, banjos and ukuleles—all uniquely American (and Hawaiian) instruments. In October of the same year, the Greater East Asia Symphonic Orchestra (DaiTōA Kōkyō Gakudan) of Japan performed Bach's violin concerto and excerpts from Bizet's *Carmen* and *L'Arlésienne* at the Hibiya Public Auditorium in central Tokyo. The Japanese did not have a problem with Western culture per se.

The axis alliance with Germany, and to a lesser extent with Italy, testified to Japan's cultural resilience during the war. The Japanese government emphasized that Japan's European allies—the Teutonics (Germans) and Latins (Italians)—shared an enthusiasm for totalitarianism, which challenged the Anglo-American claim that Western civilization fought in unison for democracy.[62] Far from hoping to build a new "pure" Asia by excluding the West, Japan aspired to demonstrate that their Eurasian empire could fuse East and West.

Russian collaboration would add credibility to such aspirations and help authenticate Japan's pan-Asianism. Valentine Morozoff, the owner of the confectionary shop in Kōbe, gave a patriotic speech shortly after Pearl Harbor and was quoted by a Japanese police report: "I feel as if I am bathed in the brilliant Japanese sunshine now that Japan is finally ready to wage war after the gloom of economic sanctions and psychological warfare. Anglo-America had long told us about the invincibility of Singapore and Pearl Harbor. But only yesterday we heard the news that their bases bowed to the superior naval force of Japan, so we are overjoyed."[63] Whether this was a sincere expression or a carefully crafted political comment to demonstrate his loyalty to the Japanese government is unknown. As soon as the Pacific War began, Japanese authorities suspected the Russian émigrés in Hokkaidō of betraying Japan and committing espionage for other nations because of the island's strategic location in relation to the Soviet

---

62. Suzuki Norihisa, "Gen-Taisen no hongen kentō" (Examination of the fundamental cause of the current world war), *Gaikō Jihō* (Diplomatic review) 940 (February 1, 1944): 12.

63. Shimizu Megumi, "Dai-Niji Sekai Taisen-ki no Hakkei Roshiajin no dōkō" (Conditions of the White Russians during World War II), in Namamura Yoshikazu, Yasui Ryōhei, Naganawa Mitsuo and Nagayo Susumu, eds., *Ikyō ni ikiru* (Yokohama: Seibun Sha, 2005), vol. 3, 71–80.

Union and the United States (via Alaska).[64] Some Russians in Nagasaki were interrogated and imprisoned by the police simply because they hosted Russians visiting from Harbin.[65] Nonetheless, during the war Russian émigrés in Japan were a valuable asset that gave Japan's pan-Asianism the luster of universalism and cosmopolitanism. Their whiteness was not dissonant with Japan's professed goal in the war. In fact, Japanese officials elicited significant contributions from Russian artists to the cause of Japan's pan-Asianism.

Two Russian ballerinas, Elena Pavlova and Olga Sapphire, incorporated Japan's pan-Asianism into their work. Elena Pavlova, the "mother of Japanese ballet," was born to an aristocratic family in present-day Tbilisi, Georgia, and arrived in Japan in 1919 with her family. She instantly became a star through her performance of Camille Saint-Saens' *Dying Swan.* Having performed at the Kiev Opera House and also the Mariinsky Theater in St. Petersburg, she opened Japan's first classical ballet school near Kamakura, and trained future Japanese principal dancers while remaining active as both a dancer and a choreographer.[66] When not teaching at her school, Elena toured Japan, Taiwan, and Korea. In public appearances she preferred to wear a kimono to accentuate her assimilation into Japanese culture. Devoted to the Russian tsar, Elena respected the Japanese emperor and applied for Japanese citizenship in 1931. In 1937 when all the members of her family also became naturalized in Japan, Elena adopted a Japanese name, Kirishima Eriko. On November 2, 1937, when Elena gave a ballet recital at the Soldiers Hall (Gunjin Kaikan) near the Imperial Palace to celebrate her family acquiring Japanese nationality, she pledged to the audience that she would continue to devote all of her talent to imperial Japan. Around this time she began to experiment with blending Western and Japanese dance. In November 1938 she choreographed and danced an original work *Ume* (Plum), a Japanese-style expression performed to Japanese and Western musical instruments. In January and November 1940 Elena danced two other new works *Oriental Fantasy* and *Goddess of Justice.* In March 1941 at the request of the Japanese Army, Elena began a northern China tour with a troupe of twelve Japanese ballerinas, musicians, and entertainers. Elena danced standard works of classical Western ballet and also improvised dances to Japanese folk songs and children's songs. It was reported that Japanese soldiers were moved

---

64. Shimizu Megumi, "Saharin kara Nihon e no bōmei—Shūetsu-ke o chūshin ni" (The Shvets family's exile from Sakhalin to Japan), in *Ikyō ni ikiru,* vol. 1, 83–84.

65. "Lyubōfi Semyōnobuna Shūetsu san ni kiku" (Interview with Lyubov Semyonova Shvets, conducted by Shimizu Megumi), in *Ikyō ni ikiru,* vol. 2, 19.

66. Akiko Tachiki, "Living with Japanese Ballet History: An interview with Asami Maki, artistic director of Asami Maki Ballet Company and the New National Theatre Ballet, Tokyo," available online at www.pcah.us/m/dance/living-with-japanese-ballet-history.pdf.

to tears, in particular by her forte *Dying Swan*. On May 2, 1941, she suddenly died of tetanus at forty-four. As a civilian employee of the Imperial Army, she received posthumous honors from the Japanese government.[67]

Olga Sapphire, who studied and danced lead at the Leningrad National Ballet Academy, came to Japan in 1936 as the wife of a Japanese diplomat she met in Moscow. While her husband quit the Japanese Foreign Ministry after they married and began a two-year teaching position at the Harbin Institute, Olga, now a naturalized Japanese citizen through marriage, began a promising career as a ballet instructor in Japan and became the only Western performer at the renowned Nihon Theater (Nichigeki) in Tokyo. As Japan's prima donna she specialized in the Russian classical repertoire but also performed Japanese dances. In May 1938 she choreographed and directed a new two-act program, *Tōyō no inshō* (Impressions of the Orient). She announced this new production would raise Japan's artistic standards to the Western level so that Japan could prove a worthy leader of the Orient. Throughout the Pacific War she regularly performed classical ballet programs at the Nichigeki. In October 1942 she danced the lead in *Scheherazade* at the sold-out Takarazuka Theater, seating capacity 2,810. In the fall of 1943, in what would be her last wartime stage appearance, she danced a new production, *Burmese Peacock*, celebrating the independence Japan had "awarded" Burma.[68]

In Manchukuo, where the national policy rhetorically upheld the cosmopolitan ideal of harmonious cooperation among the five races—the Manchu, Han Chinese, Mongol, Korean, and Japanese peoples—the Japanese officials hoped that the Russian émigrés would play a role as the sixth racial group in the state. Japanese officials and settlers appreciated the Eurasian dimension of Manchukuo provided by Russians in social, cultural, literary, and racial enterprises. Since Russian settlers in the late nineteenth century had developed the regions along the Chinese Eastern Railway (also known as the North Manchuria Railway), Russian influences in architecture and city planning were prominent. Harbin in particular had the ambiance of a European town. The colonial authority of Manchukuo welcomed Russians with its rhetoric of racial harmony and actively promoted the presence of Russians as evidence of its cosmopolitanism. Tourist pamphlets published by the South Manchuria Railway Company presented Harbin for its charming and rich Russian influences.[69] Postcards of Harbin depicted

---

67. Sorada Harumitsu, *Hakuchō no shisha Elena Pavlova* (Elena Pavlova, the Swan) (Tokyo: Yurikago Sha, 1997), 95ff; Shirahama Ken'ichirō, *Shichirigahama Pavlova Kan* (The Pavlova Mansion at Shichirigahama) (Tokyo: Bun'en Sha, 1986), 186ff.

68. Satō Toshiko, *Kitaguni kara no barerīna—Origa Sapphire* (Olga Sapphire: The Ballerina from the northern country) (Tokyo: Kasumigaseki Shuppan, 1987).

69. Institute of Developing Economies Japan External Trade Organization (IDE-JETRO), Library Digital Archives, Special Internet Exhibition "Kin-gendan Ajia no naka no Nihon (Japan in

Russian churches, stores, hotels, Russian festivals, Russians enjoying parks and rivers, and Japanese people merrily shopping with Russians and dining with Russians at a posh Western-style restaurant.[70] These scenes were chosen to show the Japanese empire happily blending with the West.

Japanese settlers and city planners in these regions actively preserved distinctive Russian tastes. The *pechka*, a Russian-style fireplace, was commonly adopted in Japanese homes as a reminder of Russian influence. Postwar memoirs of Japanese settlers in Manchukuo reflect on their friendships with Russian neighbors with affection. One Japanese woman remembered an elderly Russian couple who served her tea from a samovar whenever she slipped into their kitchen by the backdoor. Another former Japanese settler cherished the memory of two young Russian brothers whose father owned a Russian restaurant in Hsinking (Changchun): they were enrolled in a Japanese school and were very popular with their Japanese classmates. A former Japanese resident in Dalian fondly remembered a Russian family whose Easter celebration was the most anticipated event among her Japanese neighbors.[71]

Japanese authorities in Manchukuo welcomed and encouraged Russian musical talents, manifested in sacred chants, Kazak choirs, and symphonic orchestras, as enrichments of Manchukuo's cultural and ethnic diversity. The Harbin Organization (Harubin Kikan), one of the special service organizations under the auspices of the Kwantung Army, aimed to strengthen nostalgia for the old Russia and to encourage Russian residents to hope for a reconstruction of anti-Bolshevik Russia. They coordinated various arts and entertainment programs for émigré theaters and philharmonic orchestras and helped advertise them in newspapers, magazines, and radio broadcasts.

In addition, Manchukuo also invited some 8,000 Russian peasants to the Sanga (Transbaikal) region. The most distinctive group among them was the Stavorery, or the Russian Old Believers. In the early 1930s some of them had left the Primorsky Region in opposition to the Soviet collectivization of farmlands, crossed the

---

Modern and Contemporary Asia). See "Harubin (1927)," "Harubin (1937)," and "Harubin An'nai (1942)." Available online at http://d-arch.ide.go.jp/asia_archive/rare/travel.html.

70. See the collection of postcards of "Harubin," "Harubin sono 2," "Harubin sono 3," and "Harubin sono 4," in "Manshū Shashin-kan (Photo Studio of Manchuria)," available online at http://www.geocities.jp/ramopcommand/page035.html. Also see the Nara Prefectural Library Information Center, "Ehagaki Harubin (Postcards of Herbin)," available online at http://www.library.pref.nara.jp/event/booklist/W_2008_04/hitosyo09.html. Nihon University College of Humanities and Sciences Museum is building a digital archive of visual images of Harbin—ranging from postcards, posters and flyers, pamphlets and books to photos and motion pictures. For updated information, log on to http://www.chs.nihon-u.ac.jp/museum/exhibition/schedule/post_15.html.

71. Bungei Shunjū, ed., *Saredo waga "Manshū"* (My Manchuria nonetheless). See personal memoirs in chapter 1, "Manshū no haru—Ōdō Rakudō no yume" (Spring of Manchuria—dream of a peaceful land governed by the Kingly Way), 30–96.

Ussuri River, and moved into Manchuria. The Romanovka Village, one of the communities they built, was a fairytale success. In November 1936 preparations began amid the wilderness of the northern part of Manchukuo to bring in a community of 122 refugees who possessed next to nothing. By the spring of 1945, the population had increased to more than 200 residents and the village enjoyed pastoral tranquility and a modest living, with each household owning a minimum of three horses and two cows.

Since it preserved medieval Russian folk culture with traditionally built houses, costumes, ceremonies, music, and rituals, Romanovka Village gave that Manchurian region an ethereal quality that led Japanese authorities to advertise it as "the Shangri-La of Asia."[72] The Old Believer men hunted and otherwise adhered to a distinctive agrarian-community life, which was praised by the officials of Manchukuo as appropriate to the ideology of harmony. Even a book about military conflict on the Soviet-Manchurian border, published in 1939, referred to peasants living in log cabins made of birch trees, Russian wenches milking cows, boys chasing home cows and horses, and the echoes of a church bell in the village.[73] Famous journalists, painters, photographers, and writers were encouraged to visit Romanovka Village to report what they saw to the Japanese people. Ishibashi Tanzan, a liberal economist and journalist, praised Russian agrarian villages for their knowledge of herding domestic animals in hygienic, odor-free conditions, and recommended to Japanese colonizers that they emulate these Russians who kept their modest houses clean and pleasant within limited means.[74]

Once the Sino-Japanese War began, new efforts were made actively to assimilate Russian residents into the Japanese way. In 1937 the Imperial Army's Special Service Organization (Tokumu Kikan) founded the Office of the White Russians (Hakkei Rojin Jimu-kyoku), as a quasi-autonomous agency headed by former Russian military generals, which supervised their assimilation and also the improvement of their living conditions in Manchukuo. Later renamed the Russian division of the Concordia Association (Kyōwa-kai), this office took charge of all administrative matters such as residential registration, issuance of identification and passports, and distribution of rations. More important, it promoted awareness of Russians as being harmonious members of Manchukuo through education, programs, and publications. The Russian division of the Concordia Association administered Russian

---

72. Nakamura Yoshikazu, *Seinaru Roshia no rurou* (The sacred vagrancy of Russia) (Tokyo: Heibon Sha, 1997), 120–34.

73. Nakamura Satoshi, *ManSo kokkyō funsō-shi* (A history of the Soviet-Manchurian border conflicts) (Tokyo: Kaizō Sha, 1939), 381.

74. Ishibashi Tanzan, *ManSen sangyō no inshō* (My impressions of industries in Manchuria-Korea) (Tokyo: Tōyō Keizai Shinpō Sha, 1941), reprinted in *Ishibashi Tanzan zenshū* (Tokyo: Tōyō Keizai Shinpō Sha, 1972), vol. 12, 424–27.

schools, where the use of the Russian language was tolerated on the condition that in other subjects they adopted the same curriculum as Manchurian, Mongolian, and Korean schools. Russian pupils, for example, were obliged to write compositions in Russian on the theme of the racial harmony of Manchukuo.[75]

Some Russian students chose to pursue higher education in Japanese. The Nation-Building University (Kenkoku Daigaku) at Hsinking, the capital of Manchukuo, was created to train future leaders of Manchukuo: it allowed a quota of five Russian students each year. Japanese martial arts such as judo and kendo were part of the physical education curriculum. In 1938 the Harbin Medical College (Harubin Ika Daigaku) invited applications from Russian students and accepted ten students for full-time enrollment. They obtained Russian medical textbooks from the Soviet Union, with all references to communist propaganda deleted by Japanese censors, and used them as back-up references in preparing for examinations in Japanese. Between 1944 and 1945 six Russian students graduated and obtained medical licenses.[76]

Among them was Dr. Eugene (Evgeny) Aksenoff. Born in a suburb of Harbin in 1924, he attended school when Japanese language courses became mandatory after the creation of Manchukuo. While enrolled in a boarding school run by Jesuit priests, he received a private fellowship (with approval from the Manchukuo government) to attend a medical school in Tokyo. After a year at Waseda University polishing his Japanese, he entered the Jikei University School of Medicine in 1944, stayed there during the war and through the US occupation, and eventually obtained a medical license to practice in Japan. During the war the Japanese secret police asked Aksenoff to help broadcast Russian radio programs aimed at Soviet citizens. After he turned down this lucrative offer in the conviction that Japan and Germany would soon lose the war, he experimented with a stint in entertainment and played Caucasian foreigners—usually a spy—for the famed Enoken Roppa comic company. While attending medical school, he also had small roles in films such as *Harimao of Malay* and *A Man from Shanghai*.[77]

The poet Hasegawa Shun believed that Manchurian literature, as cosmopolitan as Manchukuo itself, should make a radical departure from the Western-centric norm and nurture the spirit of the Asia-centered world (*Ajia teki sekai seishin*).

---

75. Manshūkoku-shi hensan kankō-kai, ed., *Manshūkoku-shi* (A history of Manchukuo) (Tokyo: Manmō Dōhō Engo-kai, 1970), 42, 128–29, 933, 1102, 1145–46, 1243–47.

76. Matsumura Miyako, "Shinbun 'Manshū no oka nite,' ni keisai sareta Nihon kanren kiji o megutte" (Japan-related articles printed in the newspaper *On the Manchurian Hill*), *Ikyō ni ikiru*, vol. 1, 162–64.

77. "Efugeni Nikoraebicchi Akushonofu shi ni kiku" (Interview with Evgeny N. Akushonov), *Ikyō ni ikiru*, vol. 2, 3–12. He still practices today at the Azabu Clinic in Roppongi, just a few blocks away from the Russian Embassy. Available online at http://www.medtokyo.com, accessed May 2012.

Hasegawa embraced as Manchurian literary motifs such as Cossack villages in the Sanhe region, howling wolves in the primeval forests of Siberia, and the taste of vodka, all of which he declared founding elements of the Manchukuo utopia.[78] The literary journal *Manshū Rōman* (Manchurian romance), inaugurated in 1938, aimed to nurture a distinctive Manchurian literature. Russian writers, along with Chinese and Manchu writers, were all encouraged to contribute to the journal. Nikolai A. Baikov was celebrated among Japanese readers for his depictions of wild animals and hunters in the setting of Siberia's wilderness. His most popular works were *The Great Wang: Story of an Amur Tiger* (1936), a novel about the life of a tiger king ruling the Siberian taiga, and "The Tigress" (1943), a story about Natasha, a Siberian hunter who, after her husband is killed by a tiger, decides to raise a tiger cub. His translated works became so popular in Japan that he was invited to attend the Greater East Asia Literary Conference (DaiTōA Bungakusha Taikai) held in Tokyo in November 1942.

Anthologies reflecting the cosmopolitan character of Manchukuo began to be published in Japanese. A 1940 anthology of works by Manchurian residents included two Russian works. Three years later nine short stories by white Russian émigré writers in Manchukuo were published as an anthology. Their stories depicted émigré nostalgia for Imperial Russia and their despair, loneliness, and anxiety in the foreign land. Russian writers wrote about their lives in Manchukuo in tranquil seclusion, with close contact with only a few Koreans, Manchus, or Chinese.[79] Russians seldom wrote of any Japanese presence in their lives, contradicting an official report that determined the Russians were opportunistic in associating with the Japanese. This same report noted Russians, because of their intelligence and higher living standards, had an air of superiority when dealing with Koreans and Manchus.[80]

Japanese writers, both visitors and settlers in Manchukuo, used the Russians to portray the positive attributes of cosmopolitanism. Future Nobel Prize laureate in literature Kawabata Yasunari praised Kitamura Kenjirō's 1942 novel *Shunren* as the best product of Manchurian literature.[81] The story portrays a Japanese

---

78. Ozaki Hotsuki, *Kindai bungaku no shōkon—kyū shokuminchi bungaku ron* (Scars of modern Japanese literature: the colonial literature) (Tokyo: Iwanami Shoten, 1991), 232.

79. See Viktoriya Yankovskaya, "Without God, without law" (Kami mo naku okite mo nashi), and Arnesiy Nesmeerov, "Akage no Renka" (Renka, the Red-Haired) in Yamada Seizaburō, ed., *Nichi-Man-Ro zai-Man sakka tanpen-shū* (Anthology of short stories by Japanese, Manchurian, and Russian writers in Manchuria) (Tokyo: Shun'yō Dō, 1942).

80. "Hi: dai-52-gō: Botankō fukin ni okeru zai-Man Rojin saikin no dōkō ni kansuru ken" (Confidential: no. 52: Recent activities of the Manchurian Russians in Mudanjiang) (March 6, 1942) [A-7-0-0-9-9-8], DRO.

81. *Shunren* is a translation of the Chinese *chūnlián*, a special type of couplet used only during the Chinese New Year.

settler and his romantic struggles in building the state of Manchukuo. It chronicles his fight with Manchu rebels, escape from them, rescue by a Russian rancher and his maid called Natasha, and eventual return to safety. The protagonist, moved by the Russians' kindness, raises interest in the welfare of Russian émigrés and launches a project to build a pioneering village for them.[82]

Other Japanese writers depicted Russians coping with the hardships of living in Manchuria. Hinata Nobuo's *Dai-hachi-gō tentetsu ki* (The railroad switch number eight, 1941), which won the first Manchurian Literature Prize (Manshū Bunwa-Kai Shō), tells the story of a Manchu man who works for the South Manchuria Railway. With great difficulty he adjusts from the Russian way to the Japanese way after the transfer of control of the railway. His Russian wife is the widow of a former Russian colleague. Her determination to live in spite of all her difficult experiences makes her the ultimate survivor.[83] Takeuchi Shōichi in *Ryūri* (Dissipation) traces the fall of a Russian Jewish family, which gives up not only bourgeois living but family altogether in the face of Japanese takeover of Harbin. Yoshino Sadao's *Iwan no Ie* (House of Ivan) portrays the dire straits of a Russian man, a former employee of the North Manchuria Railway, and his family, through the eyes of a Japanese settler who rents a bedroom in their house.

Yokota Fumiko looked into a darker side of the Russian-Japanese relationship. *Kaze* (Wind) is about Russian and Japanese boys engaging in sinister play in a field. The story ends when a physically handicapped Russian boy experiences euphoria while holding a dead sparrow that had been toyed with and abandoned by the other boys. *Aru Kurisumasu no monogatari* (A Christmas story) portrays the inability of a young Japanese woman to understand an elderly Russian woman living in solitude in Hsinking (Changchun). Out of curiosity, she celebrates Christmas with this casual acquaintance. As they talk over candlelight, the old woman, unable to restrain herself, begins to cry. After watching the Russian woman doze off in tears, the young Japanese woman leaves, aware that the Russian's solitude is the common destiny of all émigrés in Manchuria.[84]

The Japanese authorities in Manchukuo tended to view Russian émigrés as compliant and collaborative.[85] A report from the Japanese military police (Kenpei-tai)

---

82. Kitamura Kenjirō, *Shunren* (Tokyo: Shinchō Sha, March 1942). Kawamura Minato, *Ikyō no Shōwa bungaku—"Manshū" to kindai Nihon* (Showa literature in the foreign land: Manchuria and Modern Japan) (Tokyo: Iwanami Shoten, 1990), 125–26.

83. Hinata Nobuo, "Dai-hachi-gō tentetsu ki" (The railroad switch number eight), in *Shōwa sensō bungaku zenshū* (Tokyo: Shūei Sha, 1964), vol. 1.

84. Kawamura Minato, *Bungaku kara miru 'Manshū'* (Manchuria in the Japanese literature) (Tokyo: Yoshikawa Kobunkan, 1998), 57–59, 66–69.

85. The best samples of such views can be found in the following archival collection: "DaiTōA Sensō kankei ikken jōhō shūshū kankei Botankō jōhō" (The Greater East Asia War: intelligence gatherings: Information on Mudanjiang) [A-7-0-0-9-9-8], DRO.

in Manchukuo, issued in March 1942, confirmed the good fit between Russian émigrés and Japan's pan-Asianism. The report asserted the Russian émigrés seemed to be working in accordance with the goal of pan-Asianism: they attended Shinto ceremonies and even donated to related causes. Yet the report acknowledged that the Russians longed for a true motherland and remained uncompelled by the idea of complete assimilation. Whether they liked it or not, they collaborated with Japan's Manchukuo because that was the only institution they could rely on for survival, at that moment.[86]

As the prospect of Japan's eventual defeat loomed larger, the vision of cultural coexistence with Russia under Japan's pan-Asianism gradually lost its luster. The Japanese authorities worried that Russian émigrés across the Japanese empire might betray Japan should the Soviets attack. In Tokyo in March 1944, the Japanese police brokered jobs for financially struggling Russians in an attempt to prevent them from engaging in espionage for the Soviet Union. Eighteen former peddlers of clothes, six former peddlers of tins and cosmetics, and six other Russians were all referred to new jobs at a small machine factory in Tokyo for modest daily wages of four to five yen. This way the Japanese police could keep them under surveillance.[87]

Some Russian émigrés had divided allegiances. Some in Manchuria tried to obtain Soviet citizenship because they anticipated Japan's ever deteriorating condition and eventual defeat in World War II. Some made financial donations to Japan's war cause. Others even encouraged their sons to join the Japanese Army. In this milieu Foreign Minister Shigemitsu Mamoru made a last-ditch effort to invite the Soviet Union to join Japan's Greater East Asia Coprosperity Sphere. At the Supreme Council for the Direction of the War in mid-September 1944, Shigemitsu proposed investigating what principles Japan most likely shared with the Soviet Union and how the two could work together to achieve a Eurasian principle, similar to the Pacific Charter, toward building a new order in East Asia. Shigemitsu argued that by promoting the Asian membership of the Soviet Union, Japan could and should emphasize the congruence of the Japanese and Soviet principles of "national liberation and independence for the peoples of East Asia" (*TōA minzoku no kaihō to dokuritsu*). The spirit of Japan's Greater East Asia was a mirror image of the Soviet communist principle of nationalism for Asian peoples.[88]

---

86. "Hi: dai-52-gō: Botankō fukin ni okeru zai-Man Rojin saikin no dōkō ni kansuru ken," (Confidential: no. 52: Recent activities of the Manchurian Russians in Mudanjiang) (March 6, 1942) [A-7-0-0-9-9-8], DRO.

87. Shimizu Megumi, "Dai-Niji Sekai Taisen-ki no Hakkei Roshiajin no dōkō," in Nakamura, Yasui, Naganawa and Nagayo, eds., *Ikyō ni ikiru*, vol. 3, 71–80.

88. Hatano Sumio, "Shigemitsu Mamoru to DaiTōA Kyōdō Sengen—senji gaikō to sengo kōsō" (Shigemitsu Mamoru and the Greater East Asia Declaration—his war diplomacy and postwar planning), *Kokusai Seiji* 109 (May 1995): 47–50.

Even as the vision of cultural coexistence dimmed when Stalin labeled Japan an aggressor in November 1944, Japan's strategic thinking regarding China and Korea demonstrated that the Soviet Union continued to be an integral part of Japan's blueprint for Asian reconstruction. Japanese policymakers evaluated the appeal of communist ideology to Chinese and Korean nationalists and anticipated considerable Soviet interference in China and Korea especially after the demise of Japanese empire. At a more subtle level, the undeniable Russian affinity with Asia must have made it difficult for both Japanese and Russians to envision an Asia without the Russians.

Toward the final phase of the war, diplomatic relations between Tokyo and Moscow became strained, with each side less given to expressing the truth about its intentions, particularly those relating to military planning aimed at the other. As Japan's war planners had anticipated, the Soviet Union eventually invaded the Japanese empire, and that action led to a series of events that effectively suppressed memories of Japan's interactions with Russian people and culture. The loss of Japan's cultural connection to the Eurasian world is another forgotten legacy of Japan's Eurasian-Pacific War.

Part II

THE FUTURE OF EAST ASIA AFTER THE JAPANESE EMPIRE

3

MAO'S COMMUNIST REVOLUTION

Who Will Rule China?

The Sino-Japanese War (1937–45) was no local skirmish, insignificant outside East Asia. Even before the Pacific War fully erupted, Japanese leaders expected its outcome would determine global power dynamics far beyond Asia. Were Japan to lose, Japanese leaders wondered, who would emerge to dominate China? How would that control manifest itself over East Asia in the postwar? Long attendant to the rivalry between the United States and the Soviet Union, Japanese leaders and intelligence agencies closely observed the efforts of both powers to influence China's civil war as well as the reactions among the different Chinese factions to these efforts. The strategic reflection underlying the Eurasian Pacific War cannot be fully understood without attending to the Japanese thinking and planning in the Sino-Japanese conflict.

Focused almost exclusively on Japan's battles against Chiang Kai-shek's Guomindang (GMD), studies of the Sino-Japanese War have rarely shed light on Japan's understanding of the Chinese Communist Party (CCP), even though the assessment of Chinese communists was critical to Japanese wartime policy. The standard narrative of Japan's war in China usually comprises two parts: Japan's occasional, yet substantial, military successes against Chiang Kai-shek's forces and its frustrated search for a diplomatic solution with Chiang via the Japanese puppet regime of Wang Jingwei in Nanjing. Militarily, Japan fought in both China and the Pacific, and American military preponderance in the Pacific negated the limited successes of Japan's offensives in China. Diplomatically, as long as Japan gave Wang the responsibility of mediating peace with the GMD regime, Chiang refused to take any interest. Even if peace were achieved, Chiang seemed to lack the popular support necessary to unite and revitalize China. Not only that, he did not have the trust or collaboration of Churchill, Roosevelt, or Stalin. To concentrate solely on Chiang's GMD regime in the Chinese context then impoverishes our understanding of Japan's war.[1]

Japan's wartime policy toward China developed through critical evaluations of Chinese communist forces. Japanese intellectuals saw the potential of Chinese communism to change existing government systems and observed its growth with a mixture of bewilderment and enthusiasm. As China's civil war worsened in parallel to Japan's quagmire of war, Japan's China experts, from scholars and journalists to the North China Area Army (Kita-Shina Hōmen-gun) and the South Manchuria Railway Company (SMR) Research Department, recognized the CCP's superiority over the GMD. When Japan's peace negotiations with the GMD via the Wang Jingwei regime in Nanjing ended with his death in November 1944, the Japanese government attempted a rapprochement with the CCP. As their evaluation of the CCP as the most likely unifying force of China strengthened, they paid ever greater attention to the level of influence and control the Soviet Union cast over the CCP. In the war against China, as elsewhere, the Japanese carefully watched the Soviet Union as a potential power broker who could well play a substantial role in China after the end of the Japanese empire.

In November 1944 Foreign Minister Shigemitsu Mamoru, an architect of the Greater East Asia Declaration, told Ambassador Satō Naotake in Moscow that Japan would recognize the CCP Headquarters as the Yan'an regime (*seiken*), a de facto government independent of the GMD. Shigemitsu subsequently advised the Japanese media not to print articles hostile to the CCP. The Japanese government's recognition of the CCP regime has been understood as an effort to placate Moscow and cement the Soviet-Japanese Neutrality Pact. Historian Akashi Yōji argues that the Japanese government tried to add CCP-led China to the Eurasian alliance in an effort to form a Moscow-Yan'an-Tokyo détente to counter the GMD-Washington alliance.[2]

Behind the recognition of Yan'an, however, lay a more nuanced assessment of China's future based on its relations with the Soviet Union as well as the United States. In November 1944, shortly after the Yan'an recognition, Richard Sorge and Ozaki Hotsumi were executed for their roles in what would come to be known as the Richard Sorge international spy ring. Sorge, an adviser to the Ger-

---

1. Yukiko Koshiro, "Japan's World and World War II," *Diplomatic History* 25, no. 3 (summer 2001): 437–40.

2. Akashi Yōji, "Taiheiyō Sensō makki ni okeru Nihon gunbu no En'an seiken to no wahei mosaku—sono haikei" (In search of peace—the Yan'an alternative and the Imperial Japanese Army), *Gunji Shigaku* (Journal of military history) 31, nos. 1 and 2 (September 1995): 175–85.

man Embassy in Tokyo, spied for the intelligence department of the Soviet Red Army and recruited around eighteen collaborators, including foreign residents of Tokyo (several Japanese-Americans, a German, a Finn, and a Croatian), a Japanese aristocrat, and a member of the Kwantung Army. From 1933 until his arrest in October 1941, three days after Ozaki's, Sorge relayed to the Soviet Union information from Ozaki and other collaborators on Japan's political and economic conditions, diplomacy, and most importantly, military matters concerning Japan's strategy against the Soviet Union. The executions of Ozaki and Sorge sent a cautionary message to the Soviet Union, while the Yan'an recognition was an amicable gesture to the CCP. The Yan'an recognition therefore was not likely Tokyo's open welcome of an international communist bloc under Moscow.

That summer, having lost Saipan to the United States, an island designated as a part of Japan's Absolute National Defense Sphere, Japanese policymakers felt pressured to complete Japan's self-imposed mission in Asia before the war's end: to revive Asia all by itself and purge Anglo-American interference. Japan's North China Area Army predicted that the CCP would become the ultimate unifier of China because of its greater populist appeal.[3] Even so they did not anticipate Moscow's influence would prevail in China. Surviving documents discussed in this chapter demonstrate that the Japanese government did not attempt to prop Japan's relationship with the Soviet Union by giving diplomatic recognition to the CCP. North China Area Army intelligence analysts had early indications that Chinese and Soviet communists had disparate goals—a finding that came to be shared by the Foreign Ministry in Tokyo. They concluded that Mao was not a puppet of the Soviet government, a view reinforced by his determination to keep China independent of both Washington and Moscow. Far from a conciliatory gesture to Moscow, Tokyo's appeasement of the CCP reflected its expectation that Mao had the power to check both Soviet and US ambitions and keep Asia for Asians.

While acknowledging the Soviet capacity to exist alongside Asians and to contain the United States, the Japanese government did not envision the Soviet Union as the ultimate custodian of East Asia under the banner of pan-Asianism. The Japanese government preferred to entrust the CCP under Mao with the task of keeping China for the Chinese. Examination of the hitherto unrecognized centrality of the Sino-Japanese War to Japan's Eurasian-Pacific War, reaffirms the importance of wartime Japan's Eurasian perspective.

---

3. The North China Area Army was created after the Marco Polo Bridge Incident of 1937 from elements of the China Garrison Army, Kwantung Army, and the Chōsen Army and soon became a law unto itself.

Japan's China Studies and the CCP

"The Japanese are geographically so close to the Chinese, yet know so little about them," a Chinese expert in Japan lamented in 1938. According to him the Japanese had only three extreme and simplistic reactions to the Chinese: cruel disdain for the inferior "chinks," maudlin pity for the misery of the Chinese people, and sophomoric praise for heroic Chinese revolutionaries. "When you give a talk in front of the uneducated masses," the author explained, "just insult the Chinese and praise the Japanese and you'll get thunderous applause. Don't criticize the Japanese even a bit, or you will be cursed. If your audience happens to be university students, criticize all Japanese shortcomings and elaborate Chinese virtues, and you'll be met with loud cheers. The masses are narcissistic and the intelligentsia are masochistic; both are vulgar, hopelessly stuck in stereotypical views of the Chinese."[4] Deploring the absence of any well-balanced understanding of the Chinese people, he alerted Japanese readers to the revolutionary potential of China as the Sino-Japanese War entered its second year.

After the epic success of Chinese Communist Army's Long March of 1934–36, the Japanese noted the building potential of the CCP leaders to succeed Sun Yat-sen and to complete the unfinished republican revolution. The Japanese media reported the growing strength of the CCP under the charismatic leadership of Mao Zedong and speculated that the CCP would in the end win the civil war against the GMD. Once the Sino-Japanese War broke out, the Japanese Imperial General Headquarters, the Foreign Ministry, the Kwantung Army, the SMR Research Department, and various research institutions and organizations launched serious investigations of the CCP and produced numerous secret reports. They examined the ideological goals of the CCP; studied the bureaucratic, legal, and socioeconomic systems developed in regions controlled by the CCP; and even analyzed global politics and the CCP, including the party's relations with the United States, the Soviet Union, and other communist movements across Asia.

One of Japan's leading China experts, Ozaki Hotsumi (1901–44) was a well-respected journalist and political adviser to Prime Minister Konoe Fumimaro—the latter position functioning as the cover for his covert Marxist beliefs. Ozaki attempted to make a case to the Japanese public why studying the CCP was critical for understanding the future of China, Japan, Asia, and the world. China's hardship, according to Ozaki, derived from the twin yoke of semifeudalism and semicolonialism. Whereas the former was preserved by landlords, bureaucrats, and warlords, China's semicolonialism was sustained by three economic conditions:

4. Sugiyama Heisuke, "Shina shisō taisaku-ron" (How to cope with Chinese thoughts), *Kaizō* 20, no. 10 (October 1938): 55–68.

heavy industries owned by foreign capital, a domestic financial system regulated by foreign capital, and domestic markets controlled by foreign capital. Since the imperialist powers used China's semifeudal forces as their agents to secure and enhance control over China, their only interest in preserving the semifeudal elements was to maximize the exploitation of China. China's semicolonialism and semifeudalism were symbiotic.[5] Ozaki argued that there was hope for change. Now that Chinese peasants were fighting to eradicate the feudal elements and achieve national unification, they would eventually expel all imperialist powers and achieve an anti-imperialist and antifeudal democratic revolution (*han-tei han-hōken no minshu-shugi kakumei*), and herald a new phase in China's history as well as Asia's.[6] The underlying message: CCP leadership could make such radical change possible.

Ozaki wrote both within and against prevailing Japanese academic views of China. Despite their different ideological backgrounds, Japan's pan-Asianists and Marxists had an interest in seeing China revived with an Asian-style modernity. They intently observed the CCP's growth and activities and wondered if Mao would be the one to realize their respective dreams. Japan's pan-Asianists had materially supported Sun Yat-sen's 1911 revolution and remained interested in whether the CCP would emerge as his legitimate successor. At the same time, both camps were curious about whether China's nationalist movement (*minzoku undō*) would prove a decisive factor in determining the fate of Chinese society and, if so, whether such a movement would allow collaboration with Japan's pan-Asianism and imperialism.

Japan's interference in China began with a self-imposed mission to oversee a cycle of China's death and rebirth within the larger frame of world civilization. Modern Japanese studies of Chinese history began as part of Tōyō-shi (Oriental history), a new discipline invented to rework and measure Japan's past within a cohesive entity of Asian culture and geography comparable to Europe's past. Shiratori Kurakichi, one of the first students of Leopold von Ranke and professor of history at Tokyo Imperial University from 1904 to 1925, used the framework of European Orientalists to show the limits on progress for Asia. In doing so Shiratori carefully separated Japan from China by claiming that Asia was Japan's past, not present. By arguing that modern Japan had successfully developed beyond the norm of Asia, Shiratori placed Japan at a higher stage of development than China.[7] Naitō Konan, a sinologist at Kyoto Imperial University, described a steady

5. Asada Kyōji, *Nihon chishikijin no shokuminchi ninshiki* (Japanese intellectuals and their views of colonialism) (Tokyo: Azekura Shobō, 1985), 114–18.

6. Asada Kyōji, *Nihon chishikijin no shokuminchi ninshiki*, 124–25.

7. Stefan Tanaka, *Japan's Orient: Rendering Pasts in History* (Berkeley: University of California Press, 1995), 61.

regression in the course of China's history after its peak period—from the Han dynasty to the Tang—and argued that China's glory existed only in its past. Naitō equated a nation's history to a man's life cycle, which could be divided into the stages of birth, development, and maturity. China in the early twentieth century was like a man in the final stage of senescence.[8]

Scholars of the Tōyō-shi school posited Japan as a progenitor of Asian civilization, as well as a harbinger of Asian progress; they designated Japan the custodian of Asia's past and future. In contrast they placed China in the eternal past, characterizing it as ancient, barbaric, and stagnant. Modern Japanese deliberately adopted for China the ancient name *Shina*, the appellation found in Chinese Buddhist writings brought to Japan in the early ninth century.[9] China as Shina became the object of Japan's mission to guide the ancient and uncivilized to modernity and enlightenment.

Twentieth-century Chinese political development had often passed through Japan, leading to productive cross-pollinations especially in the cultivation of communist leaders and communities. Japan was an early venue for Chinese study of Marxism. Around the time of the Russo-Japanese War, a group of Chinese began to study Marxism through a Japanese work on modern socialism.[10] The birth of the Japan Socialist Party in 1906 inspired Chinese interested in overthrowing the Qing Dynasty. Future communist leaders such as Zhou Enlai, Chen Duxiu, and Li Dazhao all studied in Japan. In 1921 the CCP was born; the Communist International tasked it with leading the Far East toward communism and nationalism. The following year saw the founding of the Japanese Communist Party, whose mission including assisting Chinese and Korean communists in their fight against Japanese imperialism. Japanese Marxists did not consider their role subsidiary. They understood that Japan, already experiencing the problems of modernity, needed a new direction of development. In contrast a revolutionary movement in search of a completely new phase in history, one whose scale and boundary could exceed Japan's progress and development, had just begun in the yet-to-modernize China. Japanese Marxists found inspiration in how China's communist movement defied the reading of modernity under which Japan denigrated China as a stagnant civilization.

Ozaki was critical of Japanese studies of China, which he labeled "Tōyō-teki Shina-ron" (Orientalist China theories). He argued that modern Japan's China studies had been developed to serve the goals of Japan's continental (and imperial-

8. Tanaka, *Japan's Orient*, 193–98.
9. Tanaka, *Japan's Orient*, 4–5.
10. Jonathan Spence, *The Search for Modern China* (New York: W.W. Norton, 1990), 260.

ist) policy. The lack of a scientific approach to Chinese studies in Japan, according to Ozaki, reflected Japan's desire to lock China into a perpetual decline because it was the only way Japan could portray itself as guardian of Orientalist China. Ozaki wrote, "In order to understand China correctly, it is vital to perceive it synthetically, not piecemeal, and to observe it in constant action. Scientific observation is important, but experimentation should not be confined to the microscopic. Neither should it be for the purpose of an autopsy." Rather, try vivisection, Ozaki insisted. China, though seemingly in a long-term near-death state, possessed vital energy and responded to the laws of kinetics (*atarashii undō hōsoku*).[11]

Different branches of Japan's China studies also aimed to develop concrete skills that would facilitate cross-cultural understanding and not just serve abstract ideology. The TōA Dōbun Shoin (East Asia Common Culture Academy) provided educational opportunities for revolutionary-minded Japanese students. Originally founded in Shanghai in 1886 by Japanese with military and commercial interests in China, the academy developed into Japan's largest overseas institution of higher learning. The founders dreamed of reviving China and developing solid Sino-Japanese trade relations so the two nations could eventually unite against western imperialism. They hoped their pan-Asian dream—coprosperity through trade—would materialize through a curriculum in which Japanese and Chinese students studied each other's society and political and economic systems in the native language: Japanese students learned about China in the Chinese language and vice versa. Subsequently sponsored by the Japanese Foreign Ministry and thereafter by the Imperial Army, Japanese students studied Chinese society through the intensive reading of Chinese publications and extensive field research; 5,000 Japanese and 864 Chinese students studied at the academy between 1900 and 1945.

The academy, vanguard of Japanese imperialism in China, ironically produced a breed of Japanese student that became increasingly interested in China's revolutionary movement. A group of Japanese and Chinese students at the academy engaged in Marxist study as well as in anti-Japanese and anti-imperialist activities, which intensified after a series of anti–foreign labor movements in the early summer of 1925.[12] By the early 1930s the academy had become a major recruiting

11. Asada Kyōji, *Nihon chishikijin no shokuminchi ninshiki*, 110–12. A different translation of this part of Ozaki's writing appears in Tanaka, *Japan's Orient*, 220.

12. On May 15, 1925, a strike at a Japanese-owned cotton mill in Shanghai resulted in the death of a Chinese laborer. At his memorial service on May 30, Chinese students and laborers clashed with British police, which led to thirteen Chinese deaths. In the following month more violent confrontations took place between the Chinese and Western and Japanese powers in Shanghai and elsewhere. The May 30 incident thus heralded a new era for China's anti-imperialist movement.

center for leftist Japanese as well as a haven for underground collaborators of the CCP and the Japanese Communist Party.[13]

The South Manchuria Railway Company (SMR) Research Department, a think tank of the Kwantung Army, also adopted a Marxist approach to the understanding of contemporary China during the critical decade of the 1930s. With its headquarters in Dalian, the research department began operations in 1907, just one year after the establishment of the SMR. For the next thirty-eight years until the end of World War II, it expanded its global research and intelligence network to Mukden (Shenyang), Harbin, Shanghai, Nanjing, New York, and Paris, and produced nearly sixty-two hundred analytical reports. One of the finest research institutions in the Japanese empire, the SMR Research Department hired prominent Marxist scholars from different factions who had fled persecution in Japan and allowed them to conduct social science research informed by Marxist concerns. Its scholars included Gushima Kanesaburō, Itō Takeo, Nakanishi Tsutomu, Itō Ritsu, and Sano Manabu. Ozaki Hotsumi, too, was once affiliated with the department. These Marxist researchers conducted socioeconomic analyses of the conditions of Manchuria and northern China and argued that the rise of the CCP was inevitable. Nakanishi, a dropout from the East Asia Common Culture Academy, joined the SMR Research Department in 1934 and became a star researcher who won the trust of, and gained free access to, the China Expeditionary Army (Shina Haken-gun). He received recognition for his study "Chūgoku Kyōsan-tō chōsa" (Research on the CCP), in which he claimed that the Chinese resistance was invincible because the masses now fought on an upward vector toward national independence, a natural development with historical inevitability because it meant liberation from the yoke of imperialism.[14]

The TōA Kenkyūjo (East Asia Institute) began in 1938 as a foundation under the auspices of the Kikaku-in (Planning Board), which served directly under the prime minister and was responsible for comprehensive policy design of wartime national mobilization. Reflecting the urgent need to pursue war goals in Asia, the institute secured ample budgets as well as extensive help from the SMR, the Mitsubishi Economic Research Association (Mitsubishi Keizai Kenkyūkai), the ministries of Finance, Foreign Affairs, Education, and Colonization (Takumushō), the army, and the navy. Under the heavy military influence of the adminis-

13. Douglas Reynolds, "Training Young China Hands: Toa Dobun Shoin and Its Precursors, 1886–1945," in Peter Duus, Ramon H. Myers, and Mark Peattie, *The Japanese Informal Empire in China, 1895–1937* (Princeton, NJ: Princeton University Press, 1989), 210–71.

14. Fukumoto Katsukiyo, "Nakanishi Tsutomu shōron" (Arguments concerning Nakanishi Tsutomu), in *Nakanishi Tsutomu jinmon chōsho* (The complete record of cross-examination of Nakanishi Tsutomu) (Tokyo: Aki Shobō, 1996), 467–77. See also Hara Kakuten, *Mantetsu Chōsa-bu to Ajia* (The South Manchuria Railway Company Research Department and Asia) (Tokyo: Sekai Shoin, 1986), 260.

tration, the institute managed to attract progressive scholars and researchers, and its thousand-some researchers and staff produced voluminous policy-oriented studies on topics ranging from the invasion of East Asia by Red imperialism (Sekishoku teikoku-shugi), relations between Chinese communism and the Soviet Union, the nature of revolutionary movements in East Asia, to the current situation of Jewish financiers as well as Islamic and Lamaist activities. Among the institute's leading accomplishments were Yamamoto Hideo's "San-min shugi minzoku riron ni kansuru kenkyū" (Studies of nationalistic theory based on the "Three Principles of the People"), and Sakai Tadao's "Shina chishiki kaikyū no minzoku-shugi shisō" (Studies of the ideology behind nationalism among Chinese intelligentsia). The institute's Chinese specialists translated original Chinese communist works such as "A seventeen-year history of the Chinese Communist Party," "The Chinese Communist Party," and "Soviet China."[15]

Toward the outbreak of the Sino-Japanese War, Japanese intellectuals became progressively more interested in the CCP, which they regarded as the agent of revolutionary change for China. Even before the SMR Research Department conducted Marxist studies on the growing importance of the CCP, the radical-progressive intellectual journal *Kaizō* regularly published articles on the CCP's latest achievements. Even after the war began, the journal printed articles on the CCP containing marked criticism of Japanese imperialism. One month before the Marco Polo Bridge Incident of July 7, 1937, that marked the start of the Sino-Japanese War, *Kaizō* featured Japanese translations of two interviews with Mao Zedong conducted respectively by American journalists Edgar Snow and Agnes Smedley. *Kaizō* often invited prominent foreigners to contribute. Snow's interview brought to light Mao's harsh criticism of Japanese imperialism and his hope the United States would assist the CCP in their joint antifascist fight. Mao was confident that when the Chinese people formed a united anti-Japanese front and when people all over the world supported the liberation of oppressed races (*minzoku*) that the war against Japanese imperialism could be won. Mao praised Chinese citizens living in the Soviet districts organized by the CCP for their spiritual strength and military preparation. Snow's interview concluded with a statement from Mao that the eventual success of the Chinese revolution should spark further popular desire for struggles against colonialism in other parts of Asia such as Cambodia, Vietnam, the Philippines, India, and eventually all over the world.[16]

---

15. Hara Kakuten, *Gendai Ajia kenkyū seiritsu-shi ron—Mantetsu, TōA Kenkyūjo, IPR no kenkyū* (A history of modern Asian studies in Japan) (Tokyo: Keisō Shobō, 1984).

16. Edgar Snow, "Chūgoku Kyōsan-tō no tai-Nichi seisaku" (CCP policy toward Japan), *Kaizō* 19, no. 6 (June 1937): 144–59.

In the Smedley interview, Mao distinguished his fight against Japanese imperialism from the struggle against global imperialism, the former being the most imminent threat to China. The formation of the second united front with the GMD, Mao explained, did not mean that the CCP endorsed bourgeois nationalism and had abandoned the goal of class struggle. Fundamental nationalistic interest (*minzoku no rieki*) and class interest should go hand in hand. Workers, peasants, and the poor, though all still lacking power and influence, were the foundation of China and also the largest class capable of resisting Japan and protecting the nation. The CCP stood for both internationalism and patriotism, he continued. When the popular front government was created, the government would propose seven conditions under which it would accept peace talks with Japan: complete equality between China and Japan, dissolution of Manchukuo, Japan's military withdrawal from northern China, suspension of Japanese flyover rights, removal of Japanese intelligence offices, abolition of arrogant and irrational attitudes exhibited by Japanese toward China, and prohibition of Japan's illegal trade. Mao admitted that it was improbable that the Japanese government would agree to these conditions and confessed that he anticipated war between China and Japan. Should war break out with still no international aid for China, Mao asserted that the Chinese people would fight the war of resistance themselves and lead Japan to the bankruptcy of its financial, economic, and political systems. At the end of the interview, Mao affirmed his endorsement of Sun Yat-sen's Three Principles. He reiterated his belief that all Chinese people, regardless of ideology and religion, would work to found a solid basis for national unification and revitalization; only then would the Chinese see a bright future.[17]

That *Kaizō* could publish such a bold, critical view on the prospect of war between China and Japan so shortly before the Marco Polo Bridge Incident shows that the media enjoyed considerable latitude even with the official censorship of communist ideas, at least until the Yokohama Incident of 1942. The editor proudly announced that readers could obtain a vivid and useful picture of Mr. Mao Zedong, the man who was exercising superb leadership with pride and flair in the mountain areas of northwestern China. This issue's focus on the communist world was confirmed by "Soren no Teiō" (The Tsar of the Soviet Union), a study by Colonel Hata Hikosaburō, the foremost Soviet expert in the Imperial Japanese Army. In contrast to the affable portrayal of Mao, Hata described how the Stalin-Trotsky rivalry after Lenin's death transformed Stalin into a dictator

17. Agnes Smedley, "Seian Jihen to KoKkyō Gassaku" (The Xian Incident and the GMD-CCP coalition), *Kaizō* 19, no. 6 (June 1937): 159–71.

whose regime presented an uncertain Soviet future.[18] For the next few years, *Kaizō* published articles on the radicalization of the CCP, its entangled relations with the GMD, and its successful mobilization of peasants for the anti-Japanese resistance. It occasionally even printed biographies of key figures within the CCP as illustrated by the July 1937 article on Zhou Enlai, who served as a matchmaker for the remarriage of the CCP and GMD.[19]

The next month *Kaizō* featured three articles on the "North China Incident" (Hoku-Shi Jihen), the official Japanese government name for the early stage of the Sino-Japanese War following the Marco Polo Bridge Incident. Ozaki Hotsumi wrote about the increasing collaboration between the CCP and the GMD. Ozaki also highlighted Chinese nationalism and democratization as two powerful forces against Japan.[20] In October 1937, *Kaizō* published a special issue on the "China Incident" (*Shina Jihen*), the new official term replacing the "North China Incident." Ozaki this time contributed an essay that called for the Japanese people to pay serious attention to the rise of the CCP. He cautioned that their interest should not be a scholarly and abstract examination of communism; the Japanese people should understand the CCP as a phenomenon within the Chinese nationalist movement (*minzoku undō*) and watch carefully as it expanded and matured in the war against Japan.[21] Another essay in this issue made much the same point, identifying Chinese communism as a true form of Chinese nationalism. The Chinese people, it argued, were demonstrating the explosive power of a burgeoning nationalism that was leading the nation toward an unprecedented progressive reconstruction.[22]

The November 1937 *Kaizō* featured the translation of Edgar Snow's transcription of Mao's autobiography.[23] The December 1937 issue contained a translation of a Chinese reporter's detailed look inside the Eighth Route Army. The story depicted the vibrant life of soldiers and how, when not studying, they played basketball and tennis. Through a streamlined curriculum, the soldiers learned

---

18. Hata Hikosaburō, "Sutārin to iu otoko" (The man named Stalin), *Kaizō* 19, no. 6 (June 1937): 1–12; Also see "Henshū dayori" (Editor's Note), in the same issue, 96.

19. Hatano Ken'ichi, "KoKkyō saikon no tateyakusha: Shū Onrai den" (Zhou Enlai: the matchmaker for the GMD-CCP remarriage) (originally written on May 31, 1937), *Kaizō* 19, no. 7 (July 1937): 86–91.

20. Ozaki Hotsumi, "Hoku-Shi mondai no shin-dankai" (The new stage in the northern Chinese issue), *Kaizō* 19, no. 8 (August 1937): 94–101.

21. Ozaki Hotsumi, "Jikyoku to tai-Shi ninshiki" (How to understand China in the current situation), *Kaizō* 19, no. 11 (October 1937): 43–50.

22. Inomata Tsunao, "Rinpō Shina no zento" (Future of China, our neighbor), *Kaizō* 19, no. 11 (October 1937): 51–75.

23. Edgar Snow, "Mō Takutō jijo-den" (An autobiography of Mao Zedong), *Kaizō* 19, no. 12 (November 1937): 362–70.

about "imperialism," "colonialism," and "revolution," and quickly became capable of discussing political matters with sophistication. The essay showed that Eighth Route Army soldiers had high morale, discipline, and enthusiasm. Most important, an egalitarianism prevailed among the soldiers and also between them and the peasants. The reporter explained that these conditions could exist because CCP leaders—Mao Zedong, Zhu De, Peng Dehuai, Lin Biao, Xiao Ke, Xu Haidong, Zhou Enlai, Ye Jianying, Liu Bocheng, Ding Ling, and many others—possessed immense talent as leaders as well as colorful personalities that gave their program a warm human touch.[24] The April 1938 *Kaizō* featured a translation of Agnes Smedley's uplifting report on the Eighth Route Army, with high praise for the soldiers' self-discipline and egalitarianism.[25] Throughout 1939 *Kaizō* continued printing articles on the CCP, highlighting its superiority to the GMD, particularly in its ability to mobilize the populace.[26]

The SMR Research Department actively examined the CCP as well. In 1939 Itō Takeo edited and published the comprehensive report "Shina kōsen-ryoku chōsa hōkoku" (A research report on China's capacity to fight a war of resistance). Later praised as one of the best contemporary Japanese studies of China, this work demonstrated how Japan's modern warfare in the first Sino-Japanese War of 1894–95 inadvertently and finally awakened the Chinese people, notably the bourgeois class, to the acute need to replace their society's antiquated structure. While China's bourgeois class grew in modernized cities under GMD control, the report harshly criticized the GMD: under its leadership China would never gain enough momentum to modernize. As long as the Chinese bourgeois collaborated with the very imperialists who made China a semicolony, no matter how they and the GMD tried to modernize China, they would never emancipate China from the yoke of imperialism, modernize, and achieve national independence.

The report gave a strikingly different, positive review of how CCP membership had increased dramatically in the countryside and achieved genuine appeal under Mao Zedong's leadership. The party mobilized people with the promise of

---

24. Zhang Guoping, "Dai-Hachiro-gun no zenbō" (A complete picture of the 8th Route Army), *Kaizō* 19, no. 15 (December 1937): 255–73.

25. Agnes Smedley, "'Kyōsan-gun jyūgun ki" (War correspondent report from the 8th Route Army), *Kaizō* 20, no. 4 (April 1938): 382–87.

26. Hatano Ken'ichi, "Shō seiken to Kyōsan-gun no kongo" (Future of the Chiang regime and CCP Army), *Kaizō* 20, no. 7 (July 1938): 72–79; Kanaka Kanae, "Kōsen Shina no naibu jōsei kentō" (Examination of China's domestic conditions in war), *Kaizō* 21, no. 1 (January 1939): 214–24; Yokota Minoru, "1940-nen no Shina" (China, 1940), *Kaizō* 21, no. 14 (December 1939): 51–57; Miyazawa Toshiyoshi, "Sonbun-shugi to Kyōsan-shugi" (The principles of Sun Yat-sen and the CCP), *Kaizō* 22, no. 1 (January 1940): 78–96; Edgar Snow, "Mō Takutō Sunou taidan" (Mao-Snow talk), *Kaizō* 22, no. 5 (March 1940): 164–77; Qing Ye, "Kokumin-tō to Chūgoku Kyōsan-tō: Chūgoku nidai seitō no hikaku" (A comparison of the GMD and the CCP), *Kaizō* 22, no. 10 (June 1940): 66–78.

democratization and national unification, along with three political goals: to achieve nationalism, fight against Japan, and abolish class. The report recommended that it was essential for Japan to understand that the Chinese fight against Japan was a people's fight to achieve revolutionary change. A military victory by Japan would never "settle the difference" between Japan and China or provide the Chinese people with any of their three political goals. This 1939 report thus concluded that Japan could never win in China militarily; the only solution Japan should seek was a political one.[27]

Japanese Military Appraisal of CCP Propaganda

How confident the Japanese people were that the war of aggression could modernize China in Japan's image remains unknown. An eerie notion of China's invincibility was already present in *Ikiteiru heitai* (Living soldiers), a novel by Ishikawa Tatsuzō that appeared in the March 1938 issue of *Chūō Kōron* (Central review), Japan's leading intellectual journal. Winner of the first Akutagawa literary prize in 1935, Ishikawa visited Nanjing on January 5, 1938, as a special war reporter for the *Chūō Kōron* and investigated the aftermath of the Nanjing Massacre. Upon returning to Japan, he completed his chilling exposé about looting, torture, rape, and killing by Japanese soldiers who had lost all sense of humanity. Though the novel managed to pass the Interior Ministry's press code, the March issue of *Chūō Kōron* received a total recall order on the day it appeared in bookstores across Japan. Ishikawa was arrested. After a public trial he received a prison sentence of four months. By December 1941 he was allowed to resume activities as an embedded reporter with the Japanese Navy. Until the original, uncensored version was published in December 1945, "Living Soldiers" remained a classic people only whispered about.

In one scene Sergeant First Class Hirao, formerly a newspaper proofreader and now a murderer in China, enters a mansion deserted by an upper-class Chinese family. Inspecting one luxurious antique after another, he expresses a bombastic, lurid romanticism for China the eternal:

> These four hundred million Chinese people are as grand and ancient as the Yangtze River. China has remained the same since the times of the

27. Minami Manshū Tetsudō Kabushiki-gaisha Chōsa-bu Shina Kōsen-ryoku Chōsa Iinkai hen, *Shina kōsen-ryoku chōsa hōkoku* (The Research Committee on China's capacity to fight a way of resistance, SMR Research Department, ed., "A research report on China's capacity to fight a war of resistance") (1940; reprint Tokyo: San'ichi Shobō, 1970), 10–15, 69–77.

> Yellow Emperor, Emperor Taizong, Yang Guifei and the like. China will never perish. Even though Chiang Kai-shek boasts of the New Life Movement, he will never ever be able to change people like these. *Likewise, no matter if we occupy the whole of China, it's a dream of a dream that we will ever make them adopt the Japanese way.* China is the way it is and the way it will be permanently. How awesome! How awesome, indeed! [The sentence in italics was deleted at the time of publication.]

In another scene Sergeant First Class Kondō, a medical doctor, indulges in drink at a bar in Shanghai, away from the hell in Nanjing, and thinks about all the dead soldiers he left behind. He tries to rationalize all the deaths as the materialistic result of a collision of three powerful forces in the course of human history—individualism, socialism, and fascism. But then, "*After a short pause, he suddenly feels a chilling sensation running through his back.*" (The sentence in italics was deleted at the time of publication.)[28] Even as he tries to deaden his emotions with nihilism, his bodily reaction suggests that he recognizes something fundamentally wrong about Japan's aggression in China. This short novel never highlights the CCP. Yet Hirao and Kondō are prescient about the eventual defeat of Japan and the ultimate triumph of the Chinese people. Chiang would not lead them to this triumph; whoever won these people's hearts would.

In the early phase of the war against China, the Japanese military labeled Chinese communists as "terrorists" who threatened Japanese interests. To extirpate communist guerrilla activities, the Japanese military adopted the notorious "three alls" (*sankō*) strategy—kill, burn, and destroy all communists. This campaign even targeted Chinese civilians whom the Japanese Army identified, without proof, as communist collaborators and sympathizers. The anticommunist fight did not blind the Japanese Army to the steady rise of the CCP's power and influence. Observing the rapid growth of the CCP's popularity in the countryside, the Japanese military began confidential studies to assess the CCP's strength and potential in order to determine whether Japan could eventually win the war in China.

While the SMR Research Department tended to produce studies with heavily Marxist interpretative frameworks, the Imperial General Headquarters conducted empirical research that examined the CCP's goals and strategies as well as its ideology, philosophy, membership, and relationship with the masses. In Beijing, the North China Area Army Headquarters, the elite Japanese command for the entire war theater in China, had been producing a series of secret reports on the CCP before the SMR Research Department even began its research.

28. Ishikawa Tatsuzō, *Ikiteiru Heitai* (Living soldiers). Uncensored original version. (Tokyo: Chūkō Bunko, 1999), 119–20 and 165–66.

The CCP captured the Japanese Army's attention with its fierce propaganda campaign to draw Japanese soldiers to the Chinese side. Between July and December 1937 the CCP began planting Japanese flyers and pamphlets in combat regions where Japanese soldiers might spot them. Hardly eye-catching to Japanese soldiers, these publications, likely written by nonnative speakers of Japanese, were replete with grammatical and idiomatic mistakes. But in early 1938 the Japanese authorities discovered that the CCP had recruited Japan experts at the instigation of Zhou Enlai and revamped and improved the quality of its propaganda. CCP propaganda materials quickly became remarkably sophisticated. They featured Japanese poems, songs, and cartoons in visually arresting layouts with photos and even statistical graphs. Since the materials exhibited a profound knowledge of Japanese folk and popular culture, including the most contemporary, the Japanese authorities suspected that the CCP had secured Japanese collaborators in their propaganda efforts. These collaborators were probably Japanese living in China with CCP sympathies or members of the Japanese Communist Party who had studied at communist universities in Moscow or Khabarovsk and been dispatched to help the CCP. It was even possible that Japanese prisoners of war had been forced to collaborate with the CCP.

By the summer of 1938, CCP propaganda fliers and booklets had become irresistible to those Japanese soldiers hungry for fun and entertainment, news, and intellectual stimulation. In November of that year, the Japanese Cabinet Information Bureau issued "Bōkyō chōsa shiryō" (Anticommunism research report), which examined the CCP's superb propaganda techniques in striking a chord with Japanese youth. The report acknowledged that the contents were rich and well conceived. Some lowbrow materials were included for their appeal to the less-educated lower-ranking Japanese soldiers. Sophisticated and intellectual materials were intended to catch the attention of the more educated within the Japanese military. The report claimed that these materials strongly suggested the writers' familiarity with contemporary Japanese society and popular culture. These fliers gave a Marxist frame to even the latest Japanese news, which demonstrated that they were smuggled in directly from Japan through some underground network. The Japanese Cabinet Information Bureau was convinced that there had to be Marxist Japanese collaborators helping the CCP to wage its propaganda campaign.[29]

The Japanese authorities soon discovered the identities of the Japanese collaborators. By December 1938 the Japanese Cabinet Information Bureau had

---

29. "Dai-Hachiro-gun to wa" (What is the Eighth Route Army?) (November 1938), in Naikaku Jōhō-bu, *BōKyō chōsa shiryō* (Japanese Cabinet Information Bureau, *Anticommunism research report*), vol. 1 (March 20, 1940), 46–51, available at Waseda University Library, Tokyo.

obtained a copy of an article written by Nosaka Sanzō (also known as Okano Susumu), a communist leader in exile. The article had been published in the *Journal of the Communist International* (the original title is unclear from the Japanese translation) that same year; it called for Japanese people to unite with Chinese people in the fight against Japanese fascism.[30] By the spring of 1939, the North China Area Army Headquarters had obtained information that Kaji Wataru and his wife Ikeda Sachiko were the central figures in the anti-Japanese propaganda effort in China.[31] Kaji Wataru, active in the proletarian literature movement, had been arrested in 1934. After being released from prison, he moved to Shanghai in 1936 to study and translate works by Lu Xun. In 1937 he translated Smedley's interview with Mao for *Kaizō*.[32] When war broke out he escaped the Japanese authority and reached Wuhan in 1938 where he joined the GMD and began an antiwar and antifascist campaign.[33] In 1939 he organized the Nihon Heishi Hansen Dōmei (Japanese Soldiers' Antiwar League) in Chongqing, which named Churchill, Roosevelt, Stalin, Mao Zedong, and Chiang Kai-shek as its executive members.

Nosaka Sanzō himself soon joined the anti-Japanese campaign in China. He left Moscow in 1940 and entered Yan'an along with Zhou Enlai and established a branch of the Japanese Soldiers' Antiwar League. Since Kaji had developed troubled relations with Chiang Kai-shek because of the latter's staunch anticommunism, he was inclined to help Nosaka's movement in Yan'an and expanded the education programs for Japanese prisoners of war into other parts of China. The new curriculum covered the basic concepts of war and peace, Marxism and Leninism, and the importance of building a new Japan. The programs fed and treated the Japanese prisoners generously. The league continued to build other branches across China's battlefields. In North China alone 223 Japanese soldiers joined the league.[34]

With all these threats arising from Japanese sympathizers with the CCP, studies of Chinese communism became a priority for the North China Area Army

---

30. S. Okano, "Shina Jihen to Nihon kokumin" (The Sino-Japanese War and the Japanese people) (December 1938), translated and reprinted in Naikaku Jōhō-bu, *BōKyō chōsa shiryō* (Japanese Cabinet Information Bureau, *Anticommunism research report*), vol. 1 (March 20, 1940), 81–90.

31. Kita-Shina Hōmen-gun Shirei-bu, "Gokuhi: Kyōsan-tō no waga gun ni taisuru shisō-teki gakai kōsaku no shinsō to kore ga bōatsu hōsaku" (The North China Area Army Headquarters, "Top secret: the CCP operation to infiltrate our army ideologically and the possible countermeasures against it") (April 5, 1939), reprinted in WIC, vol. 3, 345–48.

32. See note 17 of this chapter. In this article he was acknowledged as its translator, but only his family name, not full name, appeared.

33. Since Stalin regarded the GMD as the main force of revolution for China, he ordered the CCP to be subordinate to the GMD in first achieving the bourgeois revolution. Kaji joined the GMD in this spirit of the united front.

34. Ōmori Minoru, *Sokoku kakumei kōsaku* (The operation to revolutionize Japan) (Tokyo: Kōdansha Bunko, 1981), 162–224.

Headquarters. Northern China was strategically important because of its proximity to Manchukuo and for its role as a supplier of foodstuffs and mineral resources to Japan. Although the region was already under heavy Japanese influence, tightening control of the region held the key to Japan's further expansion in other parts of China. The North China Area Army conducted independent investigations on CCP activities and published a series of confidential reports based on these studies.

On April 5, 1939, the North China Area Army Headquarters published a top secret memorandum on the superb skills revealed by CCP propaganda. The focus was on a captured manual published by the Eighth Route Army's Political Department. The manual provided Eighth Route Army soldiers with detailed instructions on how to draw Japanese soldiers into their camp. The manual recommended that CCP soldiers recognize that most Japanese soldiers were innocent peasants forcibly drafted into the Imperial Army. The manual urged CCP soldiers to teach these Japanese soldiers that they were victims of Japan's corrupt military clique whose sole interest was its capitalistic monopoly in the world of imperialism. Japan's military officers could be reeducated, continued the manual, because they were a product of elitist education within the confines of military school. Once taught about social reality, they could learn to see what was wrong with Japan's war. The duty of CCP soldiers was to be patient with both officers and soldiers and to encourage them to open their eyes to the vices of imperialism and militarism: Japan's military-financial clique wished to prolong the fight in China in order to increase their profits from war industries and war spoils at the cost of the people's suffering. Once Japanese officers and soldiers understood the shameless scheme behind this aggressive war, they would lose their fighting spirit and want peace. To grab their attention and make them listen, the manual instructed CCP soldiers first to express sympathy for their homesickness and unhappiness with military life and then tell them that the CCP would consider Japanese soldiers as friends in a mutual fight for peace. The Japanese military analysts who examined this captured manual conceded that the CCP's psychological propaganda would be effective in tugging at Japanese soldiers' heartstrings.[35]

The CCP's propaganda skills and potential appeal to Japanese soldiers were not the only strengths the Japanese Army identified. The North China Area Army also recognized the CCP's impressive mobilization of Chinese peasants and urged examination of the CCP's success in winning their collaboration. The North China Area Army initiated its own propaganda program in December 1937 to promote

35. Kita-Shina Hōmen-gun Shirei-bu, "Gokuhi: Kyōsan-tō no waga gun ni taisuru shisō-teki gakai kōsaku no shinsō to kore ga bōatsu hōsaku" (April 5, 1939), reprinted in WIC, vol. 3, 341–81.

the region's integration under Japanese rule. Called the Hsin-min Hui (People's Renovation Society), the program aimed to educate the Chinese residents in the region on the historic and cultural meaning of Japan's pan-Asianism so they would understand the importance of collaborating with Japanese leaders toward co-prosperity and peace in Asia. Through newsletters, pamphlets, radio programs, school curricula, and organizational activities, the North China Area Army tried to convince the Chinese people of the need to assist the Japanese and fight against both the GMD and the CCP.

On New Year's Day 1938, the Hsin-min Hui distributed to local residents slogans written on strips of red paper to adorn their gates and doors:

> Support Sino-Japanese friendship.
> Oppose communism and save the country.
> Pray for the peace of the world.
>
> Build up the New Order.
> Regenerate from the beginning.
> Do not change the old family customs.
>
> The Hsin-min Hui gives the republic a new life.
> China and Japan have the same culture and the same race.
> We ought to unite together to reconstruct the Oriental race.
>
> Overthrow the corrupt evil of China—Chiang Kai-shek.
>
> The Hsin-min Hui builds a happy valley for China, Japan and Manchukuo.[36]

Although the Hsin-min Hui program attempted to show sensitivity to the local custom of seasonal celebration, few Chinese residents shared the imposed spirit of peace and friendship.

As it became clear that Japan was losing the propaganda war, it became all the more urgent for the North China Area Army to uncover the CCP's secret of winning people's hearts and minds. The North China Area Army Headquarters subsequently decided to investigate the CCP organization further, especially its command system, which had enabled such successful anti-Japanese campaigns among ordinary people.[37] In a September 1938 top secret report, the North China Area

---

36. George E. Taylor, *The Struggle for North China* (New York: Institute of Pacific Relations, 1940), available online at http://www.questia.com/library/book/the-struggle-for-north-china-by-george-e-taylor.jsp. These mottoes appear on p. 210.

37. Kita-Shina Hōmen-gun Sanbō-chō, "Gunji gokuhi: Hoku-Shi ni okeru Kyōsan-tō katsudō jōkyō no ken hōkoku" (The North China Area Army Chief of Staff, "Military top secret: report of activities of CCP forces in North China") (April 14, 1938), reprinted in WIC, vol. 2, 225–28.

Army Headquarters admitted that the CCP had successfully adopted a highly sophisticated method of mobilizing and training the Chinese masses in the anti-Japanese fight.[38]

A series of confidential reports issued by the headquarters and other Japanese authorities praised and marveled at the brilliance of CCP tactics. A secret report issued by the headquarters of the Terauchi Unit (Terauchi Butai Sanbō-bu) in November 1938 praised the Chinese communists' impressive successes in the Jin-Cha-Ji Border Region of northern China, the stronghold of the Japanese military. In a successful multilevel campaign, CCP members were now vigorously forming a regional government, organizing the local populace into political units, and implementing a series of new socioeconomic policies aimed at improving people's lives. The Terauchi secret report emphasized that these Chinese communists were particularly effective in combining anti-Japanese sentiment with the nationalist revolution (*minzoku kakumei*), sending the message straight to the hearts of the residents of all ages and classes, male and female. The Terauchi report also highly praised the CCP's humanitarian programs, including its education program. Even though literacy was not an integral part of the communist agenda, the CCP worked to wipe out illiteracy because it genuinely cared about the people. The people responded to the sincerity of the CCP by working to make the literacy project a success. People liked and respected the CCP because its army treated villagers with courtesy, respect, and discipline. The report concluded that the Japanese Army should carefully consider these attributes of the CCP in order to win the hearts of the Chinese people (*minshū no kokoro*).[39]

The Imperial General Headquarters in Tokyo could not ignore these secret reports from China, all of which communicated that the CCP was winning popular support in the countryside. In spite of the realities of the Nanjing Massacre and other atrocities and abuses committed by the Japanese Army, the official reason for war remained ostensibly an altruistic one: the establishment of the Greater East Asia Coprosperity Sphere under Sino-Japanese friendship. A Lieutenant Colonel Tanaka, known as a China expert, is said to have commented on the essence of Sino-Japanese friendship, "To feed the Chinese people—that's the beginning and also the ultimate goal [of any kind of friendship with them]."[40] The original plan was that the Japanese Army would liberate the Chinese peasants,

---

38. Kita-Shina Hōmen-gun Shirei-bu, "Gunji gokuhi: Kita-Shina Hōmen-gun senkyo chi'iki nai chian jōkyō" (The North China Area Army Headquarters, "Military top secret: the security condition in the North China Area Army-occupied areas") (September 1938), reprinted in WIC, vol. 2, 157–62.

39. Terauchi Butai Sanbō-bu, "Hoku-Shi ni okeru Kyōsan-tō oyobi Kyōsan-gun no sho-kōsaku" (CCP and GMD operations in North China) (November 18, 1938), reprinted in WIC, vol. 2, 246–53.

40. Shina Kōsen-ryoku Chōsa Iinkai, *Shina kōsen-ryoku chōsa hōkoku*, 10–15.

give them food, education, and other necessities and integrate them into the pan-Asian regional order. The CCP seemed to be doing a much better job at all of these things.

In 1938, one year after the Marco Polo Bridge Incident, *Kaizō* published a poignant essay on this matter by Sugiyama Heisuke, the political analyst known for his acid tongue. Chinese peasants, contrary to the Japanese stereotype, were spiritually mature and possessed cunning shrewdness. They could not be manipulated by any philosophy, propaganda, or politics of mere ideas or empty promises. Whoever successfully fed them would win their hearts and ultimately determine China's fate. The Japanese could never win so long as their ultimate desire was to control and dominate the Chinese and not to feed them.[41]

When the General Staff of the North China Area Army launched a new program for winning the minds of Chinese peasants for Japan's pan-Asianism, they emulated the tactics of the CCP. In April 1940 the North China Area Army Headquarters published a top secret report and circulated it among a selected group of Japanese organizations. It contained instructions on how to outdo CCP propaganda. This report fully acknowledged that the Chinese communists in Hebei Province had succeeded with political democratization of village governance and their economic program for the peasants. By establishing autonomy in the region, they brought peace and order and strengthened self-defense, winning the approval and support of the people. To compete against such accomplishments by the CCP, the report presented a list of programs that the Japanese organizations should carry out. Except for a program to teach the peasants Japanese culture, the list was a carbon copy of the programs already introduced by the CCP: education, religious freedom, and reorganization of villages into autonomous political units.[42]

In March 1940 the Imperial General Headquarters in Tokyo reworked the image of ongoing war in China and relabeled it a war of ideology (*shisō-sen*). Assisted by the consular police, the Foreign Ministry now gathered information on the CCP directly through the use of spies and intelligence agents—Caucasians (*gaijin*, particularly white Russians), Chinese, and Koreans.[43] The growing strength of CCP guerrilla operations also compelled the Japanese Army to predict their eventual success in the war against the GMD. In late September 1940 the North China

41. Sugiyama Heisuke, "Shina shisō taisaku-ron" (How to cope with Chinese ideology), *Kaizō* 20, no. 10 (October 1938): 67.

42. Tada Butai Honbu, "Gokuhi: Kahoku ni okeru shisō-sen shidō yōkō," oyobi "Fuzoku-sho" (The Tada Unit Headquarters, "Top secret: instructions on the war of ideology in North China" and "Appendix") (April 20, 1940), reprinted in WIC, vol. 5, 211–26.

43. Hoku-Shi Keimu-bu (North China Department of Police Affairs), *Shōwa 15-nen Hoku-Shi kōtō shunin kaigi-roku* (Minutes of the executive chiefs in North China, 1940) (March 1940), reprinted in WIC, vol. 10, 381.

Area Army Headquarters issued a top secret report on the military effectiveness of Chinese communist guerrilla attacks on Japanese railways and coal mines in the region and urged a serious study of their superior intelligence and ability to coordinate a complex web of operations.[44]

On October 1, 1940, the North China Area Army Headquarters issued another top secret report on the communist forces in North China. For the first time a report not only noted the continuing growth of the CCP, but also acknowledged the credibility of its long-term goal of achieving unification of China under the leadership of Mao Zedong, Zhou Enlai, and Zhu De. This military report of October 1940 reiterated earlier accounts of the ever-growing appeal of the CCP to a wide gamut of people—peasants, factory workers, intelligentsia, and radical factions. Questioning the durability of the GMD-CCP united front, the report even speculated that the CCP hoped the war against Japan would completely exhaust the GMD so that it would become easier for the CCP to single-handedly unify China under its revolutionary government. The report was one of the earliest Japanese documents that positively evaluated CCP ideology for its intricate blend of communist ideology and nationalistic sentiment. The report explained that its ideological movement (*shisō-teki katsudō*) had successfully instilled in the populace a sharp awareness of China as a nation-state (*kokka-teki naishi minzoku-teki ishiki*), which seemed to be the source of the spiritual charm of CCP propaganda. The authors of this report seemed hesitant to use the word *charm* (*miryoku*) because they added a question mark in parentheses. Perhaps they felt the word put too positive a spin on the CCP. The authors showed no hesitation later when they praised the mid-ranking party members of the CCP for possessing similar qualities to the honored rigid discipline and the self-sacrifice for a greater good of Japanese *bushidō* (the way of the samurai). The secret report concluded with a crucial recommendation to the Imperial General Headquarters: never underestimate the CCP propaganda's ability to capture the minds of Japanese soldiers.[45]

Another secret report issued in December 1940 pushed these points further. Made possible through collaboration with the Shanghai division of the SMR Research Department, this report urged the Japanese government to focus sharply on the CCP, rather than the GMD. The secret report emphasized how the CCP, under Mao Zedong's leadership, successfully combined Marxism and nationalism

---

44. Iinuma Butai Sanbō Bu, "Gunji gokuhi: Konji Kyōsan-gun no shūgeki ni kangami Kyōsan taisaku jō shōrai no kyōkun mata wa sankō to narubeki jikou" (Military top secret: recent damage caused by the CCP and its lesson for a future measurement against the CCP), reprinted in WIC, vol. 5, 557–63.

45. Kita-Shina Hōmen-gun Sanbō-bū, "Gunji gokuhi: Hoku-Shi hōmen Kyōsan seiryoku ni taisuru kansatsu" (The North China Area Army Chief of Staff, "Military top secret: observations of communist forces in North China") (October 1, 1940)," reprinted in WIC, vol. 5, 570–85.

and showed the Chinese people how the proletarian victory against capitalism would go hand in hand with China's victory against imperialism and its emancipation from oppressive semicolonial status. Like the earlier October report, this secret report argued that the CCP stirred people's patriotism, which further fueled their support for national unification under communism.

If Japan remained determined to achieve pan-Asianism in China after the model of modernization adopted in the Meiji Restoration, the report continued, how did Japan plan to prove that Japan, and not the CCP, could lead the Chinese people to this utopia of politics, economy, and culture? To demonstrate that Japan was a better agent of progress than the CCP, the report insisted, Japan should cease viewing China as merely an investment market and begin making the utmost effort to win the trust and respect of the Chinese people. Only this way could Japan possibly compete with the CCP.[46]

By this time the Japanese military recognized communism as an agent for change in China and had even come to terms with the prospect of eventual CCP victory in the civil war. In the postwar years, only the Marxist scholars at the SMR Research Department received accolades for reaching the same conclusions in the aforementioned 1938 study, "A Research Report on China's Capacity to Fight a War of Resistance" (*Shina kōsen-ryoku chōsa hōkoku*). Yet the Japanese military had recognized the full potential of the CCP before the SMR Research Department. Moreover the Japanese military unintentionally developed sympathy for the enemy's agenda of socioeconomic improvement. The North China Area Army even introduced in April 1940 plans for the so-called "Gassakusha" operation, a cooperative that encouraged mutual economic help among village members.[47]

In November 1941 members of the SMR Research Department were arrested in the Gassakusha Incident for their endorsement of the North China Area Army's plan. Their arrest was a dramatic reversal of fortune. Just a year before in the summer of 1940 the Imperial General Headquarters in Tokyo had invited several researchers from the SMR Research Department, including Nakanishi Tsutomu, to lecture on the current situation in China to around a hundred top-ranking military officials.[48] The Imperial General Headquarters and the Marxist-oriented SMR Research Department had collaborated behind the scenes and exchanged research on the CCP. Even after the crackdown on communists within the SMR Research Department, the Imperial General Headquarters did not abandon its

46. Tōshūdan Sanbō-bu, "Hi: Chūgoku Kyōsan-tō oyobi Kyōsan-gun no gaikyō" (Secret: survey of CCP and CCP forces) (December 1940), reprinted in WIC, vol. 8, 307–21.

47. Tada Butai Honbu, "Gokuhi: Kahoku ni okeru shisō-sen shidō yōkō" (The Tada Unit Headquarters, "Top secret: instructions on the war of ideology in North China") (April 20, 1940), reprinted in WIC, vol. 5, 225–26.

48. Shina Kōsen-ryoku Chōsa Iinkai, *Shina kōsen-ryoku chōsa hōkoku*, 579.

attempts to learn about and from the CCP. The Japanese military was aware that Japan's war had inadvertently energized the CCP and mobilized the masses, both politically and economically, toward modernization. Would the Soviet Union, the presumed mentor of the CCP, instruct the CCP in the war against Japan, and if so, how much assistance would it give the latter? For these questions, the role of the Soviet Union occupied an increasingly critical position in Japan's planning for the war in China.

Moscow-Yan'an Dissonance

Shortly before his arrest in November 1941, Ozaki Hotsumi called the Soviet Union a sympathizer with nationalist movements worldwide and characterized Moscow's China policy as one that encouraged China's nationalist independence and socialist revolution.[49] The North China Area Army had adopted Ozaki's view and assumed Soviet presence behind CCP operations. The Japanese government and the Imperial General Headquarters also had adhered to view of a communist monolith, with the CCP subordinate to the political machinery of the Soviet Union. They overcame that misleading stereotype rather quickly when they studied the CCP. On the eve of signing the Soviet-Japanese Neutrality Pact in April 1941, the Japanese government and the Imperial Army concluded that Yan'an and Moscow were not as intimate as previously thought.

The Japanese analysis of CCP-Soviet relations began as soon as the CCP was born in 1921. The Japanese authorities had no solid evidence that the Soviet Union was behind the Chinese-Japanese communist collaboration, or orchestrated their anti-Japanese, anti-imperialism campaigns in China. The arrest of Sano Manabu in Shanghai in 1929 and his subsequent renunciation of the Comintern in 1933 provided clarification. One of the founders of the Japanese Communist Party and also a member of its Central Committee, Sano had fled to the Soviet Union in 1923 and then relocated to Shanghai. When he returned to Japan in 1925 to rebuild the party, he was arrested and imprisoned. After his release from prison, Sano fled to Shanghai, was arrested, and brought back to Japan, where he finally renounced communism while in prison, much to the shock of the Marxist community in Japan. Known as a strong opponent of Fukumoto Kazuo, who stressed the importance of theory ("correct" Marxism) over practical means

---

49. Ozaki Hotsumi, "Taisei o saigo made tatakai nuku tame ni" (How to fight for the current system till the end), *Kaizō*, November 1941, as discussed and quoted in Asada Kyōji, *Nihon chishikijin no shokuminchi ninshiki* (Japanese intellectuals and their views of colonialism), 129.

and experience, Sano wrote a prison account in 1929 on his observations of communist movements in China.

Sano's account portrayed the CCP as distinct from the Soviet Communist Party. Sano explained that the current top priority of the CCP was not the pursuit of revolution per se, but intraparty coordination, which suggested the party's growing pains in matters of bureaucracy and command. Although Sano acknowledged the CCP's considerable achievements in agrarian land reform, warfare, and mass mobilization, he did not portray Mao Zedong as infallible. On the contrary Sano declared that Mao Zedong erred from time to time in his political judgments because his provincial background detached him from actual interactions with the world ("Inaka ni iru tame seiji-teki iken no tokidoki tadashiku nai koto ga aru"). The relationship between the Comintern and the Profintern in East Asia was not the most amicable, because of Moscow's desire to maintain good diplomatic relations with Japan.[50] Sano added that while the CCP collaboration with the Japanese Communist Party was understood as indispensable because the collapse of Japanese imperialism meant a victory for both of them, no Comintern document had ever been written on the proper relationship between the two communist parties.[51] In his 1929 prison confession, Sano gave the Japanese government an early picture of strained relations between the CCP and the Soviet Union. He later would provide more crucial intelligence on Chinese communists to the Japanese government.

These observations were corroborated by Moscow's continuing support for the GMD, whose leader, Chiang Kai-shek, was never a friend of communism. The world knew that the Soviet Union supported Chiang Kai-shek, not Mao Zedong, as the legitimate successor to Sun Yet-sen's republican revolution of 1911. When the First Congress of Toilers of the Far East took place in Moscow in January 1922, delegates from China, India, Indonesia, Japan, Korea, Mongolia, and Siberia attended and adopted the resolution that a national democratic movement, not the proletarian movement, should be the first phase of the revolutionary movement for China. In this phase the CCP was encouraged to assist the GMD in the fight against feudalistic warlords. Only after the democratic revolution became successful under GMD leadership would the proletariat launch

50. Profintern, or the Red International of Labor Unions, was an international body established in 1921 with the aim of coordinating Communist activities within trade unions across the world. Its headquarters was in Moscow.

51. "Rōya ni okeru Sano Manabu no shuki (August 22, 1929): zai Shanhai Nihon Sōryōji-kan" (Writings of Sano Manabu while in prison (August 22, 1922): The Japanese Consulate General in Shanghai), in *Nihon Kyōsan-tō kankei zakken—Sano Manabu taiho kankei* (Miscellaneous data on the Japanese Communist Party: arrest of Sano Manabu) [I-4-5-2-3-13], DRO.

the struggle of the second phase, in which they allied with the poor peasants against the bourgeoisie.[52]

The Japanese media provided a public venue for discussing China's international politics with regard to the Soviet Union and helped to clarify the political triangle formed by the Soviet Union, the GMD, and the CCP. In the early stages of the war in China, pundits insisted that the CCP was a pawn of the Soviet Union. On October 28, 1938, two months after the conclusion of the Changkufeng Incident, the *Hōchi* newspaper printed an editorial with the headline "The Soviet Union had better give up hostility [to Japan] in the Sino-Japanese War." The editorial voiced suspicions that the Soviet Union was enthusiastically aiding the CCP Army and was trying to turn the northwestern region (Seihoku chiku) into communist districts. If the Soviet Union continued such interference, the editorial argued, it would impede much of Soviet-Japanese border settlement and harm diplomatic relations with Tokyo. The *Chūgai* newspaper published an editorial on February 10, 1940, five months after the Nomonhan Incident was over, claiming that the Soviet Union continued to supply a substantial volume of weapons to the CCP as evidenced by the CCP's growing competence in the war against Japan. Even though the editorial vented frustration that Japan could not possibly manipulate the Soviet Union in the context of the Sino-Japanese War, it suggested that the Soviet Union would be more trustworthy if it stopped aid to the CCP for the sake of better diplomacy with Japan.[53] Other leading journals printed similar articles identifying Soviet aid to the CCP as the greatest obstacle in achieving peace in China.[54]

Kaizō openly questioned the nature of Mao's relationship with Stalin and vigorously debunked the myth of the communist monolith. In the Snow interview of Mao in the June 1937 issue, the journal featured Mao's lively denial that the CCP would allow China to become a Soviet colony. Mao argued that as long as communist ideology was useful for Chinese nationalism in the anti-Japanese

---

52. Spence, *Search for Modern China*, 324–25.

53. These editorials are reprinted in "Tai-So mondai ni kansuru wagakuni sho-shinbun shi no ronchō" (How the major Japanese newspapers editorialize the recent Soviet problem), in Naikaku Jōhō-bu, *Bōkyō jōhō* (Japanese Cabinet Information Bureau, *Anticommunism information*), vol. 2 (March 15, 1940), 2–3, 13.

54. Baba Hideo, "Soren no sekai seisaku" (Soviet global policy), *Nihon Hyōron* (ca. December 1939); Kinoshita Hanji, Sekai seiji ni okeru Soren no chii" (The place of the Soviet Union in world politics), *Bungei Shunjū* (ca. January 1940); Maruya Masao, "NiSso sekkin no kanō-sei to sono genkai" (The possibility and limit of Japanese-Soviet rapprochement), *Chūō Kōron* (ca. January 1940); all reprinted in "Tai-So mondai ni kansuru wagakuni sho-shinbun shi no ronchō" (How the major Japanese newspapers editorialize the recent Soviet problem), in Naikaku Jōhō-bu, *Bōkyō jōhō* (Japanese Cabinet Information Bureau, *Anticommunism information*), vol. 2 (March 15, 1940), 14–17.

struggle, the Chinese people would join with the Russian people in the fight against fascism. Mao explained to Snow his understanding that the nature of Soviet interest in China remained pragmatic and strategic. In the event that Japan invaded and occupied China, the Soviet Union would not stand aside, explained Mao, primarily because the Soviet Union would not tolerate the building of Japanese outposts in China for further invasions into Soviet territory. For that reason alone eventual Soviet involvement in the Sino-Japanese confrontation was plausible, argued Mao, implying that the Soviets would not come to aid the CCP purely for the goal of world communist revolution.[55] In this interview Mao seemed to have already established his distance from Moscow by stating that ideology alone would not automatically and unconditionally unite the CCP and Moscow.

The nature of, and reasons for, Moscow's possible interference in China remained an open question. In August 1937 *Kaizō* published an essay by Prime Minister Konoe, which calculated that Moscow would not quickly move to help China fight against Japan's advance into North China.[56] One review essay in the March 1938 issue even argued that the Soviet Union did not have a definite China policy: it proposed that as long as Stalin's regime coped with bankruptcy in domestic politics and economics, it simply did not have the capacity for foreign intervention. The author warned that once the Soviet Union increased its production levels, resolved ethnic minority problems, and became confident of its national power, it would become active in the Far East again.[57] People concerned about Moscow's strategic interest in China suspected that the Soviet Union might interfere in China regardless of its relation with the CCP. Given Moscow's keen observation of British policy in the Far East, they surmised that the Soviet Union had reason to collaborate even with Britain, the imperialist in China since the Opium War, so they together might check Japan's further advance into China.[58]

Japanese observers also reflected on the strength and durability of the bond between Moscow and the CCP. Some even wondered whether Moscow intentionally fueled GMD-CCP rivalry by supporting the GMD so as to exploit the civil war in order to promote its own interests in China. An article in the November 1937 issue of *Kaizō* bluntly pointed out that Stalin only shook hands with Chiang Kai-shek for strategic reasons: so long as Chiang checked Japan's conti-

---

55. Edgar Snow, "Chūgoku Kyōsan-tō no tai-Nichi seisaku" (CCP policy toward Japan), *Kaizō* 19, no. 6 (June 1937): 149–50 and 154.

56. Suzuki Mosaburō, "Hoku-Shi no ken'aku ka" (Deterioration of Northern China), *Kaizō* 19, no. 8 (August 1937): 104.

57. Takeo Ichi, "Soren minzoku seisaku no hatan to Tōhō-seisaku" (Bankruptcy of Soviet minority policy and far eastern policy), *Kaizō* 20, no. 3 (March 1938): 173–75.

58. Tanaka Kyūichi, "Hoku-Shi Jihen to kokusai kankei" (The Sino-Japanese War and international relations), *Kaizō* 19, no. 9 (September 1937): 85; Nakano Seigō, "Nihon wa Shina o dousuruka" (What Japan will do with China), *Kaizō* 19, no. 11 (October 1937): 98–100.

nental advance, he served Soviet interests.[59] *Kaizō* also published numerous articles in the fall of 1937 and beyond that argued the ill-conceived GMD-CCP united front favored only Mao's political success in the long run, in spite of Moscow's support for Chiang. The logic for this was simple. If the united front remained possible only if Chiang Kai-shek were to abandon anticommunism, then this conditional alliance would in effect amount to Chiang's capitulation to Mao and ultimately to the Soviet Union as well. The GMD-CCP front would thus negate any chance for Chiang's victory in an independent China. The Sino-Soviet Nonaggression Pact, signed in Nanjing on August 21, 1937, supported the existence of this very condition that many Japanese observers inferred had to exist. The treaty guaranteed Soviet munitions to the GMD in its fight against Japan's aggression, but it also firmly restrained Chiang's independent political activities for a minimum of five years. Without the option to conclude an anticommunist pact with Japan, Chiang had to let the war against Japan slide further into quagmire and allow communism to spread over his country. Several Japanese analysts argued that Chiang's alliance with Moscow was therefore inadvertently suicidal in driving him to a dead end, and that it eventually would deliver the advantage to Mao.[60]

Although Moscow's interests aligned better with those of Mao than of Chiang, Mao's alliance with Moscow did not necessarily mean China would be a communist state in the Soviet image. One contemporary Japanese analyst explained why. Since the early nineteenth century, China had been in a semicolonial state under the control of imperialist powers. The Chinese model of transforming the nation to communism would have to address this historical circumstance and therefore would differ from the Soviet formula. It could even be argued that even if Stalin were to continue to support Chiang, he might eventually find himself at a stalemate with Mao's triumph.[61]

Even after Japan and the Soviet Union reached rapprochement in the aftermath of the Nomonhan Incident of 1939, the Soviet Union increased interference in the regions of Xinjiang and Inner Mongolia where Japanese control was weak. Japanese monitors wondered whether the CCP would take this opportunity to facilitate its own expansion into the Shaanxi-Gansu-Ningxia region and eventually

---

59. Yoshioka Bunroku, "Shō Kaiseki wa seki-ka sezu" (Chiang Kai-shek will not become communist), *Kaizō* 19, no. 12 (November 1937): 240–44.

60. Shimojō Yūzō, "'Sobieto Shina' e no ugoki" (A movement toward Soviet China), *Kaizō* 19, no. 10 (October 1937): 59–70; Sugiyama Heisuke, "Gekika shi iku kokunai tairitsu" (Intensifying domestic rivalry), *Kaizō* 19, no. 12 (November 1937): 244; Hatano Kan'ichi, "Shō seiken to Kyōsan-gun no kongo" (A future of Chiang's regime and CCP Army), *Kaizō* 20, no. 7 (July 1938): 72–79.

61. Andō Hideo, "Shin-dankai ni tatsu Chūgoku Kyōsan-tō" (A new phase for the CCP), *Kaizō* 20, no. 9 (September 1938): 73–74.

Xinjiang as well.[62] Apparently unaffected by the ostensible Soviet-Japanese rapprochement, Mao Zedong did not take such actions. In another interview with Edgar Snow that appeared in *Kaizō*, Mao expressed his opinion that Moscow's new trade relationship with Japan did not mean its readiness to assist Japan's war of aggression in China. Asked about continuing US exports of war materials to Japan, Mao discounted that fact and said what mattered most was whether the United States would eventually take a decisive stance on the war of imperialism, in other words, in World War II. In this manner Mao reminded Snow that the Soviet Union had concluded the fateful nonaggression pact with Nazi Germany in August 1939. He added euphemistically that the pact at least allowed Stalin to "keep Hitler in his pocket."[63]

While the public engaged in such debates, the Japanese military and government also considered whether the CCP was a Soviet satellite and part of Moscow's plan for world revolution. In its 1938 report on the Eighth Route Army, the Japanese Cabinet Information Bureau in Tokyo defined the CCP as a Chinese branch of the Communist International. Its report of March 1939 speculated that Japan lagged behind the CCP in the ideological war because the Soviet Union gave the latter superb instruction behind the scenes. The report even claimed that the current war of ideology—Japanese pan-Asianism versus Chinese communism—was in fact one waged between Japan and the Soviet Union because Moscow had instructed the CCP to instill communism in the minds of Japanese soldiers. The Comintern was possibly using the war to set the stage for a communist revolution in Japan.[64]

The Imperial Army had suspected for some time that the military strategy of the CCP might be under Moscow's instruction. In the fall of 1938, the North China Area Army Headquarters determined that the CCP Army of northern Shaanxi Province had received direct instructions from the Soviet Union, which coordinated its military operations with another CCP Army in the northern part of Shanxi Province.[65]

---

62. Tanaka Kanae, "KoKkyō-kankei no shin-tenkai" (A new phase for the GMD-CCP Relationship), *Kaizō* 21, no. 13 (December 1939): 79–85; Yokota Minoru, "1940-nen no Shina" (China in 1940), *Kaizō* 21, no. 14, extra edition (December 1939): 53–55.

63. Edgar Snow, "Mō Takutō Sunou taidan" (Mao-Snow talk), *Kaizō* 22, no. 5 (March 1940): 174–77.

64. "Hoku-Shi Kyōsan-gun no senden senjutsu" (Propaganda strategy of CCP forces in North China) (March 1939), in Naikaku Jōhō-bu, *Bōkyō chōsa shiryō* (Japanese Cabinet Information Bureau, *Anticommunism research report*), vol. 1 (March 20, 1940), 169–83.

65. Kita-Shina Hōmen-gun Shirei-bu, "Gokuhi: Kita-Shina Hōmen-gun senkyo chiiki nai chian jōkyō" (The North China Area Army Headquarters, "Top secret: the security condition in the North China Area Army-Occupied areas") (November 25, 1938), reprinted in WIC, vol. 2, 171.

The North China Area Army Headquarters researched the CCP-Soviet propaganda campaign, and in April 1939 published a fifty-two-page top secret report. Almost six years later the Konoe Memorandum would come to draw the same conclusion. The report argued that the current Sino-Japanese war was a war of ideology between Japan and the Soviet Union and held the Soviet Union responsible for the growing war in China. The report predicted that the Soviet offensive against the Japanese Army in China would intensify along with the establishment of more Soviet districts across China. More important, the report also warned that the Soviet Union would attempt to plant revolution in the minds of Japanese settlers and soldiers in China as well as in Taiwanese and Korean subjects, would attempt to overthrow the Japanese empire, and would seek to incite communist revolutions all across East Asia. To foil such Soviet attempts, the report emphasized the importance of Japan's own ideological propaganda to refute communism.[66] At that moment the North China Area Army had not yet concluded that Chinese communism was a unique blend of nationalism and anti-imperialism.

The aforementioned top secret pamphlet on CCP propaganda issued in April 1940 also discussed Japan's war of ideology against the Soviet Union. The pamphlet recommended a close watch on Soviet citizens as well as the white (anti-Bolshevik) Russians living in China to prevent them from engaging in any subversive activities against Japan. The pamphlet also recommended a war of propaganda to expose the "evil plot" (*inbō zaiaku*) of the Soviet Union and the CCP. The secret report proposed that it would be effective to show the Chinese people how the annihilation of the CCP would prevent the eventual Soviet takeover of China as its satellite state and contribute to the preservation of China for the Chinese people.[67]

Such military claims soon lost credibility amid the growing realization among Japanese leaders that the CCP stood for Chinese nationalism first and foremost. By the time the Soviet-Japanese Neutrality Pact was concluded, the Japanese government and military had finally become convinced of Moscow-Yan'an tensions. In March 1940 the Japanese Cabinet Information Bureau in Tokyo issued a pamphlet concerning the Soviet Union and communist trends worldwide. This publication no longer treated the CCP as a pawn of the Soviet Union. Citing information obtained from the GMD (most likely through intelligence activities), the report brought to light the rising strains among factions within the CCP and

66. Kita-Shina Hōmen-gun Shirei-bu, "Gokuhi: Kyōsan-tō no waga gun ni taisuru shisō-teki gakai kōsaku no shinsō to kore ga bōatsu hōsaku" (April 5, 1939), reprinted in WIC, vol. 3, 329–32, 336.

67. Tada Butai Honbu, "Gokuhi: Kahoku ni okeru shisō-sen shidō yōkō fuzoku-sho" (Top secret: instructions on the war of ideology in North China: Appendix) (April 20, 1940), reprinted in WIC, vol. 5, 232–33, 237. See note 42 of this chapter.

explained that they arose in part due to Mao's bitter view of the Soviet Union. The report identified Mao Zedong as a central theorist of the "orthodoxy" faction, who had won the trust and confidence of party members through his energetic struggles for the party organization. Mao would continue to exercise military leadership and would steadily climb the party's bureaucratic ladder even though his political ascension had been challenged internally. The first challenger, the "Zhang Guotao faction" (or the "liquidation faction"), no longer posed a threat since it had dissolved some time ago after Zhang's risky proposal for a merger between the CCP and the GMD. The second challenger, the "Zhou Enlai faction" (or the "elder statesman faction"), consisted of people who had worked with Zhou at the Whampoa Military Academy or spent time with him in France. This faction's influence was already in decline. Some twenty members in the first tier of the party's hierarchy formed the most significant challenger, the "pro-Soviet" (or "international") faction of elite party members who had been trained in the Soviet Union. They had the confidence of the Comintern in Moscow and worked closely and willingly with members of the GMD along the line of basic Soviet directives. They were now training their sympathizers to become the party's executive members and dispatching some of them to the Red Army as political agents; they very likely would challenge Mao's status within the military as well. In theory backed by Moscow, this faction, with its intellectual rigor, would become a formidable force. The Japanese Cabinet Information Bureau predicted pro-Soviet dissidents within the CCP would further complicate Mao's relations with Stalin.[68]

Seven months later in October 1940, the top secret military report (*gunji gokuhi*) issued by the North China Area Army Headquarters urged reevaluation of the CCP as an independent agent, and not as a puppet created and "nurtured in the hands of the Soviet Union." The report quoted Stalin's "indiscreet" remarks allegedly made around July 1939 at a certain conference: "[Our plan is to] designate Outer Mongolia as a base, from which to advance revolutions into Manchuria and Korea, and also to designate Xinjiang as a revolutionary base for Central China." While admitting the insufficiency of evidence to verify the statement, including the time it was issued, the secret report stated that the North China Area Army Headquarters had growing doubts that the CCP always obeyed instructions from Moscow. The report raised many more questions about the nature of the CCP. Did the CCP coordinate with international communist forces in Outer Mongolia, Korea, and Manchuria? Had the CCP launched a military campaign of a different nature to expand its own sphere of influence so as to

---

68. "Chūgoku Kyōsan-tō no tō-nai bunpa to sono seiryoku" (Factions within the CCP and their power dynamics), (n.d.), reprinted in "Tai-So mondai ni kansuru wagakuni sho-shinbun shi no ronchō," in Naikaku Jōhō-bu, *Bōkyō jōhō* (Japanese Cabinet Information Bureau, *Anticommunism information*) vol. 2 (March 15, 1940), 95–96.

eventually gain total control of China? In that case the CCP might assist the Soviet Union in expanding into these regions. But if so, how exactly would the CCP cope with the fact that the Soviet Union continued to provide weapons mostly to the GMD Army (in the fight against the CCP) but very few to the CCP Army in the war against Japan? The secret report thus urged investigating the strategic reason for the lack of Soviet military assistance to the CCP.[69]

By the time the war with the United States broke out, Japanese military and civilian authorities were fairly confident of the mutual antipathy between Mao and Stalin. They were assured that Japan's rapprochement with the Soviet Union under the Neutrality Pact would not send the CCP any compromising messages, least of all an endorsement of a communist takeover of Japan and East Asia.

The timing coincided with a crackdown on CCP sympathizers within the Japanese governmental and semigovernmental institutes. In April 1941 seventeen bureaucrats within the Kikaku-in, the planning board responsible for comprehensive wartime policy, were arrested for communist sympathies. In November 1941 the Gassakusha Incident followed. Satō Daishirō and forty-four researchers close to him in the SMR Research Department were arrested between September 1942 and July 1943. Following the arrest of Ozaki Hotsumi in October 1941 for his role in the Sorge spy ring, Nakanishi Tsutomu, another leading China expert, was arrested in June 1942 for his role in gathering high-level intelligence and analysis from the China Expeditionary Army and passing them along to the CCP. After the editors-in-chief resigned in the wake of the Yokohama Incident of September 1942, *Kaizō* stopped publishing articles about the CCP and instead dealt almost exclusively with the GMD in its coverage of the Sino-Japanese War until the journal was closed down in July 1944. In December 1942 the Imperial General Headquarters distributed a memorandum to all Japanese troops in China that instructed them to keep an eye on all soldiers of all ranks within the Japanese military who seemed attracted to communism.[70]

Toward the Recognition of Yan'an

In parallel to the battle against the United States, the annihilation of the GMD regime, an official ally of Anglo-America, became Japan's top military priority in China. At the same time a call for a diplomatic settlement with Chiang Kai-shek

69. Kita-Shina Hōmen-gun Sanbō-bu, "Gunji gokuhi: Hoku-Shi hōmen Kyōsan seiryoku ni taisuru kansatsu" (Military top secret: observations of communist forces in North China) (October 1, 1940), reprinted in WIC, vol. 5, 571–73. See note 45 of this chapter.

70. "(Riku-Mitsu dai-3833-gō) Nihon Riku-gun no gunki oyobi fūki" (Military discipline and morals of the Imperial Japanese Army) (December 17, 1942)," reprinted in DCJ, vol. 1, 362–86.

also emerged within the Japanese government. In March 1940 the Japanese government had installed Wang Jingwei, a former leader of the GMD, as president of a pro-Japanese puppet regime in Nanjing, as an alternative to Chiang's regime relocated in Chongqing. In February 1942, at the "request" of Japanese ambassador Shigemitsu Mamoru, the Nanjing regime agreed to send emissaries to Chongqing for peace talks on Japan's behalf. While the Japanese government believed Chiang had no desire for peace with Japan, diplomatic manipulations by way of the Nanjing regime continued. The Imperial Conference (Gozen Kaigi) in December 1942 decided to abolish the unequal treaty system and move toward an equal partnership with the Nanjing regime. In January 1943 when the Nanjing regime declared war against the United States and Britain, the Japanese government announced its readiness to abolish extraterritoriality and to return Japanese concessions to China. These conciliatory policies were meant to catalyze a bigger peace: to incline the GMD regime toward compromise with the Nanjing puppet regime, pave the way toward peace between Japan and China, and ultimately achieve a settlement between Japan and Anglo-America.[71] In September 1943 the Japanese government commissioned the Nanjing regime to engage in "political [peace] operations" against the GMD. Subsequently political figures at the Nanjing regime set up numerous channels with individuals in and around the GMD regime. None was effective.

In April 1944 the Japanese military launched Operation Ichi-gō (Operation Number One, or Continental Cross-Through Operation), a major offensive against US air bases in Hunan Province, from where bombers launched raids on major Japanese cities. By December 1944 the Japanese offensive of 620,000 troops won a string of victories, successfully threatening the China-Burma-India theater and seriously damaging Chiang's resistance and credibility as a political and military leader. When the fall of Saipan in July 1944 effectively neutralized Japan's military offensive in China, the new Koiso cabinet (July 1944–April 1945) considered resuming the peace negotiations with the GMD regime, this time through a power broker named Miao Pin, a Japanese collaborator living in Shanghai with strong contacts in the GMD. The Miao Pin operation began in July 1944, and by February 1945 a Japanese liaison brought to the Japanese government Miao's proposal that a Chongqing-Tokyo rapprochement was possible on the following conditions: immediate liquidation of the Nanjing puppet regime; relocation of the GMD regime from Chongqing to Nanjing; and Japanese withdrawal from China. Only when these conditions were met would the GMD consider implementing peace initiatives for Japan and Anglo-America. Foreign Minister Shigemitsu, Army

71. Tobe Ryōichi, "Tai-Chū wahei kōsaku, 1942–45" (Japan's peace operation toward China, 1942–45), *Kokusai Seiji* (International relations) 109 (May 1995): 5–7.

Minister Sugiyama, Navy Minister Yonai, and Chief of Army Staff Umezu all opposed Miao's peace proposal, which they considered too risky. The Miao Pin operation was completely suspended in April 1945, just two days after the US invasion of Okinawa.[72] Japan's diplomatic interlude with the GMD thus ended futilely.

During the Miao Pin operation the Japanese government and the Imperial General Headquarters resumed the CCP watch that eventually led to diplomatic recognition of the CCP headquarters in Yan'an. The sensational suppression of domestic communists in the early years of the Pacific War did not mean that the Japanese government and the Imperial General Headquarters stopped paying attention to the CCP, particularly its estranged relations with the Soviet Union.[73] Under the auspices of the military and government, the SMR Research Department went on to publish translated works by Western scholars on the CCP as well as their own research.[74]

By May 1942 a top secret report reached Foreign Minister Tōgō Shigenori from Horiuchi Tateki, the Japanese consul general in Shanghai. The Japanese Consulate General in Shanghai had conducted a special investigation to determine what Mao Zedong had attempted to achieve in the ongoing rectification campaign (*seifū undō*), an intensive program to educate people in CCP-controlled regions about the necessity for socialist revolution. Besides indoctrinating people with the need to fight against both Japan and the GMD and taking control of a unified China, the special investigation discovered that the rectification campaign aimed to purge so-called Soviet-returnees (Soviet supporters) within the CCP. The secret report quoted Mao harshly criticizing elitist CCP members who denigrated local leaders for their unfamiliarity with Moscow doctrine, ridiculing them as *tubaozi*, a Chinese term for country bumpkins. The secret report identified Wang Ming as the most prominent Soviet returnee, who backed by the Comintern, had vied with Mao for the party leadership. The secret report explained that the Comintern had never liked Mao Zedong, preferring someone like Wang Ming who would execute the Comintern's orders with blind loyalty and commitment. After Mao successfully suppressed Wang's ambitions, the Soviet-returnees within the CCP came to realize they had no chance of strengthening their power base. The secret report from the Japanese Consulate General in Shanghai explained

72. Tobe Ryōichi, "Tai-Chū wahei kōsaku, 1942–45," 11–15. Also see Nomura Otojirō, "TōA Renmei to Senbu kōsaku" (The East Asian League and Miao Pin's peace move), part 1, *Seiji Keizai Shigaku* (Journal of historical studies: the politico-economic history) 310 (April 1992): 21–38.

73. Surviving archival documents on the CCP dramatically decrease in quantity for the period after Pearl Harbor. The CCP-related reports and analyses may have been destroyed for political considerations before the US military occupation began.

74. See Kusayanagi Daizō, *Jitsuroku Mantetsu Chōsa-bu* (The true history of the SMR Research Department), vol. 2 (Tokyo: Asahi Shinbun Sha, 1983), 360–61.

that the current rectification campaign showed Mao's determination to crush any remaining ambitions of the Soviet-returnees and to thus consolidate his dominance as party leader. When Mao eventually secured the independence of the CCP, the Soviet Union, rather than castigating Mao, might have to recognize him as a genius, concluded the report, apparently applauding Mao.[75]

Another top secret report, dispatched on August 27, 1942, from the Japanese consulate in Mudanjiang to the Foreign Ministry in Tokyo, further confirmed the strains between Moscow and the CCP. In the event of a war between the Soviet Union and Japan, communication would be cut off between Moscow and the communist forces in Manchuria. In that case the Comintern would likely request that the CCP establish auxiliary bases in the Greater Hinggan Mountains and allow Soviet forces to use the existing CCP bases. Even if such a scenario were to materialize, the Soviet forces might find it difficult to obtain assistance from those Chinese communists who had left the Soviet Union disillusioned with deteriorating living conditions and intraparty intrigues. The report did not find it plausible that the Comintern could effectively use these Chinese communists in southern Manchuria and northern China.[76] Indeed, nine months later, in May 1943, Stalin announced the dissolution of the Comintern for the sake of consolidating the Grand Alliance. What little remaining anxiety about the communist takeover of East Asia was now gone.

Calling the Comintern dissolution a great event, Mao welcomed the strengthening of the national communist party of each country. He reiterated his conviction that revolutionary movements could be neither exported nor imported. Despite the aid given by the Communist International, Mao declared the CCP owed its birth and development to the conscious working class of China. Put another way, he declared that the Chinese working class, not Moscow, created its own party.[77]

In 1944 while Operation Ichi-gō devastated wide areas under GMD control, the CCP successfully launched more intensive guerrilla warfare against the Japanese Army, including underground espionage activities. Japan's North China Area Army had to rediscover the same truth it had uncovered five years previously: that the CCP had achieved amazing success in mobilizing the ordinary people

---

75. "Gokuhi 1247-gō, 'Mō Takutō no Sanpū Shukusei e no kansatsu,' Zai Shanhai Nihon Sōryōjikan Tokubetsu Chōsa-han" (Top secret 1247th, 'Some observations of Mao Zedong's three rectifications campaign' by the Special Research Department of the Japanese Consulate, Shanghai), in "DaiTōA Sensō kankei ikken jōhō shūshū kankei Shanhai jōhō" (The Greater East Asia War: intelligence gatherings: information on Shanghai), vol. 2 [A-7-0-0-9-9-6], DRO.

76. "Gokuhi: Kominterun kankei" (Top secret: the Comintern file) (August 27, 1942) [A-7-0-0-9-9-8], DRO.

77. "The Comintern has long ceased to meddle in our internal affairs" (May 26, 1943), in "Selected Works of Mao Tse-tung," available online at http://www.marxists.org/reference/archive/mao/selected-works/volume-6/mswv6_36.htm.

(*minshū*), both politically and militarily, while at the same time increasing agricultural productivity, perfecting the rectification campaign, and educating the populace with propaganda.[78] Even Japan's General Staff on Intelligence (Jōhō Sanbō) in Tokyo admitted that Chinese peasant guerrillas were waging war far beyond what the conventional wisdom of the Japanese Army had thought possible. They now agreed that the better strategy would be to abandon the goal of "annihilation [*gekimetsu*] of the enemy" and to take seriously the previously proposed goal of "understanding the minds of the people" (*min-shin no haaku*). The General Staff announced that crushing the CCP Army alone could not possibly be the answer. Passive as it seemed, the best way to deal with the CCP would be to understand the party's political and economic base and to determine why the Chinese people supported the party rather than to deploy the Japanese Army and trumpet pan-Asianism.[79]

Soon the Japanese official recognition of the CCP's superior position in the Chinese civil war took form. Kondō Yasuo was appointed a senior researcher at the TōA Kenkyūjo in April 1944, only eight months after he was dismissed from his position at the Tokyo Imperial University. His dismissal had come as the result of his 1939 work, "Tenkan-ki no nōgyō" (Agriculture in the transitional period), in which he criticized Japan's failure to remedy the fundamental problem of private land ownership with an agricultural plan similar to the CCP program.[80]

By then, both the North China Area Army and the Army War Operations Plans Division of the Imperial General Headquarters had concluded that the CCP was really a political entity independent of the GMD regime and that they should support the CCP. In early June, upon the success in Operation Ichi-gō—in which the Japanese secured the railway between Beijing and Wuhan, eliminated the US air forces based in Hunan Province, and reached near part of Indochina under Japanese control—the Imperial General Headquarters made a major political shift to adopt a measure that would further debilitate the GMD. Vice Chief General Staff Lieutenant-General Hata Hikosaburō ordered Colonel Tanemura Sakō and Lieutenant Colonel Tanaka Keiji, both members of the Army War Operations Plans Division, to draft a plan to improve relations with the CCP primarily as a jolt to the GMD. The complete draft plan "Konkai no Shina sakusen ni tomonau senden yōryō narabi ni teikoku seifu seimei-an" (The outline of propaganda plan accompanying the China operation and subsequent governmental announcement) received preliminary approval from Chief of the Imperial Japanese Army General Staff Tōjō Hideki, and then went to the Imperial General

78. WHS-PPW, 494–95.
79. WHS-PPW, 510–11.
80. Hara Kakuten, *Gendai Ajia kenkyū seiritsu-shi ron*, 122–23.

Headquarters and Government Liaison Conference (Daihon'ei Seifu Renraku Kaigi), the precursor of the Supreme Council for the Direction of the War. Though several staff officers of both the army and navy criticized it for deviating from the traditional China policy, Foreign Minister Shigemitsu endorsed it and the Imperial General Headquarters and Government Liaison Conference adopted it as a formal policy on July 3, 1944, demonstrating unity within the Japanese government regarding the CCP policy.[81] From then on Japan would recognize the CCP Yan'an regime (En'an seiken). The policy also recommended avoiding derogatory labels for communism, including "Chū-Kyō," a perfunctory abbreviation of the Japanese name for the CCP, Chūgoku Kyōsan-tō.[82]

Field Marshal Hata Shunroku, commander of the Second General Army, was among those leaders who were baffled by this new Yan'an policy. On July 8 he wrote in his journal that he understood the new Yan'an policy aimed in part to win the hearts of the Chinese people and to encourage their collaboration with Japan toward Greater East Asia. He surmised that the new Yan'an policy was the government's poor attempt to flatter the Soviet Union (*Soren ni taisuru gokigen tori seisaku*). The Imperial General Headquarters and Government Liaison Conference had explained that the new China policy sought to prevent the formation of an anti-Japanese coalition among the GMD, CCP, Britain, United States, and the Soviet Union. Hata was one of those who, at that stage in the war, still took Moscow-Yan'an solidarity for granted. On August 21 Hata wrote in his journal that the worsening situation in the war in China compelled Tokyo to try anything to appease the Soviet Union, and that included the new friendly policy toward the CCP.[83] Others within the army considered the Yan'an policy to be a pro-Soviet gesture and part of a larger peace operation aimed at the United States via Moscow. Lieutenant Colonel Tanaka Keiji wrote in his memoir that he understood this new Yan'an policy as more than a gesture to win the favor of Mao Zedong. Once Japan had Mao on its side, he fumed, it would ask Mao to request Soviet Foreign Minister Vyacheslav Molotov to mediate peace between Japan and the United States.[84]

Events before and after the Yan'an recognition suggest other motivations. In the effort to develop a sound policy for dealing with the CCP, the Imperial General

---

81. Akashi Yōji, "Taiheiyō Sensō makki ni okeru Nihon gunbu no En'an seiken to no wahei mosaku—sono haikei" (In search of peace, the Yan'an alternative and the Imperial Japanese Army), *Gunji Shigaku* (Journal of military history) 31, nos. 1 and 2 (September 1995): 176–77.

82. "Tai-Shi sakusen ni tomonau senden yōryō" (Propaganda in the North China Operation) (July 3, 1944), in RJD, 28–29.

83. Itō Takashi and Terunuma Yasutaka, eds., *Zoku gendai-shi shiryō (4) Riku-gun: Hata Shunroku nisshi* (Records of modern history: second series, vol. 4, "The army: the diary of Hata Shunroku") (Tokyo: Misuzu Shobō, 1983), 477 and 482.

84. WHS-PPW, 525. Also see Akashi Yōji, 'Taiheiyō Sensō makki ni okeru Nihon gunbu no En'an seiken to no wahei mosaku—sono haikei," 177–78.

Headquarters dispatched Sano Manabu on his release from prison to Shanghai to investigate the nature of CCP. In mid-March 1944 Sano was back in Japan lecturing to members of the Army War Operations Plans Division at the Imperial General Headquarters about the current state of the CCP, including its increasing contacts with the United States. This information reached the foreign minister quickly.[85] In February 1944 the army allegedly had dispatched Nabeyama Sadachika, another former communist-turned-war collaborator to Beijing to observe CCP activities. When he returned to Tokyo in April he briefed the army that the CCP was a clean and independent regime. Although Nabeyama explained that the CCP was still under Moscow's influence, he also added that the CCP, with its ideological fallacies, was not authentically communist.[86]

On August 10, 1944, in a follow-up to the July 3 announcement by the Government Liaison Conference, the Imperial General Headquarters, in consultation with the North China Area Army Headquarters, announced that henceforth the Japanese Army would treat the CCP as the Yan'an regime, a regional government independent of the GMD. They declared that they would drop slogans such as "anticommunism" (*han-Kyō*) and "destruction of communism" (*metsu-Kyō*). The announcement explained that this new policy would appease the CCP, intensify CCP-GMD rivalry, and drive a wedge between the CCP and the anti-Japanese coalition of the United States, Great Britain, and the Soviet Union.

The new Yan'an policy seemed to have another hidden purpose unspecified by these generic explanations. In a comment attached to the announcement, the Imperial General Headquarters stated that the Yan'an regime was politically a de facto independent regime and ideologically "molting" out of communism and transforming into nationalism.[87] This clarified the Imperial General Headquarters' understanding that the CCP's revolutionary goal was to achieve nationalism, not communism, and as such its goals were not in line with Moscow's own. Unlike the GMD who, for the sake of China's rapid industrialization, condoned the continuous presence of the Western powers in China under unequal treaties, the more nationalistic CCP would be less tolerant. With the Yan'an recognition policy, the

---

85. TSWJ, vol. 2, 505–6. See the entries for March 17 and 18, 1944.

86. In his postwar memoir, Nabeyama vehemently denied the "allegation" of his collaboration with the army. He wrote that he learned only after Japan's defeat of the army's intention of using him for the CCP operation. Nabeyama also declared that the army had tried to dispatch to China Shimonaka Yasaburō of Heibon Sha and Yamamoto Mitsuhiko of Kaizō Sha along with himself. He added that the army should have known that he would not work on its behalf. Nabeyama insisted that the army did not entrust him with any such mission. Nabeyama then complained that rival members of the Japanese Communist Party deliberately spread rumors that he wanted to collaborate with the army to the intelligence section (Chōhō-bu) of the Imperial General Headquarters. See Nabeyama Sadachika, *Tenkō 15-nen* (Tokyo: Rōdō Shuppan Sha, 1949), 151–52.

87. WHS-PPW, 523–25.

Imperial General Headquarters effectively recognized the power of the CCP to keep China for Chinese, and also to keep Asia for Asians.

The synergy of Japan's Soviet-China policies materialized in the Foreign Ministry's draft proposal on special diplomatic negotiations with the Soviet Union that emerged in the wake of recognizing Yan'an. Foreign Minister Shigemitsu submitted to the Supreme Council for the Direction of the War on September 4, 1944, a list of issues Japan might discuss with the Soviet Union as well as some suggestions for how to solve them. Three days later an unspecified chief of an unspecified section within the Foreign Ministry submitted to the Supreme Council for the Direction of the War a table of possible concessions to the Soviet Union should it act favorably to Japan.[88] In all six hypothetical circumstances, the Foreign Ministry proposed that Japan should recognize the spread of Soviet influence in areas of East Asia currently under Japan's purview, including China. As stronger enticement, the Foreign Ministry even suggested Japan would support the Yan'an regime should the Soviet Union either agree to strengthen neutrality with Japan or mediate peace between Japan and the GMD. By that time the Foreign Ministry was aware of growing Moscow-Yan'an tension even as it became anxious that the Soviet Union would eventually attack Japan. Tokyo's recognition of the Yan'an regime as an ostensible gesture of goodwill to Moscow probably led the latter to worry and to wonder how much Tokyo knew of the Moscow-Yan'an relationship. When Ambassador Satō Naotake met with Foreign Minister Molotov in September 1944, Molotov, apparently uneasy about the topic of China, told Satō that the Soviet Union would continue its policy of noninterference in China and would maintain its relationship with the GMD.[89]

Hata Shunroku, who originally saw the new Yan'an policy as a poor ploy to gain Soviet favor in wartime diplomacy, learned in due course about the complexity of international politics surrounding the CCP. On November 3, 1944, Hata wrote in his journal his new understanding of the inevitable future clash between the United States and the Soviet Union. He recorded his judgment that the nature of Soviet aid to China was purely material and not at all ideological.[90] On November 7, 1944, one day after the one-year anniversary of the Greater East Asia Joint Declaration, Foreign Minister Shigemitsu Mamoru telegraphed Ambassador Satō in Moscow, informing him of Japan's recognition of the CCP as the Yan'an regime. Only the day before, the Japanese government had learned that

88. "Tai-So shisaku ni kansuru ken (an)" (Concerning the Soviet policy [draft]) (September 7, 1944), in RJD, 172–74. See Table 5.1.

89. "Satō Morotofu Kaidan no ken" (On the Sato-Molotov conference) in RJD, 190.

90. Itō Takashi and Terunuma Yasutaka, eds., *Zoku gendai-shi shiryō (4) Riku-gun: Hata Shunroku nisshi* (Records of modern history: second series, vol. 4, "The army: the diary of Hata Shunroku" (Tokyo: Misuzu Shobō, 1983), 495.

Stalin had called Japan an aggressor in his anniversary speech commemorating the Bolshevik Revolution. Thus Japan's recognition of Yan'an was likely intended to convey to the Soviets that Japan would support a viable and unified China independent of Soviet influence.

Indeed, in the same November 7 telegram, Shigemitsu instructed Ambassador Satō to tell the Soviet government that Japan's pan-Asianism fully "supported" the Soviet principle of liberating the oppressed peoples of greater East Asia. If the Soviet Union honored its principles of liberation and independence for all oppressed people, then it could not possibly meddle in China or anywhere else in Asia so long as the CCP was the vanguard of independence and nationalism for China. Shigemitsu's simultaneous endorsement of the CCP as an independent regime and of the Soviet principle of nationalistic independence, therefore, could not be interpreted as procommunist. The two messages, one to Yan'an and the other to Moscow, seemed intended to induce a balance of power in the region even the face of Japan's probable defeat.[91] The Japanese government now believed the CCP regime could eventually keep not only the Soviet Union but also the United States at arm's length while carrying on the mission of Asian-style reinvigoration and progress.[92] The neutrality pact with the Soviet Union would keep Anglo-America out of Asia. The attempted rapprochement with the CCP would in turn check the Soviet's ambition in China and create a desirable balance of power in East Asia. In this manner, the Sino-Japanese War integrated into the Pacific War, together constituting the larger Eurasian-Pacific War.[93]

---

91. Hatano Sumio, "Shigemitsu Mamoru to DaiTōA Kyōdō Sengen" *Kokusai Seiji* (International relations) 109 (May 1995): 48–49.

92. WHS-PPW, 551–57.

93. For the interrelationship between the China and Pacific theaters, see Tohmatsu Haruo, "The Strategic Correlation between the Sino-Japanese and Pacific Wars," in Mark Peattie, Edward Drea, and Hans van de Ven, eds., *The Battle for China: Essays on the Military History of the Sino-Japanese War of 1937–1945* (Stanford, CA: Stanford University Press, 2011), 423–45.

4

INTERNATIONAL RIVALRY OVER DIVIDED KOREA

Who to Replace Japan?

In reflecting on the US-Soviet rivalry in the Eurasian-Pacific War, Japanese planners attended to the interactions of the two powers with Japan's colonies and their peoples—above all Korea. No battle, in the end, took place in Korea, yet the postwar status of the peninsular country was a central strategic focus for planners in thinking though Japan's postwar survival as some sort of power. The study of Japan's World War II rarely considers the Korean Peninsula, a strategic gateway to the Eurasian continent as well as a passageway to the Pacific Ocean. Japanese colonialism has never successfully been integrated in the Pacific War narrative even though the Cairo Declaration of 1943 explicitly mentioned the Allies' resolve to defeat Japan and dismantle its colonial empire. After all, few military battles fought in the South Pacific led to direct American "liberation" of Japanese colonies, except for some small islands of the South Sea Mandates such as Saipan and Tinian. Never a battleground, Korea nonetheless occupied a highly strategic place in a confluence of the Sino-Japanese War and the Pacific War. That is, the significance of Korea emerges prominently only by looking at the full canvas of the Eurasian-Pacific War.

In the early twentieth century, Japan first transformed the Korean Peninsula into its granary and then built heavy industries in the north and linked them to the Manchurian project. Japan made Korea a supply base for Japan's military operations on the continent. Once the Sino-Japanese War began in 1937, the governor-general of Korea forced on Koreans the spirit of "a true merger of Japan and Korea into oneness" (*Nai-Sen ittai*). Korea, the thinking went, would become an inseparable part of Japan and Koreans would come to believe that Korea's fate rested with Japan. Once the Pacific War began, the Soviet-Japanese Neutrality Pact meant Japan did not have to worry about attacks on Korea from the north. As Japan's defeat loomed in the Pacific War, however, the Japanese military integrated Korea into the defense perimeter for the presumed final battle against the United States. In requesting that Japan be allowed to keep the colony if it surrendered to the United States, Japanese "peace feelers" demonstrated Japan's diplomatic determination to hold onto Korea.

Confidential research and analyses conducted by the Governor-General's Office of Korea and Japan's Chōsen Army had recognized since the early 1930s that forced assimilation programs and conscription belied the rhetoric of the true spiritual merger of Japan and Korea. Historian Miyata Setsuko has argued that the realistic appraisals made by the leaders in spite of their conspicuous arrogance and overconfidence demonstrated their understanding that their empire was not destined to last.[1] The ever-deteriorating war situation in both China and the Pacific amplified this pessimistic view. Nonetheless, Japanese leaders did not see an independent Korea arising from disparate Korean nationalists movements given the inability of these nationalists to form a united front. Instead, the Japanese believed that foreign powers might attempt to capitalize on the situation and enhance their influence in the region. The preponderance of communists among Korean nationalists led wartime Japanese leaders to give special consideration of foreign governments that might seek the custodianship of postwar Korea. They carefully followed the intricate relationships Korean nationalists cultivated with not only Moscow but also the Guomindang (GMD), the Chinese Communist Party (CCP), and Washington.

The key to unveiling the place Korea occupied in Japan's Eurasian-Pacific War is to look at how the Japanese assessed the possible influences of the Soviet Union and China on the Korean Peninsula. Since the Soviet Union shared borders with Korea, Japanese policy makers kept an eye on its clandestine interference with the colonial administration. As in the case with China, they did not desire to see a Soviet presence growing in Korea. Nor did they want a stronger American presence in Korea in the event of Japan's defeat in the Pacific War.

In thinking about the future of Korea, Japan's policymakers zeroed in on the international competition for control over Korean nationalists and tried to determine how a new regional order might emerge after Japan's supremacy was gone. Only by returning Korea to the Korean people could Japan have fulfilled its colonial duty. Too little communication and interaction, however, exacerbated misunderstandings between Japanese colonialists and Korean nationalists.

1. SHKA, 3–4.

Early War Years: Assessing Communist Influences from Abroad

Around World War I, as Japan became one of the world's top five industrialized powers, Korea also experienced full-scale industrialization. With the success of companies such as the Chōsen Spinning and Weaving Company, the Chōsen Nitrogen Fertilizer Company, the Chōsen Oil Company, heavy industry developed steadily. By 1936 heavy industry comprised 28 percent of total industrial output, with more than half a million Koreans employed in that sector alone. Although Japanese colonists had earlier discouraged higher education for colonial subjects, they soon realized that rapid industrialization required a supply of skilled laborers. The colonial government launched a program in the mid-1930s to improve the quality of vocational and technical education. While most Korean engineers were middle school graduates, 15 to 30 percent of them had a diploma from professional schools, junior colleges, or Keijō Imperial University. On the eve of the Pacific War, engineers in Korea numbered about twenty thousand, over one-third of whom were Korean.[2] Hoping that acculturation might facilitate material success, Korean youths began accepting Japanese schooling.

In 1924 Keijō Imperial University, the sixth of Japan's imperial universities, opened in Seoul. Korean engineers and technicians emerged with college and university degrees and other skilled workers began achieving positions of responsibility within factories, leading Japanese business owners and administrators to become heavily dependent on them. Along the way blossomed a Korean bourgeoisie, which included, above all, the *chaebol*, the Korean equivalent to the Japanese *zaibatsu*, or conglomerate. Handicapped by structural discrimination, Koreans nonetheless began participating in industrial enterprises and joint ventures with Japanese colonialists. By the early 1940s Korean ownership was ubiquitous in many industries, ranging from beverages, pharmaceuticals, and rice mills, to wartime processors and manufacturers of metals, chemicals, and textiles.[3]

Beyond relying on Korea for its industrial output, Japan needed the Korean Peninsula for logistical reasons. The industrial development of Korea was directly linked to military procurement of foodstuffs and munitions for the war front in

---

2. Carter J. Eckert, "Total War, Industrialization, and Social Change in Late Colonial Korea," in Peter Duus, Ramon Meyers, and Mark Peattie, eds., *The Japanese Wartime Empire, 1931–1945* (Princeton, NJ: Princeton University Press, 1996), 20–21.

3. Bruce Cumings, *Korea's Place in the Sun: A Modern History* (New York: W.W. Norton, 1998), 169–71; Carter Eckert, "Total War, Industrialization, and Social Change in Late Colonial Korea," in Duus, Myers, and Peattie, eds., *The Japanese Wartime Empire*, 4–7 and 18–23; E. Patricia Tsurumi, "Colonial Education in Korea and Taiwan," in Ramon Myers and Mark Peattie, eds., *The Japanese Colonial Empire, 1895–1945* (Princeton, NJ: Princeton University Press, 1984), 294–95, 300, and 306.

China. Munitions factories in Pyongyang and Inchon were designed to provide necessary materials in case of war in Manchuria. Railroad expansion in Korea also corresponded to the development of Japan's military strategy in China. Each train route running through the peninsula served as a link between Japan and China.[4] The military nature of Japanese control of Korea was best embodied in the eight of eleven governors-general of Korea who were either army ministers or army generals. Fully armed police forces in Korea, some fifteen thousand in number, only a third of whom were Korean, had the defensive capability of one Japanese military division. The pillar of Japan's military control was the Chōsen Army (Chōsen-gun) whose commander-in-chief possessed power equal to that of the governor-general.

Against this background, "Nai-Sen ittai"—Japan's articulated goal of "a complete merger of Japan and Korea"—never took off. The Korean economic boom in the 1930s did not encourage Koreans to be assimilated voluntarily and transformed into imperial Japanese subjects. Industrialization and urbanization propelled Koreans to search more ardently for their own modern identity. In 1934 under the tenure of Governor-General Ugaki Kazushige (1931–36), it became mandatory for colonial schools to spend more hours on Japanese language, ethics, and history. Starting in 1935 a new policy enforced student and government employee attendance at Shinto ceremonies. Ugaki's successor, Minami Jirō (1936–42), attempted to intensify Korean assimilation. In 1939 Minami issued Ordinances 19 and 20, known as *Sōshi-kaimei*, or the "Name order," requiring Koreans to relinquish their clan names and adopt Japanese family and given names. By 1944 approximately 84 percent of the population had registered Japanese family names.

The Japanese rulers were aware of the level of resistance among the Korean people and the improbability of transforming them into loyal imperial subjects. As early as December 1933, less than two years after the creation of Manchukuo, the Imperial General Headquarters in Tokyo ordered the General Staff of the Chōsen Army (Chōsen-gun Sanbō-bu) to prepare and submit semiannual secret reports on trends in Korean opinion. After the creation of Manchukuo, cases of Korean resistance temporarily dropped. The Japanese officials surmised that the Koreans were choosing to collaborate with Japan so as to benefit from the Manchurian boom. By 1936 the Chōsen Army estimated that roughly 23 percent of the Korean population were Japanese nationalists—officials and bureaucrats, intellectuals and students, the so-called Korean collaborators who supported Japan's pan-Asianism. Yet 58 percent of Koreans, mostly peasants and laborers, remained susceptible to anti-Japanese indoctrination and propaganda because,

4. SHKA, "Introduction," 4–5.

according to the Chōsen Army's interpretation, they did not possess the ability to make rational judgments. The remaining 19 percent, mostly educated, were problematic because in public they acted as if they were willing to share the spirit of Japanese nationalism, but privately they were strong Korean nationalists. They disdained Japan's policy in China and Manchuria, calling it an act of aggression (*shinryaku kōi*). They hid such hostility toward Japan only because they knew their time had not come. These fake collaborators were a potential time bomb. Worse, the Chōsen Army cautioned, their numbers were on the rise.[5]

The Chōsen Army also noticed that class-conscious labor movements were growing all over Korea. Amid the boom in military industry, Korean workers demanded higher wages and improved work conditions, and even attempted to mobilize their colleagues. Peasants, comprising 80 percent of the population in Korea, could partake in what the Chōsen Army called "pandemonium" if tenant disputes were not properly resolved. The Chōsen Army also identified as a danger leftist inclinations among students, youths, and Christians. In the first half of 1936, the Chōsen Army obtained information about a meeting of Korean work-students (*kugakusei*) who demanded the abolition of discrimination against Koreans and the reform of militarist and capitalist society.[6]

In studying these seditious thinkers, the Chōsen Army did not regard the Korean leftists in general, or the communists in particular, as posing a direct threat to the Japanese rule. The real trouble lay with various foreign powers, from which these Korean leftists received inspiration as well as instruction. The Chōsen Army's top secret report of April 1934 explained why external forces such as the Soviet Union and the CCP could shape the course of seditious activities in Korea. The report mocked Korea's historical subjugation to the Chinese, Mongol, and then Japanese races (*minzoku*) and disdainfully theorized that Koreans as a people were passive and opportunist. Koreans always waited for a favorable wind of change in international relations while doing nothing for themselves; and just now, the report continued, some Koreans secretly might be dreaming that Britain or the United States would defeat Japan and "award" independence to Korea as a windfall.[7]

This imperious view of Korean dependency developed out of not only Korea's history as a tributary nation of China, but also the manner of Korea's struggle against Japan's colonization. When Meiji Japan's "modern" ambition for Korea directly challenged China's suzerainty over Korea in the late nineteenth century,

5. Chōsen-gun Sanbō-bu (Headquarters of the Chōsen Army), "Hi: Shōwa 11-nen zen'han-ki Chōsen shisō undō gaikan" (Secret: survey of the trends of thought in Korea in the early half of 1936) (August 1936), in SKTM, 30–31.

6. "Shōwa 11-nen zen'han-ki Chōsen shisō undō gaikan" (Secret: survey of the trends of thought in Korea in the early half of 1936), in SKTM, 19–22.

7. SKTM, "Introduction," 2–3 and 6–7.

Korean politicians and intellectuals divided into pro-Japanese and pro-Chinese factions in search of a better alliance for Korea's survival. After Japan won the Sino-Japanese War of 1894–95, the Korean king turned to Russia for help and took refuge at the Russian legation in Seoul, where he remained until 1897. When Japan defeated Russia in the Russo-Japanese War of 1904–5 and made Korea a protectorate, the Japanese government secured US recognition of Japan's position in Korea. Although the Koreans tried to appeal to the Second Hague Peace Conference of 1907, it was too late to solicit supporters from the international body of justice. The Korean delegates were even denied the right to participate in the proceedings. Modern Korea's quest for a dependable ally consistently failed because the intrigues of world politics never operated on behalf of Korea.

In spite of the intensity and tenacity of Korean nationalist movements, the Japanese colonists had a low estimation of its cumulative power because it lacked a unifying organization. From early on Korean nationalists had to escape Japanese crackdowns and attempt—as in Russia, Manchuria, China, and even the United States—to keep the movement alive while searching for foreign allies and sponsors. After the brutal suppression of the March 1 Movement of 1919, activists fled the country and created provisional Korean governments in different parts of the world: the first in Vladivostok in late March, the second in the French concession in Shanghai on early April, and the third in Seoul on April 21. In September 1919 these governments merged into the Provisional Government of the Republic of Korea. Its first cabinet meeting convened in Shanghai on November 4. The Chinese GMD, their mentor and sponsor, did not recognize the Korean Provisional Government in Shanghai, but it instructed Korean leaders first to follow Sun Yat-sen's Three Principles of the People: nationalism, democracy, and welfare. Unable to establish a congruity between Sun Yat-sen's teaching and Korea's struggle against Japan, the Korean Provisional Government in Shanghai became moribund. Its first president, Syngman Rhee, who had earlier experimented with forming the Korean National Association in 1909 in Hawaii, moved back to the United States and engaged in diplomatic efforts with Washington by establishing himself as the head of a Korean exile government.

Korean nationalist movements that developed under communist auspices suffered a similar fate. Disillusioned with Wilsonian liberalism that condoned "cooperative imperialism" in East Asia, as exhibited at the Paris Peace Conference of 1919, Korean activists looked instead to the Soviet Union as the champion of the anticolonial and anti-imperialist crusade. Those who found the Korean Provisional Government in Shanghai insufficiently radical joined the communist forces. Like their noncommunist comrades, they never successfully unified. Various factions vied for formal recognition from Moscow. Two separate groups, organized and based respectively in Irkutsk and Shanghai, even had an armed confrontation in Siberia in 1921. The Comintern subsequently directed the Korean communists to establish a united front in their home country, and thus the Korean Communist Party formed in 1925. The Comintern, however, in 1928 criticized the Korean Communist Party for failing to distinguish between a proletarian revolution from below and a mere nationalist movement for social reform.[8] Korean communists/nationalists henceforth had to achieve an impossible combination of duties: overcome factionalism, expand their activities at a grassroots level, collaborate with moderate and centralist nationalists, and above all conform to Comintern directives. The fight against Japanese colonialism was not to be their immediate goal.

Nonetheless, Korean communists inside and outside Korea became increasingly active against the Japanese. In the summer of 1936, a group of Korean soldiers employed by the Manchukuo Army fled to the Soviet Union in protest of discriminatory treatment by Japanese officers. The Chōsen Army detected the presence of growing agitation within Korean intellectual circles and noted in particular the rising popularity of Marxist criticisms of Japanese affairs. The Chōsen Army discovered that Koreans regarded the February 26 Incident of 1936 in Japan as a sign of the decline of Japanese capitalism and a harbinger of a communist revolt within the Japanese military.[9] Toward the outbreak of the Sino-Japanese War in 1937, the Chōsen Army began monitoring communist influence in all kinds of movements as an integral part of its systematic study of Korean trends of thought.[10] The Chōsen Army published its findings in semiannual secret reports, each handwritten and mimeographed, fifty to a hundred pages in length, and regularly submitted them to the Imperial General Headquarters in Tokyo. All surviving reports that cover the period between 1936 and 1940 begin with an analysis of the communist movement. Each report also studied other movements from political and antimilitary to religious movements of nationalists, right-wingers, laborers, peasants, and students. The reports voiced the suspicion that most movements, one way or another, were influenced by communism. In the category of antimilitary movements, the Chōsen Army tracked expressions and messages adopted in specific Korean speeches, films, theatrical works, newspaper articles, and even fliers.

The secret report covering the first half of 1936 stated that Korean communists were now trying to resume underground activities. In that period alone 906 Korean communists were arrested in forty separate incidents. Most of them were peasant-laborers. Of twenty-six cases of Korean communist movements that

8. Cumings, *Korea's Place in the Sun*, 154–62; Carter Eckert et al., *Korea Old and New: A History* (Cambridge, MA: Harvard University Press, 1990), chap. 16, "Nationalism and Social Revolution, 1919–1931."

9. SKTM, "Introduction," 8–9.

10. SKTM, "Introduction," 9.

resulted in the imprisonment of 328 Koreans, all were involved in creating communist cells within farm villages, factories, companies, or teacher's organizations, or were implicated in attempting to reorganize the Korean Communist Party.[11] In the condescending manner typical of the Japanese colonialists, the secret report blamed the Koreans' lack of high intelligence for their growing fascination with communism. Whereas Japanese intelligentsia tended to be attracted to communism for its scholarly value, Koreans, mostly "uneducated and unintelligent," easily succumbed to the communism because its call for "independence for the oppressed race" sounded good. Such a degrading view had an element of sour grapes because the Chōsen Army was painfully aware that communism, unlike Japan's pan-Asianism, appealed to a wide gamut of Koreans from peasants and factory workers to university students and intellectuals.

Rather than ascertaining the nature of communism's appeal to the Korean people, as extensive field studies conducted in China did in investigating the CCP, the Chōsen Army looked for external factors igniting and fueling the communist movement in Korea. The Chōsen Army suspected that even noncommunist nationalist movements and innocuous organizations of Korean scientists, farmers, craftsmen and merchants, and teachers had links with foreign agents in Vladivostok, Manchukuo, Shanghai, Nanjing, and even North America. Possible external influences on the Korean communists included the Third International, the Pan-Pacific Trade Union Secretariat (an auxiliary of the Red International of Labor Unions [Profintern]), the Japanese Communist Party, and various CCP factions active in Manchuria and Shanghai.[12] The Chōsen Army deemed the Soviet Union and, to a lesser degree, the CCP to be the most influential. The report assumed that they aggressively ushered the exile movement into Korea by smuggling in activists and agents. The Chōsen Army suspected that the Soviet Union was intensifying its manipulation of the Korean communist movement in spite of the delicate and complex diplomatic dance with Japan.

Concerned about international networks, the Chōsen Army also monitored the activity of Korean communists overseas. The case of Lee Jong revealed a complex web of communist movements that spanned Korea and Japan. He unionized Korean servants in the Setagaya district of Tokyo, fled back to Korea, and was arrested along with a Japanese professor from Keijō Imperial University for

11. Chōsen-gun Sanbō-bu (Headquarters of the Chōsen Army), "Hi: Shōwa 11-nen zenhan-ki Chōsen shisō undō gaikan" (Secret: survey of the trends of thought in Korea in the early half of 1936) (August 1936), SKTM, 6–10.

12. In the secret report, the original Japanese referred to the Pan-Pacific Trade Union Secretariat as *Taiheiyō Sekishoku Rōdō Kumiai* (the Pacific Red Labor Union). It is most likely a mistaken combination of "Han Taiheiyō Rōdō Kumiai Shoki-kyoku" (The Pan Pacific Trade Union Secretariat) and "Sekishoku Rōdō Kumiai International" (The Red International of Labor Unions).

attempting to unionize peasants in a farming village. After his release from the prison, he returned to Japan as a factory worker under an alias but was again arrested while working underground. Korean communists in Manchukuo and Shanghai were also used by the CCP to turn Korea and Manchuria into communist districts after their own image. Organizations such as the Japanese language club, the inventors' association, and the association for Korean agricultural produce did not escape the Chōsen Army's suspicion of harboring communist connections.

The Chōsen Army discovered that over time many more Korean nationalists hoped for the outbreak of war between Japan and the Soviet Union. These nationalists believed such a war would bring Soviet victory and the downfall of Japan, which would ostensibly herald a golden age in East Asia and the liberation of the Chinese and Korean people. Some noncommunist nationalists hoped that strengthening the Anglo-American alliance would further estrange Japan from the international community. Even these noncommunists seemed to desire a Soviet-Japanese war, which they hoped would provide opportunities to stage anti-Japanese uprisings in Manchuria or Korea.

By 1936 anti-Japanese and pro-Soviet rumors and graffiti throughout Korea expressed these very sentiments. Out of all the rumors recorded in the Chōsen Army's semiannual secret reports, there was only one brief mention of the United States: a short poem insinuating that a US-Japanese conflict meant American victory circulated in a circle of affluent old gentlemen in Gyeonggi-do. All other rumors focused on the Soviet Union. In January 1936, on the twelfth anniversary of passing of Vladimir Lenin, graffiti discovered on the wall of a public toilet at a train station in Masan read: "We the red youths will observe the anniversary of Lenin; all the communist parties of the world unite under the red flag; overthrow Japanese imperialism; hurrah and hurrah for Lenin's anniversary." In February graffiti appeared on the wall of a toilet at a public market near Pusan: "Very soon the Soviet-Japanese war will break out, all the Koreans will unite and stand against [Japan, expurgated in the original], March the 1st is approaching, Hurrah for Korean independence."

Throughout 1936 rumors that the Soviet-Japanese war would break out inside the year were everywhere, from the south to the north of the Korean Peninsula. In Gyeongsang-namdo and Gyeongsang-bukdo, Koreans whispered that Japan, though pressured in northern China, was recklessly plotting to start a second world war, but the war between Japan-Manchukuo and the Soviet Union would surely result in Japan's defeat. In Gyeonggi-do, residents near Seoul murmured that within a year Japan would go to war against a united force of the Soviet Union and the United States, and that they must start saving cash for such an emergency. In Gangwon-do a fifty-year-old peddler was said to tell several locals the following:

in light of the recent military clash on the Soviet-Manchurian border, the Soviet-Japanese war seems inevitable in the near future; a second world war will begin and Japan will have to fight against the entire world, so Japan is preparing to draft Korean men. In Chungcheong-namdo and Gyeongsang-namdo, locals speculated that rebels within the Japanese military had staged the February 26th Incident in Japan in order to remove obstacles to starting a war against the Soviet Union. In Jeolla-namdo rumors swirled that the Japanese Navy was investigating the port of Mokpo with the intention of converting it to a transportation hub in the event of a Soviet-Japanese war.[13]

Some Koreans expressed uneasiness about the uncertain outcome of such a war. Some feared that the Japanese Army would draft Korean youths; others talked of how the Korean Peninsula would become rubble as a main battlefield in East Asia. Individuals in different regions expressed the apprehension that even if Japan were defeated, that fate of Korea remained unknown. Rather than becoming an independent nation, they feared, the nation might become a protectorate of the Soviet Union.[14] Prevailing pessimism about the Soviet-Japanese war was nonetheless peppered with some hope that it would destroy the status quo in Korea. After the outbreak of the Sino-Japanese War in July 1937, the Chōsen Army arrested a Korean for saying, "No matter how much Japan tries to strengthen its military, there is no way that Japan can win a two-front war against China and the Soviet Union. Japan should make an effort to make peace with China rather than trying to achieve something unrealistic."[15]

During the first half of 1939, the Chōsen Army observed that the organized communist movement in Korea was in decline, as its leaders had either been arrested or been through ideological conversion after which they renounced communism (*tenkō*). But underground movements remained active. Students formed secret organizations and others maintained contact with comrades outside Korea. They all seemed to be cautiously biding their time. The arrests recorded in the secret report of August 1939 included Park Ihn-chan, a communist who spread rumors that the Sino-Japanese War would exhaust Japan's finances and lead to its defeat; Kim Jeong-oh, a Christian priest and a communist who taught Korean children that Japan's war in China was suicidal and that Japan's defeat would lead to the birth of a communist Korea; and a group of four Korean youths arrested

---

13. Chōsen-gun Sanbō-bu, "Hi: Shōwa 11-nen zenhan-ki Chōsen shisō undō gaikan furoku (August 1936)" (Secret: survey of the trends of thought in Korea in the early half of 1936: appendix), SKTM, 70–75.

14. Chōsen-gun Sanbō-bu, "Hi: Shōwa 11-nen zenhan-ki Chōsen shisō undō gaikan furoku (August 1936)," 72–74.

15. Chōsen-gun Sanbō-bu, "Hi: Shōwa 13-nen kōhan-ki Chōsen shisō undō gaikyō (February 1939)" (Secret: survey of the trends of thought in Korea in the second half of 1938), SKTM, 130.

for attempting to go to the Soviet Union to enroll in the Moscow Communist University.[16]

The same 1939 report took note of the working relationship between Kim Il-sung's men in Manchuria and the Soviet Union. The Japanese authorities had placed the Soviet-Korean border under intense surveillance, as the region provided points of contact for Korean communists and Soviet agents. The Chōsen Army discovered increasing activity along this border. In February 1939 a Korean, with instructions from a Soviet agent, posed as a political exile and entered Korea from Vladivostok, only to be arrested at Rajin (Rason). In June Kim Il-sung's men in Manchuria were arrested for having smuggled men into Korea to conduct an antiwar propaganda campaign as well as to organize Korean farmers and factory workers into unions. The Chōsen Army reported that some of the farmers and workers successfully met with four top officials of the Kim Il-sung faction along the Korean-Manchurian border and discussed how to rebuild the Red Farmers' Union (Sekinō Kumiai).[17]

In 1939 and 1940 the Chōsen Army discovered that cross-ideological anti-Japanese movements were intensifying as foreign influences contesting Japan's war of aggression in China attempted to tap Korean anti-Japanese sentiment. The Korean exile movement in China became invigorated by Chiang Kai-shek's contemplation of a united front of Korean nationalists and the GMD.[18] Twenty-three Westerners residing in Korea received copies of an article from the *World Outlook* in Nashville, Tennessee, that denounced Japan's invasion of China and praised Chiang Kai-shek's war against Japan. A teacher at a Chinese school in Hwanghae-do received, probably by mistake, a letter allegedly from the "League of [Japanese] Soldiers within the headquarters of the Kwantung Army against the war of invasion." Fearing arrest for antiwar activity, he voluntarily submitted it to the Japanese authorities. This letter alerted the Chōsen Army that some Japanese might be infiltrating Korea to support the anti-Japanese movement.[19]

The Chōsen Army's secret report for the period of the first half of 1940, 104 pages in length, carefully examined the communist movement that now played an integral role in the nationalist movement for independence. The Chōsen Army concluded that extremely radical factions remained active underground and that they took advantage of rapid changes in international relations. The Chōsen Army

16. Chōsen-gun Sanbō-bu, "Hi: Shōwa 14-nen zenhan-ki Chōsen shisō undō gaikyō (August 31, 1939)" (Secret: survey of the trends of thought in Korea in the early half of 1939), SKTM, 169–70.

17. Chōsen-gun Sanbō-bu, "Hi: Shōwa 14-nen zenhan-ki Chōsen shisō undō gaikyō (August 31, 1939)," 171.

18. Carter Eckert et al., *Korea Old and New: A History*, 323–24.

19. Chōsen-gun Sanbō-bu, "Hi: Shōwa 14-nen kōhan-ki Chōsen shisō undō gaikyō (February 28, 1940)" (Secret: survey of the trends of thought in Korea in the second half of 1939), SKTM, 240–42.

arrested members of a reading club, a secret society organized by editors of a newspaper, a study group of young farmers, a farmers' union, and even a secret society of students of the elite Keijō Imperial University. They were arrested for contributing to internal disturbances that they hoped would lead to Japan's defeat as well as Korean independence and communist revolution.

Several years into the Sino-Japanese War, the Chōsen Army discovered the CCP's growing interference in the communist activities in Korea. The Chōsen Army now had intelligence reports that Korean exiles, under instructions from the CCP, had reentered Korea to carry out clandestine operations on behalf of Yan'an. Their activities most likely consisted of praising China's Soviet districts and touting the Soviet Union as a model for Korea. The Chōsen Army's analysis concluded that the CCP must have seen a good opportunity to deploy their propaganda in Korea. By that time the Japanese military had begun recruiting Korean volunteers for the war against China, which rekindled the Koreans' fierce antiwar and anti-Japanese sentiments. A secret communist society, the New People's Club (Shinjin Kurabu) in Gyeonggi-do, led by the chief editor of a newspaper and joined by five others, exemplified growing Korean sympathy for, as well as ties with, the CCP. It criticized Korean volunteers of the Japanese Army as a regrettable case of Korean collaboration with the Japanese invasion in China and argued that the only way for Korea to resist Japan was to achieve a communist revolution. Propaganda denouncing Japan's war in China urged Koreans not to waste their lives by volunteering for the Japanese military.[20]

A three-day meeting of the Department of Japanese Police Administration for North China that began on March 22, 1940, raised concerns about the disturbing alliance between Korean nationalists and the CCP. Executive police chiefs described growing Korean propaganda operations on China's war front. In the CCP-controlled region, Japanese soldiers and Korean volunteers had retrieved a heavy volume of Korean nationalist-communist (*minzoku-sekika*) flyers, which appealed to the Koreans living in Japanese occupied territories to stop fighting for Japan. The Japanese police chiefs also confirmed that several Korean communists served in the Eighth Route Army as officers or interpreters. Influential Koreans had also participated in other CCP armies and had fought against the Japanese Army in North China. One executive police chief recommended that the Japanese police continue investigating the motives of these Koreans. If their motives were nationalistic, with the goal of achieving communist independence for Korea, then Japan should be cautious about their alliance with the CCP. On the other hand, if their motives were "merely impulsive" and not guided by hopes of

---

20. Chōsen-gun Sanbō-bu, "Hi: Shōwa 15-nen zenhan-ki Chōsen shisō undō gaikyō (August 1940)" (Secret: survey of the trends of thought in Korea in the early half of 1940), SKTM, 297–301.

specific achievements for Korea, then their alliance with the CCP should not be cause for worry. Thus he recommended a wait-and-see attitude toward Korean communist collaboration with the CCP.[21]

The Japanese had grounds for believing that the Koreans would have difficulty forming coalitions with the Chinese. One month earlier on February 27, 1940, the Japanese Foreign Ministry had convened a three-day meeting in Beijing, inviting the Japanese consulate police chiefs in occupied North China to discuss the security screening of Japanese and non-Japanese. Koreans, whose population in the Japanese occupied territory in North China had been increasing since the Manchurian Incident, had been closely monitored, not because they were communists, but because some were employed as anti-Chinese spies by Japan. The police chiefs reported that many Korean migrants were vagabonds and unemployed, who transacted in illegal goods for a living. After the outbreak of the Sino-Japanese War, approximately 1,350 Koreans moved into Japanese jurisdictions and behaved as if they, like the Japanese, were superior to the Chinese. The number of delinquent Koreans recently had decreased, thanks to tightening Japanese regulations, while the number of hard-working Koreans increased. Of 9,969 classified as the latter, many worked as company employees, bankers, store and office clerks, entertainers, and employees at Japanese government offices.[22] These Koreans seemed willing to collaborate with the Japanese. Japanese police stations in various regions hired a small number of Koreans as intelligence agents who collected information on communists, anti-Japanese terrorists, Soviet citizens and their collaborators, and even people working for the GMD-CCP united front. Some even infiltrated the CCP Army and monitored its military planning. Pro-Japanese Korean spies reported on some forty Korean "lawless factions" in China as well. Having escaped Japanese persecution in the aftermath of the March 1 Incident of 1919, members of these factions lived as exiles in Tianjin and other foreign settlements in China. Some later even had opportunities to study at the Moscow Communist University or the Chinese military academy.[23]

One assistant police inspector from Qingdao even praised the Koreans in his jurisdiction as "patriotic" (pro-Japanese). Although his watch list included seven former nationalists and one former communist, this police inspector stated that the Koreans had become loyal subjects of the empire and actively collaborated

21. Hoku-Shi Keimu-bu (North China Department of Police Affairs), *Shōwa 15-nen Hoku-Shi kōtō shunin kaigi-roku* (Minutes of the executive chiefs in North China, 1940) (March 1940), reprinted in WIC, vol. 10, 412–15.

22. Zai-Chūka Minkoku (Pekin) Nihon Teikoku Taishikan Keisatsu (The Police Department of the Japanese Embassy, the Republic of China), "Bugai-hi Hoku-Shi Ryōji-kan keisatsu shochō kaigi-roku" (Confidential: the minutes of the meeting of the Police Chiefs, the Japanese Consulates in North China), no. 1 (1940), WIC, vol. 10, 34–35.

23. Hoku-Shi Keimu-bu, *Shōwa 15-nen Hoku-Shi kōtō shunin kaigi-roku* (March 1940), 381–83.

with Japan's war efforts by soliciting financial donations to the war cause and visiting military hospitals to comfort wounded soldiers. Some even received commendations from the minister of the Imperial Navy.[24] He believed it was unlikely that the Koreans would ally themselves with the Chinese rather than the Japanese. The majority of those attending the meeting were not so optimistic. Questions remained as to how the Koreans might organize a powerful anti-Japanese movement, and with which foreign nation's assistance.

Understanding International Ambitions for Korea: The View from 1944

As the war in China dragged on and Japan's prospects in the Pacific War worsened, Japan exploited Korea further. While the Korean Peninsula itself escaped becoming a battleground, Korea bore a heavy toll as a supplier of resources to the two war fronts in China and the Pacific. Labor and military conscriptions uprooted some 4 million Korean men and women to the battlegrounds as soldiers and comfort women as well as to factories and mines outside Korea as laborers. Those remaining in Korea suffered from ever-deteriorating living conditions, political repression, and forced Japanization. Korean farmers, coping with the pressure to export agricultural products amid droughts and shortages of farmhands, were driven to petition, protest, sabotage, and even to commit violence against colonial officials. Domestic agitation threatened to become a security risk at any moment.

Amid this internal crisis the Governor-General's Office became convinced by mid-1944 that the larger challenge to Japanese colonialism came from foreign powers. The Governor-General's Office did not think that these foreign powers would altruistically help the Koreans achieve independence. It suspected that the Soviet Union was manipulating Korean communists, especially in Manchuria, for its own interests. By then it was common knowledge among Japanese leaders that the CCP was not under Soviet control, so they presumed that the CCP had its own goals in Korea, separate from those of the Soviets. The race by the powers to control the peninsula seemed underway. At this stage of war, Japan's most fundamental security issue, according to the Governor-General's Office, was to address which foreign influence would be most likely fill the power vacuum after Japan was gone.

In September 1944 the Governor-General's Office submitted a classified report on the state of Korea in the war to the special session of the 85th Imperial Diet in

---

24. Hoku-Shi Keimu-bu, *Shōwa 15-nen Hoku-Shi kōtō shunin kaigi-roku*, 416.

Tokyo. The 183-page report analyzed miscellaneous conditions ranging from the food supply, transportation, savings, security and defense preparations such as student mobilization, the detailed examination of the results of a military draft test taken by Korean men, and the productivity of aircraft, steel, coal and other industries. The primary intention of the report was to alert the Japanese government to growing anti-Japanese sentiment in Korea, as people became wearied of the controlled economy, shortages of food and other goods, and above all the prolonged war. Koreans knew that the Allied powers were overwhelmingly superior, so anti-Japanese rumors, "blasphemies" against the emperor, and seditious statements proliferated everywhere. Koreans talked about Japan's inevitable defeat and their nation's subsequent independence. The Governor-General's Office warned that this rebellious discontent might precipitate into an unexpectedly dangerous situation before the war's conclusion. Now that the US air raids were intensifying even in southern Korea, these rebels might look for a major turning point in Japan's war to launch subversive riots and a nationwide uprising. The report explained how the office made efforts to improve general conditions in Korea in order to avoid such a security situation.[25] The governor-general's report encouraged the Japanese government to listen to Koreans, especially the intellectuals, youths, and students, and to gain an understanding of their sincere demands such as the abolition of discrimination between Japanese and Koreans.[26] From the governor-general's point of view, Japan's noblesse oblige required it to work harder to achieve the assimilation of Koreans into Japanese imperial subjects. Therefore, Korean independence was out of the question.

Some Korean activists pursued legal avenues to achieve rights. Since 1919 the National Association (Kokumin Kyōkai) had futilely demanded that Imperial Japanese Diet grant them suffrage. On December 8, 1941 when the Pacific War broke out, the National Association requested that the governor-general of Korea realize the complete integration of Korea and Japan toward the goals of the Greater East Asia Coprosperity Sphere. The Governor-General's Office suspected that previously politically inactive Koreans would join the National Association's suffrage movement and demand their rights now that they were fulfilling the three basic duties of imperial subjects—military service, compulsory education, and tax payment. If Korea and Japan were completely integrated, many forms of discrimination would be abolished accordingly such that the Koreans would receive suffrage, the right to travel freely between Korea and Japan, and equal pay for officials.[27]

25. IDS, 53–54.
26. IDS, 54.
27. IDS, 57–59.

TABLE 4.1 Arrests for seditious activities in Korea, 1939–44

YEAR	NATIONALIST	COMMUNIST	STUDENT	RELIGIOUS	OTHERS	TOTAL ARRESTS
1939	36 (256)	28 (646)	6 (26)	18 (105)	7 (9)	95 (1042)
1940	29 (72)	31 (668)	16 (121)	24 (329)	3 (3)	103 (1193)
1941	73 (176)	20 (158)	48 (203)	34 (206)	57 (118)	232 (861)
1942	33 (237)	25 (141)	57 (409)	34 (317)	34 (38)	183 (1142)
1943	46 (204)	23 (151)	46 (198)	58 (211)	149 (238)	322 (1002)
1944 Jan-Jun	51 (140)	2 (12)	16 (42)	8 (56)	55 (87)	132 (337)
Total	268 (1085)	129 (1776)	189 (999)	176 (1224)	305 (493)	1067 (5577)

Number of cases (number of individuals)

Source: IDS, 67–68.

Despite the rhetoric, the governor-general knew that a complete unification would not be a satisfactory solution in the eyes of Koreans. More and more Koreans were ratcheting up their efforts to achieve independence. This knowledge had prompted the Governor-General's Office to study the changing nature of Korean nationalism as a factor in Japan's war against China and the United States. It tried to ascertain which leader, or which faction of the Korean nationalists, backed by which foreign power, would most likely emerge as the major challenger of Japanese colonialism. By 1944 the governor-general had determined that the Korean communists remained the prime force behind the independence movement even though yearly trends of arrests during the war showed that Korean nationalists with noncommunist or anticommunist ideological affiliations were on the rise. In 1939 and 1940, 62 percent and 56 percent of the arrests respectively were of communists, but in 1941 nationalist arrests counted for 20.4 percent and communist arrests dropped to 18.4 percent. Each year after that the nationalist arrests exceeded the communist arrests. In the first half of 1944, nationalist arrests rose to 42 percent, while communist arrests sank to 3.6 percent.

These figures alone did not support the argument that noncommunist Koreans were emerging as the central force in the independence movement. As indicated in table 4.1, student arrests were not specified by ideological preference, but it was common knowledge that those in higher education tended to be leftist. By looking at the total number of arrests from 1939 to June 1944, even without factoring in the leftist inclinations of students, there were 1,085 nationalists as opposed to 1,776 communists; these numbers suggested that the communists had been more successful in mobilizing sympathizers.[28] The governor-general of Korea was aware that the sharp decline in communist arrests in 1941 and again in early

28. IDS, 65–71.

TABLE 4.2 Arrests of Soviet spies in Korea, August 1944

		NATIONALITY OF INDIVIDUALS			
	NUMBER OF CASES	JAPANESE	KOREANS	CHINESE	NUMBER OF INDIVIDUALS
1934	1		1	1	2
1935	7		11		11
1936	8		14		14
Until June 1937	1		7		7
From July 1937	9	1	15		16
1938	13	1	15		16
1939	8	10	5		15
1940	29	9	25		34
Until Dec 7, 1941	19	3	22		25
After Dec 8, 1941	1	1			1
1942	9		12		12
1943	11		11		11
Until July 1944	4		4		4
Total	120	25	142	1	168

Source: IDS, 79–80.

1944 must have been linked to their mass exodus to Manchuria, China, or the Soviet Union. Rather than seeing Korea as a breeding ground of revolutionaries, the Governor-General's Office concluded that the true challenge to Japanese colonialism was building outside Korea.

The governor-general of Korea had noticed that with the outbreak of the Pacific War the Soviet Union resumed intense intelligence and espionage operations in Korea in the pursuit of its own national interests. The governor-general's 1944 secret report devoted considerable space to analysis of Soviet activities in Korea. The Soviet Union had a historical and strategic interest in securing the Korean Peninsula as a gateway to warm water. In fact, according to the Governor-General's Office's investigation, since the creation of Manchukuo the Soviet Union had continued operating the most extensive espionage activities in Korea employing Korean agents. Of 168 individuals arrested as Soviet spies between January 1934 and July 1944, 25 (14.9 percent) were Japanese and 142 (84.5 percent) were Koreans. Only one Soviet spy captured in Korea was Chinese.

As demonstrated in the 1939 secret report by the Chōsen Army, the Japanese authorities had long monitored Kim Il-sung as a Soviet agent rather than as a nationalist with an autonomous agenda for Korean independence and revolution. In late July 1941 the Japanese consulate in Mudanjiang dispatched to Tokyo a confidential report that the Soviets had instructed a guerrilla group of Korean communists, headed by Kim Il-sung and Choe Hyon, to reenter Manchuria to engage in anti-Japanese plots.[29] Concurring that Korean communists in Manchuria were guerrillas dispatched by the Soviet Union to strategic locations in northern Korea, the Governor-General's Office was convinced, nonetheless, that the Soviet Union pursued its own strategic interests and not a communist revolution. By 1944 Soviet spies no longer merely engaged in disturbing the colonial order and agitated the populace. Highly trained Soviet intelligence agents, mostly Koreans, had been most active along the northern Korean and Russian border, around important Japanese military bases as well as pivotal transportation centers. The Governor-General's Office suspected that the Soviets now collected information on Japan's possible intent to launch an attack on the Soviet Union. Since January 1943 seventy-five Korean military spies for the Soviet Union had been counted crossing the border. Three were shot to death and five were arrested. Two Japanese policemen were also killed in shootouts.

The 1944 report of the Governor-General's Office also revealed that the Soviet intelligence agents, mostly Koreans, had penetrated deep into Korean society. Some had settled in specific locations equipped with sophisticated short-wave transmitters and others had become sleeper agents. From 1943 through the summer of 1944, according to the findings of the Governor-General's Office, fifteen Soviet spies were arrested for illegal entry into Korea. The office indicated a concern in the report that their methods of entering Korea had become highly clever in recent years. Rather than crossing the border, they reached the east coast of the Korean Peninsula by sea and landed in sparsely populated coastal areas. They were also becoming more aggressive. They would exchange fire with the military police or police officers or even kidnap local residents as hostages. Most alarmingly, continued the report, Soviet sleeper agents in Korea had recently become active, successfully avoiding dragnets and were looking for the perfect time to deploy. In addition the Soviet embassy in Seoul also employed spies among its diplomatic staff. According to the Governor-General's Office, all signs indicated Moscow's growing interest in deploying military forces, ousting Japan, and capturing Korea for its own use.[30]

China also remained a serious challenge to Japan's rule in Korea. In the same 1944 report the Governor-General's Office provided substantial analysis of China's involvement in Korea. China, like the Soviet Union, had a historical interest in "overseeing" Korea. The Sino-Japanese War of 1894–95 had been fought over

---

29. "Kimitsu: Roku-gatsu bun Botankō-shō chian jōkyō gaikyō hōkoku no ken (July 21, 1941)" (Top secret: on the report of security in the Mudanjiang Province in June [July 21, 1941]), in "DaiTōA Sensō kankei ikken jōhō shūshū kankei Botankō jōhō" (The Greater East Asia War: intelligence gatherings: information on Mudanjiang) [A-7-0-0-9-9-8], DRO.

30. IDS, 73–76.

the control of Korea. The Qing Dynasty had insisted on China's suzerainty over Korea, while Japan asserted its superior claim to Korea based on the Treaty of Kanghwa of 1876, Korea's first "Western style" treaty with another "modern" nation, Japan. When Japan won the Sino-Japanese War and the two nations concluded the Treaty of Shimonoseki, China had agreed to withdraw its troops from Korea and to recognize Japan's claim on the peninsula.

In the 1944 report to the Imperial Diet, the governor-general gave a full picture of how China, not the Soviet Union, had been the most dynamic venue for Korean exile nationalists. Two factions competed in China under Chiang Kai-shek's wing—the Korean Nationalist Party under the leadership of Kim Ku and the communist-supported Korean Revolutionary Party under the leadership of Kim Won-bong. After the Sino-Japanese War began, the idea of a united front emerged but never materialized in any specific actions. Kim Ku established his influence in Chongqing, the capital of the GMD regime, with the Korean Restoration Army, one of the largest Korean military units ever organized in China.[31] Kim had ambitions of gaining formal recognition of his Provisional Korean Government from the GMD government, the United States, Britain, and the Soviet Union. Chiang Kai-shek was willing to support the Korean Restoration Army insofar as it contributed to his military strength, but he refused to recognize it as the official army of the Korean Provisional Government. In November 1941, Chiang Kai-shek revoked the Korean Provisional Government's right to command the Korean Restoration Army and placed the army directly under his own command. Once Japan began the war against the United States, Chiang continued this pattern of handling Korean nationalists under his influence.

Despite such overt control over Kim, the Governor-General's Office did not see Chiang Kai-shek as a serious threat to Japan's supremacy in Korea. The 1944 report argued that Chiang Kai-shek was possibly ambitious enough to become the first world leader to recognize Korean independence, preferably under Kim Ku's leadership, after the collapse of the Japanese empire. However, not much interested in Korea's independence per se, Chiang had been only tantalizing Kim Ku with the policy that the GMD would support his Provisional Government as long as the latter adopted Sun Yat-sen's Three Principles of the People as the guiding philosophy for Korea. Given this unrealistic and incoherent scenario, the governor-general was convinced that Kim Ku had to be out of the Korean leadership race.[32]

31. IDS, 59–60.

32. Suzuki Masayuki, "Chōsen minzoku kaihō undō o meguru kokusai kankei: Chūgoku Kyōsan-tō oyobi Chūgoku seifu o chūshin ni" (International relations surrounding the Korean nationalist movement: with a focus on the GMD regime and the CCP), in Nakamura Katsunori, ed., *Kindai Nihon seiji no shosō—jidai ni yoru tenkai to kōsatsu* (Aspects of modern Japanese politics at different periods) (Tokyo: Keiō Tsūshin, 1989), 325–30.

Kim Won-bong, the exiled communist leader in China, seemed to be no better situated to lead Korea to independence. In October 1938, he consolidated his units into the Korean Volunteer Corps and fought the anti-Japanese war in China. Kim faced an internal split among the Korean communists over their disagreement in interpreting the Moscow-imposed legitimacy of the GMD-CCP united front. One faction that remained under Kim's leadership honored the GMD-CCP alliance and looked to the GMD regime for instructions. Another faction, the far leftist, abandoned Kim and joined Koreans who had worked directly with the CCP. In addition to these factions, a considerable number of Koreans in North China had served in the Eighth Route Army.

Compared to the GMD, the CCP under Mao's leadership had a clearer policy toward Korea—to fulfill China's historic noblesse oblige toward Korea. Back in 1920, young Mao, disturbed by China's "loss" of Korea and Taiwan to Japanese imperialism, wrote to his friends studying in France, calling for Chinese understanding of the importance of "helping Korea to its independence" based on the principle of "collective happiness of humankind."[33] The continuing Japanese aggression in China in parallel to its worsening colonial exploitation of Korea must have kindled the CCP's interest in China's historical claims to "protect" Korea. In August 1935 the CCP called for a united front in the common fight against Japan. In "For the mobilization of all the nation's forces for victory in the war of resistance" (August 25, 1937), Mao wrote that to overthrow Japanese imperialism, "mobilize the Mongolian, the Hui and all other minority nationalities, in accordance with the principle of national self-determination and autonomy, in the common fight against Japan. . . . Unite with the worker and peasant masses of Korea and Japan against Japanese imperialism."[34]

In January 1941 the CCP assisted exiled Korean communists in forming the North China Korean Youth Federation (Hwabuk Choson Chongnyon Yonhaphoe), which was later renamed the North China Korean Independence League (Hwabuk Choson Tongnip Tongmaeng) in August 1942. The purpose of both the federation and the league remained the same: to build up a Korean army against Japan, emancipate Korea from Japan's exploitation, and reconstruct it under the guidance of the CCP.[35] The Governor-General's Office obtained follow-up information that the North China Korean Independence League had founded the North China

---

33. Michael Hunt, *The Genesis of Chinese Communist Foreign Policy* (New York: Columbia University Press, 1996), 75 and 79.

34. "For the Mobilization of All the Nation's Forces for Victory in the War of Resistance" (August 25, 1937), in "Selected Works of Mao Tse-tung" (Peking: Foreign Language Press), available online at http://www.marxists.org/reference/archive/mao/selected-works/volume-2/mswv2_02.htm.

35. Chong-Sik Lee, *The Politics of Korean Nationalism* (Berkeley: University of California Press, 1963), 216–17, 221.

Korean Independent Military-Political School to train future military and political leaders for an independent Korea. Not only that, Korean communists in North China also began working closely with the Japanese communists of the Antiwar League in producing anti-Japanese propaganda. The 1944 report of the Governor-General's Office explained how Korean communists had also successfully persuaded Korean volunteers with the Japanese Army fighting in China to desert the Japanese war effort and join them.[36]

In spite of these increasing challenges from the CCP, the Governor-General's Office did not consider the CCP a serious contender for the new ruler of Korea. The governor-general suspected that the CCP could not work side by side with the Korean communists toward Korean independence any more than the Soviet Union could. For example, the North China Korean Youth Federation's Manifesto declared they should work for China first: "We are appealing to all Koreans who are scattered in north China and all over China to *help the Chinese antiwar effort* effectively, and thus bring victory through common operations with the Chinese compatriots. . . . *We must participate in the Chinese national unity and assist the Chinese as well as learn together with them*, and ultimately we will form a Korean anti-Japanese national united front" (emphasis added).[37]

Knowing that Korean communists in China had to set aside their desire for Korean independence and had prioritized China's objectives, the Governor-General's Office tracked CCP activities in Korea and tried to determine what they aimed to achieve in the peninsula. From December 1938 on, there were frequent incidents of arson and sabotage at war factories, major companies, and markets across all of Korea. After July 1941 military trains were constantly obstructed. The office determined that the CCP, and not Korean communists, was responsible for this sabotage, and by late August 1941 it had arrested a group of Chinese spies in Hamgyeong-bukdo who were affiliated with the Eighth Route Army of the CCP. Further investigation led to the arrest of seventy more spies in 1942, forty-nine in 1943, and seven in 1944. The Governor-General's Office concluded that the CCP's growing ambition was to use Korea as a strategic base for its anti-Japanese campaign.

These Chinese saboteurs, dispatched by the Eighth Route Army, had entered Korea legally as Chinese draft laborers. Others had entered Korea illegally, posing as laborers, shopkeepers, and vegetable peddlers. They engaged in arson, obstructed trains, and relayed military information via coded messages or wireless transmitters. Some returned to China after successfully gathering information in

36. IDS, 61–62.

37. Dae-Sook Suh, *Documents of Korean Communism 1918–1948* (Princeton, NJ: Princeton University Press, 1970), 412–13.

Korea. The major acts of arson took place in Hamgyeong-bukdo in January 1942, and Gyeonggi-do in June 1943, causing more than 7 million yen in damages and leading to the arrest of forty-two men working for the CCP. Based on the arrest of a group of Chinese youths in Hwanghae-do in July 1943, the governor-general discovered that since March of that year, the CCP had intensified its propaganda efforts aimed at recruiting Chinese residents in Korea for its own revolutionary purposes.[38]

Considering Korea's geographical location this strategy made sense. According to Japanese government statistics for 1936, of 14,485 foreigners (excluding Japanese) residing in Korea, 12,510 were Chinese, making up 86.4 percent of all foreign residents.[39] Turning these Chinese residents in Korea into CCP supporters would be a reasonable way to back up the Chinese communist campaign just across the Korean border in Manchuria. These Chinese could also spy for the CCP in Korea. As a result of this intense propaganda campaign, more and more Chinese residents in Korea were inclined to support the CCP. The 1944 report of the Governor-General's Office explained that sympathy for communist ideology alone did not engender this support. Collaboration with the CCP also stemmed from provincial loyalty because many of these Chinese residents in Korea originally came from Shandong, the province infested with the Eighth Route Army. In some cases collaboration was forced on the Chinese residents. When Chinese residents discovered that their families and relatives back in China were being held hostage by the CCP, they would return to China, surrender themselves to the CCP, and provide information on Korea. They would then be sent back to Korea on missions assigned by the CCP.

The Governor-General's Office also suspected that the CCP had another objective in Korea. Through the expanded underground networks it built all over Korea, the CCP conducted economic and industrial espionage with the goal of procuring critical war materials for their own military bases in China and Manchuria. The CCP controlled illegal traders and used them to ship sulfur, niter, and mercury out of Korea to their bases. The Governor-General's Office arrested at least 118 people involved in illegal trafficking. Between 1937 and 1944 the arrests of CCP-related spies exceeded Soviet cases. Only one Japanese individual was arrested for working for the CCP, whereas twenty-five Japanese were arrested for working for the Soviet Union. With few exceptions, the CCP did not employ Koreans for espionage activities; CCP spies in Korea were predominantly

38. IDS, 76–78.

39. "Kaku gaichi ni okeru gaikokujin kankei tōkei hōkoku no ken: Chōsen Sōtoku-fu, December 1936" (Statistical report on foreign residents in Japanese colonies: the Governor General's Office, Korea), in *Zai-Honpō gaikokujin ni kansuru tōkei chōsa zakken* (Miscellaneous statistical data on foreign residents in Japan), vol. 1 [K-3-7-0-15], DRO.

TABLE 4.3 Arrests of CCP spies in Korea, August 1944

		NATIONALITY OF INDIVIDUALS			
	NUMBER OF CASES	JAPANESE	KOREANS	CHINESE	NUMBER OF INDIVIDUALS
1937	4		2	15	17
1938	3			8	8
1939	1		2		2
1940	1	1			1
Until Dec 7 1941	1			2	2
After Dec 8 1941	1			2	2
1942	9			70	70
1943	10			49	49
Until July 1944	6		1	6	7
Total	36	1	5	152	158

Source: IDS, 81.

Chinese.[40] The CCP did not yet possess the capacity to compete against the Soviet Union for the control and leadership of Korea.

The report spent relatively little time analyzing US involvement. Historically the United States had had little interest in Korea. Since the early twentieth century, the United States had recognized Japanese control of Korea in exchange for Japanese recognition of American control of the Philippines. America's interests in Korea had been limited to missionary activities and some minor business opportunities. The United States conducted no significant intelligence activities in Korea: typical Anglo-American intelligence activities in Korea involved diplomats conducting legal information gathering or Christian missionaries engaging in antiwar propaganda campaigns. The US government also hired Korean exiles in America as broadcasters who talked to the Korean people about independence, the adversities suffered by the Axis powers, and especially the ever-deteriorating condition of Japan's war.

Beginning in March 1943 the Governor-General's Office arrested Koreans who had received American-sponsored propaganda broadcasts and passed them on to others. Unlike its inclusion of data on Soviet and CCP spies, the report provided no statistics about Anglo-American spies in Korea, most likely indicating an insignificant number of arrests. The 1944 report only noted that Anglo-America used submarines to approach the Korean coasts and sometimes even made contact with fishermen to gather intelligence.[41] The governor-general did

40. IDS, 76–78.
41. IDS, 78–79.

not even present an analysis of possible goals of the United States and Britain in Korea.

Japanese officials in Tokyo remained skeptical even about Washington's willingness to endorse an independent Korea in the distant future, much less support the Korean nationalist movement. Before Pearl Harbor, some Koreans, especially Christians, were pro-Western and praised Anglo-American economic strength, but that alone was not powerful enough to draw the US government into supporting Korean independence. The Governor-General's Office, as well as the Chōsen Army, knew that Syngman Rhee's Korean government in exile had never been taken seriously by the US government. In fact, Rhee and the "American group" had to endure American paternalism. They also had a poor reputation among fellow Koreans. According to one Korean observer, "These were all 'gentlemen.' Most of them spoke good English. They actually expected to get Korean independence by being able to speak persuasive English!"[42] Though the governor-general's report recommended "duly careful control" over the content of Rhee's shortwave broadcastings to Korean listeners, it did not raise the possibility that Rhee might pose a threat to Japanese colonialism.[43]

The Japanese Ministry of Foreign Affairs conducted its own intelligence gathering on Rhee's activities in the United States and drew the same conclusions. In August 1944 the Dōmei News Agency dispatched to the Foreign Ministry a series of "enemy news" reports concerning Rhee, all of which portrayed a shaky relationship between Rhee and Washington. These news sources in the United States did not portray Rhee as a capable and pragmatic leader. *The Army News* (Los Angeles, August 15, 1944) reported Rhee's dissatisfaction with the United States and other Allied nations because they were not enthusiastic about the idea of Korean independence. Rhee's spokesman insisted that the United States and other Allied nations should approve the Provisional Government of Korea immediately, assist its army, and allow it to join the Allied forces' operation against Japan. Although the spokesman admitted that Rhee's army still required serious organization, training, and build-up, once it was ready, it would be powerful enough to crush the Japanese military in Korea and Manchuria. Based on this optimistic claim, Rhee's spokesman pleaded for the Allied nations' recognition of the Korean Provisional Government.

Following the story about Rhee's discord with the US government, the Dōmei News Agency in Lisbon dispatched to Tokyo an article from *News Chronicle* on August 22, 1944. Rhee's Korean exile government in the United States asserted that the Allied nations' rejection of Korea's offer of military collaboration had

---

42. Cumings, *Korea's Place in the Sun*, 158–59.
43. IDS, 59, 62–63.

severely impeded the war in the Far East. Rhee complained that the Allied nations had not made any efforts toward realizing the spirit of the Cairo Declaration of November 27, 1943, in which the three Great Powers—Great Britain, the United States, and Chiang Kai-shek's China—declared that they were all mindful of the enslavement of the people of Korea and agreed "in due course Korea shall become free and independent." According to the article summary, Rhee expressed disappointment that the Allied forces took no interest in his bold plan to transform the entire Korean Peninsula into a battlefield where his army of ten thousand well-trained and well-equipped soldiers would wage brilliant anti-Japanese guerrilla warfare. The article demonstrated his naïveté about the geopolitical complexities of Korea. It was becoming clear to Japanese officials that Rhee would never be able to found an independent Korea.

The final report of the series, sent by the Dōmei News Agency to the Japanese Foreign Ministry on August 31, 1944, described a recent dinner party sponsored by the *New York Herald Tribune* in honor of the Korean desire for independence. Syngman Rhee and several other Asian dignitaries from the GMD government and the Philippines attended. Before the dinner party, Rhee had paid a visit to Fiorello LaGuardia, mayor of New York City, asking him to support the plan for the Korean army, to which LaGuardia had nodded favorably. Rhee then had headed to the dinner party where he gave an eloquent speech on Korean independence.[44] As long as Washington's relations with Rhee continued in this patronizing manner, which he seemed to enjoy, the United States did not pose much danger for Japan's Korea.

At the same time the Japanese Ministry of Foreign Affairs also tracked the rise in American interest in Korea. Through 1944 the US government gradually realized the strategic implications of the power vacuum that would be created in Korea by the demise of the Japanese empire. The American media too began discussing how the United States should collaborate with Britain, the Soviet Union, and even possibly Chiang's China in determining the proper disposition of postwar Korea. As Japanese policymakers saw it, the United States, a latecomer with no strong ties to the nationalist activists in Korea, was on its way to join the race for postwar control of Korea. They speculated that even if the US government had been aware of the growing covert operations by the CCP, it would not have regarded the CCP as capable of exercising any substantial influence over Korea.

---

44. Dōmei Tsūshin Sha nai Jōhō-kyoku tekisei jōhō" (Enemy news intercepted by the information section of the Domei News Agency), "Chōsen dokuritsu undō" (Korean Independence Movement) (August 15, 1944), "Chōsen Rinji Seifu daihyō no kujō" (Complaints by the representatives of the Korean Provisional Government) (August 22, 1944), and "Chōsen Dokuritsu Kisei Taikai" (Conference for Korean Independence) (August 31, 1944)." All in "DaiTōA Sensō kankei ikken jōhō shūshū kankei" (The Greater East Asia War: intelligence gatherings) [A-7-0-0-9-9], DRO.

As the Japanese Foreign Ministry understood it, the Soviet Union subsequently came to loom as the greatest challenge to US influence over Korea, and the United States became increasingly nervous about how aggressively the Soviet Union might attempt to determine the fate of postwar Korea.

Some historians have argued that the US government dropped its historical indifference to Korea much earlier. Only a few months after Pearl Harbor, the US State Department already was worried about the impact of Soviet involvement in Korea on Pacific security.[45] In March 1944 the Inter-Divisional Areas Committee on the Far East in Washington prepared a memorandum emphasizing that "the United States should have the most important and largest role in the operation and in military government (in Korea)." The American planners did not support either a trusteeship or a zonal system of military occupation by foreign powers. By the summer of 1944 some officials within the State Department articulated concerns that Soviet forces would invade Manchuria and Korea once it entered the war against Japan, so they recommended that the Office of Strategic Services (OSS) organize various Korean groups for pro-US paramilitary activity to thwart such Soviet ambitions.[46]

Stalin decided to be cautious with Washington on the issue of Korea. In a December 1944 meeting with W. Averell Harriman, US ambassador to the Soviet Union, Stalin offered a list of compensations he would like to receive in exchange for opening a second front in the Far East. These conditions paved the way for the Yalta Agreement. He indicated the Kurile Islands, the southern part of Sakhalin, the leases of Lushunkou (Port Arthur) and Dalian, as well as control of both the Chinese Eastern Railway (also known as the North Manchuria Railway) and South Manchuria Railway, but he carefully omitted mentioning Korea. At the Yalta Conference in February 1945, Roosevelt and Stalin agreed only vaguely on a trusteeship for Korea for a short period, as if to avoid any further diplomatic complication before the war's end.

While recognizing the preponderance of communist influence among Korean nationalists and their willingness to collaborate with the Soviet Union and even the CCP to defeat Japanese colonialism, Japanese analysts sensed that such close communist ties did not necessarily mean that Korea would become Moscow's catalyst for an East Asian communist revolution. Examinations of the relationship between the CCP and the Soviet Union had led the Japanese to conclude that Moscow did not have the capacity to orchestrate communist movements all over East Asia. In pursuing its national (and imperialist) interest in the same

45. Cumings, *Korea's Place in the Sun*, 188.

46. Gye-Dong Kim, *Foreign Intervention in Korea* (Aldershot, England; Brookfield, VT: Dartmouth Pub. Co., 1993), 15 and 20–22.

manner as tsarist Russia, Moscow sooner or later might collide with the Korean communists over the issue of self-determination. The Japanese policymakers also began suspecting that the United States, disturbed by growing Soviet interest in Korea, had become ready to secure Korea for its own sphere of influence after the war. As the US Army advanced northward in the Pacific and got closer to Japan's mainland, the Japanese leaders hoped a US-Soviet balance of power would emerge in Korea after the demise of the Japanese empire so that neither the Soviet Union nor the United States would be hegemonic in the region. As the determination of US and Soviet intentions for Korea became more pressing, understanding Korean nationalist movements and their goals became even less of a priority for the Japanese leaders—a distinct approach from Japan's China policy, which concentrated on Chinese nationalists.

Part III

ENDING THE WAR AND BEYOND

5

COLD WAR RISING

Observing US-Soviet Dissonance

The MAGIC-ULTRA reports generated in early to mid-1945 from Washington's intercepts of Japanese encrypted communications depict the Japanese government as a desperate seeker of Soviet peace mediation. Backed by the testimony of Japanese leaders at the Tokyo War Crimes Trial, these reports established that Japanese leaders made futile efforts to persuade the Soviet Union to remain neutral or to mediate peace with the United States. Historians have portrayed Japan's approach to the Soviet Union as a tragic mistake. Akira Iriye argued that Japan at this point in the war should have abandoned the pan-Asian crusade and reoriented the nation back to Wilsonianism. If the Japanese had approached Washington rather than Moscow, according to Iriye, they would have found the United States willing and ready with a peace plan.[1]

Little-studied documents, in contrast, reveal that the Japanese policymakers were skeptical of Moscow's interest in neutrality. They regarded the Russian presence in East Asia as a natural factor and took that as a given in considering Asia's future after the war; Japan's policies toward China and Korea always involved calculations of Soviet influence. On the one hand, the neutrality pact made sense in that the Soviet marginality in the Anglo-American world made Soviet assistance to the United States in the Pacific unlikely. On the other hand, Japanese leaders regarded Stalin as an archetypal imperialist and a geopolitical tactician with territorial ambitions in the Far East; in other words, a successor to Alexander

1. Akira Iriye, *Power and Culture* (Cambridge, MA: Harvard University Press, 1981), 170, 214, 222, 225.

III and Nicolai II of Imperial Russia. The two military clashes at Changkufeng and Nomonhan were costly lessons that taught the Japanese about the overwhelming Soviet military power.

Matsuoka Yōsuke knew all this. While in semiretirement during the Pacific War, he was once asked privately whether the neutrality pact with the Soviet Union was a mistake. Matsuoka rebuked the questioner, saying that defending Japan's interests was the last thing Stalin was pleased to do. Knowing that, he still concluded the pact because it was the only way to secure Japan's territorial integrity on the continent.[2] Other military leaders shared this view. On December 18, 1941, only ten days after Pearl Harbor, and barely eight months after the signing of the Soviet-Japanese Neutrality Pact, General Hata Shunroku recorded in his journal his conviction that the Soviets would eventually break the pact and enter the war against Japan. He added that this was the common understanding among top Japanese military leaders.[3]

Having cultivated a rich cultural, ideological, military, and diplomatic relationship with the Soviet Union, the Japanese, under a pro-Moscow façade, were shrewd speculators about Soviet strategic motives and intentions. Even though the Foreign Ministry proposed offering the Soviet Union various concessions in exchange for actions favorable to Japan in the war, the ministry did not necessarily do so out of desperation. They knew the Soviet Union had its own national interest to pursue and therefore would not maintain neutrality long.

By early 1945, with Japan's military defeat in the Pacific theater looming, groups of Japanese officials and civilians stationed in the neutral nations in Europe began clandestine negotiations with the United States. Their private attempts were unsuccessful, and there seemed no chance left for peace with the United States. Amid such a predicament, different groups of Japanese war planners investigated the war's progress from another angle. They attended to Moscow and Washington's competing ambitions to shape a new world order after the war. In such a scenario Soviet ambitions in East Asia might limit and contain US ambitions—a prospect very similar to the intention behind the neutrality pact. Neutral or not, the Soviet Union might be a useful buffer against the United States. With that prospect in mind, Japanese planners began studying the Allies' various blueprints for East Asia after the collapse of the Japanese empire.

---

2. Matsuoka Yōsuke Denki Kankō-kai, *Matsuoka Yōsuke—sono hito to shōgai* (Tokyo: Kōdansha, 1974), 1097.

3. "Hata Shunroku nikki" (The diary of Hata Shunroku), in *Zoku gendai-shi shiryō (4) Riku-gun* (Contemporary History Documents [4] the Army) (Tokyo: Misuzu Shobō, 1983), 329, quoted in Nakayama Takashi, "Nihon no sensō sakusen shidō ni okeru Soren yōin, 1941–45," *Seiji Keizai Shigaku*, no. 333 (March 1994), 44.

Could Japan end both the Pacific and continental theaters of the war while securing a substantial place for the nation in whatever the postwar geopolitical situation might be? This question animated Japanese planners, whose sustained reflections refute their postwar image as drained leaders unable to reflect on Japan's future strategic place. Generally rejecting mere survival as insufficient, planners disagreed about what the future could hold. Some planners envisioned that ending the war with the United States quickly would allow Japan to remain an empire, with Korea if nothing else. More realpolitik-oriented leaders speculated, before the war ended, about whether an alliance with the Soviet Union or one with the United States would best allow Japan to recover quickly. Others argued that Japan ought to remain neutral or play both ends against each other, regardless of the outcome of the war. All these planners confronted fundamental questions about how to end Japan's war to the best effect: to whom ought Japan surrender, in which theater, and at what time? They shared the conviction that choosing the optimal manner and timing of the end of the war could allow Japan to remain a substantial power or, at least, retain the foundations for rebuilding to become a power again.

Diplomatic Charades with the Soviet Union

By September 1943 the Japanese government had adopted two principal policies in regard to the Soviet Union: improving friendship with the Soviet Union in the effort to avoid at all costs a Soviet war against Japan and mediating peace between the Soviet Union and Germany. Although Japan had secured Soviet neutrality in Chinese affairs, it became less likely Germany and the Soviet Union would achieve peace, especially as the Soviet Union gained an increasingly favorable position in the war in Europe. In spite of these circumstances, on August 19, 1944, the Supreme Council for the Direction of the War, under the leadership of Foreign Minister Shigemitsu, opted to strive to separate the Soviet Union from the Anglo-American alliance by inviting the former to join Japan and Germany in the Axis alliance. In attendance were Emperor Hirohito, Prime Minister Koiso, Minister of the Navy Yonai, Foreign Minister Shigemitsu, Minister of War Sugiyama, Chief of Naval Staff Oikawa, Chief of Army Staff Umezu (the core six members of the Council), and Vice Chief of Army Staff Hata, Vice Chief of Naval Staff Itō, Chief of the Cabinet Secretariat Tanaka, and two more representatives from the army and navy.[4]

---

4. "Saikō Sensō Shidō Kaigi yōryō (Gozen Kaigi)" (Minutes of the Supreme Council for the Direction of the War [the Imperial Conference]), August 19, 1944, in RJD, 44–46.

By the summer of 1944, the US military had undertaken the invasion of Normandy against Germany in the European theater, and the war in the Pacific theater had taken a decisive turn against Japan. Japanese leaders began to reexamine Soviet neutrality in Asia, its risks, and possible abrogation. Just two weeks after its creation, the Supreme Council for the Direction of the War met in the presence of Emperor Hirohito on August 19, 1944, and Foreign Minister Shigemitsu Mamoru stated the difficulty of keeping the Soviets on Japan's side.

The accompanying report, "Sekai jōsei handan" (Evaluations of world affairs), distributed at this meeting carried the signatures of all six core members of the Supreme Council for the Direction of the War. Soviet intentions were not too favorable to Japan. Acknowledging the eventual possibility of a US invasion of mainland Japan, the report presented a harsh appraisal of the likelihood of a Soviet-German peace and questioned whether the Soviet Union would maintain neutrality with Japan given Moscow's rising confidence and ambition in world politics. While the Soviets' long-term goal was to increase its political influence in the postwar management of world affairs, its current priority was defeating Germany. To achieve that goal the Soviets would not hesitate to continue collaborating with the United States and Britain through the Grand Alliance in spite of ideological differences. The report continued that Soviet ambitions were focused in the European war theater, including unification of the Slavs and expansion of influence in the Balkans and the Mediterranean. Therefore the Soviet Union should want to maintain peace in the Far East for some time. The report concluded that the Soviet entry into the war against Japan would occur only under extraordinary circumstances.[5] Although the report did not speculate on what might happen after the defeat of Germany, as early as the summer of 1944 the Supreme Council for the Direction of the War discussed the likelihood of the Soviet abrogation of neutrality.

The Japanese Foreign Ministry also investigated Soviet intentions toward Japan. By the fall of 1944, the Foreign Ministry was ostensibly working on a new Soviet policy in a concerted effort to secure comity with the Soviet Union through diplomatic negotiations. Planners at the Foreign Ministry suggested to the Supreme Council for the Direction of the War that Japan should maintain a cautious attitude toward Moscow and prepare for the unpredictable. As early as February 1943, Morishima Gorō, a diplomat at the Moscow Embassy, had warned Tokyo that the Soviets did not intend to remain neutral for very long. To his surprise top officials at the Foreign Ministry responded that this appraisal was already a common assumption in Tokyo. In September 1944 Morishima again returned to Tokyo and briefed top Foreign Ministry officials on the Soviet readiness to enter

5. "Besshi sekai jōsei handan" (Appendix: evaluations of world affairs) (August 19, 1944)," in RJD, 51–53.

the war again Japan. Both times Morishima discovered that his briefing was not considered news.[6]

On September 6 and 7, 1944, the Japanese Foreign Ministry submitted to the Supreme Council for the Direction of the War draft proposals on possible Japanese concessions to Moscow in different global scenarios, including one in which Soviet attitudes toward Japan deteriorate and war becomes a possibility. In the table submitted on September 7, the Foreign Ministry identified six different scenarios: (1) the Neutrality Pact is maintained; (2) the Neutrality Pact is confirmed and the Nonaggression Pact is signed; (3) Soviet-German peace is achieved due to Japanese mediation; (4) Japanese-Guomindang (GMD) peace is achieved due to Soviet mediation; (5) Germany either concludes a single peace or collapses, and Japan attempts to end the war by way of the Neutrality Pact; and (6) the Soviet Union adopts a hostile stance toward Japan due to a change in world affairs and Japan attempts to avoid a Soviet-Japanese war.

In response to these scenarios, the Foreign Ministry recommended considering a wide range of concessions to the Soviet Union: passage rights through the Tsugaru Strait (between Honshū and Hokkaidō, both part of Japan proper), commercial rights in Manchuria, permission for the Soviets to expand in China and other regions in the Japanese empire, rights concerning the North Manchuria Railway, fishing rights, as well as concessions in southern Manchuria and the Kurile islands. Two other possible concessions were Japanese acquiescence to breaking the Anti-Comintern Pact and withdrawal from the Axis Pact. Of these possible concessions, the commercial rights in Manchuria were particularly lucrative. Its main industrial centers had railways, mines, stockpiles of Japanese weapons and equipment, power-generating equipment, transformers, electrical motors, laboratories and hospitals, and the latest machine tools. The Foreign Ministry's proposal remained vague as to how many of these Japanese properties would be transferred to the Soviet Union.

Under the Foreign Ministry's proposal, if the Soviets were to maintain neutrality, Japan would give the Soviets considerable concessions—including passage rights in the Tsugaru Strait along with other miscellaneous rights in Japanese-Manchurian-Soviet trade and commercial issues. If the Soviets were to defeat Germany and mediate peace between Japan and the United States, Japanese concessions would be greater, including passage rights in the Tsugaru Strait, rights in Japanese-Manchurian-Soviet trade and commercial issues, fishing rights, abolition of the Anti-Comintern Pact with Germany, and "Japanese permission" for Soviet influence to expand in China and other areas within the Japanese empire.

---

6. Morishima Gorō, *Kunō suru chū-So taishi-kan* (The Japanese Embassy in Moscow in dilemma) (Tokyo: Minato Shuppan, 1952), 41, 108–10.

TABLE 5.1 A draft proposal on Japanese concessions to the Soviet Union in the process of Soviet-Japanese negotiations

SIX DIFFERENT SCENARIOS

1. The Neutrality Pact is maintained.
2. The Neutrality Pact is confirmed and the Nonaggression Pact is signed.
3. Soviet-German peace is achieved due to Japanese mediation.
4. Japanese-GMD peace is achieved due to Soviet mediation.
5. Germany either concludes a single peace or collapses, and Japan initiates to end the war by way of the Neutrality Pact.
6. The Soviet Union adopts hostile attitudes toward Japan due to a change in world affairs and Japan attempts to avoid the Soviet-Japanese war.

TEN DIFFERENT CONCESSIONS

A. Soviet passage right of the Tsugaru Strait and other miscellaneous rights.
B. Japanese-Manchurian-Soviet trade and commercial issue.
C. Permission for the Soviets' influence to expand in China and other areas within the Japanese empire. (*) indicates Japan's support for the Yan'an regime (the CCP regime) as an added bonus. (**) indicates Japan's approval of Soviet expansion into the Indian Ocean.
D. Soviet right to the North Manchuria Railway.
E. Soviet rights in Manchuria.
F. Soviet fishing rights.
G. Soviet right to southern Sakhalin.
H. Soviet right to the Kurile Islands.
I. Abolition of the Anti-Comintern Pact
J. Abolition of the Axis Pact.

♣	Try to respect Soviet demands as much as possible.
♦	Respect Soviet intentions.
++	Allow most of the concessions.
+	Allow partial concessions.
↕	Consider Soviet demands.
?	Do not include this concession in negotiations.

	1	2	3	4	5	6
A	♣	♦	♦	♦	♦	♦
B	♣	♦	♦	♦	♦	♦
C	+ (**)	++ (*)(**)	+ (**)	♦(*)(**)	♦	♦
D	?	?	?	?	↕	+
E	?	?	?	?	+	+
						INCLUDE TRANSFER OF PART OF MANCHURIA TO SOVIETS
F	?	↕	?	♦	♦	♣
G	?	?	?	?	↕	♦
H	?	?	?	?	↕	↕
I	?	♦	♦	♦	♦	♦
J	?	?	↕	?	♣	♣

Source: "Tai-So shisaku ni kansuru ken (an)" (Concerning the Soviet policy [draft]) (September 7, 1944), in RJD, 172–74.

In this scenario, the most favorable to Japan, the Foreign Ministry did not make Korea a possible concession.

The tepid concessions the Foreign Ministry was prepared to award to the Soviet Union in order to avoid the outbreak of Soviet-Japanese war is curious. The recommended concessions did not differ radically from those of other scenarios. In this worst-case scenario the Japanese showed less enthusiasm for giving the Soviets fishing rights than if the Soviets were to mediate peace with the United States. The major difference in concessions for these cases was that Japan, in order to avoid the war, would be ready to respect Soviet intentions toward southern Sakhalin. Again Korea was not placed on the bargaining table even in an effort to prevent the Soviet entry into the war.[7] The lukewarm enthusiasm expressed by this Foreign Ministry proposal seems to imply that Japan believed it was unlikely they could entice the Soviet Union.

The Imperial Army adopted a slightly different approach to the Soviet Union. In September 1944 when Morishima Gorō briefed Tokyo on the improbability of Soviet-German peace, he added that the Soviet government had not specified what it hoped to gain from Japanese-controlled China. The Japanese government read this as a sign that the Soviet Union hoped to obtain a free hand in Chinese matters in the future and therefore was vigilant about a possible Anglo-American return to China after the war.[8] With this input the Imperial Army considered turning the southern part of Sakhalin and northern part of Manchukuo into bargaining chips in the negotiations with the Soviet Union. They even considered the complete demilitarization of Manchuria.

By late October 1944, when the Japanese Navy suffered a fatal defeat by the US forces at Leyte Gulf, the Japanese government had lost any hope that Japan's continental empire would survive intact. On November 6, 1944, Stalin called Japan an aggressor in his anniversary speech commemorating the Bolshevik revolution. Ten days later when the Supreme Council for the Direction of the War met, Lieutenant General Hata Hikosaburō, vice chief of staff of the Imperial General Headquarters, expressed to Prime Minister Koiso Kuniaki that the Soviet Union would sooner or later nullify the neutrality act.[9] The Ministry of Foreign Affairs shared this judgment. About that time Japanese diplomats in Europe began giving Tokyo regular intelligence reports on Soviet intentions and assessments about the timing of an attack on Manchuria.[10]

---

7. "Tai-So shisaku ni kansuru ken (an)" (Concerning the Soviet policy [draft]) (September 7, 1944), in RJD, 172–74.

8. See the entry of September 21, 1944, in TSWJ, vol. 2, 586–87.

9. See the entry of November 16, 1944, in TSWJ, vol. 2, 608–9.

10. "Dai-Niji Ōshū Taisen kankei ikken—sengo keiei mondai" (The Second European Great War—postwar management) (1944), especially vol. 3 [A 7-0-0-8-43]; "Dai-Niji Ōshū Taisen kankei

When the Supreme Council for the Direction of the War met between May 11 and 14, 1945, its members discussed the final stage of Soviet policy. They agreed to initiate a new round of negotiations with Moscow. The ostensible objectives were to demonstrate that Japan had tried its utmost to prevent Soviet entry into the war against Japan, foster pro-Japanese attitudes in the Soviet Union, and secure Soviet peace mediation in concluding the war. To encourage serious Soviet engagement with these requests, Foreign Minister Tōgō Shigenori suggested the need to demonstrate Japan's readiness to make larger concessions to the Soviet Union than ever before: to relinquish the southern part of Sakhalin and Japanese fishing rights, to open the Tsugaru Strait to Soviet passage, to transfer the North Manchuria Railway to the Soviet Union, to recognize the Soviet sphere of influence in Inner Mongolia, to lease Lushunkou and Dalian to the Soviet Union, and even to transfer northern parts of the Kurile islands and neutralize southern Manchuria. In spite of all these extravagant offers, Tōgō and the rest of the Japanese leaders agreed that Japan would keep Korea even after the war.[11]

Considering that authorities in Korea had already begun studying international impacts of the demise of Japan's colonial administration, the Japanese government did not appear too serious in "purchasing Soviet assistance in peace mediation" with these offers. As historian Constantine V. Pleshakov explains, these Japanese concessions were similar to those President Franklin Roosevelt offered Stalin at Yalta and that they were also exactly where Stalin wanted to establish a Soviet sphere of influence in East Asia. Pleshakov argues that Stalin chose not to accept these Japanese offers for two reasons: he wanted postwar friendship with the West, and he wanted to take revenge against Japan for the humiliation incurred in the Russo-Japanese War. Pleshakov nonetheless speculates about what would have happened had Stalin accepted the Japanese offers, decided not to enter the war against Japan, and mediated the war's end with the United States.[12] Not only the CCP and the GMD but also the US government, all wary of the prospect of a growing Soviet preeminence in the Far East, might have counteroffered different concessions to the Soviet Union, inadvertently turning Stalin into the kingmaker of the Far East at this final stage of the war.

The Soviet reception of these Japanese offers was cold. In June 1945, during talks with Soviet ambassador Yakov Malik, former prime minister Hirota Kōki offered to neutralize Manchuria and relinquish Japanese fishing rights, in exchange

---

ikken—sengo keiei mondai Ei-Bei-Soren kanren" (The Second European Great War: postwar management—UK-US-Soviet relations) (1944) [A-7-0-0-8-43-1], DRO.

11. JC, vol. 2, 448–53.

12. Constantine Pleshakov, "Taiheiyō Sensō: Sutārin no ketsudan" (The Pacific War and Stalin's Decision), in Hosoya Chihiro, Honma Nagayo, Iriye Akira, and Hatano Sumio, eds., *Taiheiyō Sensō* (The Pacific War) (Tokyo: Tokyo Daigaku Shuppan-kai, 1993), 191–94.

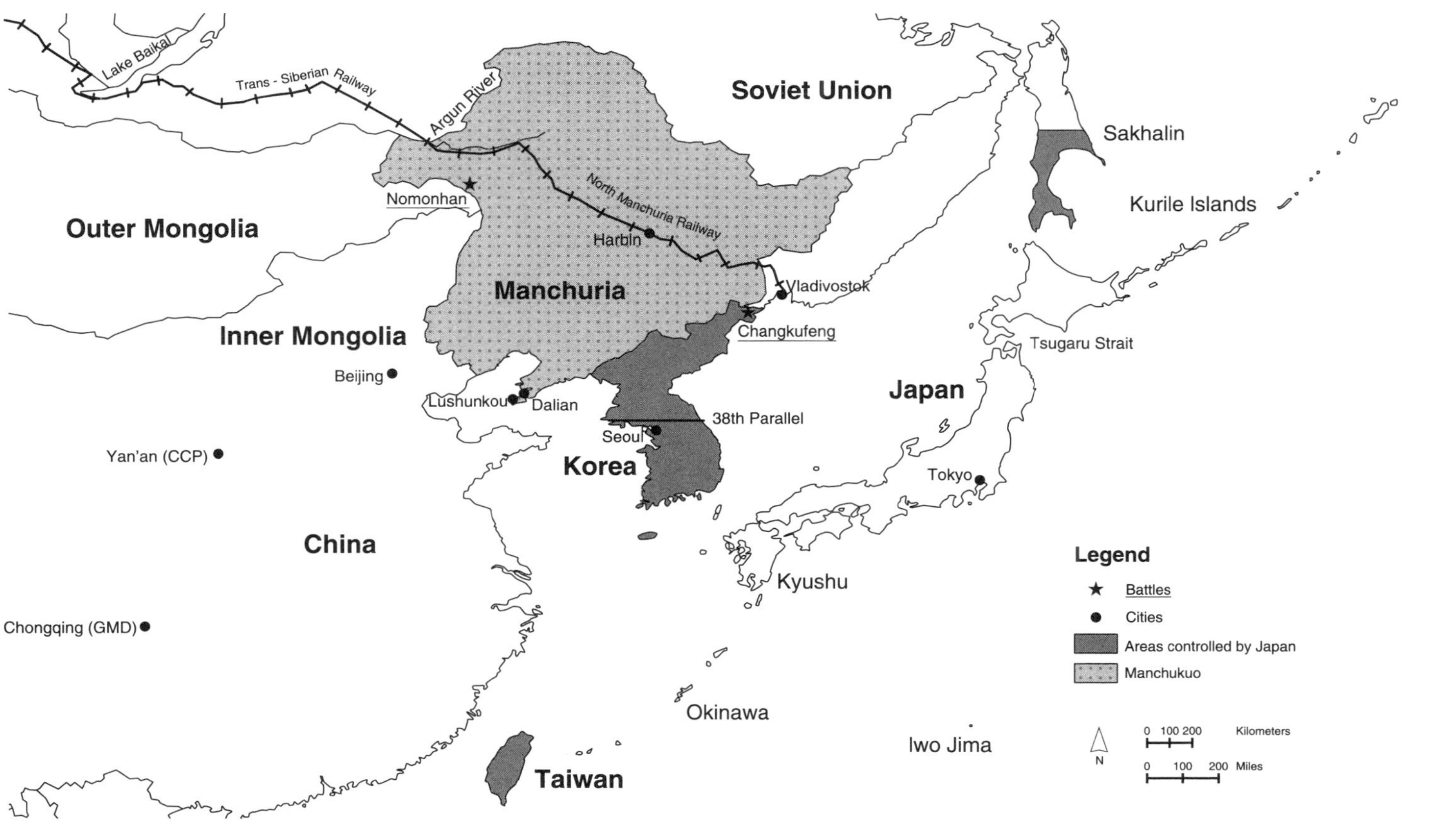

MAP 5.1 The Japanese Empire with Regard to Soviet Considerations in World War II, Based on ESR1 World Data, 1945. In May 1945, Foreign Minister Tōgō proposed a list of maximum possible concessions to the Soviets, including the North Manchuria Railway, leases of Lushunkou and Dalian, and the opening of the Tsugaru Strait for Russian passage.

Sources: Myongsuu Kong, Colgate University, and Takashi Yasukawa, Tokyo.

for the Soviet Union supplying Japan with oil. The neutralization of Manchuria and the subsequent withdrawal of the Japanese Army after the war were the greatest wartime concessions Japan was willing to make to the Soviet Union.[13] Nevertheless, the June 29, 1945, meeting in which the Japanese made the offer to neutralize Manchuria was the last because Malik, who had agreed to convey the Japanese proposal to the Soviet government, was unable to meet Hirota again because of his health problems. In July Satō Naotake, Japanese ambassador to the Soviet Union, tried to follow up on the talks with Foreign Minister Molotov but failed. That same month saw the failure of Prince Konoe Fumimaro's attempt to visit Moscow as a secret envoy to request peace mediation between Japan and the United States.

Throughout these negotiations with Moscow, Japanese policymakers were actually never as desperate to buy Soviet favor as postwar scholars have argued. Despite its apparent willingness to explore wide-ranging concessions to the Soviet Union, the Japanese government never included Korea in any list of offers. As Pleshakov points out, the Japanese government, aware of Imperial Russia's historical interest in the Far East, suspected Stalin's territorial ambition for the Korean Peninsula as a gateway to warm water, and they attempted to predict his next geopolitical moves.[14] The Governor-General's Office in Korea had already reported to the Imperial Diet in September 1944 that their monitoring of the Soviet Union's interactions with Korean communists suggested that the Soviets had no interest in an independent Korea. If the Japanese government had been desperate enough to obtain Soviet assistance in achieving peace, it could have made Korea a concession. But Tokyo did not make this choice in its diplomatic game with Moscow.

Japan's half-hearted approach to the Soviet Union can also be seen in Ambassador Satō's experience. During this critical time in Soviet-Japanese diplomacy, Tokyo instructed him not to initiate any diplomatic overtures with Moscow. Satō did not initially share Tokyo's assessment of Moscow, so it was late July 1945 when he finally realized that the Soviet Union would not mediate peace for Japan. He

---

13. "NiSso gaikō kōshō kiroku" (Records of Japanese-Soviet diplomatic negotiations) in JC, vol. 2, 572–75 and 579–81. Nakayama Takashi, "Nihon no sensō sakusen shidō ni okeru Soren yōin, 1941–1945," *Seiji Keizai Shigaku* (March 1994), 49, 52. For English-language scholarship on these Japanese concessions (with slightly different listings from Nakayama's), see George Lensen, *The Strange Neutrality: Soviet-Japanese Relations during the Second World War, 1941–1945* (Tallahassee, FL: The Diplomatic Press, 1972), 134–35, especially footnote (b).

14. For the view of Stalin as a geopolitical tactician, see Constantine V. Pleshakov, "Taiheiyō Sensō: Stārin no ketsudan"(The Pacific War and Stalin's Decision), in Hosoya, Honma, Iriye, Hatano, eds., *Taiheiyō Sensō*, 185–89; also see his "Yaruta Taisei no keisei to Soren" (Formation of the Yalta system and the Soviet Union), in Hosoya Chihiro, Iriye Akira, Gotō Ken'ichi, and Hatano Sumio, eds., *Taiheiyō Sensō no shūketsu: Ajia Taiheiyō no sengo keisei* (The close of the Pacific War and a formation of postwar Asia and the Pacific) (Tokyo: Kashiwa Shobō, 1997), 412–18.

tried to convince the Japanese government of his "critical discovery," a "profound insight" for which he later received many accolades in the postwar period.[15] In truth the government in Tokyo had long been preparing for this possibility.

In spite of his important post, Satō was kept out of the loop. An elite diplomat to France, Switzerland, Luxemburg, and Belgium, Satō enjoyed an aristocratic lifestyle in Moscow. He was a liberal diplomat with an old-fashioned samurai spirit and a deep love for Western culture. His flamboyance and lack of political or ideological commitment to any single value or principle made him peculiarly suited to be the Japanese ambassador to Moscow during the murkiest time in the war.[16]

Japanese Peace Feelers and the United States

In early 1945, while the Japanese government played diplomatic charades with the Soviet Union, a small circle of individuals began to make various attempts to come to peace with the United States in an anti-Soviet spirit. So-called "peace feelers," this group of Japanese military and diplomatic officers as well as journalists and businessmen were stationed in the neutral nations in Europe and had various connections with several European power brokers. They initiated private operations through channels in Sweden and Switzerland, and they all proposed that Japan forge a truce with the United States as soon as possible. The Japanese government did not commission them: their efforts were voluntary, local, and unrelated to one another. There was no uniform command system orchestrating their actions. Moreover, given their diverse careers and backgrounds, it is hard to detect any common ideals or visions of a future that might have united them. The US government ultimately determined that they did not represent formal offers of surrender from Tokyo. In the end their efforts with the United States came to naught, just as Japanese diplomacy gained nothing from the Soviet Union.

---

15. Upon Japan's surrender, Satō was detained at the embassy until April 1946. According to his memoir, the detention was never too painful, since he was allowed to keep his favorite chef with him and continue the same lifestyle as before. After he returned to Japan, he successfully ran for the Japanese Diet and was appointed chairman of the Upper House. He believed in the "middle-of-the-road" course for postwar Japan. He befriended the Supreme Commander for the Allied Powers (SCAP) leaders, promoted Japan's participation in the United Nations, vehemently opposed leftist propaganda, supported anticommunist bills, proposed emperor worship through Shintoism, yet rejected right-wing ultranationalism.

16. Morishima Gorō, *Kunō suru chū-So taishi-kan*, 26–27. Also see Satō Naotake, *Futatsu no Roshia* (Two faces of Russia) (Tokyo: Sekai no Nihon Sha, 1948); Satō Naotake, *Kaiko hachijyū-nen* (Reminiscence of my eighty years) (Tokyo: Jiji Tsūshin Sha, 1963); Kurihara Ken, ed., *Satō Naotake no menboku* (Satō Naotake's pride) (Tokyo: Hara Shobō, 1981).

In the postwar period these peace feelers received accolades for their heroic attempts to end the war, make peace with the United States, and spare the nation from annihilation. Scholars have argued whether the United States would have eventually succeeded in bringing Japan to capitulation had it kept communication alive with them. The motives and goals of those peace feelers, however, were not as simple and altruistic as ending the war in the Pacific theater. They hoped that the United States would allow Japan to preserve its national polity under the emperor in exchange for Japan's capitulation. They also believed that the United States would allow postwar Japan to redevelop as a capitalist-industrialized liberal power; therefore, they reasoned that since Japan had no natural resources it should be allowed to retain Korea and Taiwan after the war in order to secure raw materials and foodstuffs. In this regard their vision was congruent with the government's Soviet diplomacy in that both resolved to keep Korea as Japan's territory. Since those peace feelers were convinced that the integration of an economically stable Japan into a US-led world market would benefit both Japan and the United States, they were hopeful about their peace-making attempts.

Their approach was reminiscent of Japan's diplomacy in the 1920s that followed Wilsonianism—a cooperative approach to capitalist development of the world adopted by the great powers at both the Versailles and Washington Conferences in lieu of competitive imperialism. Aware even during World War II of the prospect of US-Soviet rivalry, the peace feelers anticipated that the United States, in order to ward off the Soviet and communist menaces, would see a need to make peace with and realign with Japan. In this scenario the United States, in the spirit of cooperative imperialism, would condone Japan's continued rule of Taiwan and Korea. The peace feelers reckoned that the US government would seriously consider their terms out of its support for a revival of capitalist Japan and also out of fear of the Soviet Union's rise.

Their early attempts began in mid-September 1944, after the fall of Saipan, the keystone of Japan's inner defense perimeter. Suzuki Bunshirō, a Japanese journalist, approached his friend Widar Bagge, a Swedish diplomat in Tokyo to discuss whether and how Sweden, a neutral nation in World War II, might mediate between Japan and Anglo-America in an effort to end the war. Suzuki suggested that Japan could renounce all the territories occupied during the war, including Manchuria. Korea and Taiwan, however, should remain under the Japanese control because, according to Suzuki, they were Japanese territories long before the hostilities began. After both Shigemitsu and Tōgō, the former and current foreign ministers, made known their support for Swedish mediation, Bagge returned to Stockholm in May 1945 and met with Okamoto Suemasa, the Japanese minister to Sweden, to prepare for a clandestine operation. Meanwhile Major-General Onodera Makoto, military attaché in Stockholm, initiated a separate peace attempt by approaching Prince Carl Bernadotte, a minor member of the Swedish royal family. Unable to coordinate the separate attempts by the army and the Foreign Ministry, much less their terms of negotiations, Foreign Minister Tōgō requested that Bagge not initiate any contact with any party. Thus the Bagge operation came to end by May 23. The Onodera operation ended as well.[17]

Although Onodera never specified proposed terms for peace, Bagge met at least once with Herschel V. Johnson, the US minister to Sweden, and conveyed Japanese desires for peace.[18] According to Okamoto's memoir, Bagge told Johnson about the Japanese hope of retaining Korea and Taiwan as territories after the war and personally endorsed the idea based on Japan's "excellent" record of administration in Korea and Taiwan. Johnson disagreed, referring to the Cairo Declaration of November 1943, which had already determined the disposition of the Japanese colonies after the war. Under the Cairo Declaration, Great Britain, the United States, and China had jointly agreed that Taiwan should be restored to the Republic of China and Korea should become free and independent "in due course."[19] Furthermore Johnson added that if the Koreans proved to lack the ability for self-governance, the United States would provide them with proper aid and guidance toward eventual independence.[20] The US saw absolutely no reason why Japan should be allowed to remain the "leader" of Asia.

The Japanese peace feelers showed resolve in keeping Korea in other negotiation attempts with the United States that took place in Switzerland. In late April 1945 Commander Fujimura Yoshirō, a Japanese naval attaché in Bern, approached Allen Dulles, Bern station chief of the Office of Strategic Services (OSS), a US intelligence agency established during World War II to coordinate espionage activities, and attempted to propose initiating peace discussions. In May 1945 Fujimura commissioned Dr. Friedrich Wilhelm Hack, the German arms trader and authority on the Far East, to convey Japan's conditions for terminating the war to Dulles. According to Fujimura's own account, he insisted that postsurrender Japan should retain Korea and Taiwan. He hoped that Hack would explain to Dulles on his behalf that, just like New Mexico after its annexation to the United

17. JC, vol. 1, 328–30.

18. Kobayashi Tatsuo, "Tai-Suwēden wahei kōsaku" (Peace operation in Sweden), in Nihon Gaikō Gakkai ed. (Society for the Study of Japanese Diplomacy), *Taiheiyō Sensō shūketu ron* (On the conclusion of the Pacific War) (Tokyo: Tokyo Daigaku Shuppan-kai, 1958), 493.

19. The Cairo Declaration (November 27, 1943) states as follows: "Japan shall be stripped of all the islands in the Pacific which she has seized or occupied since the beginning of the first World War in 1914, and that all the territories Japan has stolen from the Chinese, such as Manchuria, Formosa, and the Pescadores, shall be restored to the Republic of China. . . . The aforesaid three great powers, mindful of the enslavement of the people of Korea, are determined that in due course Korea shall become free and independent."

20. Kobayashi Tatsuo, "Tai-Suwēden wahei kōsaku," 500. Also see JC, vol. 1, 342.

States, Korea and Taiwan had developed culturally and economically as they were integrated into Japanese territory. Japan also depended on Korea and Taiwan's agricultural production to feed its populace. Although Hack replied the disposition of Korea had already been determined at Cairo and Yalta, Fujimura was steadfast that Hack should press Dulles to acknowledge the geographical inseparability of Japan and Korea. Specifically Fujimura emphasized that Japan could not supply itself with essential foodstuffs and was dependent on Korea for sugar and rice. He further insisted that Japan needed to retain some of its merchant marine for necessary food imports.[21]

From early June 1945, Lieutenant General Okamoto Kiyotomi, an army attaché seeing no future for Germany after its unconditional surrender in the previous month, began pondering peace overtures with the United States. Toward that end he worked in Basel with Kitamura Kōjirō, a director of the Bank for International Settlements, and another bank official named Yoshimura Kan. He kept the Imperial General Headquarters updated with their peace-making efforts until early August. In mid-June Kitamura and Yoshimura met Per Jacobsson, a Swedish economic adviser to Kitamura, and indicated that the Japanese government might negotiate for peace on two conditions: that the emperor institution and the imperial Japanese constitution remain intact and that Korea and Taiwan remain Japanese territories. Subsequently Jacobsson met with Allen Dulles in Wiesbaden, Germany. The American record has a slightly different version of events. It indicates the Yoshimura-Kitamura-Jacobsson meeting took place in mid-July. According to the American version, when Yoshimura and Kitamura raised the question of maintaining Japanese territorial integrity, they apparently did not mean to include Manchuria, Korea, or Taiwan. Throughout the discussions with Jacobsson, the Japanese officials stressed only two points: the preservation of the emperor and the possibility of returning to the constitution promulgated in 1889. Either way Dulles did not comment on the disposition of Japanese territories.[22]

Meanwhile Kase Shun'ichi, the Japanese minister in Bern, had informed the Foreign Ministry of his own peace overtures. On May 11 Kase contacted an anti-Nazi German source with connections to the OSS and made known his desire to arrange for a termination of war through direct talks with the United States and Britain rather than through negotiations with the Soviet Union. Kase explained

21. JC, vol. 2, 423–24. Also see the American record on Fujimura's request, "Confidential: Memorandum for the President (4 June 1945)," NARA, Record Group 226, Microfilm Publication Number 1642, "Records of the OSS: Washington Director's Office Administrative Files, 1941–1945," Roll 62, Frames 870–72.

22. JC, vol. 2, 412–13. The American source is "Confidential: The Memorandum for the President: Japanese Peace Feelers (16 July 1945)," NARA, Record Group 226, Microfilm Publication Number 1642, Roll 62, Frames 893–95.

that he did not want to see Soviet prestige increased in East Asia as a result of Soviet peace mediation between Japan and the United States. No longer mentioning any desire to keep parts of Japan's colonies, Kase added that Japan's only condition for surrender would be to retain the emperor as a safeguard against communist revolution at home.[23] In early June Kase met Kitamura, learned of Lieutenant General Okamoto's separate peace effort, and acknowledged his effort. Then in late June Kase contacted Naval Attaché Commander Fujimura and instructed him to work with him. Kase's personal attempt to coordinate the intragovernmental actions hardly meant that the Foreign Ministry synchronized its peace effort with the Imperial Army and Navy, because around that time it ostensibly was seeking Soviet mediation for peace.

Japanese peace feelers outside of Sweden and Switzerland also made attempts to contact the United States. On April 11, 1945 an OSS representative relayed to the White House information reportedly sent to the Vatican on April 6. Lorenzo Tatewaki Toda, the Japanese Apostolic Delegate in Yokohama, had proposed to "comfort" the Japanese emperor with a message that "the Holy See will not abandon its attempt at mediation" of the war in the Pacific.[24] On May 7, 1945, the OSS representative in Lisbon reported that Inoue Masutarō, counselor at the Japanese legation in Portugal, had approached and asked a local agent to contact US representatives and to convey Japan's readiness to cease hostilities based on shared American and Japanese interests against the Soviet Union.[25] In the end the US government decided that the peace feelers did not properly represent the Japanese government and chose not to pursue communications with them.

Historians have often considered the actions of these Japanese peace feelers as the best and most heroic attempts to end the war in a prompt manner since, they argue, Japan could hardly have persuaded the Soviet Union to be neutral or to mediate peace with the United States.[26] This reasoning makes sense only if the United States at that stage of World War II had been ready to recognize Japan as a possible buffer against communism in light of growing Soviet power in Asia and if they had been willing to acquiesce to Japan's demands.

Given Washington's declared refusal to negotiate a conditional peace with the Axis powers, a shared anticommunism alone would not have driven Washington

23. "Top Secret: Memorandum for the President (12 May 1945)," NARA, Record Group 226, Microfilm Publication Number 1642, Roll 62, Frames 834–36.

24. "Confidential: Memorandum for the President (11 April, 1945)," Central Intelligence Agency, Library, Center for the Study of Intelligence, "Memoranda for the President: Japanese Feelers," available online at https://www.cia.gov/library/center-for-the-study-of-intelligence/kent-csi/vol9no3/html/v09i3a06p_0001.htm.

25. "Top Secret: Memorandum for the President (31 May 1945)," NARA, Record Group 226, Microfilm Publication Number 1642, Roll 62, Frames 861–63.

26. Akira Iriye, *Power and Culture*, 170 and 220–25.

to seek a mutual friendship with Japan. The Japanese peace feelers should have known that diplomatic efforts to terminate warfare in exchange for the right to retain Korea and Taiwan had little chance of success with the United States. The US and British governments had already declared at the Casablanca Conference of January 1943 that they would fight to deprive Germany and Japan of all military power in order to achieve a lasting world peace. The only acceptable peace with the Axis Powers would be one of "unconditional surrender." The peace feelers' hopes that the US government might be willing to work toward a negotiated peace despite its Casablanca declaration rested on their estimation that Washington's annoyance at the prospect of Moscow's intervention in the Pacific War would lead it to deal directly with Japan. The peace feelers should have kept in mind that the Soviets were planning to come to war against Japan without Washington's overt objection.

More problematic was the peace feelers' insistence that Japan be allowed to keep Korea after the war, the same stipulation Foreign Ministry made in negotiations with the Soviet Union. Japanese authorities in Korea were by then fully aware of the difficulty of retaining Korea as a colony because of pressures within and without. With Soviet influence growing stronger on the peninsula, these peace feelers might have hoped that the US government would tacitly approve Japan's continuing presence in Korea as an anticommunist buffer. Unlike earlier in the twentieth century, the United States no longer anticipated Japan would remain an imperialist power after the war. They did not expect that Japan, already exhausted to the point of collapse, would have the resources to wage an anticommunist struggle from Korea. It did not seem to occur to the peace feelers that the US government might prefer to contain communism by placing Korea under its direct control after the war. Moreover, the US government was as ambitious about establishing control over Japan as creating a new order in East Asia. These peace feelers failed to understand that the United States, regardless of its attitude toward the Soviet Union, had no intention of welcoming Japan back to the traditional Wilsonian world order, under which the League of Nations had acknowledged the legitimacy of Japan's colonial empire. Their peace proposals to the United States lacked realistic evaluations of Japan's international standing and its capabilities in the last phase of the war.

To elucidate the visions and calculations that might have motivated these peace feelers to favor accommodation with the United States, the case of Major-General Onodera Makoto, military attaché to Sweden, may be of some help. His earlier involvement in Operation Stella Polaris, the anti-Soviet operation initiated by the Finns, had drawn him to the network of pro-US Europeans, which gave him a chance to consider peace with the United States. Operation Stella Polaris was a clandestine operation in which Finnish signals intelligence records, equipment, and personnel were transported into Sweden in the fall of 1944. Finland was about to surrender to the Soviet Union and the possibility of Soviet occupation was imminent. In early September 1944, Captain Albert Wilman, assistant attaché of the Finnish Navy visited Onodera, a colleague within a circle of Axis officers stationed in Stockholm. Wilman requested Japan's assistance in financing Finnish guerrilla warfare against the invading Soviet forces. In exchange he proposed that the Finnish Army would transfer all the signals intelligence records, including American and Soviet, in its possession to Japan and continue to provide Japan with Soviet-related intelligence. Wilman added that several Finnish military officers were already inclined toward supporting the United States. According to a postwar memoir written by his wife, Onodera reported this offer to the Imperial General Headquarters in Tokyo and is said to have received approval for assisting the Finnish Army. Though he kept this transaction a secret from the Japanese consul in Sweden for fear of leaks, Onodera is said to have handed 300,000 kroner to the Finnish Army as requested.[27]

As this episode shows, Onodera's anti-Soviet activities did not arise from an active pro-American stance in support of capitalism and American-style democracy. Neither did he seem to be acting from an informed perspective about the situation within Japan's colonial empire or the war in China. These European operations did not emerge from nor engender a concrete vision of Asia after the war.

Moscow-Washington Dissonance and Competing Visions for a Postwar World

With the offers to the United States by various peace feelers faltering, and the possibility of Soviet entry into the war ever more likely, Japan seemed without recourse. Some who favored peace negotiations with the United States became vocally anticommunist and attempted to purge ostensibly pro-Soviet leaders. Yoshida Shigeru, former ambassador to Italy and Britain and head of the so-called "Yohansen group," a loose cluster of anticommunist and pro-Anglo-American peace feelers in Japan, was a central figure in this movement. As part of his "pacifist plot" to end the war with the United States, he led the drafting of what became known as the Konoe memorandum.

In mid-February 1945 Prince Konoe Fumimaro alerted Emperor Hirohito in this memorandum to the danger of communist revolution under Soviet leadership in China, Manchuria, Korea, Taiwan, and Japan. In a private meeting with

27. Onodera Yuriko, "Stella Polaris sakusen to Nihon (Operation Stella Polaris and Japan)," *Gunji Shigaku* 27, no. 4 (March 1992): 73–79.

Emperor Hirohito, Konoe accused the military group Tōsei-ha (Control faction) of scheming to foment communist revolution in Japan. To prevent such a tragedy, Prince Konoe urged Emperor Hirohito to end the war before the Soviet entry and to make peace with the United States.[28] Subsequently the military police arrested Yoshida for slandering the Imperial Army as overly pro-Soviet, a position, the claim went, that would likely drive Japan to annihilation. Even Emperor Hirohito is said to have been bewildered by this oversimplified view of the Imperial Army. Thanks to General Anami Korechika's final judgment after a long deliberation within the Imperial Army, Yoshida was never prosecuted. After his release from prison, Yoshida remained politically nonactive until the war's end, when he eventually served as prime minister several times in postwar Japan.

Yoshida and Konoe's "wisdom" hardly derived from the mainstream view within the wartime Japanese government. Since Konoe had earlier endorsed the four-nation alliance with the Soviet Union, his turnabout at this late stage in the war intrigued the inner political circle. An aristocrat who had studied socialism in his youth, Konoe became pan-Asianist when he witnessed Japan being denied full access to the Anglo-American-led world order at the Paris Peace Conference and at the Washington and London Naval Conferences. Given this history, Konoe's motivations in proposing friendship with the United States may not have necessarily been ideological. As historian Torii Tami has pointed out, Konoe may have issued this warning only to document himself as an anticommunist crusader and to secure his survival in the foreseeable event of American conquest and occupation of Japan. Kido Kōichi, Lord Keeper of the Privy Seal, even suspected that Prince Konoe was plotting to escape from war responsibility by acting pro-American and by ascribing war crimes to pro-Soviet officers within the Imperial Army.[29]

Konoe's ascription of unified communist leadership to Moscow also looks strange given that the view of a monolithic communist force had by then been largely dismissed within the government and military. After having conducted studies of Chinese, Korean, and Japanese communists and their relationships with Moscow as well with each other, the Japanese military and civil government had concluded that the various national communists differed in ideological interpretations, goals, methodologies, and leadership. It is doubtful, therefore, that Konoe believed in Moscow's singular ability to mastermind all communist movements across Asia. Konoe's noncommittal attitude toward Moscow became apparent when five months later, in early July 1945, he agreed to act as a secret

---

28. Torii Tami, *Shōwa 20-nen* (1945), vol. 1, no. 2 (Tokyo: Sōshi Sha, 1986), chapter 7.
29. Torii Tami, *Shōwa 20-nen*, vol. 1, no. 2 (Tokyo: Sōshi Sha, 1986), 57–77.

envoy to Moscow to request peace mediation between Japan and the United States.

Unsurprisingly the Konoe memorandum failed to stir up anti-Soviet and pro-US sentiment within the government. The Japanese government, instead of pondering capitulation, cautiously studied how the United States and the Soviet Union were competing for control in postwar East Asia and came to favor a "balance-off-our enemies" strategy for ending the war. Even in the final stage of the war, government and military officials, as well as civilians, viewed world politics and international relations not along ideological lines but as modulated by US-Soviet power dynamics. Japanese politicians had earlier tried and failed to position the Soviet Union as a deterrent against the United States by way of the four-nation alliance. Acutely aware that the Soviets would likely break neutrality given the changing war circumstances in Europe, Japanese experts inside and outside the decision-making loop shifted to investigating how to situate Japan halfway between the United States and the Soviet Union amid their growing differences regarding the postwar disposition of East Asia.

From the outset of the Pacific War, Japanese intellectuals offered proposals on how to keep equal distance from the United States and the Soviet Union. On December 8, 1941, the day of Pearl Harbor (Japan time), Kokusai-hō Gakkai (Japanese Society of International Law) became a foundation endowed by businesses and other groups to offer a forum for discussing a peacekeeping mechanism for the Greater East Asia Coprosperity Sphere. Yokota Kisaburō, a law professor at Tokyo Imperial University and a future chief justice of Japan's Supreme Court (1960–66), recommended that postwar Japan should participate in a collective security system under a joint leadership of the United States, Britain, and the Soviet Union. Yokota later viewed the United Nations as a positive departure from the League of Nations because the newer organization's member nations had diverse ideological systems, diplomatic styles, and worldviews. Although Yokota suspected that the growing US-Soviet rift would impede the smooth operation of the United Nations, he endorsed the revolutionary new system of international laws, including the concept of collective security, and began drafting a blueprint for a "pacifist" Japan as a member of the United Nations.[30] Ishibashi Tanzan, a liberal procapitalist economist, also recommended that postwar Japan join such a collective peacekeeping organization. He suggested that Japan pay extra attention to the intentions of *both* the United States and the Soviet Union, try to

---

30. See Takenaka Yoshihiko, "Kokusaihō-gakusha no 'sengo kōsō'—'DaiTōA kokusai hō' kara 'Kokuren shinkō' e"(Postwar visions of wartime scholars in international law: from the pursuit of the greater East Asia international law to idealization of the United Nation), *Kokusai Seiji* (International Relations), vol. 109 (May 1995).

maintain a balance of power between the two, and promote a new open-door policy in the Far East.[31]

Since the outbreak of war in Europe in 1939, the Japanese Foreign Ministry had investigated Allied intentions for the postwar world order. The Foreign Ministry had amassed arguments, analyses, and information on forecasts for World War II dispatched by their diplomats stationed in Germany, the Soviet Union, and neutral nations such as Sweden, Switzerland, Vatican City, Portugal, and Turkey. Japanese diplomats regularly sent copies of significant articles printed in major Western (predominantly English-language) newspapers and journals. The list of newspapers and journals was long and extensive, including the *New York Times, Daily Mail, Reader's Digest, Daily Telegraph, Manchester Guardian, Observer, Times* (of London), *Sunday Times, News Chronicle, Saturday Evening Post, Life, New York American, Svenska Dagbladet, TASS, Pravda*, and *La Nación*.

The Imperial General Headquarters in Tokyo also had its own channel of gathering paper-based information from abroad. As early as October 1942, the Imperial General Headquarters entrusted three Japanese businessmen—Honma Jirō of Mitsui Steamship Company, Satō Kichinosuke of Mitsui & Company, and Inoue Yōichirō of Mitsubishi Corporation—to serve as part-time military attachés in Stockholm.[32] The Imperial General Headquarters received reports from them and other military attachés stationed in neutral nations such as Argentine, Spain, and Switzerland. Even the general headquarters of the China Expeditionary Army relied on periodicals and newspapers for the latest information, in addition to regular espionage activities and secret telegrams. The China Expeditionary Army created a monthly list of latest news from the war theaters in the Pacific and also Europe (especially the German-Soviet war) as well as from Japan, the United States, Britain, China, the Soviet Union, Germany, and Italy, and also regions such as the Middle East, South America, and Nanpō (Southeast Asia and South West Pacific). After synthesizing them, the China Expeditionary Army attempted to put together a snapshot of global trends.

The government regarded the media as an important source of information that could supplement intelligence gathering. Unlike the top secrets obtained via espionage activities and decoding signals intelligence, information from sources such as newspapers, magazines, and public broadcasting—news analyses, editorials, opinions from the readers, and even cartoons, jokes, and satires about events

31. Masuda Hiroshi, "DaiTōA Kyōei-ken hitei to henkaku no ronri—Ishibashi Tanzan no baai" (Arguments concerning a rejection of the Greater East Asia Coprosperity Sphere and a radical departure from it—a case of Ishibashi Tanzan), in Nakamura Katsunori, ed., *Kindai Nihon seiji no shosō* (Aspects of modern Japanese politics) (Tokyo: Keiō Tsūshin, 1989), 194–97.

32. Onodera Yuriko, "Stella Polaris sakusen to Nihon (Operation Stella Polaris and Japan)," *Gunji Shigaku* 27, no. 4 (March 1992): 74.

and leaders of the war—provided a window to both official and public mentalities concerning the war. The Japanese analysts looked for traces of white propaganda in these paper-based media. According to navy intelligence officer Lieutenant Colonel Imai Nobuhiko, intelligence analysts not only determined the accuracy of information but also attempted to detect layers of intentionality behind the dissemination of news to the world.[33]

The information thus obtained was not wasted. Since the Foreign Ministry, the Imperial Army, and Navy, shared the latest news from Allied media among themselves, the amount of information available to the Japanese decision-makers was considerable. They used these sources to put together comprehensive studies of Allied plans for the postwar world order. Based on the latest world news, they formed the "balance-off" prediction—that neither the Soviet Union nor the United States would be hegemonic in postwar East Asia. For example, the Foreign Ministry's secret document "Bei-Ei-So sengo taisaku no kenkyū" (Studies on US-British-Soviet approaches to postwar management), covering the period from July 1943 to February 1944, analyzed the three nations' respective war goals as well as their visions and plans for the postwar world order. In putting together these reports, the Foreign Ministry also referred to research by the TōA Kenkyūjo (East Asian Institute) and the Dōmei News Agency.[34]

Moreover, the Foreign Ministry regularly published and distributed news summaries and digests on international relations to a limited nongovernment audience. The research department (*chōsa-bu*) of the Foreign Ministry published monthly journals: *Kokusai Jijyō* (International affairs), which analyzed trends in world politics primarily in Europe; and *So-Mō sōsho* (The Soviet-Mongol series), which analyzed Soviet domestic politics and diplomacy toward the United States.

Informed by these sources, leading national newspapers and intellectual journals such as *Kaizō* and *Gaikō Jihō* (Diplomatic review) were able to keep Japanese readers abreast of political dynamics in Europe and Asia. The standard of news made available to the Japanese public contradicts the conventional image of wartime Japanese as kept in the dark and fed only government propaganda. During the war the Special Higher Police (Tokkō) in each prefecture routinely produced investigative reports on domestic "peace preservation" (i.e., control of antigovernmental thoughts and behaviors) for the Home Ministry. These reports

---

33. Kotani Ken, "Nihon-gun to interijensu—seikou to shippai no jirei kara" (The Japanese military and intelligence activities—cases of successes and failures), *Bōei Kenkyūjo Kiyō* (the National Institute for Defense Studies Report) 11, no. 1 (November 2008): 45–49; Ken Kotani, *Japanese Intelligence in World War II* (Oxford: Osprey, 2009), 92–93.

34. Gaimushō Chōsa-kyoku Dai-ichi kachō (First Section Chief, Research Department, Foreign Ministry), "Bei-Ei-So sengo taisaku no kenkyū, 1943-nen 7-gatsu yori 1944-nen 2-gatsu ni itaru" (Studies on US-British-Soviet approaches to postwar management, from July 1943 to February 1944) (February 1944), available at Waseda University Library, Tokyo.

showed that a diverse range of citizens speculated on Japan's dealings with the United States, the Soviet Union, Chiang Kai-shek, and Mao Zedong based on fairly accurate assessments of world politics.[35] Discussion of Japan's fate in ever-complicated world politics was not just for the elites; it was a national occupation.

The Japanese media often expressed skepticism about the longevity of the US-Soviet Grand Alliance in maintaining postwar international order. Even before the Moscow Foreign Ministries Conference concluded in November 1943, Japanese scholars and journalists noted Anglo-American unease with growing Soviet influence in the Mediterranean, North Africa, and the Balkans.[36] Communist successes in Poland and Egypt and the rise of Charles de Gaulle of France suggested further discord in the Great Alliance to them.[37] De Gaulle had difficult relationships with Anglo-American allies. Fearful of seeing postwar France subjugated to Anglo-American domination, De Gaulle began dealing independently with Stalin in August 1944 and in December that year they signed the French-Soviet treaty of alliance and mutual assistance. De Gaulle hoped to obtain Soviet support for French fight against Nazi Germany in exchange for recognizing the Soviet-sponsored government in Poland.[38] De Gaulle saw his association with the Soviet Union as a way to check Anglo-American control over France.

These developments did not lead Japanese observers to anticipate a breakup of the Grand Alliance; such a course would only defuse its antifascist and anti-Japanese pressure. Japanese observers considered Roosevelt, Stalin, and Churchill to be three Machiavellians who would act as allies, at least until the defeat of Germany. They had to wait and see whether such a compromise would survive in the Asian theater.[39]

---

35. Toward the war's end, especially the period between the issuance of the Potsdam Proclamation and August 15, the Japanese government found diverse public attitudes toward the Allies', Japan's reason for not accepting the Potsdam Proclamation, US-Soviet rivalry, the Soviet entry into the war, and the atomic bombs. See chapter 7 and chapter 8 for further analysis of the popular perception of Japan's war, particularly its ending. NRPP.

36. Matsuda Michikazu, "Mosukuwa Sangoku Gaisō Kaidan" (The Moscow Foreign Ministers Conference), *Gaikō Jihō* (Diplomatic review) 938 (January 1, 1944): 5–12; Yoneda Minoru, "Soren tai-Ei-Bei no ichidai mondai" (The major issue concerning Soviet relations with Britain and the United States), *Gaikō Jihō* 942 (March 1, 1944): 5–14.

37. Naomi Zenzō, "Kōsaku suru Bei-Ei-So sangoku no seiryaku" (Clashes of political maneuvers of Britain, the United States and the Soviet Union), *Gaikō Jihō* 945 (May 1, 1944): 25–31.

38. Michael Gueldry, *France and European Integration: Toward a Transnational Polity?* (New York: Praeger, 2001), 148–49.

39. Suzukawa Isao, "Kebekku kara Mosukuwa made" (From Quebec to Moscow), in Asahi Shinbun-sha Chūō Chōsa-kai, eds., *Asahi TōA Nenpō* (Asahi East Asian Annual Report) vol. 3 (1944), 191–203.

The Japanese media also attended to how Washington and Moscow attempted to assume world leadership. At the Moscow Foreign Ministries Conference, the United States, Britain, the Soviet Union, and the GMD government of China agreed to establish a security organization for a postwar world based on the principle of equal sovereignty. The road was rocky from the outset. In December 1944 Soviet Foreign Minister V. M. Molotov secured the right for the Soviet government to send representatives of all sixteen Soviet Republics with sixteen individual votes to any international conference. One of the articles reporting this development explained it as Moscow's tactic to secure a bloc vote and thus to expand its international influence.[40] There was a British precedent: at the Paris Peace Conference in 1919, Britain had successfully invited members of its empire to join the League of Nations Commission to cast bloc votes for Britain. At the San Francisco Conference of April 1945, called to discuss a peacekeeping mechanism under the leadership of the United Nations, the United States managed to send twenty-one small nations from the Western Hemisphere to counter Soviet bloc votes. Japanese articles derided the folly of the two rival powers jockeying for dominance during discussions about postwar peace.[41] Japanese readers became all the more uncertain about choosing between the two for their country's postwar course.

The Foreign Ministry of Japan studied Western media reports to learn about the complexity of Anglo-American-Soviet rivalries and collaborations in building a postwar order in East Asia.[42] An article in the June 1, 1944, issue of *Foreign Policy Reports* (New York), sent to Tokyo as confidential, predicted an experimental international administration of Korea and possibly Manchuria. It conceded the difficulty of coordinating the separate national interests of the Big Four nations,

---

40. Inabara Katsuji, "Roshia no gaikō kōsei o miru" (Observations of Soviet diplomatic offensives), *Gaikō Jihō* 941 (February 15, 1944): 7–8; Yoneda Minoru, "Soren tai-Ei-Bei no ichidai mondai" (Soviet's big problem with Anglo-America), *Gaikō Jihō* 942 (March 1, 1944): 12.

41. Komuro Makoto, "Okashii Han-Sūjiku Ren'mei an" (Ludicrous plan for the Anti-Axis League), *Gaikō Jihō* 950 (October 1, 1944): 1–4; Nishizawa Ei'ichi, "San Furanshisuko Kaigi no shōtai" (Truth about the San Francisco Conference), *Gaikō Jihō* 955 (March 1, 1945): 11–15; Komuro Makoto, "Bei-Ei sekai seifuku no gensō" (Anglo-American illusion about world conquest); Matsuda Michikazu, "San Furanshisuko Han-Sūjiku Kaigi no hontai" (True nature of the anti-Axis San Francisco Conference); Tamura Kōsaku, "San Furanshisuko Kaigi ni kansuru kōsatsu" (Reflections on the San Francisco Conference); Yoshizawa Seijirō, "Danbāton Ōkusu an ni tsuite no ni san no dansō" (Several thoughts on the Dumbarton Oaks Plan), all in *Gaikō Jihō* 956 (April 1, 1945): 1–5, 6–13, 13–18, 39–43, respectively.

42. "Dai-Niji Ōshū Taisen kankei ikken sengo keiei mondai" (The Second European Great War: postwar management (1944), vol. 1–4 [A-7-0-0-8-43]; "Dai-Niji Ōshū Taisen kankei ikken—sengo keiei mondai Ei-Bei-Soren kanren" (The Second European Great War: postwar management—UK-US-Soviet relations) [A-7-0-0-8-43-1], DRO.

especially given Russia's security interests in wider East Asia.[43] In mid-September 1944, the Japanese Foreign Ministry received a confidential copy of a *Reader's Digest* article, "What Is Our Future in Asia?," published earlier that July by veteran American journalist Demaree Bess, a ten-year resident of China. This article revealed how the United States foresaw problems in achieving such a balance of power in the Far East, because the United States "cannot expect Soviet Russia to underwrite the regime in China which makes war upon Chinese communists." Bess cautioned that the defeat of Japan would create a dangerous political vacuum in the rich and vast territory, making the "Pacific peace" an extremely fragile one. More specifically, he predicted the difficulty lying ahead between the United States and the Soviet Union concerning the disposition of the "vast and potentially rich territory" after Japan's defeat. Bess wrote that "the Pacific (and the Far Eastern) peace which follows Japan's defeat will be an extremely uneasy peace."[44]

Subsequently a summary of Walter Lippmann's prophetic article, published in *Dagens Nyheter*, was dispatched as confidential from Stockholm to Tokyo in late November 1944. In light of Russia's "expansionist" policy in China, only a continued Russian-American alliance would prevent turbulence in the northern Pacific, mused Lippmann. Should they compete for "hegemony in Central and eastern Europe, or in the colonies, in Asia and Africa," Lippmann worried, "they are unable to resist united regeneration of Germany's and Japan's military power."[45] Lippmann saw a burgeoning postwar cold war politics and identified a "chance" for Japan's survival in such a world.

Korea had become a delicate issue on which the Western powers tested the durability of the Grand Alliance, the Japanese observers noticed. Washington and Moscow had not made any overt commitment to the peninsula's future, but each increasingly worried about the other's interest in Korea.[46] There were numerous historical precedents for a divided Korea. Before the outbreak of the Sino-Japanese War of 1894–95, a British official had proposed to the Japanese government that Japan occupy southern Korea and China occupy northern Korea, with Seoul as a

---

43. "Tokubetsu Lison no. 126" and Lawrence Rosinger, "Disposition of the Japanese Empire," *Foreign Policy Reports* (June 1, 1944), in "DaiTōA Sensō kankei ikken jōhō shūshū kankei" (The Greater East Asia War: intelligence gatherings) [A-7-0-0-99], DRO.

44. "Tokubetsu Lisbon no. 139" and Demaree Bess, 'What Is Our Future in Asia,' *Reader's Digest* (July 1944), in "DaiTōA Sensō kankei ikken jōhō shūshū kankei" (The Greater East Asia War: intelligence gatherings) (sent on September 12, 1944) [A-7-0-0-9-9], DRO.

45. "Hi: Sutokkuhorumu Okamoto Kōshi yori Honsho" (Secret: from Minister Okamoto, Stockholm, to the Foreign Ministry) (November 23–29, 1944), and "Stockholm No. 43 (Hi)[Confidential])," in "Dai-Niji Ōshū Taisen kankei ikken—sengo keiei mondai Ei Bei Soren kanren" (The Second European Great War: postwar management—UK-US-Soviet relations) [A-7-0-0-8-43-1], DRO.

46. Kathryn Weathersby, "Soviet Aims in Korea and the Origins of the Korean War, 1945–1950: New Evidence from Russian Archives," Cold War International History Project, Woodrow Wilson International Center for Scholars (November 1993), 6–7.

neutral zone. In 1896 and 1903 the Japanese and Russian governments, in an effort to avert a military confrontation, discussed dividing Korea along the thirty-eighth parallel.[47]

As early as January 1944, the Foreign Ministry in Tokyo received a copy of an *American Mercury* journal article that discussed Washington's plan for an Allied Pacific Control Council to govern defeated Japan. The US government declared that it favored restoring "political freedom to Korea." The task would require extreme finesse, argued the article, because the US government would not support Korea's "freedom" to choose a communist government.[48] Since Japanese officials knew about the preponderance of Korean leftist-nationalists they could anticipate frictions between these Koreans and Washington now that the latter had shown an interest in the construction of postwar Korea. Likewise, given the activities of Soviet spies in Korea, Washington's interest in Korea would likely raise concerns. Officially Tokyo adhered to a Soviet policy that insisted on keeping Korea as Japan's territory after the war, but the Foreign Ministry must have been painfully aware of the diminishing likelihood of this occurring given rising US and Soviet ambitions in the peninsula.

Between late summer and fall of 1944, the Japanese Ministry of Foreign Affairs received articles confirming Washington's growing differences with Moscow over the postwar disposition of Korea. These articles explained how the collapse of the Japanese empire would create a power vacuum in Korea, which the United States and the Soviet Union worried the other would attempt to fill. The confidential summary of the *Foreign Policy Reports* article (June 1, 1944) dispatched from Lisbon to Tokyo set forth the scenario. Lawrence Rosinger, a member of the Institute of Pacific Relations, discussed the difficulties of dismantling the Japanese empire and reconstructing the East Asian order. Taiwan and Manchuria, long under Japanese rule, may have developed their own identities and might not want to be "reintegrated into a single united China." Korea presented an equally sensitive case. Although the Cairo Declaration promised Korean "independence in due course," Korea at the end of the war might not possess the economic or political wherewithal for autonomy and self-rule. If the current communist-led armed resistance continued to grow until the end of the war, and if it were to organize itself into a regime, an international organization such as

47. See Morita Yoshio, *Chōsen shūsen no kiroku: Bei-So ryōgun no shinchū to Nihonjin no nikiage* (A record of the fall of Colonial Korea: US-Soviet military advances and Japanese withdrawal) (Tokyo: Gan'nandō Shoten, 1964), 157. See Nagaoka Shinjirō, "Nan-Sen to Hoku-Sen—sono shiteki kōsatsu (Examining the historical backgrounds of South and North Koreas)," *Nihon Rekishi*, vol. 64 (September, 1953). Also see Bruce Cumings, *The Origins of the Korean War: Liberation and the Emergence of Separate Regimes, 1945–1947* (Princeton, NJ: Princeton University Press, 1981), 121.

48. "Plans for a Vanquished Japan [*American Mercury* (January 1944)]," in "DaiTōA Sensō kankei ikken jōhō shūshū kankei," DRO.

the United Nations might declare that regime the de facto government of post-Japan Korea. An independent communist Korea would hardly suit US interests.

Rosinger proposed three alternatives for postwar Korea: occupation by a single foreign power, governance by an international authority, or the establishment of a *noncommunist* independent Korean regime (emphasis added by Rosinger). The first alternative would be the most controversial because the United States, Britain, China, and the Soviet Union would each demand a share of the control of Korea and oppose the selection of a sole nation to occupy Korea. Rosinger believed that because the Russians had a "deep security interest" in Manchuria and Korea and wanted to be in an "important position to influence their future," the Soviet Union would be the most aggressive nation in demanding unilateral control. The second alternative, occupation by an international body, was hypothetical because the world community had never experimented with the long-term international administration of an industrialized nation such as Korea. Korea thus presented a different case from the territories governed by the League of Nations mandates. Rosinger recommended a third alternative—government by a noncommunist regime—as the best, regardless of the will of the Korean people. During the transition from Japanese administration to such a regime, Korea would have to be under military occupation for six months to a year, in which period Korea would be prepared for a representative administration. Rosinger did not specify whether the United States would take up the military occupation of Korea. But so long as Japanese rule was overthrown, Rosinger maintained, Korea would be a better place.[49]

In the face of US-Soviet interests in Korea, the Japanese government at least adhered to the policy of preserving Korea's territorial integrity and took measures to cement the Japanese identity of the Korean people. Both the Governor-General's Office in Korea and the Japanese government worked to speed up the full merger of Korea and Japan, rewarding Koreans' (forced) participation in Japan's war efforts by granting rights and equality. On December 22, 1944, the Japanese cabinet passed a resolution concerning the improvement of the social environment for colonial subjects in Korea and Taiwan, on the basis of which the following were promised: freedom of travel to Japan proper, better police conduct, improvement in labor management, better schooling and employment, and a greater chance for them to become Japanese in Japan proper. Subsequently the cabinet established a committee to investigate how to improve the political status of Koreans and Taiwanese. By April 1, 1945, a new election law passed. While this new election law did not grant universal suffrage to Korean voters, it allowed eli-

---

49. "Tokubetsu Lisbon no. 126" and Rosinger, "Disposition of the Japanese Empire" (sent August 23, 1944), in "DaiTōA Sensō kankei ikken jōhō shūshū kankei," DRO.

gible Korean voters, males over twenty-five who had paid more than fifteen yen as direct tax to the Japanese nation for more than one year, to elect ten members to the House of Peers and twenty-three members to the House of Representatives of the Imperial Diet.[50]

Japan's assimilation program maintained that Japan and Korea remained one political and cultural entity free from ideological fault lines. Even as the fall of the Japanese empire was imminent, Japanese leaders and war planners exhibited no preference for either the United States or the Soviet Union as a new occupier of Korea after the war. Nor could they possibly predict which nation had a better chance of exerting a larger influence in postwar Korea. In pre-1945 analyses of Korea, Japanese colonialists had been concerned about Korean expectations of a Soviet arrival in Korea and subsequent liberation from Japanese control. Japanese colonialists knew that leftist Koreans had aggressively organized nationalist movements with broad popular support, but the Japanese also knew that these communists had complicated relationships with the Soviet Union and the Chinese Communist Party (CCP) that prevented them from uniting. Korean communists had since July 1942 fought with the CCP against Japan in Manchuria and northern Korea. As the war dragged on, however, they became increasingly divided into two factions, one under Soviet and another under CCP leadership. On the other end of the political spectrum, exiled Korean nationalists formed the Korean Provisional Government at Chongqing.[51] And Syngman Rhee continued representing his exile government in the United States where he received only tepid support.[52]

The 1944 report of the governor-general of Korea had informed the Eighty-fifth Imperial Diet session in Tokyo of ever-intensifying international intelligence activities in Korea. By then the Soviet Union, the CCP, the United States, Britain, and the GMD government all were already conducting covert operations, each "assisting" Korea's "independence" movement.[53] In August that year the Japanese authority in Seoul discovered that Korean communists had high expectations of a Soviet attack on Japan and believed that this meant their revolutionary movement would gain momentum.[54] Meanwhile, except for Christian converts, the United States had no community of American collaborators within Korean society

50. Morita Yoshio, "Chōsen ni okeru Nihon tōchi no shūen" (The end of Japanese administration in Korea), *Kokusai Seiji*, no. 2 (1962), 84–85.

51. Morita Yoshio, "Chōsen ni okeru Nihon tōchi no shūen," 83. See chapter 4 for detailed analysis.

52. The Japanese Foreign Ministry's knowledge of Washington's stale relations with Rhee was recorded in a series of entries of August-December 1944 in the file "*Dōmei Tsūshin Sha-nai Jōhō-kyoku, Tekisei jōhō*" (Domei News Agency, Information Bureau—enemy information) in "DaiTōA Sensō kankei ikken jōhō shūshū kankei" (The Greater East Asia War: information gatherings) [A-7-0-0-9-9], DRO. See chapter 4 for detailed analysis.

53. IDS, 73–81.

54. IDS, 67, 69–70. Also see SKTM, 9, 73, 171.

or across East Asia. The Japanese authority had suspected that Korean receptiveness to American influence was hardly comparable to their amenability to Soviet and communist influences.

Notwithstanding, the United States and the Soviet Union seemed to endorse a balance of power in postwar Korea. At Yalta they vaguely agreed on FDR's proposal for a joint trusteeship of the peninsula. At Potsdam they avoided the issue of stationing forces during the trusteeship and exchanged only thin military plans to "liberate" Korea, leaving the postwar status of the peninsula largely undecided.[55]

Korea aside, the US-Soviet rivalry would have its greatest impact on the disposition of Japan after the war. The Japanese Foreign Ministry learned from a variety of Western sources that the US government was concerned about which nations would control postwar Japan. As discussed earlier, an *American Mercury* article that reached Tokyo in early 1944 introduced one of Washington's earliest proposals for an Allied Pacific Control Council to govern defeated Japan. Possible council members included the United States, Britain, China, Australia, New Zealand, Canada, the Netherlands, and the Soviet Union. The proposal specified that the Soviet Union could only join the occupation if it entered the Pacific conflict. In March 1944 Okamoto Suemasa, Japan's minister to Sweden, forwarded an article from *Svenska Dagbladet* that suggested an Anglo-American interest in turning defeated Japan into a bastion of anticommunism in Asia.[56] In this case the Soviet Union would be excluded from the occupation of Japan. In late 1944 Tokyo received another news article on the creation of an Allied Pacific Control Council. The chief members would be the United States, Great Britain, China, and also the Soviet Union. This article cautioned that the Soviet Union's membership depended on it entering the war against Japan.[57] As long as the Soviet Union stayed out of the war against Japan, it would not have the legitimacy to share control over postwar Japan.

Imperial Navy's Rear Admiral Takagi Sōkichi outlined a possible route to survival for Japan. Since 1943 he had insisted on an end to the unwinnable war. His reasoning reflected his keen awareness of evolving tensions in international politics and Japan's desperate need to find a way to survive in such a world. He encouraged Japan to regard the rise of Soviet influence not as a threat to Japan but as a counterforce to the United States in the postwar era. On March 13, 1945,

---

55. Kathryn Weathersby, "Soviet Aims in Korea and the Origins of the Korean War, 1945–1950," 8. Also see *FRUS, the Conference of Berlin (The Potsdam Conference)*, vol. 2, 345–53, 408.

56. "Hi: Sutokkuhorumu Okamoto Kōshi yori Honsho" (Secret: From Minister Okamoto, Stockholm, to the Foreign Ministry) (March 21–22, 1944), in "DaiTōA Sensō kankei ikken jōhō shūshū kankei," DRO.

57. "Plans for a Vanquished Japan [*American Mercury* (January 1944)]," in "DaiTōA Sensō kankei ikken jōhō shūshū kankei," DRO.

Takagi completed "Chūkan hōkoku an" (Draft intermediary report), an analysis of the global politics besieging Japan in the war.[58] Although Takagi predicted that the Big Three—the Soviet Union, the United States, and the United Kingdom—would stand together until the end of the war in East Asia, he surmised that the United States could not win the war against Japan and simultaneously establish hegemony over Japan proper, Korea, Manchuria, and northern China. Regardless of how the war ended, anticipated Soviet interference in the region would thwart US ambitions. Takagi insisted that Japan should not disregard the Soviet factor from any large-scale perspective of postwar peacemaking, no matter Japan's chances for peace with the United States.

Takagi proposed that Japan optimally should consider separate approaches to each of the Big Three nations tailored to their respective motives, goals, and aspirations in world politics. In the spirit of traditional friendship between the British and Japanese navies, Takagi praised "the kingdom" for having the best understanding of Japan's national polity, the emperor system. Takagi preferred Britain to the United States as a partner for Japan because of its capitalist system, international prestige, as well as its cultural and intellectual proximity to Japan. Yet he acknowledged Britain's waning power in sharp contrast to that of the United States and the Soviet Union and stated that Britain would not be able to finance Japan's postwar recovery.[59]

Takagi characterized the United States by its ambition to establish a US-centric capitalist world after the war. For the United States to achieve these goals, Takagi predicted that the United States would very likely aid Japan's reconstruction and integrate Japan into its global network. As part of the American system, Japan would quickly recover as a capitalist society and regain credibility in the international community. On the other hand, America's postwar hegemony in Asia would mean the denial of Japan's traditional stake in China and the prohibition against Japanese efforts to reclaim regional leadership. Japan's only chance to overcome these disadvantages, according to Takagi, would be when Washington found it impossible to deal single-handedly with Moscow's objection to America's hegemony in Asia and sought assistance from Japan. Only then might Japan be able to regain ground in Asia with Washington's backing.[60]

Takagi then discussed how rapprochement with the Soviet Union might also benefit Japan. Acknowledging that Japan could learn from the Soviets' advanced socialist system, he cautioned that the long-term effects of alliance with the

58. Takagi Sōkichi, "Chūkan hōkoku an" (Draft intermediary report) (March 13, 1945) (handwritten draft), in *Takagi Sōkichi Shōshō shiryō* (Rear Admiral Takagi Sokichi Papers) [Kai-gun 9-Takagi 3], MAL.

59. Takagi, "Chūkan hōkoku an," 35–36.

60. Takagi, "Chūkan hōkoku an," 6, 33–34.

Soviet Union would be more unpredictable because the Soviet Union lacked international credibility and its revolutionary propaganda always had a destabilizing effect. If the Soviet Union were to lose Stalin's leadership the nation might plunge into chaos.[61] Nonetheless, Takagi asserted that Japan should not underestimate the power of a shared Soviet-Japanese desire to check Anglo-American expansion in Asia.[62]

Takagi's proposed minimum conditions for Japan's cease-fire included the preservation of the emperor system, maintenance of industrial capacity, continuation of the police force, and the continued possession of Korea and Taiwan under Japan's sovereignty. In addition, Takagi proposed concessions to the Soviet Union such as the southern part of Sakhalin. He also suggested that the northern part of Manchuria might be placed under joint Soviet-Japanese control with the condition that its sovereignty would eventually revert to China.[63]

Takagi's proposal—to favor overtly neither the United States nor the Soviet Union—amounted to a form of risk management reminiscent of a strategy medieval samurai commanders employed during civil wars. In fourteenth-century Japan when civil war divided the nation into forces of the samurai regime and forces of the imperial court, it was common for members of the same clan to take opposite sides deliberately. The intentional division of allegiance within a clan did not rest on conflicts of principle; the division was aimed at guaranteeing that one part of the family would be on the winning side regardless of the outcome of the civil war. The strategy was to leverage risk by siding with *both* rivals. Despite apparent family breaches, split families shared an understanding that the conflict was superficial.[64]

As the Japanese Foreign Ministry soon learned, the United States was investigating the tactical advantages of a potential surrender by Japan. A *Washington Evening Post* article of May 2, 1945 stated that Japan was convinced of Soviet entry into the war and its subsequent intervention in the settlement of Asian affairs. The article surmised that Japan "preferred" to surrender to "Anglo-Americans in Chungking [*sic*]" because of Japan's desire to salvage its economic power.[65] Since this article was written amid Japanese peace feeler efforts, their proposals may have provided the basis for its speculations. Nine days after the Japanese

61. Takagi, "Chūkan hōkoku an," 25–26, 32.

62. Takagi, "Chūkan hōkoku an," 31–32.

63. Takagi, "Chūkan hōkoku an," 41–43. Moreover, he added that under sufficiently pressing circumstances, Japan would provide the Allied forces a labor force in exchange for supplies of foodstuff, fuel, and construction materials.

64. George Sansom, *A History of Japan, 1334–1615* (Stanford, CA: Stanford University Press, 1961), 53, 74.

65. "Peace Rumors Concerning Japan (US Collection), Zurich, May 2 (Dōmei)," in "DaiTōa Sensō kankei ikken jōhō shūshū kankei."

Foreign Ministry obtained the copy of this article via Zurich, it discovered that the Americans were attempting to discern whether Japan had hidden intentions. A Reuters report, dispatched to Tokyo on May 11, 1945, revealed that the United States now speculated that Japan might use the Soviet card against it. The report asked, "Might not Japan, surrounded by enemies, prefer to offer unconditional surrender hoping by shortening the war to secure better terms? The difficulty here is that Russia's Far Eastern Policy is still unpredictable and that the Japanese Government has some reason to hope that profound disagreements between the Allies may create a diplomatic situation in which Japan can maneuver and bargain its way toward concessions."[66]

After the Yalta Conference, where Stalin confirmed his commitment to enter the war against Japan, the United States grew increasingly alarmed about Soviet ambitions for Korea. General Douglas MacArthur suspected that the Soviet Army intended to acquire all of Manchuria and Korea. Secretary of War Henry Stimson believed that "Russia is militarily capable of defeating the Japanese and occupying Karafuto, Manchuria, Korea and Northern China before it would be possible for the US military forces to occupy these areas." Concerned about such Soviet military potential, former president Herbert Hoover even wrote to Stimson on May 15 that the United States should promptly offer the Japanese peace on specified terms before the Soviets captured substantial war spoils in East Asia.[67]

When Takagi drafted a second peace proposal in June 28, 1945, he suggested Japan pursue two-stage negotiations with the Soviet Union and Anglo-America.[68] Takagi proposed making the first attempt with the Soviet Union in early July, and then the second with Sweden, in late July to early August, to request peace mediation with Britain. Only when the Japanese government failed to persuade the Soviets to remain neutral at least until April 1946 would it begin contacting the peace feelers in Sweden or Switzerland and consider dispatching a special envoy to Britain for detailed negotiations.[69] Even though Takagi did not propose direct negotiations with the United States, he effectively proposed several indirect lines of communication to Washington.

Takagi's proposed terms did not seem to compel the United States and the Soviet Union to offer Japan any advantage in ending the war. As concessions to the Soviets, Takagi proposed that Japan would recognize the following:

---

66. "London, May 11 (Reuters) in 'Peace rumors concerning Japan (US collection),'" in "Dai-TōA Sensō kankei ikken jōhō shūshū kankei."

67. Tsuyoshi Hasegawa, *Racing the Enemy* (Cambridge, MA: Belknap Press, 2005), 41, 78–79.

68. Takagi, "Jikyoku shūshū taisaku (miteikō bassui)" (Proposal to settle the current state of affairs [unfinished and excerpted]) (June 1945) (handwritten draft), in *Takagi Sōkichi Shōshō shiryō* (Kai-gun 9-Takagi 53), MAL.

69. Takagi, "Jikyoku shūshū taisaku (miteikō bassui)," 8, 11.

demilitarization along the Manchurian-Soviet border; Soviet influence in Mongolia, Xinjiang, Tibet, Middle East, and India; transfer of strategic railways in Manchuria to the Soviets; Soviet rights to military overflights over Manchuria and northern China; transfer of leasing rights of the Kwantung territory; return of southern half of Sakhalin; and recognition of Soviet's (or the CCP's) special rights in Manchuria and northern China. In contrast, Takagi proposed few concessions and demanded much more from the United States. As concessions to the United States, he proposed Japan immediately withdraw from occupied regions; reduce its military power; cede overseas territory, including the mandated territories; pay indemnity; dissolve secret societies and right-wing organizations in Japanese society; and deal with Japanese war criminals. As Japanese "demands" in return for a cease-fire with the United States, Takagi proposed the continuity of the emperor system, possession of Japan's mainland and adjacent islands; maintenance of people's living standards; continued possession of Korea and Taiwan; rejection of the Allied occupation; maintenance of Japan's own police force; and, independence for East Asian nations.[70]

Takagi concluded with the Allies' likely demands on Japan: unconditional surrender; effective or permanent disarmament; trial of Japanese war criminals; abandonment of and subsequent demilitarization in all the occupied territories; secession of the colonies; self-rule (and future independence) for Korea; return of Manchuria; establishment of the democratic government; military occupation; prohibition of air and heavy industries; indemnity; dissolution of reactionary national polity; and Allied interference in educational and religious matters.[71] Takagi ended the draft there.

Ryū Shintarō, European correspondent for the *Asahi* newspaper, wrote in early July 1945 to Shimomura Hiroshi, director of the Japanese Cabinet Information Bureau, saying that the Soviet Union would demand Sakhalin, Manchuria, and Korea either as spoils of a victory against Japan or as a condition for maintaining neutrality with Japan. Ryū urged that, rather than giving these territories up to the Soviets, Japan should immediately surrender to the United States and let them all fall under the US sphere of influence. Ryū hoped that such readiness would move the United States to grant Japan a conditional surrender.[72] In con-

70. Takagi, "Jikyoku shūshū taisaku (miteikō bassui)," 8–13.

71. Takagi, "Jikyoku shūshū taisaku (miteikō bassui)," 19–20.

72. The copy of Ryū's letter was transmitted top secret to Tokyo by Kase Shun'ichi, Minister to Switzerland. See "Kase Kōshi yori Tōgō Gaimu Daijin" (A memo from Minister Kase to Foreign Minister Togo) (July 9, 1945)," in "DaiTōA Sensō kankei ikken—Suwēden, Suisu, Bachikan nado ni okeru shūsen kōsaku" (The Greater East Asia War: peace operations in Sweden, Switzerland, Vatican, etc.) [A-7-0-0-9-66], DRO. Also see Odaka Tomoo, "Sumiyaka ni NiKkan kankei no chōsei o hakare" (Repair Japanese-Korean relations promptly), *Hwarahng* 1, no. 1 (April 1953): 18–23. Odaka, professor at the University of Tokyo, mused: had the Japanese government decided to accept

trast, under Takagi's proposal, Japan's surrender to the United States before Soviet entry into the war was not an option. In June 1945 Ashida Hitoshi, diplomat before the war and prime minister in 1948, predicted the uncertainty of the post-war world in his journal: "I have no clue as to who (which political bloc) will carry Japan's future, a few years from now on."[73]

China Intrigue

The proposals of both the Foreign Ministry and Takagi to the Soviet Union included Japanese concessions of various rights in China and Manchuria to the Soviet Union, but Japanese planners never included similar terms in the proposed offer to the United States. Why did they seemingly offer to promote Soviet interests in China?

Based on abundant overseas intelligence activities, the Japanese government had, by the spring of 1944, learned about a possible rapprochement between the CCP and Washington.[74] An alliance and the assistance it promised might enable the CCP to emerge as the victor in China by winning the war against not only Japan but the GMD. Too much reliance on US assistance would make the Yan'an regime vulnerable to demands and pressures from Washington and place all of entire postwar East Asia in the American sphere of influence. Japanese policy-makers, aware of the growing schism between Moscow and Yan'an, also investigated whether or how the Soviets would react to Washington's alignment with Yan'an. Japanese policymakers tracked US-Soviet competition over China in order to anticipate the East Asian order that would emerge after the collapse of the Japanese empire and Japan's possibility for survival.

The Imperial General Headquarters, along with the Foreign Ministry, had studied Chinese politics in order to develop an overview of China's foreign relations. Through the course of the war Japan's attention shifted from the GMD to the CCP. In the earlier phase of the Sino-Japanese War, Japan's top priority had been the war against Chiang Kai-shek's army. This condition gradually changed as Japan learned more about the CCP. The Japanese Army deployed the atrocious "three alls" campaigns (*sankō*) to root out communist guerrillas.[75] By 1943 the

the Potsdam Proclamation on August 6, instead of August 9, the Soviet Union would have lost the opportunity to enter the war against Japan and the tragedy of divided Korea at the Thirty-eighth parallel would not have occurred.

73. Hatano Sumio, "Sengo gaikō to sengo kōsō" (Wartime diplomacy and postwar planning), in Hosoyo, Gotō, and Hatano, eds., *Taiheiyō Sensō no shūketsu: Ajia Taiheiyō no sengo keisei,* 30.

74. Imperial General Headquarters, "Jyūkei no haisen ni tomonau En'an gawa no seijiteki kōsei" (Political rise of Yan'an and decline of Chungking) (February 22, 1944), in Usui Katsumi and Inaba Masao, eds., *Gendai-shi shiryō, 38, Taiheiyō Sensō 4* (Tokyo: Misuzu Shobō, 1972), 326–27.

75. WHS-PPW, 319–34, 504–12, 523–26.

Japanese Army had conceded the impossibility of containing CCP guerrillas in northeast China. In the spring of 1944, the Imperial General Headquarters acknowledged that the CCP was establishing a semi-independent regime in the northwest. In May 1944, *TōA* (East Asia), a publication of the TōA-kai, the advisory body commissioned by the Ministry of Greater Asia, published an article that portrayed America's dilemma in choosing between Chiang Kai-shek and Mao Zedong. This article equated Chiang Kai-shek with Drazha Mihailovich, the military leader of southwest Yugoslavia who disapproved of partisan warfare by civilians and preferred the prewar brand of Yugoslav dictatorship. Chiang seemed destined to be abandoned by the United States. The article argued that Mao, the Marshal Tito of Asia, would also be an impossible partner for the United States. To make the story more complex, the Soviet Union had betrayed both the GMD and the CCP in their fight against Japan, the worst breach of trust being the Soviet-Japanese Neutrality Pact. Why had the GMD Army's invasion of Outer Mongolia in late 1943 been followed by a visit to Moscow by T. V. Soong, the foremost pro-American politician within the GMD? Why was the GMD influence growing in "Red Xinjiang"? All these cases indicated increasing complications among the United States, Soviet Union, the GMD, and the CCP.[76]

The Japanese government did not worry that tensions between Moscow and the Yan'an regime, officially recognized by Japan in July 1944, would push Chiang Kai-shek and Mao Zedong toward coalition or that these strains would drive the CCP closer to Washington. When US observers headed for Yan'an in July and November 1944, the Imperial General Headquarters did not consider these visits as signs of a honeymoon between the Americans and the CCP. On the contrary, they discovered CCP leaders had some unease about the United States.[77]

Since the summer of 1944, Mao had tried to obtain US military assistance in expanding CCP bases and waging the civil war against the GMD. On July 4, 1944, Mao celebrated American Independence Day and declared that "the work which we Communists are carrying on today is the very same work which was carried on earlier in America by Washington, Jefferson, and Lincoln; it will certainly obtain, and indeed has already obtained, the sympathy of democratic America."[78] The Imperial General Headquarters learned that Mao, while persistent about obtaining American assistance, remained suspicious of Washington's motives for continuing aid to the GMD regime amid the CCP's rapid expansion of its bases across China.

---

76. "KoKkyō kankei no tenbō" (Prospects for GMD-CCP Relations), *TōA* 17, no. 5 (May 1944): 26–42.

77. Michael Hunt, *The Genesis of Chinese Communist Foreign Policy* (New York: Columbia University Press, 1996), 145–50 and 155–57. See chapter 3 for detailed analysis.

78. Hunt, *The Genesis of Chinese Communist Foreign Policy*, 153–54.

The situation developed quickly. A November 1944 intelligence report informed the Imperial General Headquarters of the CCP struggle to secure military assistance, especially in the air war against Japan, from the United States. Only after the CCP secured US military assistance did the Soviet Union step in and pledge to conclude a new military alliance with the CCP and to provide it with aircraft, munitions, and technological support. The Soviet Union had wanted to test Washington's commitment to the CCP and, more importantly, the CCP's willingness to accept aid from Washington. The events revealed in this secret report highlighted the cruel reality that the CCP would not receive what it wanted from either nation, especially its "ideological motherland." The intelligence report also disclosed that top CCP leaders Zhu De and Peng Dehuai had telegrammed Yan'an that US aid was helping the GMD regime build military industries in areas rich in natural resources so it could eventually attack the CCP and even the Soviet Union.[79] In search of military allies, Mao increasingly found himself caught in the power intrigues between Washington and Moscow. The Imperial General Headquarters saw how the United States and the Soviet Union checked each other in vying for control of the CCP.

The January 1945 issue of *Shina* (China), a journal published by TōA Dōbun Kai (East Asia Common Culture Society), presented a similar picture of the two powers' entanglement over China. The United States wanted to control China as an overseas market and the Soviet Union wanted to integrate China into its defense perimeter. As already demonstrated in Eastern Europe and the Balkans, the Soviet Union would readily crush nationalism in Asia to expand its own sphere of influence, starting with Iran, India, Outer Mongolia, and Xinjiang Province. The article predicted increasing dissonance between the United States and the Soviet Union over their respective interests in China as the war came to an end.[80]

The Japanese government continued attempts to distinguish all four players—the GMD, the CCP, the United States, and the Soviet Union—and to calculate the interests and goals of each as independent factors in the Chinese theater. On January 20, 1945, the Imperial General Headquarters completed "Teikoku Riku-Kai-gun sakusen seisaku taikō" (Grand proposal for Imperial Army-Navy strategic maneuvers), in which the army and the navy proposed joint military operations. This proposal did not consider the Soviet factor. Nevertheless, the new plan proposed a significant change in the China operation. On January 22 the

79. Imperial General Headquarters, "Saikin Bei-En gunji-teki torikime seiritsu to So-En gunji dōmei teiketsu setsu ni tsuite" (Recent arguments concerning the US-Yan'an military agreement and the conclusion of Soviet-Yan'an military alliance) (November 29, 1944), in Usui Katsumi and Inaba Masao, eds., *Gendai-shi shiryō, 38, Taiheiyō Sensō 4*, 330.

80. Maita Minoru, "Shina ni okeru Beikoku to Soren" (The United States and the Soviet Union in China), *Shina* 36, no. 1 (January 1945): 1–8.

Imperial General Headquarters issued Continental Order 1228 to the China Expeditionary Army Commander to consider the US forces, not the GMD forces, as the primary enemy. The new mission for the China Expeditionary Army was to strengthen its holdings in central and south China and to crush the US forces should they attempt to advance to China. There was no specific mention of CCP forces.[81]

The Konoe memorandum of February 14, 1945, warning of the spread of communist revolution across Asia, was an odd interlude in light of such realist assessments of the CCP and the Soviet Union. In his warning to Emperor Hirohito, Prince Konoe claimed that Japanese communists stationed at Yan'an and the so-called pro-Soviet faction within the Japanese Imperial Army were *all* under Moscow's leadership, fighting side by side with Chinese, Korean, and Taiwanese communists. Few in Tokyo by then would have found a joint Moscow-Yan'an attempt at a communist takeover of Asia credible.

The Soviet government had declared in early 1945 its refusal to support the CCP because of the latter's lack of ideological authenticity. Later, in an April 1945 meeting with Patrick Hurley, Roosevelt's special envoy to Yan'an, Stalin disdainfully called Mao a "margarine Marxist." In a secret meeting with Harry Hopkins on June 25, 1945, where he stated that the Soviets were ready to enter the war in Asia by August 8, Stalin reaffirmed that Chiang Kai-shek was a more desirable leader than Mao of unified China. He even promised that should the Soviet Army enter Manchuria and other areas of China he would let Chiang Kai-shek, not Mao, administer civil politics.[82]

Washington began to gauge Soviet intentions and plans for East Asia especially should the Soviet Union enter the war. On May 12, 1945, Acting Secretary of State Joseph Grew met with W. Averell Harriman, Assistant Secretary of War John McCloy, State Department Soviet expert Charles Bohlen, and Secretary of the Navy James Forrestal. Grew questioned whether the Soviet Union would demand participation in the occupation of Japan as a result of its entry into the war in Asia. To deal with this uncertainty, Grew said that the State Department wanted to demand that the Soviet government make three pledges as prerequisites to its entry into the war: a pledge to influence the CCP toward the unification of China under the GMD regime; a pledge to endorse the return of Manchuria to China, as

81. CCCO, vol. 10, 12, 31.

82. See Sergei Tikhvinsky (Tikhvinskii)'s comment, in Hosoya, Honma, Iriye, and Hatano, eds., *Taiheiyō Sensō*, 644–45. In this comment made at an international academic conference held in Japan in November 1991, Tikhvinsky, an orientalist, historian, and merited diplomat of the Soviet Union, added that the record of the Hopkins-Stalin meeting on June 25, 1945, had recently been declassified in the United States and would become available in the Soviet Union upon congressional approval.

specified in the Cairo Declaration; and a pledge to support the trusteeship of Korea under the United States, Britain, China, and the Soviet Union.[83]

Shortly afterward, the so-called *Amerasia* Affair of June 1945 made the CCP wary of America's intentions. On June 6 the FBI arrested six American citizens on charges that they had passed top secret US government documents to the CCP. Those arrested were "pro-communist" editors and diplomats affiliated with *Amerasia,* an American journal specializing in contemporary Asian issues. On June 25 *Jiefang Ribao,* the official newspaper of the CCP, printed harsh criticism of the reactionary faction in Washington for its blatant anticommunist stance.[84] Historian Michael Hunt argues that Mao, in spite of all these developments, remained flexible and even opportunistic, depending on "his reading of the fluid circumstances" in world politics, in his adherence to the military plan to collaborate with the Allied Forces in the final stage of the war. Mao thought he could still harness American military and political ascendancy in the Pacific, and thus remained in touch with US military representatives in mid-1945.[85]

Around the time of the *Amerasia* Affair, the worsening battle situation in Okinawa forced the Imperial General Headquarters to redirect China strategy in the Pacific War context. On April 22, General Anami expressed his desire to see peace in China in the face of the twin obstacles: the Soviet announcement of not renewing the neutrality pact and the US preponderance in the battle of Okinawa. Anami proposed conducting parallel peace operations with the GMD and CCP regimes under the command of General Okamura Yasuji, commander-in-chief of the China Expeditionary Army. In the meantime, the Imperial General Headquarters issued a new China operation under the series of Continental Orders 1335 (May 28) and 1339 to 1341 (all May 30). Based on these orders, the China Expeditionary Army created a new plan "Shina Haken-gun tai-Bei sakusen keikaku taikō" (The outline of the China Expeditionary Army's strategy against the United States). The major goal of this plan was to stop US forces and defend Japanese strategic bases if they were to land on the Yangtze River Delta and advance inland along the Yangtze River. The plan also tasked the Kwantung Army to prepare an anti-Soviet defense operation (*tai-So bōei sakusen junbi*) in northern Korea.

Toward the final stage of the war in China, the United States became defined as the main enemy there, with the Soviet Union as a secondary, potential threat. The GMD and the CCP retreated in the background of Japan's comprehensive picture of the war. This June outline of China strategy contained only a few references

83. Tsuyoshi Hasegawa, *Racing the Enemy*, 76.

84. Katō Kōichi, "Chūgoku Kyōsan-tō no tai-Bei ninshiki to Soren no tai-Nichi sansen mondai, 1944–1945" (CCP's views of the United States and the Soviet entry into the war against Japan, 1944–1945), *Rekishigaku Kenkyū* (Journal of historical studies) 751 (July 2001): 42–43.

85. Hunt, *The Genesis of Chinese Communist Foreign Policy*, 156–57.

to the GMD forces insofar as the Thirteenth and Twenty-third Armies of the China Expeditionary Army were to use the minimum force against them in order to reduce unnecessary war fronts (*fuyō sen'men o shūshuku suru*). There were no instructions on how to deal with the CCP forces. The new plan saw no possibility of US-Chinese joint military operations against the Japanese.[86]

The Army War Operations Plan Division's top secret war journal (*Kimitsu sensō nisshi*) included reflections from May 31, 1945, about how the Soviet Union would like relations among the Soviet Union, China, the United States, and Japan to evolve in East Asia, and whether Japan could accept such a vision.[87] On June 8, 1945, the Supreme Council for the Direction of the War met with Emperor Hirohito to discuss the basic principle in guiding the war in the future (*kongo torubeki sensō shidō no kihon taikō*). The outcome of the fundamental scenario for the Chinese war front proposed by the Supreme Council for the Direction of the War seemed dismal. As the council unanimously understood, the GMD, while exhausted by unpredictable Soviet intentions as well as the battle against the CCP, continued to hope to exploit the alliance with the United States in executing the war against Japan and in enhancing its own status in the international community. Once the US forces intensified its offensive against Japan after the fall of 1945, the GMD would likely deploy all-out counteroffensives against Japan, threatening the Japanese war front on the continent. The CCP would simultaneously intensify its guerrilla warfare on the Japanese occupied territories. In spite of all this, the Supreme Council for the Direction of the War pointed to the increasing Anglo-American rivalry with the Soviet Union as well as the growing Anglo-American dissonance with the GMD and presented forecasts detrimental to the GMD. These were the continuation of civil war after World War II, the establishment of American hegemony in East Asia (in the event of America's complete victory), the growing influence of the CCP, and also increasing pressure from the Soviet Union. The Supreme Council for the Direction of the War concluded that although achieving a separate peace with the GMD seemed improbable, Japan should continue to offer the GMD a chance for peace negotiations in the same spirit of fairness as before.[88] The Supreme Council for the Direction of the War did not specify who might emerge ruler of a unified China.

Into the final phase of the war, major Japanese newspapers printed articles on the superior position of the CCP in the civil war against the GMD. Favorable

---

86. Bōei-chō Bōei-kenkyūjo Senshi-shitsu, ed., Senshi sōsho, *Shōwa 20-nen no Shina Haken-gun*, vol. 2 (The Defense Agency, The Defense Research Institute, Military History Department, ed., War history series—the China Expeditionary Army in 1945, vol. 2) (Tokyo: Asagumo Shinbun Sha, 1973), 434–49.

87. TSWJ, vol. 2, 722–23.

88. "Kongo torubeki sensō shidō no kihon taikō" (The basic principle in guiding the war in the future), June 8, 1945, in RJD, 265–73.

reports on the CCP continued to appear until the end. On July 27, 1945, just one day after the issuance of the Potsdam Proclamation, *Asahi* printed an article on the CCP and an editorial on the future of East Asia. The article reported that the future of China could never be gauged as a simplistic rivalry between the US-GMD camp and the Soviet-CCP camp because there were multiple elements of contention among all these four players. The CCP, nevertheless, had made some significant strides. At the Seventh Congress of the CCP in Yan'an (April–June 1945), Mao had won endorsements from frustrated GMD supporters by attacking the GMD dictatorship. Mao had also become increasingly hostile to the United States, now a potential invader and divider of China. Although the CCP had previously agreed to accommodate possible anti-Japanese US military operations along the coast of China, Mao had reversed this decision and was now organizing popular movements to oppose US landings in China by cultivating fear of America. The news thus implicitly praised the CCP for winning the minds of the Chinese and for its determination to keep China for the Chinese.[89]

Mao, meanwhile, kept his distance from both Moscow and Washington. As Michael Hunt argues, Mao Zedong expected Japan's defeat in the Pacific War, but he also feared that the rise of American and Soviet power in the Far East would follow. Mao worried that collisions with Soviet ideology and Soviet military strategy in East Asia would harm his party's survival and growth. As he observed the gradual collapse of the Grand Alliance, Mao contemplated harnessing US power to check the Soviet Union. At the same time Mao was careful *not* to allow the United States any room for postwar colonial expansion or any chance to obtain complete command of the Pacific. As Hunt puts it, "Mao's quest for foreign affairs autonomy—reflected in a distancing from Moscow and an attempted rapprochement with the United States—had set the old international affairs orthodoxy in limbo."[90]

The intricacies of China's republican revolution of 1911 meant that the GMD's official allies were the Soviet Union and the United States, though Stalin and Chiang were never close. To complicate matters the Soviet Union was also the ideological motherland of the CCP, even though Stalin never treated Mao Zedong as a worthy comrade. A Soviet military presence in Manchuria would not necessarily benefit the CCP since Korean and Chinese communists fighting in Manchuria, insofar as they were handpicked by Moscow for their non-Maoist revolutionary goals, identified with Stalin, not Mao.[91]

89. "En'an Seiken no nerai" (Goal of the Yan'an policy), *Asahi Shinbun* (July 27, 1945).

90. Hunt, *The Genesis of Chinese Communist Foreign Policy*, 145–50 and 155–57.

91. Suzuki Masayuki, "Manshū Chōsen no kakumei-teki renkei: Manshū kō-Nichi tōsō to Chōsen kaihō-go no kakumei naisen (A Manchurian-Korean revolutionary linkage: the anti-Japanese movement in Manchuria and the post-liberation Civil War in Korea), in *Iwanami Kōza kindai Nihon*

The Japanese government pursued two incongruous strategies involving China: support for Soviet interests in Manchuria and acquiescence to the rise of the CCP. One likely effect of these approaches in a vacuum left by Japan's defeat would be mutual Soviet-CCP discomfort, which Japanese leaders hoped would dampen both their influences. These approaches would also likely leave the United States with little room to intervene in China. Provided the Soviets attacked Manchukuo, Japanese policymakers and strategists could thus expect the emergence of a delicate balance of power in China.[92] Reckoning with the prospect of losing the war against the United States, Japan had already abandoned its pan-Asian dream. Japan's Eurasian world began to be eclipsed by the American military preeminence in the Pacific. If a chain reaction caused by a Soviet attack on Japan could keep the United States off the Eurasian continent after the demise of Japan's colonial empire, however, some of Japan's original war aims might be salvaged. Japanese leaders surreptitiously began to anticipate a Soviet attack.

---

to shokumin-chi (6): Teikō to kutsujyū (The Iwanami lecture series: Japan and colonialism, vol. 6 "Resistance and subjugation") (Tokyo: Iwanami Shoten, 1993), 29–59.

92. For the argument that Japan's China policy was based on the classic power politics, see Hatano Sumio, "Senji gaikō to sengo kōsō" (Wartime diplomacy and postwar planning), in Hosoya, Iriye, Gotō and Hatano, eds., *Taiheiyō Sensō no shūketsu*, 18–24.

6

MILITARY SHOWDOWN

Ending the War without Two-Front Battles

American scholars remain divided in their assessments of the nature and degree of Japan's defense preparedness in Kyūshū in the summer of 1945. Some claim that Japan dramatically expanded its defense forces on Kyūshū, so they were ready to meet an American invasion and could cause large US casualties in the event of land battle. Others argue that the Japanese preparations were far from complete. The inflated American evaluation of Japan's defense preparation in Kyūshū has been a critical factor in justifying the use of the atomic bombs *in place of* the mainland invasion: the atomic bombs were necessary to avoid a tragically high number of casualties inevitably resulting from Japan's determination to defend the homeland.[1]

Conventional wisdom holds that the Imperial General Headquarters was determined to fight the final battle against the United States even while holding on to a dim hope for Soviet neutrality. However, hitherto little used military records present a very different picture. A May 13, 1945, entry in the top secret journal of the Imperial General Headquarters Army War Operations Plans Division states, "Overall, *there is no determination for the final battle against the United States or in the continent* [against the Soviet Union]. The only focus is on protracted withdrawal (*jikyū kōtai*). This is true with the planning for China, Manchuria and Korea. This is awe-inspiring (*osorubeshi*)" (emphasis added).[2] The next entry on

1. For a survey of the major positions, see J. Samuel Walker, "The Decision to Use the Bomb: A Historiographical Update," in Michael Hogan, ed., *Hiroshima in History and Memory* (Cambridge: Cambridge University Press, 1996), 28–29.

2. TSWJ, vol. 2, 717.

May 20th records War Minister Anami Korechika's statement that he had adopted a new policy of "turning darkness into brightness [*yami o akarumi e*]," with the first step having already been successfully implemented in Manchuria.[3] The entry of June 8, 1945, reports that the 10:00 a.m. Imperial Conference proceeded smoothly as planned (*yotei dōri sura sura to torihakobu*). Hiranuma Kiichirō, president of the Privy Council, gave his favorite speech on the moral principle of fighting until the end. Yet the record keeper called Hiranuma an "ardent advocate for peace" and reported that the purpose of the Imperial Conference had been sufficiently fulfilled by participants chanting and reconfirming the official goals of Japan's war.[4] This break in the fourth wall suggests that, as was common among politicians and diplomats in the war, the Japanese war leaders said one thing at top-level meetings where consensus needed to be hammered out but said or recorded the opposite on other occasions. Even when the official records of the Supreme Council for the Direction of the War or Imperial Conference discussed the final mainland battle, they did not necessarily reflect the complexity of the state of affairs within the government.

As the prospect of two-front assault became more likely, the Imperial General Headquarters regularly updated its estimates of how a Soviet advance might interact with further US penetration into the Japanese empire. In such calculations Korea became the contested stage. While some archival documents mention strategic plans to fight both the United States and the Soviet Union to keep Korea, other documents reveal efforts to work out what the combined effects of US and Soviet military operations would mean for Korea. Japanese strategists predicted Korea would be invaded by the United States from the south and the Soviet Union from the north and would end up being occupied by both and divided into two separate entities. Far from being only determined to fight the final battle against the United States or the Soviet Union or both, the Imperial General Headquarters attempted to look beyond the collapse of Japan's colonial empire.

The Improbability of Two-Front Attacks

Throughout the war, the army and the navy never succeeded in coordinating their battle capabilities in the Pacific theater against the United States. Even after Japan started facing stalemates in the early offensive strategies against the Allied nations, the army gave priority to the war in China and avoided interventions in military operations in the Pacific Ocean. The army-navy cooperative strategy

3. TSWJ, vol. 2, 717.
4. The entry of June 8, 1945, TSWJ, vol. 2, 728.

in the South Pacific Ocean adopted by the Imperial General Headquarters in mid-November 1942 bore little fruit.

On March 5, 1943, the Imperial General Headquarters formally adopted "Teikoku Riku-gun sōgō sakusen shidō keikaku" (the Army comprehensive operation guidance plan), in which the army developed for the first time a comprehensive operational plan for the army as a whole. Now both the army and the navy considered the Southeast area as part of the main battlefield, with an aim to keep the areas west of Lae-Salamaua and north of the central part of Solomon Islands. Confronting the military disadvantages in the central Solomons in early August, however, the army and the navy insisted on separate defense line retreat plans in the Pacific. On September 30, with approval from Emperor Hirohito, the government and the Imperial General Headquarters adopted "Kongo torubeki sensō shidō no taikō" (the Principle in guiding the war in the future) and shifted to a new strategy involving the "Absolute Defense Sphere" (*zettai kokubō ken*). While a significant shift in defensive strategy in the Pacific, this strategy still did not materialize into army-navy unity concerning Pacific defense. The army still wanted to prioritize the defense of the Mariana to Caroline Islands and the navy the Marshall Islands; the difference in priorities left some areas in the designated defense sphere unprotected.

On November 8, 1943, in response to the US attacks on Wake Island and the north Solomon Islands since early October, the army agreed to dispatch to the defense of the central Pacific Ocean approximately forty infantry battalions extracted from Japan proper, Korea, Manchuria, and China. About that time, the army was drawing up a new plan, Operation Ichi-gō (Operation Number One, or Continental Cross-Through Operation), an attempt to create a corridor in mainland China to prevent US air forces in China from raiding Japan proper and to launch a new offensive operation on the continent. Subsequently the army postponed dispatching armed forces to the Pacific Ocean.

Only in February 1944 did the Operations Sections of the army and the navy finally agree on the urgent need to send soldiers to the Truk and Mariana areas to enhance the Absolute National Defense Sphere. Only then did the army make a serious commitment to the battle in the Pacific. Five months later, the Absolute Defense Sphere already began to crumble with the loss of Saipan to the US forces.[5]

5. Yashiro Noriaki, "Taiheiyō Sensō chūki ni okeru Nihon no senryaku—shu-senjō taru Taiheiyō ni okeru sakusen senryaku no kisū," a paper submitted to the National Institute for Defense Studies International Forum on War History, 8th Forum, 2009. Its abridged English version is Noriaki Yashiro, "Japanese Strategy in the Second Phase of the Pacific War." Both texts are available online at http://www.nids.go.jp/event/forum/j2009.html (for the original Japanese) or http://www.nids.go.jp/english/event/forum/e2009.html (for the English version).

The delay in adopting the "Pacific First" view did not conversely mean a ratcheting up of the military build-up against the Soviet Union on the continent. In late November 1943 the Imperial General Headquarters' Fifth Section, which collected information on Russia, conducted a comprehensive survey of the Soviets' preparation for war against Japan. The Imperial General Headquarters began working on Operation Otsu-gō, a plan for a two-front war against the United States and the Soviet Union.[6] When Soviet troops provoked the Kwantung Army by repeatedly crossing the Argun River on the Soviet-Manchurian border in the summer of 1944, neither the Imperial Army nor the Kwantung Army responded, abiding by the policy of "keeping peace and status quo." They inferred that the Soviets were testing Japanese preparedness in response to such maneuvers and intensified their intelligence operations to better predict the timing of a future Soviet attack on Manchukuo.

Mid-ranking officials of the Kwantung Army were frustrated that top-ranking officials exhibited no sense of urgency concerning the impending Soviet attack. One major of the Kwantung Army reminisced after the war that no matter how many times his department prepared analyses of the dangerous level of Soviet war preparation, the Kwantung Army Headquarters sent only tepid warnings to Tokyo. The Imperial General Headquarters in Tokyo did not take such reports at face value either. Its Tokyo-based Fifth Section received reports directly from its own intelligence sources in China and Manchukuo, from which it learned of the latest Soviet troop movements and drew its own conclusions.[7] It appears that both the Imperial General Headquarters in Tokyo and the headquarters of the Kwantung Army downplayed the signs of impending Soviet attack so as to maintain the strategic façade of peace with the Soviet Union on the front lines. So long as the Soviets were not yet ready to launch a massive all-out assault, they continued moving troops to meet the United States.

By early August 1944 Lieutenant Colonel Kusachi Teigo, chief of the Kwantung Army's Operations Plans Division, presented the Imperial General Headquarters with a set of six strategic plans against anticipated Soviet assaults on Manchuria and beyond. Only one plan proposed a counteroffensive to push the Soviet Army back over the Manchukuo-Mongolian border toward Lake Baikal. This plan, based on an aggressive strategy predating the Nomonhan Incident, was not in serious contention. The remaining five plans all suggested passive defensive strategies. One plan to defend the entire border of Manchuria against Soviet attack was rejected as unfeasible. Another plan suggested withdrawal from the Manchurian plains and a protracted war to defend only the Kwantung region and Korea.

---

6. See the entry of November 26, 1943, in TSWJ, vol. 2, 453.
7. WHS-KA, 282–83, 322–23, 338–39.

Another plan suggested withdrawing completely from Manchuria and defending only the Korean-Manchurian border. The plan to abandon all of Manchuria risked deserting a million Japanese settlers residing in Manchukuo and abdicating Japan's self-imposed responsibility for the defense of Manchukuo.[8]

The defense of Manchuria became less tenable when the elite 26th Division was transferred to fight in the Philippines, which left a serious void. Further troop redeployments to serve as reinforcements elsewhere cost the Kwantung Army dearly. In 1944 alone more than ten divisions and units were diverted from the Kwantung Army to the South Pacific, the Philippines, Ryukyu Islands, and China, reducing its fighting ability by one-third. Most of its air power was transferred to the battlefields in the Philippines, the bombing of Chongqing, and elsewhere.

The Imperial General Headquarters' apparent inertia in the face of the predicted Soviet attack did not mean that it was more prepared to fight a final battle against the United States, although it drew up detailed plans to counter a US invasion of Japan proper. By the beginning of 1945, the Imperial General Headquarters began working in earnest on the prospect of two-front assaults by the United States and the Soviet Union. On January 1, 1945, the Imperial General Headquarters War Operations Plans Division set up two grand war plans: a plan for concluding the war (*shūsen kōsaku*) and a plan for postwar management (*sengo keiei hōsaku*).

As the US forces moved north toward the Japanese mainland, the Imperial General Headquarters' foremost concern was to identify where the US troops would begin the first major land invasion. On January 5, 1945, the Imperial General Headquarters estimated that US forces might land on the southeastern coast of China sometime after June 1945. Based on this new timeline, the Imperial General Headquarters instructed the China Expeditionary Army to change focus from the Guomindang (GMD) forces in Chongqing to the US forces as the primary enemy (Continental Order 1228). The Southern Expeditionary Army, headquartered in Saigon, was repositioned to thwart any US advance toward Japan proper and possibly the Chinese continent (Continental Order 1236). Okinawa, Shanghai, and the Shandong Peninsula, the Ogasawara islands, and Iwo Jima were all considered possible locations for US invasions. On February 3 the Imperial General Headquarters issued a similar order to the Tenth Area Army in Taiwan (Continental Order 1242).[9]

The Imperial General Headquarters worked to pinpoint the possible timing of US operations. The earliest estimate of the timing of US landings in Japan was given on January 16, 1945, by Colonel Sugita Ichiji, formerly the head of the

---

8. WHS-KA, 278–79.
9. CCCO, vol. 10, 12–13, 30–31, 39–40, 47–48; WHS-KA, 290–91.

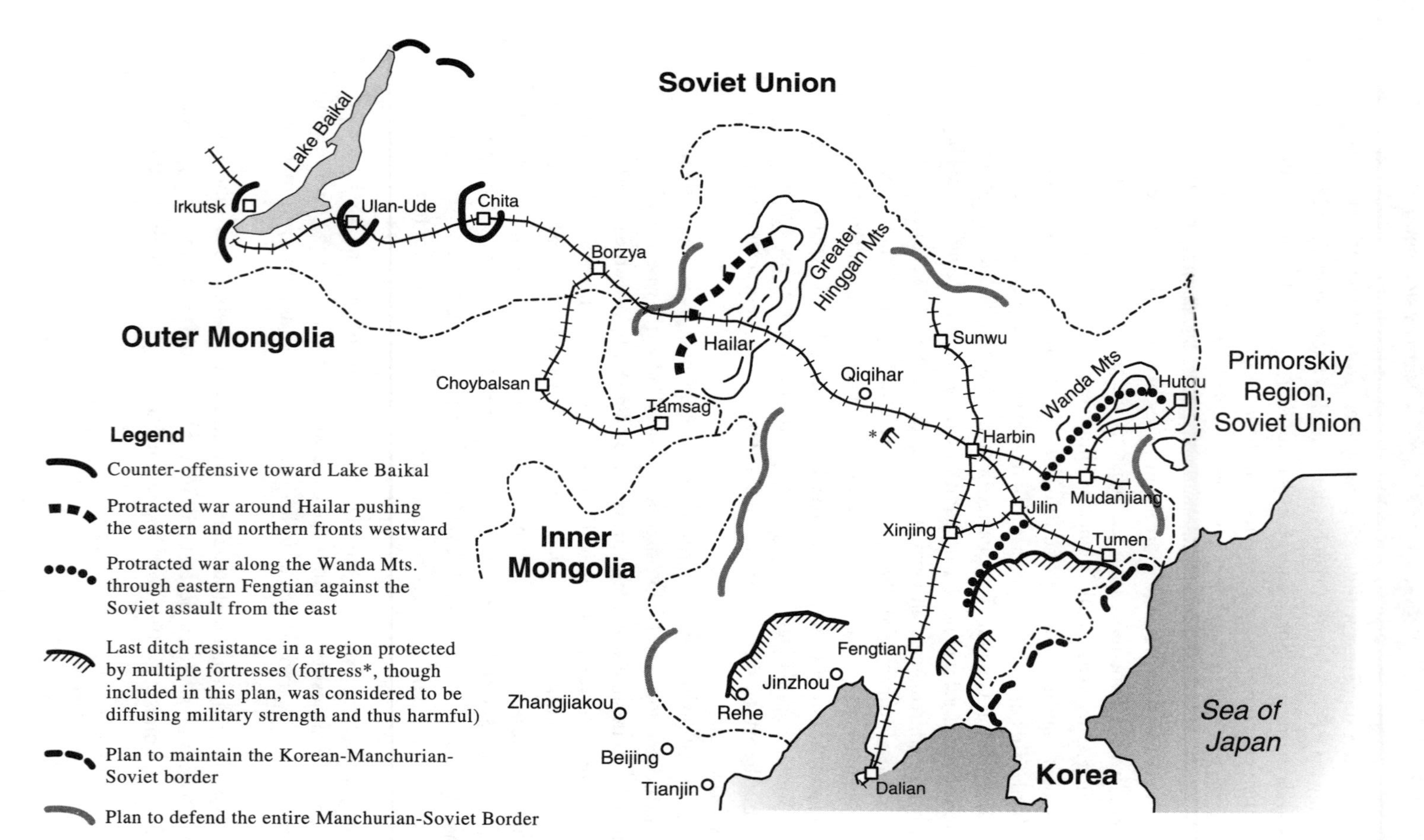

MAP 6.1 The Kwantung Army's Six Strategic Plans against Anticipated Soviet Attack on Manchuria and Beyond, Early August 1944.

Source: Courtesy of the Military History Department, the National Institute for Defense Studies, Tokyo. Adopted from Senshi Sōsho: Kantō-gun (War History Series: The Kwantung Army), vol. 2 (Tokyo, 1974), 279. Adapted by Myongsun Kong, Colgate University, and Takashi Yasukawa, Tokyo.

European/US Section, Imperial General Staff, and then head of operations for the Imperial General Staff. Colonel Sugita explained at a meeting that US landings in mainland Japan would most likely take place in the fall of 1945. He provided a timetable for when US forces would reach specific destinations: the Ogasawara islands between January and February; Taiwan and Okinawa by March and April; the southeastern coast of China by February or March; the Kurile islands by May; Shanghai by April or May; the Andaman and Nicobar Islands in the Bay of Bengal within January; Malay and Sumatra by February; Singapore by May; and Hong Kong by February. Sugita then explained how the defenses of mainland Japan should be prepared in light of this schedule of enemy advances. He identified as possible US targets Kyūshū, Shanghai, Ogasawara, Okinawa, Taiwan, and southeastern China. At this stage the list did not include Korea.[10] On January 19 the Operations Division provided a revised estimate, which predicted that US forces planned to complete the enclosure of Japan by the fall of 1945 and would attempt a mainland operation by the spring of 1946.[11]

On January 20 the Imperial General Headquarters completed "Teikoku Riku-Kai-gun sakusen keikaku taikō" (Grand proposal for Imperial Army-Navy strategic maneuvers), which set a timeline to complete preparations for Operation Ketsu-gō, the final homeland battle against the United States, by the early fall of 1945. On February 7 the Operations Plans Division specified that the US invasion of Japan proper would most likely take place after August or September 1945, regardless whether it occurred after the capture of Okinawa or landings in China. On February 22, three days after the US landing on Iwo Jima, the Imperial General Headquarters revised its early estimate for the invasion of mainland Japan to the fall of 1945 or later.[12]

By the Yalta Conference, the Imperial General Headquarters closely monitored the Soviet moves against Japan in conjunction with the study of US military strategy. According to the conventional account, Japanese policymakers never learned that Roosevelt and Stalin confirmed at Yalta that the Soviets would enter into the war against Japan. Instead they maintained a naïve expectation that Soviet neutrality would last. Japanese documents demonstrate this was not the case. On February 7, just three days after the Yalta Conference began, the Operation Plans Division issued an estimate that the US landing in mainland Japan would occur after August or September, and the commander of military police (*kenpei-shirei-kan*) briefed General Umezu Yoshijirō, chief of army staff, that the Soviet Union very likely would abrogate the neutrality pact.[13] Indeed by February 8 (Japan

10. TSWJ, vol. 2, 650–52.
11. TSWJ, vol. 2, 653.
12. TSWJ, vol. 2, 672.
13. TSWJ, vol. 2, 663–64.

time), the Imperial General Headquarters already had obtained intelligence that Roosevelt, Churchill, and Stalin had met at Yalta to discuss the postwar management of the world. Within three days after the end of the conference, by February 14, it had obtained intelligence on the basic agreement among Roosevelt, Stalin and Churchill at Yalta regarding the postwar disposition of Germany, Poland, and Yugoslavia, and the creation of a world peace organization.[14]

On the following day, February 15, the Supreme Council for the Direction of the War issued a summary report, the tenth publication in the "Sekai jōsei handan" (Evaluations of world affairs) series, declaring that the US government, in a serious bid to end the war in a short period of time, had attempted to enlist the Soviet Union into war against Japan. The report predicted that it was highly likely that the Soviet Union would break the neutrality pact the coming spring. The report even anticipated that, regardless of progress in the European war theater, the Soviet Union, when it judged Japan's national strength to be exceptionally weakened, would ignite the war against Japan in order to secure postwar influence over the management of East Asia.[15] By late February the Imperial Army attaché in Moscow had informed Tokyo of an increased volume of military trains moving to the Far East, which suggested the acceleration of Soviet military preparation for war against Japan.[16]

General Tōjō Hideki, the former premier, believed that the Soviets would attack Japan in response to, or even in conjunction with, US operations against Japan. On February 16, he told the chief of the War Operations Plans Division to raise the alert level in response to any Soviet military moves after April, when Stalin was likely to abrogate the neutrality pact, and then again around the expected time of US landings in Japan. General Tōjō cryptically added that Japan's Soviet policy, though not without some errors in judgment, had thus far brought a good outcome (*kekka wa ryōkō nari*).[17] To understand what the general could have possibly meant, it is necessary to identify strategic benefits Japan could gain by acting like a good friend of Stalin regardless of what he might be planning.

On March 20 the War Operations Plans Division—the Twentieth Group (20-*pan*)—and the Military Service Division (*Gunmu-bu*) met to discuss an unspecified new Soviet policy, which they agreed to recommend strongly to the Foreign Ministry.[18] Throughout March, four existing regiments and three newly formed regiments were extracted from the Kwangtung Army and restationed in

---

14. TSWJ, vol. 2, 664, 667.

15. The Supreme Council for the Direction of the War's 10th report, "Sekai jōsei handan" (Evaluations of world affairs) (February 15, 1945)," in RJD, 230–31.

16. WHS-KA, 323.

17. TSWJ, vol. 2, 669.

18. TSWJ, vol. 2, 690.

Japan proper and in southern Korea against US offensives. To reinforce the ever-thinning Kwantung Army, the Imperial General Headquarters examined the possibility of transferring troops from the China Expeditionary Army to Manchuria. The extraction of soldiers from combat regions in China to noncombat regions in Manchuria was controversial and a decision in support of this plan was not made until late May (Continental Orders 1335, 1337, 1338). Even in the face of the growing vulnerability of Manchukuo to an impending Soviet offensive, the Imperial General Headquarters bluntly ordered the Kwantung Army to try its best to keep up its appearance as an impressive force (*gaimen-teki kyōdai gunbi no iyō o hoji*) to serve as passive deterrence against the Soviet forces.[19]

On April 16, eleven days after Soviet Foreign Minister Molotov announced the Soviet intention not to renew the neutrality pact, the Imperial General Headquarters began a revised study of the timing of a Soviet attack on Japan in order to "promptly prepare to perfect a measurement for that" (*kore ga taiō sochi no kyūsoku naru kanpeki*).[20] The record of April 16, 1945, in the top secret war journal kept by the Army War Operations Plans Division acknowledged the rapid reinforcement of Soviet forces in the Far East and urged military planners to fine tune the prediction of the timing for Soviet entry into the war. The record contained not a single word about the need to prepare a Japanese counteroffensive against the Soviet forces. The entry of April 16 ended with the following comment: the crucial key to accomplishing the goal of the Greater East Asia War is to predict precisely when the Soviet attack will occur and to carry out the quick and proper response and measure to the Soviet attack.[21] From the Japanese perspective, the Soviet entry into the war against Japan would mean Japan's defeat but it might also thwart America's singular takeover of Japan's colonial empire and its hegemony of postwar East Asia.

On April 25 the Imperial General Headquarters completed "Sekai jōsei handan an" (Preliminary evaluations of world affairs) and estimated the Soviets would attack Japan in early fall of 1945, or whenever the condition of Japan's war worsened, regardless of the situation in Europe.[22] Lieutenant Colonel Asai Isamu, military attaché to Moscow, who observed increased military activity from the window of a trans-Siberian train as he rushed back to Japan on Tokyo's request, validated this assessment. On April 27 Asai telegraphed Lieutenant General Kawabe Torashirō, vice chief of the army general staff, reporting that the heavy volume

---

19. WHS-KA, 371–77; CCCO, vol. 10, 154–56.

20. TSWJ, vol. 2, 703.

21. See the entry of April 16, 1945, TSWJ, vol. 2, 702–3.

22. Nakayama Takashi, "Nihon no sensō sakusen shidō ni okeru Soren yōin" (The Soviet factor on Japan's conduct of war and military operations in 1941–1945), *Seiji Keizai Shigaku* (Journal of historical studies) 333 (March 1994), 52.

of military traffic on the trans-Siberian Railroad convinced him that the Soviet preparation for war against Japan was not only inevitable, but well underway. Asai then estimated that the Soviet Army would take approximately two months to transport twenty divisions to the Far Eastern front.[23]

It now seemed to Japanese military observers that Soviet forces were prepared to attack Manchuria much sooner than the predicted US northern offensive against mainland Japan. Yet the Imperial General Headquarters focused on Japanese defenses against the US forces, while acting in accordance with its policy of passively maintaining peace with the Soviets. By May 1945 the Imperial General Headquarters determined that the dynamics of the US and Soviet offensives against Japan were competing, rather than coordinated, actions. They calculated that Soviet military operations against Japan could be triggered by various US operations in East Asia and thus the two assaults would work at cross-purposes. In "Draft intermediary report of May 13, 1945," Takagi Sōkichi predicted that the United States, once it decisively won the war, would try to establish hegemony over northern China, Manchuria, and Korea. The Soviet Union would then intervene to derail such US attempts.[24]

According to the Imperial General Headquarters analysis, there were two possible triggers for Soviet entry into the war against Japan: a US military offensive against Japan that threatened Soviet interests; and any indication of Japan's imminent surrender to the United States. In response to the first, Soviet forces would be mobilized to check US military operations. In response to the second, Soviet forces would be mobilized to prevent Japan from surrendering exclusively to the United States. The Imperial General Headquarters outlined six scenarios. Three scenarios detailed US actions that would directly threaten Soviet interests. The first would be if US forces were to land at strategic locations in either central or northern China and thus be ready to advance inland. The second would be if US forces were to land in southern Korea and gain momentum to advance northward. The third scenario would be if US forces were to penetrate deep into the Sea of Japan and attempt to land on strategic locations along the coast of Japan. In addition, the Imperial General Headquarters identified three scenarios that might lead the Soviet forces to intervene before Japanese surrender to the United States. The first would be the successful US invasion of mainland Japan. The second would be US air raids annihilating Japan's national power without a mainland invasion. The third would be Japan's domestic sentiment that Japan should seek peace with the United States.[25] (The second scenario, it turned out, is strikingly

23. WHS-KA, 323–25.
24. Takagi Sōkichi, *Chūkan hōkoku an* (March 13, 1945), 25.
25. WHS-KA, 327–28.

close to the actual sequence of events—the United States dropped an atomic bomb on Hiroshima on August 6 and the Soviet entry into the war against Japan on August 8.)

The Imperial General Headquarters' estimates revolved around Soviet readiness to act in order to prevent the United States' complete victory over Japan. The estimated timing for US invasion remained unchanged: the fall or later, but never in the "early fall" of 1945. Less than three weeks after the initiation of Operation Ketsu-gō, the comprehensive defense planning against the US invasion of mainland Japan, the Imperial General Headquarters completed the analysis that the Soviet attack would take place *prior to* the US invasion.

On May 26, 1945, the Seventeenth Area Army of Korea (Dai-17 Hōmen-gun), which took over the task of Korean defense from the Chōsen Army in February 1945, received a confidential intelligence report from Shanghai on US approaches to the Chinese Communist Party (CCP) concerning the coordination of military operations.[26] The intelligence gathered from Yan'an and from the CCP political division in Shanghai revealed that Lieutenant General Albert Wedemeyer, the commander of US forces in China, had visited Yan'an in early May 1945. During this visit he disclosed and discussed Fleet Admiral William Halsey's recent activities with the CCP leaders.[27] Almost three months before, in late February 1945, the CCP leaders already had concluded that US forces would most likely land on the central and southern coasts of China as part of the offensive against mainland Japan. They had even conceived of a plan to link a CCP military offensive with the landing of US forces. The CCP had had ample time since then to determine whether or how it would assist the US operation in China. This intelligence report seemed key to ascertaining Mao's readiness to collaborate with Washington in finishing off their common enemy, Japan.

According to this intelligence report, Wedemeyer purportedly introduced a US plan to land near the port of Lianyungang and requested coordinated military assistance from the CCP in the event of US landings on the China coast. Wedemeyer explained that such an operation was indispensable for isolating Japan proper from the continent before a successful invasion of Japan proper. Wedemeyer also explained that US forces planned to invade Korea (though the original text included a question mark at this point) by air as well as amphibiously. The CCP leaders, according to the Japanese intelligence report, counterproposed that

26. "Bei-gun no shinkō hōkō ni kansuru chōhō" (Intelligence concerning the movement of US forces) (May 27, 1945), in Dai-17 Hōmen-gun Sanbō-bu Sakusen-han (The Seventeenth Area Army Staff Operations Plans Division), *Kimitsu sakusen nisshi (otsu tsuzuri)* (The top secret strategic planning journal [series B]) (May 1945), MAL.

27. From the Japanese text it is not clear whether Wedemeyer met with only one or more than one individual.

US forces provide the CCP Army with weapons and ammunition before finalizing the plan for landing. They also requested that US forces, after landing in China, not intervene in political matters in regions under CCP control, and withdraw from China as soon as they achieved their original military goal. They also made a fourth request, which was not thoroughly decoded from the original Chinese, so its content remains unknown. The Japanese intelligence report said that no resolution was reached regarding these counterproposals.[28]

Archival records in the United States have no record of a Wedemeyer visit to Yan'an or any meeting with the CCP leaders in May. The most relevant information is found in the following document, but note that the meeting took place in April, not May:

> Within the past two or three weeks there has been held in Yenan, in Shensi Province, North of the Yellow River bend, the first congress of the Chinese Communist Party. . . . This congress has been attended by Mr. J. S. Service, political adviser for the Commanding General, U. S. Forces, China Theater, who was present in the capacity of an observer. Mr. Service has not yet returned to this Headquarters. Upon his return it is believed that he will have information which may have a direct and important bearing on the subject here under consideration.[29]

As this discrepancy might well imply, the Japanese authorities could not verify the accuracy of the above intelligence report concerning US-CCP military collaboration. Indeed the US plan to land on the east coast of China as part of the US invasion of mainland Japan had been canceled in the fall of 1944, so it is unlikely that Wedemeyer brought up the moribund plan in the spring of 1945. In the spring of 1945, however, Wedemeyer did work on a revised plan for the China theater, Operation Carbonado, which called for a rapid advance of US forces from the Philippines to the coast of China in August 1945 to seize Fort Bayard on the Liuchow Peninsula, about 250 miles southwest of Canton, and begin attacking from the Kweilin-Liuchow area with a final assault on Canton on November 1. Additional combat aircraft, including the US Tenth Air Force from India, would arrive in China to prepare for Carbonado.[30] The intelligence report of May 26,

---

28. "Bei-gun no shinkō hōkō ni kansuru chōhō."

29. In the Wedemeyer Collection at the Hoover Institution Archives, Stanford University, there are no documents indicating Wedemeyer's visit to Yan'an during this period. The document quoted in the main text is "A Study: Chinese Communists in Relation to Planned Military Operations in China," 2nd draft, 3 April 1945, 17 pages, including appendix, on p. 6. Wedemeyer Collection, Box 87, folder 7. Hoover Institute Archives, Stanford University, California. (Courtesy of Ms. Carol A. Leadenham, Assistant Archivist for Reference.)

30. Mark D. Sherry, "China Defensive: The U.S. Army Campaigns of World War II," U.S. Army Center of Military History Publication 72–38, available online at http://www.history.army.mil;

1945, therefore, might have referred to Operation Carbonado. Despite the complexity of the situation, the Japanese report captured the difficulties the US forces would face in using China as a base for its attack on the Japanese mainland.

About a month after Germany surrendered, the Supreme Council for the Direction of the War convened with Emperor Hirohito on June 8 to consider a basic principle in guiding the war. Foreign Minister Tōgō explained in the presence of the emperor how the United States was trying to force Japan's unconditional surrender in a short period of time. While rifts might emerge among the United States, Britain, and the Soviet Union on the issues of Europe, Middle East, and the world peace organization, Tōgō argued that Japan should not count on the dissolution of that coalition. For all their divisions, the Allies knew that world peace depended on their amity, and they needed victory for their own postwar planning.

Tōgō was most lucid when he explained the growing Soviet hostility toward Japan. Since the Soviet Union had called Japan an aggressor the previous November and announced that it would not renew the neutrality pact with Japan in April, "it has adopted a free hand in entering a state of bellicosity with Japan at any time." Given Soviet confidence about eventual Japanese defeat in the face of American military supremacy, and its unwillingness to negotiate with the loser, Japan's diplomacy with Moscow would become more and more deadlocked. The Soviet entry into the war against Japan would be fatal to Japan, continued Tōgō, and winning favorable neutrality with the Soviet Union was likely "impossible." He concluded that any policy based on assumptions of Moscow's friendship was simply unrealistic.[31]

The military leaders who attended this meeting seem to have agreed with Tōgō on both the improbability of a breakup of the Grand Alliance before the war's end and the inevitability of Soviet war on Japan. The military evaluation of the Soviet forces, more damning than Tōgō's statement, concluded that the Soviets had completed the military buildup of the Far Eastern front and were ready to enter the war against Japan at any minute. Even after all this was said, no military leader spoke of a need to stop or repel the Soviet offensive. On the contrary, Lieutenant General Kawabe Torashirō, vice chief of the army general staff, declared in front of Emperor Hirohito that the Japanese military would adhere to the fundamental policy of "keeping peace and status quo" (*seihitsu hoji*) with the Soviets

---

Theresa L. Kraus, "China Offensive: The U.S. Army Campaigns of World War II" U.S. Army Center of Military History Publication 72-39, available online at http://www.history.army.mil.

31. "Kongo torubeki sensō shidō no kihon taikō ni kanshi Gozen Kaigi keika gaiyō" (Summary report on the Imperial Conference on "The basic principle in guiding the war in the future"), in RJD, 263 and 272–73.

at all costs, which suggested there would be no Japanese military response to the Soviet's first blow.[32]

The June 8 meeting produced a special report, "Kongo torubeki sensō shidō no kihon taikō" (The basic principle in guiding the war in the future), signed by all participants: Suzuki Kantarō (prime minister), Hiranuma Kiichirō (president of the Privy Council), Yonai Mitsumasa (minister of the navy), Anami Korechika (minister of war), Toyoda Teijirō (minister of munitions), Ishiguro Tada'atsu (minister of agriculture and commerce), Tōgō Shigenori (minister of foreign affairs and minister of Great Asia), Toyoda Soemu (chief of naval staff), and Kawabe Torashirō (vice chief of the army general staff).[33]

The section "Sekai jōsei handan" (Evaluations of world affairs) analyzed US and Soviet attitudes toward Japan and reiterated that after President Roosevelt's death in April, the US government, with its supremacy in materiel, was trying to finish the war against Japan as quickly as possible. The United States would continue the marriage of convenience with the Soviet Union in order to maintain the Grand Alliance through the war.

Stressing the imminence of Soviet military action against Japan, the report concluded that the Soviet Union was prepared diplomatically and militarily to enter a hostile relationship with Japan at any time. Since the Soviets had already built up forces in the Far East, thus applying more pressure on Japan, it appeared very likely that it would move against Japan as soon as Japan's situation deteriorated severely. The Soviets would wait until then in order to achieve its ambitions in East Asia with the minimum sacrifice. The timing for Soviet military mobilization would not be earlier, continued the report, because the Soviet Union was waiting for the best moment to check the rise of the United States in East Asia, which could be when US forces landed in Japan proper or on the central and northern coasts of China. The report's most crucial assessment: in light of the meteorological conditions of northern Manchuria, which were suitable for its military operations, and the speed of buildup of Soviet soldiers in the Far East, the timing of the Soviet attack would be most likely either the summer or fall or later.

The report continued with the war situation in China. The GMD was strengthening its forces "in the American style" and was likely to push against Japan beginning in the fall, in parallel to US military operations against Japan. The CCP, on the other hand, would intensify attacks in areas occupied by Japan. Considering the current relations between the GMD and the United States, it was improbable that Japan could achieve peace with China. At the same time China was troubled by US ambitions for East Asian hegemony should the United States achieve

32. "Kongo torubeki sensō shidō no kihon taikō ni kanshi Gozen Kaigi keika gaiyō," 276.
33. "Kongo torubeki sensō shidō no kihon taikō ni kanshi Gozen Kaigi keika gaiyō," 265–70.

complete victory against Japan. The growing presence of the CCP and pressure from the Soviet Union added uncertainty to China's future.

Recognizing that Japan was poised between survival and extinction because the United States was quickly trying to finish the war, the report reiterated that Japan needed to be vigilant about Soviet attitudes toward Japan. The Japanese empire should resolve to win and promptly carry out the *political and military strategies* (*sei-senryaku shisaku o dankō*) (emphasis added).[34] These unspecified strategies possibly referenced the policy of "keeping peace and status quo" (*seihitsu hoji*) with the Soviet Union while waiting passively for its military operation.

A revised report on the evaluation of the war's progress issued on July 1, 1945, by the Imperial General Headquarters updated estimates for the US mainland invasion based on the US Navy's capacity. They calculated that both aerial and coastal invasions would occur between late fall of 1945 and early spring of 1946.[35] Comparisons with the US Army's Olympic plan for the Kyūshū invasion scheduled in November 1945 and the Coronet plan for the Kanto invasion in the spring of 1946 show that Japanese predictions of the US plans for the landing were nearly perfect in terms of the timing, specific locations of landing points, and strategic purposes. Historian Alvin Coox has marveled at the congruence between actual US planning and Japanese countermeasures, which in his words "extended to plotting the anticipated timings and locations of landing points in scary detail."[36] He argues that the Japanese defensive countermeasures were the result of tactical and strategic common sense, not Japanese counterintelligence in the Philippines.[37]

The Seventeenth Area Army in Korea contributed to intelligence efforts on US plans for the invasion of mainland Japan. On May 27 the Seventeenth Area Army received several confidential reports from Shanghai. One told of a certain Richardson of the US Army instructing his staff to study a plan to land on Kujū-kurihama Beach in Chiba near Tokyo. Another related how Fleet Admiral Chester Nimitz, Allied commander-in-chief of the Pacific Ocean arena, planned on heavy aerial bombing of Kyūshū ahead of a landing there.[38] Although the Seventeenth

---

34. "Sekai jōsei handan," in RJD, 267–68; also in WHS-KA, 326.

35. Daihon'ei Rikugun-bu (The Imperial General Headquarters, the Division of the Army), *Shōwa 21-nen haru-goro o medo to suru jōsei handan* (Studies of estimated conditions in the spring of 1946) (July 1, 1945), 2–3, MAL.

36. Alvin Coox, "Needless Fear: The Compromise of U.S. Plans to Invade Japan in 1945," *Journal of Military History* 64 (April 2000): 435.

37. "OLYMPIC and CORONET: G-II Estimate of the Enemy Situation (April 25, 1945)," Records of the War Department General and Special Staffs, Operation Division (RG 165), NARA. See Coox, "Needless Fear," 411–37. Also see WHS-PMB, vol. 2, 442–43, for the Japanese side attributing the brilliant congruence to solid strategic calculations.

38. Dai-17 Hōmen-gun Sanbō-bu Sakusen-han, *Kimitsu sakusen nisshi*. See the entry of May 27.

Area Army determined that it could not verify the accuracy of these reports, the timing and contents of these reports were not wide off the mark. The reference to the Kujūkurihama beach corresponds to Operation Coronet, the invasion of Honshū at the Kantō Plain, scheduled for March 1, 1946. Indeed, on May 25 the Joint Chiefs of Staff in Washington approved and ordered further military operations against Japan, including the landing on Kyūshū scheduled for November 1, 1945, in a directive issued to General Douglas MacArthur, commander in chief, US Army Forces Pacific, and Fleet Admiral Nimitz.[39]

While the congruence could be attributed to solid Japanese strategic calculations, top military leaders in Japan were far from building an adequate defense in Kyūshū in terms of equipment, training, and building of fortresses.[40] The mobilization of troops in Kyūshū itself does not indicate that Japan was preparing exclusively for a final battle against the United States. The scale and prominence of the defense preparations against a US invasion have served to obfuscate the strategic anticipation, shared among numerous different wartime planners, that the Soviets would indeed enter the war, as well as Japanese accuracy about the timing of that entry.

Evincing the careful attention paid to the Soviets, and not just the Americans, the July 1 report predicted the military strategies of all of US, British, Chinese, and Soviet forces against Japan and also the political development of these nations, including US-Soviet tensions, the GMD-CCP conflicts, as well as futures of Southeast Asia. While its scope of analysis extended to the spring of 1946, the report projected a peak in military operations from summer to fall of 1945. While it mentioned the defense of mainland Japan against the United States as the decisive battle in the final stage of the war, it simultaneously envisioned a US and Soviet two-front assault on Japan's continental empire and anticipated their attempts to check each other's East Asian ambitions. Nowhere did this report indicate a desperate need for a defense build-up against US and Soviet forces.

The report stated that the enemy US forces would attempt to end the war expeditiously by intensifying attacks on mainland Japan by air and sea. The United States would do so without requesting or receiving Soviet assistance. The report predicted that Kyūshū would be the first region of attack and Kantō the final battle. The attack on Kyūshū would occur in September 1945 if the United States planned to mobilize thirty or so divisions. If it waited to secure fifty or so divisions for the Kyūshū operation, then the attack would not occur until the spring of 1946.[41]

---

39. Gar Alperovitz, *The Decision to Use the Atomic Bomb* (New York: Vintage Books, 1996), 63.
40. WHS-PMB, vol. 2, 447–49.
41. *Shōwa 21-nen haru-goro o medo to suru jōsei handan*, 1–3.

The July 1 report also focused on impending Soviet military operations in East Asia. Considering the rapid military buildup in the Soviet Far East between late February and late June, the report estimated that the Soviet forces would be ready to mobilize before the end of 1945 to respond to any situation in East Asia. Estimates became much more precise. The primary triggers for Soviet military operations would be US landings in southern Korea and a subsequent northern advance or a US offensive on China, be it US landings in central or northern China. The report identified as another possible trigger any sign of Japan's surrender to the United States. The report explained that the US invasion of mainland Japan (Kyūshū) would surely send a signal to the Soviet Union and compel the latter to attack Manchuria and Korea. In the May 27 intelligence report, the Seventeenth Area Army had predicted a US plan to deploy heavy aerial bombing in Kyūshū prior to the actual invasion. This July 1 report added that even without an actual mainland invasion, America's air raids would trigger Soviet military deployment for fear of Japan's surrender to the United States without Soviet entry into the war, the same prediction made earlier.[42]

Once the Soviet Union decided to join in battle, the report argued, the preponderance of Soviet forces would allow them to achieve Soviet political and—parenthetically, in the original—military goals in an extremely short period of time. It predicted that the Soviet assault would be deep and wide based on the military buildup and positioning of the Soviet troops. Once the Soviet forces entered the war, their superior air power would be directed at annihilating Japan's air bases in Manchuria, Korea, Inner-Mongolia-Xinjiang, and northern China. After destroying the transportation networks and fortresses in these regions, the Soviets would quickly launch all-out assaults in Manchuria with their principal forces and simultaneously attack northern Korea and Mongolia-Xinquian, perhaps even Sakhalin with their remaining forces.[43]

The report reiterated that US-Soviet military deployment would set off a chain reaction in Chinese politics as well. With consideration of their effect on the political war in China and other regions, the US forces aimed to land on the Chinese continent and move inland. The Anglo-American military buildup in China would probably take place gradually after the summer of 1945. The GMD and CCP forces might then in the fall or winter of 1945 launch massive anti-Japanese operations in central or southern China. Meanwhile Soviet forces would most likely attempt to capture politically and economically strategic locations and secure a trans-Manchurian route into northern Korea. The Soviet military advance into Manchuria and beyond would enhance the CCP's stance against the

---

42. *Shōwa 21-nen haru-goro o medo to suru jōsei handan*, 14–15, MAL.
43. *Shōwa 21-nen haru-goro o medo to suru jōsei handa*, 7–8, MAL.

GMD in the race for control of China. The United States would also attempt to foster its own political and economic system in the regions it captured. At that point the United States and the Soviet Union would no longer be able to hide their respective political objectives for China, which would deepen their mutual antipathy.[44]

In spite of setting out these anticipated scenarios, the report suggested no Japanese countermeasures. The report simply concluded that only by establishing a posture of "waiting" while crushing the enemy would Japan be able to exploit the built-in dilemmas and contradictions of the Americans and the Soviets and turn the war situation favorable to Japan. The resulting conditions would contribute to Japan's victory even when the Allies demanded unconditional surrender.[45] The Imperial General Headquarters did not believe a final mainland battle against the United States to be a likely conclusion to the war.

Korean Gambit

The July 1 report's greatest insight concerned how both Moscow and Washington would compete for control over the Korean Peninsula even before the war's conclusion. The Imperial General Headquarters' analysis went even further. Since early 1945 it had estimated that as a result of near-simultaneous attacks on Korea by US and Soviet forces the peninsula would be occupied by both of them—the southern half by the United States and the northern half by the Soviet Union. Aware that Japan could not fight both to retain Korea, the Japanese strategists developed scenarios on how the United States and the Soviet Union might advance into the peninsula and occupy various regions beyond the end of the war.

The Soviet Union and the CCP had developed international networks across Manchuria and Korea, whereas the United States apparently had made no attempts to join its lukewarm support for Chiang Kai-shek to its tepid interest in Syngman Rhee. Washington would find it difficult to select a native Korean leader, with grassroots support, who would assist US interests not only in Korea but in East Asia. Japanese policymakers reasoned that if the United States were to catch up with the Soviet Union in securing Korea it would be through a military operation. Henceforth Japanese strategists zeroed in on US-Soviet military stratagems.

Until 1942 the Chōsen Army served as the rear guard for the war in China and prepared for a possible war with the Soviet Union. In the Pacific War context, too, Korea served as a fundamental military supply base. After January 1943, when

44. *Shōwa 21-nen haru-goro o medo to suru jōsei handan*, 3–5, 18–20, MAL.
45. *Shōwa 21-nen haru-goro o medo to suru jōsei handa*, 24, MAL.

the elite Twentieth Division in Seoul was dispatched to New Guinea, Japan heavily mobilized Korea and frequently moved troops in and out of the peninsula. While the new Thirtieth Division and 101st Regiment were added to the peninsular defense, the newly formed Forty-ninth Division in Seoul was dispatched to Burma in February 1944, and the Thirtieth Regiment was dispatched to the Philippines in May 1944.[46] The more soldiers Korea sent to the battlefields in the Pacific, the more soldiers it received from outside into the peninsula. As a result the total number of soldiers stationed in Korea, including Korean volunteers and draftees, dramatically increased over the Pacific War. By the end of 1941, there were 46,000 men; by the end of 1943, there were 59,000 men, and by the end of 1944 there were 68,000. Eventually the total would reach 347,000 by August 1945.

The number of soldiers alone indicated Japan's determination to defend Korea against the United States.[47] After Japan's decisive loss at the battle of Leyte Gulf in October 1944, the United States emerged as a direct military threat to Korea as US forces inched closer to Taiwan and the coasts of China, Korea, and Japan proper. Around that time, the Imperial General Headquarters in Tokyo, discarding the earlier determination to retain Korea, began a study of the hypothetical two-front assault on Korea in the final stage of the war, one by the United States from the south and the other by the Soviet Union from the north.

January 1945 was a turning point in Japan's military planning for Korea. On January 16, 1945, when Colonel Sugita Ichiji provided the aforementioned timetable for US landings in mainland Japan, he did not include Korea in the scenario. The Ogasawara Islands, Taiwan, Okinawa and even the Kurile Islands, and the southern coast of China were regarded as potential landing points for US forces, as they approached mainland Japan, but Sugita excluded Korea as a possible target of US military attack.[48] On January 20, 1945, when the Imperial General Headquarters adopted "Teikoku Riku-Kai-gun sakusen keikaku taikō" (Grand proposal for Imperial Army-Navy strategic maneuvers), it again omitted the entire Korean Peninsula from Japan's final defense perimeter against the US offensive.[49]

Shortly after that the strategic significance of Korea changed dramatically. Without explanation the Imperial General Headquarters suddenly revised its earlier proposal and included Korea among estimated targets of a series of US invasions. Henceforth the defense of Korea became fully integrated into the defense of Japan proper. More specifically the defense of southern Korea and

---

46. Morita Yoshio, *Chōsen shūsen no kiroku: Bei-So ryōgun no shinchū to Nihonjin no hikiage* (A record of the fall of Colonial Korea: US-Soviet military advances and Japanese withdrawal) (Tokyo: Gen'nandō Shoten, 1964), 13.

47. Morita Yoshio, *Chōsen shūsen no kiroku*, 23.

48. TSWJ, vol. 2, 650–52.

49. Nakayama Takashi, "Nihon no sensō sakusen shidō ni okeru Soren yōin," 51.

the defense of Kyūshū became integrated into one strategy. Continental Order 1242, issued on February 3, 1945, designated the defense perimeter of Japan as Taiwan, the Nansei Islands, Korea and the coast of China.[50] The Imperial General Headquarters disbanded the Chōsen Army and established the new Seventeenth Area Army to lead the Korean defense against the United States, effective February 11.[51] Subsequently Continental Order 1245, issued on February 6, 1945, declared that the central focus on strategic preparation in Korea was now in the southern part, against US invasion, and it also transferred the responsibility for Korea's strategic planning against the Soviet Union to the Kwantung Army in Manchuria.[52] Japan henceforth adopted a dual strategy for Korea—one against the United States and another against the Soviet Union—and focused on how the peninsula would turn into a stage for US-Soviet competition for control before the war's end.

Cheju Island became the focal point of Korea's defense preparation against the United States. The largest island in Korea, Cheju Island was 1,845 square kilometers (almost twice as large as Hong Kong), with a population of 230,000. A beautiful oval volcanic island, Cheju Island was marginally self-sufficient in food supply, exporting cereals, importing rice, and engaging in cattle breeding and abundant fishing. Since Pearl Harbor, Cheju Island had been one of the most "peaceful and stable" territories within the peninsula, according to the Chōsen Army report. The island thus attracted Korean returnees, migrant laborers who left mainland Japan as the US air raids intensified. The island had two hundred or so Japanese soldiers, equipped with poor transportation and communication facilities.[53] As the B-29s began bombing the southern coast of Korea parallel to the air raids on mainland Japan, more and more soldiers were sent to Cheju Island. The 111th Division was transferred from Harbin and the 108th Division was transferred from Japan.[54] By February 1945 the number of soldiers stationed on Cheju Island had risen to 1,000, eventually reaching 60,668 by August 1945. At the end of the war, Cheju Island alone contained 17.5 percent of all the soldiers positioned in all of Korea.[55] To maintain a sustainable population on the

50. CCCO, vol. 10, 47–48.

51. "Dai-17 Hōmen-gun" (The Seventeenth Area Army), *Sakusen junbi shi (dai-ichi-an)* (History of operation planning [the first draft]) (n.d.), 11, MAL.

52. CCCO, vol. 10, 52–54.

53. Chōsen-gun Zanmu Seiri-bu (The Chōsen Army Postwar Liquidation Adjustment Office), "Chōsen ni okeru sensō junbi" (War preparation in Korea) (February 1946), SHKA, 147–50 and 155–57.

54. The new 127th Brigade was set in Pusan; the 120th Division was transferred from Manchuria to Taegu. In addition the 5th Air Division (Dai-5 *Kokūtai*) was transferred from China to defend Korea and the naval units fell under a unified command system of the Seventeenth Area Army Commander.

55. Morita Yoshio, *Chōsen shūsen no kiroku*, 23–25.

island, the Seventeenth Area Army planned to evacuate some 50,000 civilian islanders to mainland Korea. However, US attacks by air and submarines prevented the safe transportation of these noncombatant residents, so the Seventeenth Area Army revoked the plan and decided to keep them on the island to aid the Japanese Army in the event of a US landing.[56] When the war ended on August 18, 1945, there were 117,000 soldiers positioned in northern Korea, as opposed to some 230,000 men stationed in southern Korea. The number of soldiers stationed on Cheju Island alone—60,668—was approximately 52 percent of the entire defense in the north.[57]

The heavy defense buildup in southern Korea, particularly on Cheju Island, should not be regarded as Japan's desperate final resolve to fight the US forces, as it necessitated a defense reduction in northern Korea against the Soviet Union and inevitably upped the ante for Japan's defeat anyway. The Imperial General Headquarters had by then anticipated an eventual Soviet attack on Manchuria and beyond and it even had concluded that the Soviet's massive attack would most likely occur *before* the US invasion of Kyūshū. Contradictory as it was, the reverse was made the official view in the case of Cheju Island: the US attack on southern Korea would occur *first*, followed by the Soviet attack from the north. This official view served as a pretext to justify the heavy focus on southern Korea and the neglect of northern Korea, which made sense in the context of the policy of "keeping peace and status quo" (*seihitsu hoji*) with the Soviet Union.

On March 12, 1945, the Imperial General Headquarters met with the chief of the Seventeenth Area Army Staff Operations Plans Division and discussed the defense plan for Korea as part of the comprehensive plan for Japan proper. The principal mission assigned to the Seventeenth Area Army was to crush the invading enemy from the south (that is, the United States) and defend the Korean Peninsula.[58] The Imperial General Headquarters and the Seventeenth Area Army were fully aware that defense cuts in northern Korea never meant that the Soviet threat was gone. On April 5 just shortly after the US landings on Okinawa, the Soviet government announced that it would not renew the Soviet-Japanese Neutrality Pact when it expired in the following year. Moscow's determination to enter the war against Japan became increasingly clear, as did the US threat to the mainland Japan. While its main assignment was to resist and push back US offensives, the Seventeenth Area Army continued observing Soviet military moves to ascertain the exact timing of the Soviet attack from the north.

---

56. Morita Yoshio, *Chōsen shūsen no kiroku*, 15–18.
57. Morita Yoshio, *Chōsen shūsen no kiroku*, 23–25.
58. Dai-17 Hōmen-gun (The Seventeenth Area Army), "Hondo sakusen kiroku" (Record of the mainland operation), vol. 5 (October 1946), SHKA, 217–20.

On April 8 the Imperial General Headquarters announced Operation Ketsu-gō, a comprehensive plan for Japan's operation against the US mainland invasion by land and air estimated to take place by the fall of 1945. This comprehensive defense plan contained seven regional operations, and Korea was the only colony fully integrated into the overall defense of mainland Japan: Operation Ketsu 1 against a US landing on the Kurile Islands as well as any US advance to the Sōya and Tsugaru Straits; Operation Ketsu 2 against the landing of smaller US forces in northern Japan; Operation Ketsu 3 against any major US landing in the Tokyo metropolitan area via the Bay of Tokyo; Operation Ketsu 4 against the landing of smaller US forces in the Tōkai region via the Bay of Ise; Operation Ketsu 5 against the landing of smaller US forces in the Chūgoku region via the Setouchi Inland Sea; Operation Ketsu 6 against a major US landing in Kyūshū and any offensive across the Korea Strait; and Operation Ketsu 7 against the landing of smaller US forces in Korea via the Korea Strait. The comprehensive guideline for Operation Ketsu-gō set a timetable for completion of defense preparations. During the first stage (April to July 1945), the preliminary defense would be built; during the second stage (August to September 1945), the defense would be strengthened; and during the third stage (October 1945 and beyond), the full defense preparation should be complete.[59]

As for the Korean defense, the Seventeenth Area Army Staff Operations Plans Division took responsibility for perfecting a detailed strategy for Operation Ketsu 7, and it did so based on the following predictions of US landings in Korea sometime after August 1945. First US forces would land on northern Kyūshū and establish a base. If not they would directly assault Cheju Island and capture it as a base for movement between northern Kyūshū and southern Korea across the Korea Strait. Then US forces would attack small islands in southern Korea, land at Pusan, and advance to the center of the peninsula. On the basis of this estimate of US operations, the preliminary defense preparation in southern Korea took off, scheduled to be completed by the end of August 1945. Full defense preparations were scheduled to be in place by the end of October 1945, the estimated timing for the US invasion of Kyūshū.[60]

In February 1945 the Kwantung Army adopted a plan to abandon all the strategic bases along the Manchurian-Soviet border and to retreat southward (toward the Manchurian-Korean border) to build multiple fortresses for launching "last-ditch resistance."[61] (See map 6.1 for these plans.) The Seventeenth Area Army in

---

59. WHS-PMB, vol. 1, 305–7.
60. Chōsen-gun Zanmu Seiri-bu, "Chōsen ni okeru sensō junbi," 163–66.
61. "Dai-17 Hōmen-gun," *Sakusen junbi shi (dai-ichi-an)*, 17–18, MAL.

Korea agreed to supply the Kwantung Army with some fifteen hundred soldiers and fifteen thousand workers from the Korean Peninsula for building fortresses in southern Manchuria starting in May 1945.[62] As a result northern Korea became increasingly vulnerable to direct attack on Seoul from Wonsan by Soviet forces.[63] In late April the Seventeenth Area Army Staff Operations Plans Division recognized new movements by the Soviet Air Force. Japanese ships navigating the Sea of Japan noticed that they were being overflown by Soviet aircraft. On May 4 the Seventeenth Area Army received a telegram from the Kwantung Army, recommending vigilance for a possible shift in operations by the Soviet Air Force because the family of a certain commander seemed ready to relocate for his new assignment. Subsequently the Seventeenth Area Army Staff Officer expressed a need to coordinate with the Kwantung Army in planning the north-south dual operation in Korea, rather than placing excess emphasis on the south.[64] The Imperial General Headquarters, too, estimated that the Soviet Army, once it attacked Manchuria, would quickly advance into northern Korea. A US advance into southern Korea would occur almost simultaneously as part of the invasion of mainland Japan in the fall of 1945, or even prior to that. It even added a revised analysis that the Soviet deployment might occur (without US military action in Korea) when the Soviet Union felt its interests in Korea were threatened by the United States.[65]

On May 30 the Imperial General Headquarters issued Continental Orders 1337–1341 in preparation for both a US invasion of southern Korea and Soviet deployment in Manchuria and northern Korea. Continental Order 1337 ordered General Umezu Yoshijirō, chief of army staff, to arrive in southern Manchuria and Korea in early June and to give instructions on the continental strategy to the commanders in chief of Kwantung Army, the China Expeditionary Army, and the Seventeenth Area Army. Continental Order 1338 commissioned the China Expeditionary Army to transfer one military unit to the Manchuria-Northern Korean region under the command of the Kwantung Army. Continental Order 1339, a more specific order to prepare for US and Soviet operations, charged the commander of the Seventeenth Area Army with annihilating the invading enemy (the United States) in southern Korea and ordered the commander of the Kwantung Army to crush the advancing US forces and also to "carry out the strategic preparation against the Soviet forces in northern Korea" (*HokuSen ni okeru tai-So sakusen junbi o jisshi subeshi*). Continental Orders 1340 and 1341 instructed the

62. "Chōsen-gun gaiyō-shi" (A concise history of the Chōsen Army) (n.d.), SHKA, 167–68.

63. "Dai-17 Hōmen-gun," *Sakusen junbi shi (dai-ichi-an)*, 35–37, MAL.

64. Dai-17 Hōmen-gun Sanbō-bu Sakusen-han, *Kimitsu sakusen nisshi*. See the entries of May 4, 8, 9, and 20.

65. WHS-KA, 327–28.

Kwantung Army and the China Expeditionary Army also to prepare for Soviet operations.[66]

What was "the strategic preparation against the Soviet forces in northern Korea"? The likely answer to that question was possibly in an attachment of Continental Order 1340 titled "Summary of Strategy against the Soviet Union in Manchuria and Korea." Unfortunately the attachment, most likely destroyed, is no longer available as part of the order.[67] Continental Instruction 2494 (May 30, 1945) provided a detailed estimate of the course of Soviet military operations in Korea: the Soviets would hit not only Pyeongan-bukdo, the province bordering Manchuria, and Hamgyeong-bukdo, the province bordering with the Soviet Union, but also Hamgyeong-namdo and Hwanghae-do, both located south of these provinces. This estimate reflected the Imperial General Headquarters' assessment of how the Soviet offensive would be swift in mobility and wide in scope.[68]

On July 13, the Imperial General Headquarters issued Continental Instructions 2521 and 2522, as follow-ups to Continental Orders 1339 and 1340 of May 30. These two instructions once again heavily emphasized defense against the hypothetical US military assault on southern Korea and called for much less preparation against the visibly growing Soviet military presence in the north of Korea. Continental Instruction 2521 set out military operations on Cheju Island against the enemy (US forces) in the following manner: when the prospect of *enemy* invasion loomed, the commander of the Seventeenth Area Army would move more troops onto the island and fortify the Fifty-eighth Army, and then launch offensive attacks and crush the *enemy's* attempt at turning the island into air and naval bases. In contrast Continental Instruction 2522, which concerned the Soviet attack on Korea, called for passive actions as follows: "Based on the basic outline of Operation Otsu, the Thirty-fourth Army, even if it cannot crush the advancing Soviet forces at the fortresses on the Hamgyeong-namdo Plain (Kan'nan Heiya), should attempt with its main force to prevent the enemy (US forces) from charging into Pyongyang, and with part of its force attempt to prevent the enemy from charging toward Seoul."[69] The big picture emerging from the two Continental Instructions taken together is the containment of US forces on Cheju Island and mild resistance against the southward advance of the Soviet forces.

---

66. CCCO, vol. 10, 154–58.

67. WHS-KA, 378.

68. CCCO, vol. 10, 318–19.

69. CCCO, vol. 10, 339. The four characters transliterated as "Kan'nan Heiya" appearing in Continental Instruction 2522 do not match any actual place name in Korea, but the first two Chinese characters are most likely an abbreviation of the name "Hamgyeong-namdo" and the last two characters mean plain or flat land. Since Continental Instruction 2494, which concerns projections of a Soviet attack on Korea, explicitly names Hamgyeong-namdo, this seems a reasonable interpretation.

Although the Japanese military ruled out immediate armed confrontation between the United States and the Soviet Union over Korea, they did not fail to predict the political complications that would arise from the near simultaneous advances of their military forces into the peninsula. The July 1 report, the comprehensive evaluation by the Imperial General Headquarters of the war's progress, addressed the competition between the United States and the Soviet Union in establishing their respective political and economic systems in regions they captured from Japanese control. The report predicted that the US government would try to win popular support by advertising its readiness to grant Korea independence. The Soviet government, too, would attempt to gain control over Korea. However, it mentioned nothing about the postwar status of Korea. In stark contrast with the comparatively detailed vision of the growth of CCP leadership in divided China, the Imperial General Headquarters remained silent about which Korean leaders the Soviet and US forces would most likely align with when they marched into the peninsula. It merely reiterated that US and Soviet forces would not likely engage each other due to the mutual desire to return to normalcy after the war.

Around this time Japanese strategists had come to grasp the possibility that the powers would carve up the peninsula. From intelligence reports they noted references to the "Korean border settlement" and "zoning." Since the Japanese were aware how defeated Germany had been quickly separated into four zones of occupation under American, British, French, and Soviet military administration, with Berlin divided into four sectors, it would not have been difficult for them to imagine that these phrases—"border settlement" and "zoning"—possibly meant drawing a new border within Korea, or dividing Korea into several occupied zones as part of a multinational trusteeship.

The Japanese special service organization in Shanghai, the Ume Kikan (Plum Blossom Agency), played a particular role in gathering information on the postwar settlement of Korea.[70] On July 1, 1945, the Ume Kikan sent a confidential telegram to the Imperial General Headquarters, the Imperial Army, the Kwantung Army, the China Expeditionary Army, the North China Area Army, and the Korean Seventeenth Area Army, informing them of a set of seven proposals the Soviet Politburo on the Far East (Kyokutō Seiji-kyoku) had allegedly submitted to the Central Committee concerning the postwar disposition of Korea.

Although the accuracy of this intelligence report cannot be determined without the corresponding Soviet archival documents, this document shows that Japanese

70. For the records on this organization, see: MIS, Ume Kikan, Espionage Organization, 1944.10.16 (RG 319, Box 1793); OSS, Kunming, Ume Kikan-Japanese Supra Spy Organization, 1944.10 (RG 226, Entry 173, Box 10); Army Staff, report on the Ume Kikan, 1947 (RG 319, Box 1793), NARA.

leaders were aware that Stalin and FDR had discussed Korea at Yalta. The report suggested an outline of Soviet planning for Korea that seems relatively congruent with actual developments. The first point proposed that based on the decision at Yalta, the United States, Britain, the Soviet Union, and the GMD regime would recognize Korea as an independent nation. After the war the United States, Britain, and the GMD regime should not revoke their approval of "Korea's border settlement," but should honor the mutual agreement. The second point advocated that in the event of establishing a provisional government in Korea, the General Headquarters of the Korean National Liberation Movement (Chōsen Minzoku Kaihō Undō Sōhonbu) that might refer to the Korean National Liberation and Struggle Alliance (Choson Minjok Haebang Tujaeng Tongmaeng), should be the organizational core. The third point proposed that volunteer corps at Yan'an and Chongqing should be recognized as the Korean Independent Army (Kankoku Dokuritu-gun) and that it would not reorganize or disarm itself after the war. The fourth point called for an international guarantee from Britain, the United States, the Soviet Union, France, and China that the General Headquarters of the so-called "Korean National Liberation Movement" would be reorganized based on the will of the Korean people. The fifth point demanded that the United States, Britain, France, and China would all see to it that the independent Korean government pursued a friendly policy toward the Soviet Union. The sixth point demanded that after the establishment of "Korean border," the armed forces of the Allied powers would all withdraw within a mutually agreed period of time. Finally the seventh point demanded that the Korean representatives should entrust the world peace conference to deal with the issues of a "border settlement" and the withdrawal of the Allied forces from Korea in a manner fair to all.[71]

On the following day, July 2, the Ume Kikan dispatched another confidential telegram to the Imperial Army, the Imperial General Headquarters, the China Expeditionary Army, the North China Area Army, the Kwantung Army, and the Seventeeth Area Army. The telegram reported that the Central Committee of the Soviet Union (Soren Kyōsan-tō Chūō Seiji-kyoku) intended to "oppose any proposal for new border demarcations or military zoning (gunji-teki bunkai) of Japan's colonies pre-arranged by the United States, Britain and the GMD regime." The Ume Kikan speculated that the Soviet Central Committee might have proposed to support the (united) independence movement in both Korea and Taiwan. The Soviets would be motivated by the integration of these new (pro-Soviet) "institutions" into the supply line of the Far Eastern Red Army, which they could then use to build a large defense perimeter for the Soviet Far East. The confiden-

---

71. Dai-17 Hōmen-gun Sanbō-bu Sakusen-han, *Kimitsu sakusen nisshi*. See the entry of July 1, 1945, confidential telegram no. 728.

tial telegram even revealed how the Soviets had a proposal to prevent Anglo-America from establishing capitalist dominance in a post-surrender Japan.[72]

On July 3 the Ume Kikan dispatched a third confidential telegram. The TASS news agency had reported a certain Soviet leader's comments, including one about Moscow's intention to approve the independence of (unified) China and Korea.[73] At previous conferences Stalin had made it clear that he did not think Korea ready for independence and had endorsed trusteeship by the United States, Britain, China, and the Soviet Union. Seeing rising US ambitions in Korea, he might have thought it worthwhile to let go of Korea, on the assumption that the majority of Koreans preferred a communist government.

In spite of Syngman Rhee's repeated pleas for US assistance and the rising concern within the State Department about Soviet military operations, the United States never considered a military assault on Korea prior to Japan's surrender. While the US Navy proposed operations to capture airbases in China and Korea, from which the US Army Air Force would carry out attacks against Japan, the US Army determined such side operations to be time-consuming and instead supported a large-scale thrust directly against the Japanese homeland. Ultimately the army's viewpoint triumphed.[74] The US Joint Chiefs of Staff never worked on a plan for a specific military operation in Korea. The Soviet Union also did not have information on US military planning for Korea. Only on July 24, two days before the Potsdam Proclamation was issued, did Soviet general Alexei Antonov ask US general George C. Marshall and admiral Ernest King about a possible US landing on Korean shores in coordination with the Soviet offensive. Marshall replied that the US government did not have a plan for any such amphibious operations, which would require a great number of assault ships. King also added that any attack on Korea would be determined only after the landing on Kyūshū and securing control over the Sea of Japan.[75]

Yet the United States grew increasingly alarmed about Stalin's ambitions for Korea after the Yalta Conference where he confirmed his commitment to enter the war against Japan. Former president Herbert Hoover wrote to Secretary of War Henry Stimson on May 15 that the United States should promptly offer the Japanese peace upon specified terms before the Soviets captured Manchuria, Korea,

---

72. Dai-17 Hōmen-gun Sanbō-bu Sakusen-han, *Kimitsu sakusen nisshi.* See the entry of July 2, 1945, confidential telegram no. 729.

73. Dai-17 Hōmen-gun Sanbō-bu Sakusen-han, *Kimitsu sakusen nisshi.* See the entry of July 3, 1945, confidential telegram no. 751.

74. John Skates, *The Invasion of Japan: Alternative to the Bomb* (Columbia: University of South Carolina Press, 1994), 44, 46–48, and 53–54.

75. "Tripartite military meeting, July 24, 1934," Foreign Relations of the United States 1945, Conference of Berlin (Potsdam), vol. 2, 351–55, quoted in Gye-dong Kim, *Foreign Intervention in Korea*, 25–26.

and north China.[76] According to Stimson in his letter to Joseph Grew, acting secretary of state, the War Department believed that Russia was militarily capable of defeating the Japanese and occupying Sakhalin, Manchuria, Korea and Northern China before US military forces could occupy these areas. In the War Department's estimate, only in the Kuriles would the United States be in a position to circumvent Russian initiative. If the United States were to occupy these islands to forestall Russian designs, cautioned Stimson, it would be at the direct expense of the campaign to defeat Japan and would involve an unacceptable cost in American lives.[77]

General Douglas MacArthur in Manila and Fleet Admiral Chester W. Nimitz in Guam began, in May 1945, preparing preliminary plans for the occupation of Japan and Korea in Operation Blacklist. After the attack on Kyūshū under Olympic, the Sixth Army would be given the task of occupying southern Japan under Operation Blacklist. The Eighth Army was designated to occupy the northern half of Japan after Operation Coronet. Then the Tenth Army, a component of the mainland invasion force, would be assigned to occupy Korea. No consideration was yet given to the possible presence of other nations as occupying forces.[78]

When Harry Hopkins, President Roosevelt's chief diplomatic adviser, had a series of meetings with Stalin in Moscow between May 26 and June 6, they covered the Far Eastern issue at the third meeting. Stalin raised the possibility of discussing the "zones of operation for the armies and zones of occupation in Japan." Hopkins subsequently cabled Truman, "The Marshal expects that Russia will share in the actual occupation of Japan and wants an agreement with the British and us as to occupation zones." Hopkins suggested Stalin discuss the matter at the upcoming conference in Potsdam. Stalin said that the Soviet Union did not intend to infringe on Chinese sovereignty over Manchuria or any other parts of China, whereas Stalin endorsed four-power trusteeship for Korea.[79]

The Soviet archival record indicates that in June 1945, two officials of the Second Far Eastern Department of the Soviet Foreign Ministry wrote a reference paper on the Korean question. It brought up five points regarding the future of Korea, based on the history of great power rivalries over Korea from the nineteenth century through the recent Allied agreements on the Korean issue at Cairo and

---

76. Tsuyoshi Hasegawa, *Racing the Enemy*, 78.

77. Tsuyoshi Hasegawa, *Racing the Enemy*, 79.

78. Gye-Dong Kim, *Foreign Intervention in Korea*, 41; U.S. Army Forces Pacific, "Basic Outline Plan for Blacklist Operations to Occupy Japan Proper and Korea after Surrender or Collapse," August 8, 1945 (Combined Arms Research Library, U.S. Army Command and General Staff College, Fort Leavenworth, KS, Digital Library), available online at www.cgsc.edu/carl/.

79. Tsuyoshi Hasegawa, *Racing the Enemy*, 82–84.

Yalta. The first and second points addressed the Soviet Union's determination to keep Japan out of Korea after the war. The third point stated a desire to establish friendly and close relations between the Soviet Union and an independent Korea, a condition crucial for the security of the Soviet Union in the Far East. The fourth point indicated the difficulties of doing so because of the conflicting interests of the United States and China. The fifth point recommended that if a trusteeship were to be established, the Soviet Union must participate in it in a prominent manner.[80]

The Ume Kikan proved never too far off the mark in tracking the US-Soviet race for postwar control of Korea. In early summer the Soviet government was intrigued by the diminution of Japanese defenses in Manchuria. According to a report published in TASS on July 3, 1945, which was intercepted by the Imperial General Headquarters, the Soviet leaders questioned why the Japanese Army did not transfer a million Japanese soldiers currently stationed in China to the Manchurian defense against a Soviet attack.[81] By this time troop movements would suggest Japanese no longer had intentions of defending Manchuria or Korea but rather waited for the Soviet mobilization as the onset of a race against the United States for postwar control of East Asia.

On July 26 the Potsdam Proclamation was issued in the name of the United States, Britain, and Chiang Kai-shek's China. The *Asahi* editorial of July 27 predicted the impending Soviet attack on Japan. Questioning the hallowed Western announcement that the Potsdam Conference successfully brought about a clear agreement on East Asia, the editorial argued that it was simply impossible to assume that the United States and the Soviet Union were now ready to solve the East Asian issue together. The East Asian issue, particularly with regard to China, was so historically and diplomatically complex that it could not possibly be "solved" by the (Western) victors with their respective interests in "war spoils." If the United States, Britain, and the Soviet Union truly had reached some kind of agreement regarding East Asia, speculated the editorial, it must have been strictly limited to the issue of Soviet entry into the war against Japan and subsequent coordination on US-Soviet policy in China. Even if that were the case, the editorial continued, there must be intensive strategic calculations on both sides: the United States must be trying to obtain Soviet recognition of its supremacy in postwar East Asia in exchange for its acquiescence of the Soviet entry into the war against

80. Kathryn Weathersby, "Soviet Aims in Korea and the Origins of the Korean War, 1945–1950: New Evidence from Russian Archives," *Cold War International History Project, Woodrow Wilson International Center for Scholars* (November 1993), 6–7.

81. See the confidential telegram, dispatched on July 2 from Shanghai and received on July 3, in Dai-17 Hōmen-gun Sanbō-bu Sakusen-han, *Kimitsu sakusen nisshi* (July 1945).

Japan, and the Soviet Union must be wanting to maintain its complete independence in planning and carrying out the war against Japan. Either way, as the United States and the Soviet Union moved forward to take the China matter in their own hands, the end of Japan's pan-Asianism seemed near, implied the editorial.[82]

On July 28, during a press conference, Prime Minister Suzuki Kantarō issued a statement that Japan would not comment on the Potsdam Proclamation.

82. "TōA mondai no jūdai-ka" (East Asian problem becomes ever more serious), *Asahi Shinbun* (July 27, 1945), 1.

7

JAPAN'S SURRENDER

Views of the Nation

Colonel Tanemura Sakō, a central member of the Army War Operations Plans Division since December 1939, is sometimes understood as a military planner fanatically determined to fight the final battle against the United States. His postwar affiliation with the Japanese Communist Party after his return from a labor camp in Siberia in 1950 gave his former colleagues and observers alike an opportunity to scapegoat him for the worst in Japan's war.[1] Contrary to such postwar slanders, his two proposals, "Kongo no tai-So shisaku ni taisuru iken" (My personal opinions on the Soviet policy) and "Tai-So gaikō kōshō yōkō" (Outline of the Soviet negotiations), both dated April 29, 1945, laid out his vision for when and how to end the war.[2] Far from an irrational militarist, Tanemura was an informed strategist aware that Japan had neither the power to keep the Soviets neutral nor a policy to manipulate them into any pro-Japanese position. He advocated concluding the war at the most opportune moment when the United States and the Soviet Union were poised to check each other's ambitions for postwar supremacy.

Tanemura identified Anglo-America as Japan's ultimate enemy. Tanemura maintained that Japan should strive to fulfill the original goal of the war: to keep Anglo-America out of Asia and to keep Asia for the Asians. Japan's recognition of the Yan'an regime should serve to achieve such a goal because the Soviet Union

1. Tsuyoshi Hasegawa, *Racing the Enemy: Stalin, Truman, and the Surrender of Japan* (Cambridge, MA: Belknap Press, 2005), 59–60.
2. Compare the argument in Tsuyoshi Hasegawa, *Racing the Enemy*, 59.

would find it easier to expand into China. But this did not mean surrendering China to the Soviet Union, explained Tanemura. Since the Chinese Communist Party (CCP) stood for the Chinese people, not for the Soviet Union, once the war was over, the CCP would likely cut its ties with the Soviet Union and move on.

With regard to the Soviet capacity to frustrate the US advance into East Asia, Tanemura argued that the Japanese government should let the Soviet Union have as much influence as possible in determining the postwar disposition of Southeast Asia while the Japanese Army still occupied the area. Japan should also let the Soviet Union gain as much as possible from the Japanese empire through negotiation and avoid fighting the Soviets by any means necessary. Tanemura proposed the critical actions Japan had to take toward the end of the war: "If, in the process of negotiating with the Soviets, they force [*kyōyō*] us to begin the path toward ending the war by either offering mediation [*chūkai*] or using intimidation [*dōkatsu*] by hitting hard our weak spot, we should be prepared to comply with it."[3]

Tanemura's proposal implied that Japan should surrender when the Soviets attacked Manchuria and Korea without waiting for the US assault on mainland Japan. Conversely Japan should continue fighting against the United States until the Soviet entered the war. Ending the war *before* the Soviet attack had no place in his strategic thinking. Since Japanese planners and strategists had developed a vision for postwar East Asia *as the outcome of* anticipated Soviet participation in the war, Tanemura's strategy was no outlier.

The final phase of Japan's Eurasian-Pacific War began with Japan's dismissal of the Potsdam Proclamation on July 27 and concluded with Japan's decision to accept it on August 10, almost immediately after the anticipated Soviet entry into the war against Japan. Upon hearing the news of the Soviet Army invading Manchukuo, Prince Konoe Fumimaro is said to have exclaimed: "This must be a godsent gift. We can now end the war." His reaction is incongruent with the politician who until that moment was supposedly ready to go to Moscow as a special envoy of Emperor Hirohito for peace talks. The news of the Soviet declaration of war, far from paralyzing the Japanese government, set in motion Japan's final decision-making process toward surrender. Within thirty hours the Supreme Council for the Direction of the War had reached a consensus to surrender through the acceptance of the Potsdam Proclamation.

The United States, in the meanwhile, had an unanticipated and unprecedented project to shorten, if not end, the war. On July 14, two days before Operation

3. Tanemura Taisa (Colonel Tanemura), "Kongo no tai-So shisaku ni taisuru iken" (My personal opinions on the Soviet policy) and "Tai-So gaikō kōshō yōkō" (Outline of the Soviet negotiations) (April 29, 1945), in RJD, 343–52.

Trinity, the first atomic bomb test, in New Mexico, a train left Los Alamos carrying a heavy steel box containing uranium-235 and major components of Little Boy. The box arrived at the San Francisco Naval Shipyard at Hunter's Point. On July 16, two hours before the successful explosion of a plutonium bomb at the Trinity test site, the box had been loaded aboard the USS *Indianapolis*, a lightly armored battle cruiser having fought in both the Iwo Jima and Okinawa campaigns. Exactly one hour after the completion of the test, at 5:29 a.m., the *Indianapolis* departed San Francisco Bay, heading for Tinian, the small island adjacent to Saipan that had been turned into the critical point of origin for the firebombing raids over Japanese cities. The *Indianapolis* covered five thousand miles at a record speed and reached Tinian on July 26, the day the Potsdam Proclamation was issued. Meanwhile, two days earlier, on July 24 Lieutenant General Leslie Groves, in charge of the Manhattan Project, had begun pressing to speed up the delivery of Fat Man, the second atomic bomb. Between July 26 and 28, special planes left Kirtland Air Force Base, New Mexico, for Tinian, carrying the Fat Man plutonium core and its bomb assemblies.

Thus regardless of how the Japanese government was going to respond to the Potsdam Proclamation, all necessary components for the two atomic bombs flowed into Tinian. The final Little Boy weapon was assembled and ready by August 1, one day before the Potsdam Conference concluded. On the following day, on August 2, all the Fat Man bomb components arrived at Tinian. Subsequently the date for its use was set for August 11.[4] Only after using these two atomic bombs in Hiroshima and Nagasaki did the US government for the first time show any willingness to communicate directly with Tokyo. At this critical moment in bringing Japan's war to an end, the Soviet Union was suddenly absent, choosing instead to continue its offensive against Japan until September 5. In the final days of Japan's Eurasian-Pacific War, the United States alone defined the nature and terms of Japan's surrender.

From *Mokusatsu* to Surrender: The Final Twenty Days of Japan's War

The Potsdam Proclamation, issued on July 26, 1945, in the names of Truman, Chiang Kai-shek, and Churchill, purported to offer Japan an "opportunity to end

4. Stanley Goldberg, "Racing to the Finish: the Decision to Bomb Hiroshima and Nagassaki," *Journal of American-East Asian Relations* 4, no. 2 (summer 1995): 126–27; Carey Sublette, "The Nuclear Weapon Archives: The Guide to Nuclear Weapons," available online at http://nuclearweaponarchive.org. See Section 8.1.3 "Little Boy" and Section 8.1.4 "Fat Man." Also see Michael Gordin, *Five Days in August: How World War II Became a Nuclear War* (Princeton, NJ: Princeton University Press, 2007).

this war" and threatened that its continuation would "mean the inevitable and complete destruction of the Japanese armed forces and just as inevitably the utter devastation of the Japanese homeland." The proclamation laid out the non-negotiable terms of surrender. The hard measures required of Japan included a complete abolition of militarism; reduction of Japanese territory; repatriation of Japanese soldiers stationed abroad; and the Allied occupation of Japan. The soft measures that demonstrated regard for Japan's survival were guarantees that the Japanese would not be "enslaved as a race or destroyed as a nation"; the establishment of democracy; permission for Japanese industries and trade to resume on a global basis; and a withdrawal of occupying forces upon achieving these objectives. The proclamation concluded, "We call upon the government of Japan to proclaim now the unconditional surrender of all Japanese armed forces, and to provide proper and adequate assurances of their good faith in such action. The alternative for Japan is prompt and utter destruction."

Shortly before the Potsdam Proclamation, the Japanese government made several diplomatic overtures to Moscow. On July 12 Foreign Minister Tōgō instructed Satō Naotake, the Japanese ambassador in Moscow, to inform Foreign Minister Molotov that Emperor Hirohito would like to send Prince Konoe Fumimaro as a special envoy to Moscow for peace talks. Molotov, on his way to Potsdam, designated Deputy Foreign Minister Solomon Lozovsky to meet with Satō. On July 18 Lozovsky informed Satō that Stalin found the imperial message lacking in any concrete proposals so he was unable to comment on Konoe's mission. Subsequently Tōgō instructed Satō to convey that the Japanese government, though still hoping for Soviet mediation, could not propose specific peace terms so Prince Konoe would express its concrete intentions after his arrival in Moscow. On July 25 just one day before the issuance of the Potsdam Proclamation, Satō met with Lozovsky. This second message was equally vague. A jittery Satō reported to Tokyo the improbability of Soviet peace mediation.

The Japanese government's decision not to respond to the Potsdam Proclamation upon its issuance is widely regarded as a serious blunder. Prime Minister Suzuki's announcement that Japan had no immediate comment on the proclamation is said to have been interpreted by the Allies as Japan's determination to fight against the United States until its own annihilation—as yet another sign of Japan's fanaticism and irrationalism. The conventional postwar narrative also accuses the Japanese government of not taking seriously enough the Allies' explicit warning in point five of the Proclamation, "We shall brook no delay," and specifically the phrase "prompt and utter destruction" in the concluding part, which seems in retrospect to insinuate impending nuclear catastrophe.

As far as the official record is concerned, including the anthology of materials related to Japan's path to the end of World War II, selected and compiled by the

Foreign Ministry and published in 1990, the decision-making process in which Prime Minister Suzuki came to issue the infamous *mokusatsu* statement remains vague. Some cabinet members seem to have interpreted the Potsdam Proclamation as offering terms for a conditional surrender. Vice Minister of Foreign Affairs Matsumoto Shun'ichi was aware of the so-called Zacharias broadcast on July 21, 1945, in which Navy Captain Ellis Zacharias, a specialist on psychological warfare, made an offer that Japan's surrender would be based on the Atlantic Charter and as such not unconditional. Matsumoto interpreted the Potsdam Proclamation as the Allies' statement of the *conditions* for Japan's surrender in line with the Zacharias's broadcast. Indeed, while the articles one to four of the Proclamation showed the Allies' resolution to conquer Japan, articles five to twelve indicated the "conditions" of unconditional surrender, with article five explicitly stating that "following are our terms." With certain guarantees seemingly given to Japan upon surrender, Matsumoto concluded that Japan should accept the terms as they stood and obtained his colleagues' consensus on this interpretation. On the morning of July 27, Matsumoto reported that the Allied nations had issued the Potsdam Proclamation as a last chance for Japan to demonstrate contrition (*hansei*) through the acceptance of its terms and to end the war. Foreign Minister Tōgō concurred.[5]

At the Supreme Council for the Direction of the War that afternoon, Tōgō is said to have stated that the Potsdam Proclamation was the Allies' offer of a "conditional" surrender so Japan should not openly and instantly reject it. According to the postwar memoir by Shimomura Hiroshi (Kainan), then director of information, Tōgō explained that the American public, increasingly wary of further bloodshed, now clamored for an end to the war such that some even claimed insisting on an unconditional surrender was inappropriate. That was why, according to Tōgō, the United States now offered a "conditional surrender (jōken an)" at the Potsdam Conference. He is said to have even speculated that the United States requested the Soviet Union participate in issuing the proclamation.

Tōgō then asked other ministers for their views about printing the Potsdam Proclamation in newspapers to inform the Japanese public. Minister of War Anami said if the government decided to reveal the proclamation to the public at all, he hoped the government would develop a solid counterargument to the proclamation and print it along with the proclamation to show the people how the government was going to deal with it. After the deliberation, Tōgō decided it was better for the Japanese government not to express an opinion on the proclamation immediately and instead to continue to study the terms and to pursue Soviet

5. "Matsumoto Shun'ichi shuki (Matsumoto Shun'ichi memorandum), reprinted in JC, vol. 2, 692–93; Ōmori Minoru, *Sengo hishi* (Secret history of Japan's postwar), vol. 2 , 117, 137–43.

diplomacy. Prime Minister Suzuki agreed that Japan should show no provocative reaction to the Allies but simply print the proclamation as news with no comment.[6] Subsequently the cabinet made a final decision to announce publicly that the government would not comment on the Potsdam Proclamation. The following morning some newspapers reporting the story used the strong word *mokusatsu*, an act of dismissing another's opinion and deed as trivial. Tōgō, disturbed by the press distortion, requested that Suzuki do something about it. By that time Suzuki had given in to military pressure and announced that he would indeed ignore and dismiss the Potsdam Proclamation as a trivial matter in the statement widely published and broadcast on July 30. This is the account provided in 1990 by the Foreign Ministry's official history.[7]

No other official records are available concerning how Japanese policymakers, particularly the Supreme Council for the Direction of the War, discussed the Potsdam Proclamation and reached the decision not to comment. While the proclamation indeed provided specific assurances of how Japan could survive as a nation after the war, thus seemingly making it easier for Japan to capitulate, it was vague about the consequences of Japan's surrender. Read carefully, the Potsdam Proclamation contains key omissions and several ambiguous expressions that probably concerned Japanese leaders. Numerous historians have pointed out that the proclamation did not mention the postwar status of the imperial institution, whether it would be abolished or allowed to continue, or the fate of Emperor Hirohito. If Emperor Hirohito were deemed a critical part of Japanese militarism, then the complete removal of "the authority and influence of those who deceived and misled the people of Japan into embarking on world conquest" would also mean the elimination of the emperor.[8]

The Japanese government's decision not to "comment" should not be understood as its failure to realize the urgency of the matter. The top secret war journal of the Army War Operations Plan Division recorded the Potsdam Proclamation as the "Anglo-American-Chinese declaration" (Ei-Bei-Shi seimei), and added the Japanese expression *saigo tsūchō* in parenthesis.[9] "Saigo tsūchō" means ultimatum—a

---

6. Shimomura Kainan, *Shūsen-ki* (The record of war's end), 1949, reprinted in JC, vol. 2, 696–97.

7. JC, vol. 2, 680–83.

8. Some US historians have argued that President Truman and Secretary of State James Byrnes were unwilling to make a firm statement in the Potsdam Proclamation that would assure the continuity of the emperor system. Former undersecretary of state William Castle explained that because they wanted to experiment with the atomic bomb they chose not to offer assurances to Japan, which made it difficult for Japan to surrender, so the war would continue long enough to allow the United States an opportunity to conduct the nuclear test. Gar Alperovitz, *The Decision to Use the Atomic Bomb* (New York: Vintage, 1996), 312–15. Originally published as Alperovitz, *The Decision to Use the Atomic Bomb and the Architecture of an American Myth* (New York: Knopf, 1995).

9. TSWJ, vol. 2, 745–46.

final diplomatic demand made from one party to another that, if rejected, implies the threat of termination of further "peaceful" negotiation. Choosing this specific phrase, Tanemura Sakō, the journal keeper, did not fail to notice the imminent threat promised in the proclamation and also the solid determination of the United States to see the war's end quickly. In light of this recorded interpretation, it is impossible to imagine that the members of the Supreme Council for the Direction of the War were blind to such circumstances.

Why then did the Japanese government choose not to respond to the Potsdam Proclamation? Certainly the Soviet Union was not yet at war with Japan so it could not take part in the Allies' disposition of Japan. Might the lack of Soviet participation in the Potsdam Proclamation signal something more? While other historians have suggested that Japan's nonresponse represented a hope that the war might end through Soviet peace mediation, it was highly unlikely that the Japanese government interpreted the absence of Stalin as a signatory in this way given the ongoing Japanese observation of the war's progress. Around the issuance of the Potsdam Proclamation Foreign Minister Tōgō's commitment to the Konoe mission to Moscow remained elusive, and Tokyo had just learned of the improbability of Soviet mediation from Ambassador Satō. Given their understanding of how unlikely Soviet peace mediation now was, Japanese policymakers could well have interpreted the exclusion of the Soviets from the Potsdam Proclamation as signaling a US strategic calculation that it might secure and define Japan's surrender unilaterally and dispose of Japan's empire without Soviet interference. Japanese policymakers had long sought to avoid such a unilateral end of the war.

To Japanese readers the following expressions in the proclamation could have supported such an interpretation: "The Japanese Government shall remove all obstacles to the revival and strengthening of *democratic tendencies* among the Japanese people. Freedom of speech, of religion, and of *thought*, as well as respect for the fundamental human rights shall be established" (emphasis added). "Democracy" in the context of Japan's Eurasian-Pacific War was not necessarily congruent with the American definition of "democracy" because Japanese leaders saw the seeds of democracy in the CCP's populist appeal and understood the Soviets to have yet another distinct form. Nonetheless "democracy" and "freedom of thought" in the context of the Potsdam Proclamation could have easily been read as "American democracy" and "postwar Japan's obligation to follow the American way." In this reading the "strengthening of democratic tendencies among the Japanese people" must have appeared to the Japanese as Washington's readiness to be the sole occupier of Japan.

Japanese policymakers had observed that discussions about the nature of the postwar governments of Korea and China revealed tensions between Moscow and Washington. Without Stalin among the cosigners, the Potsdam Proclamation indeed looked like America's declaration that vanquished Japan would follow the American way. Stalin, in fact, was said to have been frustrated with the way Washington unilaterally handled the issuance of the Potsdam Proclamation and, unwilling to see Japan pressured into surrender without Soviet presence, was therefore all the more determined to enter the war in East Asia.[10] The Japanese government might well have concluded that the Potsdam Proclamation served as a likely catalyst for the Soviet entry into the war in Asia.

Not only government officials noticed the absence of the Soviets from the proclamation. A wide range of ordinary citizens, male and female, of different social, occupational, and geographical backgrounds, held informed views and opinions concerning the end of Japan's war and subsequent fate of their nation. Preliminary investigative reports by the military police Kenpei-tai in various prefectures showed that Japanese citizens, based on what they derived from newspapers and other sources, intently discussed the meaning of Stalin's absence from the Potsdam Proclamation. The average Japanese citizen could easily figure out that the simplest reason was because the Soviet Union was not at war with Japan.[11] They, too, attempted to ascertain whether the Potsdam Proclamation disguised a hidden agenda.

A July 30, 1945, report from the Kōbe City told of a male acupuncturist discussing with his client that Chiang Kai-shek's signing of the Potsdam Proclamation meant nothing much given his parasitical relationship with the Anglo-Americans. Meanwhile he interpreted Stalin's absence as a sign of discord among the Allied nations.[12] Similar views were heard in other parts of Japan. In Kōbe, Matsuoka Junkichi, a member of the House of Peers, suspected that the United States had reason to hasten Japan's surrender without Soviet assistance, due to growing difficulties with the Soviet Union in solving the postwar disposition in Europe.

The military police issued a top secret report on August 4, two days before the United States dropped the atomic bomb on Hiroshima, which analyzed public opinion in Tokyo on the Potsdam Proclamation. The report described a general tendency to regard the contents of the Potsdam Proclamation as an enemy plot to lure Japan into further predicaments. Some said the "terms" of Japan's surrender were unacceptable. Others said that Japan, with absolutely no prospect for a

---

10. Tsuyoshi Hasegawa, *Racing the Enemy*, 160–63.

11. "Ryūgen higo hassei kenkyo hyō, Kyūshū oyobi Yamaguchi" (Charts of incidents related to rumors and gossip, Kyūshū and Yamaguchi) (July 20, 1945), Hyōgo (July 30) and Ōita (August 2), in "Japanese Army and Navy Archives, 1868–1945," M 5041, Roll 220, Frame 90929 [Microfilm Collection], LOC.

12. "Japanese Army and Navy Archives, 1868–1945," M 5041, Roll 220, Frames 90937–38 [Microfilm Collection], LOC.

victory, should take this opportunity to quit the war and surrender.[13] The same military police report revealed that some people in economic and financial circles said that Japan should take advantage of the "Three-Nations Proclamation" and launch diplomatic negotiations: they argued that since the proclamation seemed to be an offer of conditional surrender, it was a sign of US desperation to end the war without Soviet assistance so the United States might be willing to negotiate further. Top political leaders such as Hiranuma Kiichirō, president of the Privy Council, and former prime minister Okada Keisuke were said to have whispered that the Japanese government should have done more than just ignore the proclamation even if it were mere propaganda.[14]

Some citizens believed that the very fact that the government deliberately announced that it would not comment on the proclamation indicated that the government did take it seriously. These people even speculated that the Japanese government had secret plans. Some politicians and journalists demanded that the Japanese government, if it wanted to continue fighting, should issue a counterproclamation to the Allied nations. If it would not do so, then the government had to be secretly exploring a byway toward peace. Some people, including right-wing leader Sasakawa Ryōichi, also suspected that the government, secretly wanting peace despite its official stance, was carefully monitoring public reactions to the government's decision to ignore the proclamation. Some other right-wingers saw the government's failure to comment as weak-kneed and called for boosting fighting morale. One member of an ultranationalist organization commented that Japan should attempt a political alliance with the Soviet Union: "The Japanese people want friendship with the Soviet Union and we [the ultranationalists] also believe it necessary to utilize the Soviet Union as part of the strategy. Although ideologically we are not compatible with the Soviet Union, we have to collaborate with them politically."[15]

People in media and finance expressed surprise that Stalin was not among the signers and urged caution as to what the Soviet Union would do next behind Japan's back. A president of the newspaper *Kōbe shinbun* argued that just as Britain and the United States were investigating Japan's intentions, the Soviet Union too was closely observing Japan's behavior in order to conceive some plot against it.[16]

---

13. Kenpei Shirei-kan (Military Police Headquarters), *Shōwa 20-nen 8-gatsu Potsudamu Sengen ni taisuru kokunai no dōkō (gokuhi)* (The Public response to the Potsdam Proclamation, August 1945 [Top Secret]), i, 5, MAL.

14. Kenpei Shirei-kan, *Shōwa 20-nen 8-gatsu Potsudamu Sengen ni taisuru koku-nai no dōkō*, 1–2.

15. Kenpei Shirei-kan, *Shōwa 20-nen 8-gatsu Potsudamu Sengen ni taisuru koku-nai no dōkō*, 2–4, 14, 26.

16. "Ryūgen higo hassei kenkyo hyō, Hyōgo" (Charts of incidents related to rumors and gossip, Hyōgo) (July 30), Japanese Army and Navy Archives, M 5041, Roll 220, Frames 90933–34 [Microfilm Collection], LOC.

One executive adviser to a munitions company expressed concern that the Soviet Union would sooner or later join the proclamation and apply pressure on Japan.[17]

Former and current communists and leftists likewise kept an eye on the Soviets' next step. Comments by leftists were recorded at length. Some were possibly in-prison interviews conducted by the military police. One former leader of the Japanese Communist Party—possibly Sano Manabu—explained that the most important issue was what the Soviet Union would do from this point on. Soviet diplomacy toward Japan would probably harden because the Soviets planned to use Japan as a pawn in its long-term East Asian policy, the ultimate goal of which was to capture China and support the rise of the CCP. He continued that because the Soviet Union had regarded Japan's defeat as inevitable since the battle of Okinawa, it planned to capture Japan and use it as a buffer against the United States in the Pacific. To avoid that outcome Japan should surrender when the "moment was ripe" (*jukushi no toki*), once the Soviet forces deployed against Japan.[18]

A former employee at the Oriental Photographic Industry (Orientaru Shashin Kōgyō) with a record of arrest for "communist thinking" expressed that it was wrong to assume that the Soviet Union would just stand on the sidelines and quietly watch Anglo-America's unilateral disposition of the Japanese empire. He too predicted that Japan's decisive move would be made only once the Soviets joined the Japanese in battle: "Before Anglo-America enforces the invasion of mainland Japan, the Soviets will enter the war against Japan and move southward in Manchuria and Korea. It's at that moment that Japan confronts the true crisis. That's when Japan needs a prudent response."[19] A former executive of Zenkyō Sasshin Dōmei, the militant faction of labor union branching out of the Japanese Communist Party, recalled the Japanese media report that Stalin had met with T. V. Soong, China's minister of foreign affairs, just before Potsdam. They presumably made an arrangement concerning postwar Sino-Soviet relations, which must have involved a disposition of Japanese interests in China. He explained, "Stalin is cunning and shrewd; just remember how he did not immediately install a communist regime in Poland but established a pro-Soviet democratic nation, thus outdoing Anglo-America. Stalin might do the same with Japan." He continued, "Stalin might first terminate diplomatic relations with Japan or militarily occupy the Soviet-Japanese border region as a security measure; either way once he takes control over Japan, he would establish a democratic regime but allow the

17. Kenpei Shirei-kan, *Shōwa 20-nen 8-gatsu Potsudamu Sengen ni taisuru kokunai no dōkō*, 13–14.

18. Kenpei Shirei-kan, *Shōwa 20-nen 8-gatsu Potsudamu Sengen ni taisuru kokunai no dōkō*, 35–37.

19. Kenpei Shirei-kan, *Shōwa 20-nen 8-gatsu Potsudamu Sengen ni taisuru koku-nai no dōkō*, 38–39.

continuity of the imperial institution in the same manner as he did in Romania. This is how he outsmarts Anglo-America."[20]

If even people outside the government could speculate so incisively on the power politics surrounding the Potsdam Proclamation, then it is plausible that policymakers reasoned that Japan's "no comment" would probably set off a chain reaction of global events that would expedite Moscow's actions against Japan. Prime Minister Suzuki's decision not to correct, but instead to adopt, the media's term of *mokusatsu* may have been a calculated one.

On July 30 (Moscow time), the day Satō met Deputy Foreign Minister Lozovsky again, he telegrammed Tōgō, recommending the cancellation of the government's plan to dispatch the Konoe peace mission to Moscow and suggesting that the government instead speak directly with the United States. Satō explained his reasoning based on indices of rising US-Soviet tension. Stalin apparently had not known beforehand about the contents of the Potsdam Proclamation and so he had to be irritated by the Anglo-American determination to impose unconditional surrender on Japan without Soviet involvement. Satō added that Stalin knew his own ability to pressure Anglo-America in Manchuria, China, and Korea after Japan's surrender, so he needed no Japanese diplomatic assistance in expanding Soviet influence in these regions; therefore, Japan's peace overtures with Moscow would be of no avail. On the other hand, the United States by then must have obtained information about Japan's proposal to send a mission to Moscow so it would try to block the Soviets gaining postwar prestige by mediating peace in the Pacific War. Henceforth the United States would be more accommodating, unilaterally, to Japan's peace offer. Satō thus insisted that Japan should immediately surrender to the United States. Tōgō bluntly responded he should be patient and continue to press the Kremlin.[21]

At this juncture of the war's final stage, Tōgō, fully aware that Stalin would not respond to the Japanese request, seemed to act as if he were buying time and waiting for the Soviets to step in. Perhaps he needed to embellish this gesture of naïve anticipation with a touch of authenticity for the moment when the Soviet Union finally entered the war against Japan. As discussed later in this chapter, Tōgō called the moment totally unexpected and yet declined to meet with the Soviet Ambassador Malik who intended to hand him the declaration of war. Only after the Japanese government decided to surrender did he agree to meet with Malik and tell him that the war was over.

The Imperial General Headquarters' records of military planning and activities are curiously scarce for the month of July. The war history series compiled by the

20. Kenpei Shirei-kan, *Shōwa 20-nen 8-gatsu Potsudamu Sengen ni taisuru kokunai no dōkō*, 37–38.
21. JC, vol. 2, 707–10.

Military History Department at the National Institute for Defense Studies in Tokyo does not fill the gaps. The volumes on the defense of Kyūshū, the Kantō Plain, and the Kwantung Army do not even provide information on the general activities of the Japanese Army in July. The same is true of the records of the Seventeenth Area Army in Korea. In these records the narrative resumes abruptly on August 9, three days after Hiroshima. The narrative reopens with the Japanese military response to the Soviet blitz.

Ten Continental Orders were issued in July, mostly to regroup forces throughout Japan, Southeast Asia, Korea, and Manchuria. The movement of soldiers and their units both inside and outside Japan picked up considerably. The strategy behind these moves is hardly clear. Continental Orders 1360 through 1363, issued on July 11, reconstituted the Air Communication and Control Squadrons, Navy Volunteer Corps, and Transportation Corps in the Kansai-San'in and Kyūshū regions. Continental Order 1364 of July 15 reconstituted the noncombatant units in the Burma theater. Continental Order 1365 of July 16 reconstituted the units in the Hokkaidō region, particularly those assigned to defend the Tsugaru Strait, Sōya, and Nemuro. Continental Orders 1366 of July 18, 1367 of July 20, and 1368 of July 26, reconstituted the units in the Kantō and Tōhoku regions as well as the Indochina, Malaya, and Burma theaters. Continental Order 1369 issued on July 30 was the most comprehensive and the largest-scale order for the reconstitution of the Kwantung Army. On August 4 two additional Continental Orders—1370 and 1371—were issued for the further reconstitution of units in Southeast Asia. On August 7, one day after Hiroshima, Continental Order 1373 instructed the reconstitution of units in western Japan and Korea, with no reference to the nuclear attack at all. None of these orders explained any specific instructions concerning the reason and strategy behind these reconstitutions.[22]

According to the top secret war journal of the Army War Operations Plans Division of the Imperial General Headquarters, the daily activities of the government and the military between July 27 and 30 demonstrated Japan's continuing focus on the Soviet Union and China in spite of these orders for troop reformations throughout the Japanese empire.[23] On Friday July 27 Foreign Minister Tōgō explained the Potsdam Proclamation to the members of the Supreme Council for the Direction of the War. Later that afternoon the regular cabinet meeting discussed Japan's response. According to Colonel Tanemura Sakō, who kept the journal, the discussion centered on whether to disclose the Potsdam Proclamation to the Japanese public. After long deliberation they decided to broadcast the

22. CCCO, vol. 10, 183–205.
23. TSWJ, vol. 2, 745–47.

content during the daily seven o'clock radio news. Tanemura did not record anything more about the Potsdam Proclamation.

On Saturday July 28 the journal recorded that the top leaders addressed what to do about China. Minister of War Anami offered a preferred timetable for shifting focus from the operation against the Guomindang (GMD) to the operation against the United States and also his decision to centralize the Japanese administration of China. In the afternoon a group of vice ministers discussed the Chinese economy along the lines of Anami's proposal. On Sunday July 29 Tanemura briefed Vice Chief of the Army General Staff Kawabe Torashirō on an unspecified China issue.

On the afternoon of Monday July 30, the Army War Operations Plans Division listened to the Fifth Section's analysis of the Potsdam Proclamation as well as of the rapid increase in Soviet military strength in the Far East. Tanemura injected his personal opinion: "Those in the Fifth and Second Sections kept on repeating Japan's desperate need to rely on Soviet diplomacy in the face of the inevitable defeat by the United States. I scolded them and emphasized the importance of 'good strategic planning and good fighting [*zen-bō zen-sen*].'" This interjection indicates that not everyone in the Imperial General Headquarters agreed on the impossibility of Soviet diplomacy. Tanemura also noted a peculiar attitude among the Japanese public: even though July 30 was the national holiday commemorating the Meiji Emperor's passing in 1912, no households were hoisting the Japanese flag. He interpreted this as a sign that the people no longer regarded *kokutai* (national polity) as relevant. This description counters the conventional image that all Japan, ordinary citizens and leaders alike, were ready at this late stage in the war to uphold the emperor system as well as the imperial institution. Japan after Suzuki's *mokusatsu* of the Potsdam Proclamation was not uniformly determined to keep on fighting until the last soldier perished. The final few days of July passed uneventfully.

On Tuesday July 31, the last entry in the top secret war journal until August 9, recorded that the cabinet held a briefing session on the Soviet military buildup in the Far East as well as a "false propaganda broadcast" on a Japanese peace offer to the United States.[24] Representatives from the Imperial General Headquarters had gone to the Ministry of Greater East Asia (DaiTōA-shō) and briefed the vice minister and the bureau chief on the operation aimed at the GMD and the centralization of the Japanese administration of China. Tanemura ended the entry

24. Though the nature of the said broadcast is unspecified in the journal, it may be related to the so-called Zacharias broadcast on July 21, 1945. See U.S. Dept. of State, *Foreign Relations of the United States: Conference of Berlin (Potsdam) 1945*, vol. 2, 1260–61.

with a mention of his new assignment in Korea under Continental Order 1369: he would become chief (*shunin*) of the Staff Operations Plans Division of the Seventeenth Area Army of Korea.[25]

Around the same time several officers within the Imperial General Headquarters were reassigned in and out of Korea and Manchuria. On July 21 Colonel Sugita Ichiji, an expert on the United States,[26] left Tokyo for Korea to become the senior staff member of the Seventeenth Area Army Command.[27] Shortly before his new assignment, Tanemura had learned from the Russian section chief that the Soviet forces would most likely enter the war against Japan around August 10, based on the recent increase in the number of soldiers positioned in the Far East. On August 4 Tanemura left Tokyo for Nanam, the military base in northern Korea just seventy miles east of the Soviet border. According to his memoir Tanemura told his successor: "The only thing to think about is what Japan should do when the Soviet Union enters the war against Japan. I withhold expressing my opinion on that regard. Please carefully think what should be the answer."[28] As his final action in Korea would demonstrate, he implied that surrender was the only viable option.

Soviet Entry into the War and the American Use of the Atomic Bombs

On August 6 the United States dropped the atomic bomb on Hiroshima. Official Japanese documents, both military and diplomatic, hardly portray the atomic bombs as a force that compelled Japan's surrender. On August 7, one day after Hiroshima, Prime Minister Suzuki called a cabinet meeting. The discussion was not whether to surrender because of the shock of the atomic bomb. The meeting concerned how to "respond" to what US President Truman announced as the use of an atomic bomb. Anami reported that the Imperial General Headquarters had sent a scientific investigation team to Hiroshima to verify that a uranium bomb had been used. Tōgō called it a serious violation of international law and proposed that Japan should register a strong protest through the International

25. TSWJ, vol. 2, 745–48. Tanemura wrote that he would join the Chōsen Army. Since it had been disbanded in February 1945, it is obvious he meant the Seventeenth Area Army of Korea.

26. Sugita was a military attaché in the United States and Britain between 1937–38, member of the General Staff, Military Affairs, the European and U.S. Section in 1939, and the 25th Army Intelligence Officer during the Malaya Campaign.

27. TSWJ, vol. 2, 743.

28. Tanemura Sakō, *Daihon'ei kimitsu nisshi* (The Imperial General Headquarters secret journal) (Tokyo: Daiyamondo Sha, 1952), 250–51.

Red Cross. Even at that very moment Tōgō was pressing Ambassador Satō to discuss the special peace mission with Molotov. Tōgō's actions did not indicate any urgency to surrender immediately.[29] The atomic bomb itself did not precipitate a Japanese decision to surrender.

News of the Soviet attack, in contrast, served as the catalyst for the Supreme Council for the Direction of the War to form within thirty hours a consensus to surrender and to accept the Potsdam Proclamation. Molotov had read the Soviet declaration of war against Japan by the time he delivered it to Satō on August 8 at 5:00 p.m. Moscow time (11:00 p.m. on August 8, Tokyo time). Citing Japan's refusal to accept the Potsdam Proclamation, the declaration asserted that Japan's request for Moscow's peace mediation was groundless and therefore, at the proposal of the Allies, the Soviet government joined the war against Japan in order to hasten the end of war and the coming of peace. According to the declaration, the Soviet Union would enter a state of war with Japan as of August 9, but it did not specify whether this was Moscow time or otherwise. By the time Molotov handed the declaration to Satō, it was already close to midnight of August 8–9 on the Trans-Baikal Front and the First and Second Far Eastern Fronts, which were six to seven hours ahead of Moscow time. Satō's telegram reporting the Soviet declaration never even reached Tokyo.[30]

Within an hour the Trans-Baikal Army and the First and Second Far Eastern Armies crossed the Manchurian border on all fronts. The Soviet Far East Command launched its massive attack on Japanese positions in Manchuria. Reconnaissance units, forward detachments, and advanced guard units of the Trans-Baikal Front crossed the border into Inner Mongolia and Manchuria. The Soviet campaign of meticulously planned strategic offensives began in not only Manchuria but also Korea, Sakhalin Island, and the Kurile islands with of a force of more than 1.5 million men.[31] Tokyo first learned of the initial assault two and half hours later when the Dōmei News Agency intercepted a Moscow radio broadcast stating that the Soviet government had handed a declaration of war to Japanese ambassador Satō.

The final log of the top secret war journal, which was resumed on August 9 by Lieutenant Colonel Takeshita Masahiko of Military Affairs Section, Ministry of War, depicted the Soviet declaration of war against Japan as the decisive reason for an emergency meeting of the Supreme Council for the Direction of the War. According to the entry, Takeshita received a phone call at 7:10 a.m. with the

---

29. Tsuyoshi Hasegawa, *Racing the Enemy*, 184–85.

30. Tsuyoshi Hasegawa, *Racing the Enemy*, 189–90.

31. David Glantz, *August Storm: The Soviet 1945 Strategic Offensive in Manchuria* (Fort Leavenworth, KS: Combat Studies Institute, 1983), available online at http://cgsc.contentdm.oclc.org/.

message that the Soviets had declared war, so he had to attend the office immediately.[32]

Earlier at his residence Foreign Minister Tōgō had convened three top Foreign Ministry officials and they had come to a consensus that Japan should accept the Potsdam Proclamation. Around 8:00 a.m. Tōgō then visited Prime Minister Suzuki's residence and informed him of the Foreign Ministry proposal. With Suzuki, Tōgō, Anami, Yonai, Umezu, and Toyoda in attendance, the top secret Supreme Council for the Direction of the War meeting began at 10:30 a.m. According to the memo taken by Umezu, Prime Minister Suzuki stated that the purpose of the meeting was to discuss measures to adopt in response to the Soviet entry into the war.

At the meeting Tōgō stated for the record that the Soviet entry into the war was an event no one could possibly predict (*So no san'sen wa mattaku yoki dekizarishi*), an unlikely assessment. To punctuate his bewilderment, he added, or fabricated, that Foreign Minister Molotov in Moscow had just offered at 5:00 p.m. of August 8 to meet with Ambassador Satō in regard to Japan's proposed peace envoy. In reality Molotov had handed Satō the Soviet declaration of war at that time. Tōgō's reference to the Soviet offer for a meeting may have meant Soviet Ambassador Malik's request for a meeting on August 9 to deliver the Soviet declaration of war. No matter whether he feigned shock and devastation at the news, Tōgō's reaction provided a standard narrative for postwar generations.

The discussion at the Supreme Council for the Direction of the War meeting, revealed on the following day by Anami to Takeshita for recording purposes, tilted toward a termination of war. Yonai said that as Japan could not win the war, it had to accept the Potsdam Proclamation and end the war.[33] Both Yonai and Tōgō proposed a peace negotiation along the lines of the Potsdam Proclamation, with the fundamental interpretation that the proclamation guaranteed preservation of the emperor system. Anami presented an alternative, the army's peace proposal, with the following four conditions: preservation of *kokutai*, self-disarmament, no occupation of Japan, and no war trial. Umezu and Toyoda seconded Anami's proposal. During this meeting Vice Admiral Ōnishi Takijirō, vice chief of naval staff, stopped by and confidentially asked Anami to restrain Yonai's pacifist attitude. Anami replied that he understood, but he added that he preferred to proceed as if he did not hear the request.[34]

Thus approximately twelve hours after the Soviet declaration of war against Japan, the Japanese government was already discussing acceptance of the Pots-

32. TSWJ, vol. 2, 751–52.
33. RJD, 282–83.
34. TSWJ, vol. 2, 753–54.

dam Proclamation. At 11:30 a.m., news of the second atomic bomb reached the Supreme Council for the Direction of the War. The news of Nagasaki had little impact on the substance of the discussion of the day, which had already been defined by the Soviet declaration of war.[35] The meeting ended at 1:30 p.m., lasting ninety minutes longer than originally scheduled.

After the Supreme Council for the Direction of the War meeting, the cabinet meeting began. After a recess at 5:30 p.m., the meeting resumed at 6:30 p.m. and ended at 10:20 p.m. The focus shifted toward whether to follow the Tōgō proposal or the Anami proposal in accepting the Potsdam Proclamation. Various ministers reported on the nation's fighting capacity and food production levels and pointed at the difficulty of continuing the war. No one dared to be the first to advocate terminating the war. Frustrated, Anami interrupted. According to the top secret war journal, Anami said that all these comments (concerning Japan's physical decline) were plain facts that did not need to be repeated.[36] Later during the Imperial Conference, which lasted from 11:50 p.m. until 2:20 a.m., Emperor Hirohito expressed his support for the Tōgō proposal. In making the so-called sacred decision (*seidan*), Emperor Hirohito thus forged a formal consensus that Japan begin a process toward surrender.[37] Twenty-eight hours had passed since the Soviets joined the war against Japan.

Around 4:00 a.m., August 10, Tōgō returned to the Foreign Ministry to draft a text of surrender to telegraph to Ministers Kase Shun'ichi in Switzerland and Okamoto Suemasa in Sweden. Between 6:45 a.m. and 10:15 a.m., five telegrams were dispatched containing Japan's decision to accept the Potsdam Proclamation including the interpretation that the "said Declaration does not comprise any demand which prejudices the prerogatives of His Majesty as a sovereign ruler" (original in English).[38] Kase's mission was to convey the message to the US and Chinese governments and Okamoto's mission was to do so with the British and Soviet governments.

Tōgō in these communications never mentioned the two atomic bombs as the reason for Japan's decision to accept the Potsdam Proclamation. MAGIC intercepts of Japanese cables also showed that the atomic bomb was neither mentioned in the Japanese Army General Staff message to Japan's military attachés in Sweden, Switzerland, and Portugal, nor cited as a reason for the surrender.[39] The first telegram Tōgō sent to Kase in Switzerland and Okamoto in Sweden at 6:45 a.m. on August 10 simply mentioned Japan's readiness to accept the Potsdam Proclamation.

---

35. Tsuyoshi Hasegawa, *Racing the Enemy*, 204.
36. TSWJ, vol. 2, 752.
37. TSWJ, vol. 2, 753–56.
38. JC, vol. 2, 813–20.
39. Alperovitz, *The Decision to Use the Atomic Bomb*, 418–19.

The second telegram sent to both at 7:15 a.m. specifically mentioned that the failure to bring peace via the Soviet government precipitated the Japanese decision (see the appendix).[40]

The top secret war journal did not mention the second atomic bomb at all in the entry for August 9. From then until August 15, there were only two instances in the top secret war journal on the *genshi bakudan* (atomic bomb). At least on August 10 Emperor Hirohito commented at the Imperial Conference that the emergence of the atomic bomb had increased the risk of leading the nation to annihilation so he preferred the war to end.[41] But on August 14 Field Marshal Hata Shunroku, upon returning to Tokyo from Hiroshima, briefed the army that the bomb's power of destruction was not as much as enemy propaganda claimed (*taishita koto ni arazaru*).[42] The so-called "shock" of the atomic bombs and its impact on the decision to surrender were not uniformly felt among the political leaders.

Only after Tōgō had sent these cables to Switzerland and Sweden, affirming Japan's readiness for surrender with the Allies, did he agree to meet with Yakov Malik, the Soviet ambassador to Japan. Malik had requested a meeting with Tōgō on August 9 to deliver the Soviet declaration of war. But Tōgō made him wait until the following day. At 11:15 a.m. the meeting began and Malik read the declaration of war, retroactive to August 9. Tōgō replied that he understood. He added that the Japanese government had already accepted the Potsdam Proclamation with the understanding that it would not change the emperor's prerogative. The Soviet declaration of war, Tōgō pointed out, was based on Moscow's erroneous assumption that Japan had rejected the Potsdam Proclamation. Referring to Konoe's attempted peace mission, Tōgō continued that Japan had never given up on ending the war through the good offices of the Soviet Union so it had waited for a reply from Moscow before deciding what to do with the Potsdam Proclamation. Given its desire for peace, explained Tōgō, Japan saw no technical reason to fight against the Soviet Union.

At this juncture in Japan's war the scenario drawn by many of Japan's war planners and strategists became tangible: as the Soviets entered the war against Japan, Japan finally showed its readiness to end the war without fighting back. When Malik delivered the declaration of war, Tōgō approached this moment with aplomb. While implying Soviet perfidy against Japan, Tōgō never expressed overt hostility to the Soviet Union. On the contrary he even offered continuing friendship between the two nations. Although the surviving record does not

40. JC, vol. 2, 815–18.

41. TSWJ, vol. 2, 756. Cf. Tsuyoshi Hasegawa, *Racing the Enemy*, 213.

42. TSWJ, vol. 2, 761.

describe Malik's reaction to this news, Malik agreed that the Soviets had indeed declared war based on the assumption of Japan's refusal to surrender. But Malik also alluded that Truman, too, had justified the use of the atomic bombs based on the false assumption that Japan had refused to surrender, so the Soviet Union should not be the sole party blamed for jumping the gun. Regardless Malik promised to convey this matter to the Soviet government. Tōgō replied that the formal message of surrender would arrive in Moscow via Sweden and requested Soviet endorsement of the emperor's prerogative based on the two nations' friendship and continuing diplomatic relationship. Tōgō again implied his disappointment that the Soviet government did not mediate peace for Japan, but also expressed his hope that from this point on the Soviet government would communicate with Tokyo prior to making any grave decisions with the third party—the United States.[43]

By then Soviet troops had begun sweeping into Manchuria and Korea. As the numerous directives had instructed, the Japanese troops withdrew and put up only sporadic resistance. Since the Japanese government never counterdeclared war against the Soviet Union, the urgent tasks at hand were bringing the war to an end and keeping damage to a minimum. However, the Soviet government unexpectedly terminated communication with the Japanese government. The Soviet Union, which had figured so strongly in Japan's war plans, vanished from the bargaining table and Japan suddenly found itself negotiating exclusively with the US government on the manner and nature of Japan's surrender.

On the morning of August 10 (the evening of August 10, Japan time), the US government intercepted the Dōmei news broadcast containing Japan's readiness to surrender ahead of the formal announcement delivered by the Swiss government. Henceforth the United States, in preparing to accept Japan's surrender, focused solely on the interpretation of the Japanese government's request that the Potsdam Proclamation would "not comprise any demand which prejudices the prerogatives of His Majesty as a sovereign ruler." Based on the technical interpretation of that phrase, the US policymakers debated whether to accept Japan's offer of a "conditional" surrender. By this point the fate of Japan's colonial empire—the Eurasian dimension of the war—was only a marginal issue.

While Secretary of State James Byrnes opposed the idea of accepting Japan's offer as a conditional acceptance of the Potsdam Proclamation, President Truman, along with his Chief of Staff Admiral William Leahy and Secretary of War Henry Stimson, favored acceptance of Japan's surrender. Stimson felt it necessary to be flexible regarding Japan's surrender in light of the advancing Soviet Army. He wanted Japan's surrender before the Soviets gained too much influence in the war.

43. JC, vol. 2, 752–55.

A compromise with Japan would be necessary. In his words, "It was of great importance to get the [Japanese] homeland into our hands before the Russians could put in any substantial claim to occupy and help rule it."[44] Byrnes understood the danger and agreed to the ambiguous phrasing proposed by Secretary of the Navy James Forrestal: that the US government would indicate willingness to accept Japan's offer yet ensure that the intents and purposes of the Potsdam Proclamation be thoroughly preserved. What mattered at that juncture—even after the use of the second atomic bomb—was securing Japan's surrender under American initiative and containing Soviet military operations. Byrnes drafted a reply to the Japanese government.

The Byrnes note was completed at 2:00 p.m. It stipulated that "from the moment of surrender the authority of the emperor and the Japanese Government to rule the state shall be subject to the Supreme Commander of the Allied Powers." The US government offered Tokyo the same conciliatory condition stipulated in the Potsdam Proclamation that "the ultimate form of government of Japan shall . . . be established by the freely expressed will of the Japanese people."[45] The implicit message was that the ultimate form of the Japanese government would conform exclusively to American desires. The note was subsequently sent to London, Chongqing, and Moscow at 3:45 p.m.

Tension between Washington and Moscow soon became apparent. In Moscow, on the evening of August 10, Molotov met with Averell Harriman and Clark Kerr, the US and British ambassadors to Moscow, to discuss Japan's surrender. Pointing out that the Japanese offer made its surrender conditional, Molotov explained that the ongoing Soviet military operation demonstrated Moscow's "concrete rejection." In the middle of this meeting, a dispatch arrived from Washington asking whether the Soviet government would endorse the Byrnes note. At 2:00 a.m. August 11, Molotov told Harriman that the Soviets would accept the Byrnes note on the condition that the Allied powers reach an agreement as to who would be "the candidacy or candidacies for representation of the Allied High Command to which the Japanese emperor and the Japanese government are to be subordinated." Harriman replied that it had to be General Douglas MacArthur, who commanded US Army forces in the Pacific and Far East. Molotov suggested that the occupation of Japan might have two supreme commanders, Marshal Aleksandr Vasilevsky, commander-in-chief of Soviet forces in the Far East, and General MacArthur. Harriman dismissed the proposal, countering that the United States

44. Tsuyoshi Hasegawa, *Racing the Enemy*, 220.

45. Article 12 of the Potsdam Proclamation reads: "The occupying forces of the Allies shall be withdrawn from Japan as soon as these objectives have been accomplished and there has been established in accordance with the freely expressed will of the Japanese people a peacefully inclined and responsible government."

had carried the main burden of fighting for four years, while the Soviet Union had been fighting for only the past two days. Shortly after the meeting, Harriman received a telephone call from Stalin's office with the message that the Soviet government would approve the Byrnes note with the hope that it would be at least consulted on the candidacy (not the candidacies) of the supreme commander.[46]

Around 0:45 a.m., August 12 (Tokyo time), the radio room of the Foreign Ministry intercepted the military broadcast from San Francisco concerning the four nations' reply to the Japanese offer to surrender. After examining the Byrnes note all night in order to decipher whether the Allies fundamentally agreed with Japan's proposal on the emperor system, Prime Minister Suzuki and Foreign Minister Tōgō agreed to accept the Allies' reply. At 11:00 a.m., Tōgō met with Emperor Hirohito and reported their decision to him, and the latter concurred.[47] At a 3:00 p.m. meeting, Minister of War Anami, Minister of Home Affairs Abe Genki, and Minister of Justice Matsuzaka Hiromasa all argued that that Byrnes note was still vague about the postsurrender status of the emperor system and proposed double-checking with the Allies for clarification. Meanwhile, between 3:00 and 5:20 p.m., an imperial meeting (*kōzoku kaigi*) was also convened where Emperor Hirohito presided over all male adult members of the imperial family. Emperor Hirohito expressed his firm resolve to bring peace. According to the top secret war journal, when Anami met with Emperor Hirohito, the latter said, "Do not worry, Anami. I have a firm conviction [that everything will be all right]" (*Anami shinpai suruna. Chin niwa kakushō ga aru*). It was rare for the Emperor to address a subject by his surname. Such an intimate tone possibly demonstrated Hirohito's conviction that he would survive after Japan's surrender, even as a useful pawn in a rising competition between the United States and the Soviet Union.[48]

The following day, August 13, saw no consensus within the Japanese government about how to respond to the Byrnes note. Anami requested two more days for deliberation, but Suzuki is said to have explained to a navy officer who seconded Anami in the following manner: "If we don't act now, the Russians will penetrate not only Manchuria and Korea but northern Japan as well. . . . We must act now, while our chief adversary is still only the United States."[49] Suzuki subsequently announced his intension of seeking the second "sacred decision." On August 14 the Imperial Conference convened at 10:50 a.m. Emperor Hirohito announced around noon that he considered the reply—the Byrnes note—to be acceptable. It was past 11:00 p.m. when the Japanese government finalized the note to the

46. JC, vol. 2, 848–50; Tsuyoshi Hasegawa, *Racing the Enemy*, 225–27.

47. JC, vol. 3, 851–75, 880, 886–88.

48. TSWJ, vol. 2, 757–58.

49. The Pacific War Research Society, *Japan's Longest Day* (Tokyo: Kodansha International, 1968), 73. The original Japanese title is *Nihon no ichiban nagai hi* (Tokyo: Bungei Shunjū, 1965).

governments of the United States, Britain, China, and the Soviet Union. Japan expressed its desire with reference to the execution of the provisions of the Potsdam Proclamation. The US government considered this August 14 note as Japan's formal acceptance of the Potsdam Proclamation and the Byrnes note and subsequently sent Tokyo instructions through the Swiss government concerning a truce.

Collapse of Japan's Continental Empire

In the final few days toward the end of the war, bilateral communication between Tokyo and Washington defined the nature of Japan's surrender. The two nations focused so much on the future of the emperor system that they neglected the fate of Japan's continental empire, much less Japan's commitment and responsibility to it. Stalin, a symbol of the confluence of the wars in the Pacific and Eurasia, had become absorbed in the last phase of the Soviet military operation against Japan and let the United States single-handedly define the nature of Japan's surrender and ascend as the sole conqueror of Japan, if not the heir to the Japanese empire. These circumstances facilitated the postwar creation of the "Pacific War narrative," in which Japan's long and complex war with Eurasian-Pacific dimensions was simplified, preempted by a linear history of Japan's military clash with the United States that started with Pearl Harbor and ended with Hiroshima and Nagasaki.

The American use of the atomic bombs, far from serving to "conclude" the war per se, played a dominant role in engendering the myth by driving the Soviet Union out of the parley. General Robert Eichelberger, commander general of the Eighth Army in occupied Japan, testified in 1949 about America's ascendance as sole conqueror of Japan. He was convinced that the B-29s and the two atomic bombs had worked effectively to "add to the prestige of the United States" even before MacArthur arrived in Japan on August 30. Since then, said Eichelberger, the United States had quickly secured a place in the hearts of the Japanese because they were "bright enough" to realize that the Americans were better than the Russians.[50] In a sense Eichelberger confessed that the United States had indeed competed against the Soviet Union for control of Japan and "won" the race at the war's end. In his view the atomic bombs enhanced American glory in the eyes of the Soviets as well as the Japanese; they had an effect on the current enemy in World War II as well as the future enemy in the incipient cold war.

---

50. Yukiko Koshiro, *Trans-Pacific Racisms and the U.S. Occupation of Japan* (New York: Columbia University Press, 1999), 37.

Just as Japan began coping with surrender to the United States, the final episode of Japan's war—the collapse of the colonial empire—played out with the Soviet Union. The Japanese government never declared war against the Soviet Union; it only criticized the Soviet declaration of war as a violation of the neutrality pact that should have remained in effect until April 1946. No scenario by Japanese strategists clearly anticipated that the Soviets would continue their offensive even after Japan's surrender. Even without playing the mediator, Stalin still could have taken diplomatic advantage of Japan's strategic stalemate on the Soviet-Japanese front by arranging Japan's surrender and determining the postwar disposition of the Japanese empire to the Soviet advantage. Perhaps thinking that the termination of war would deprive Soviet forces of the chance to further expand operations and occupy strategic locations across the Japanese empire, Stalin instead pushed for more offensive operations. The American demonstration of nuclear capabilities likely also compelled Stalin to counteract with his military resolve in Asia.

The Soviet armies on all three fronts quickly penetrated the Japanese empire. The Soviet military operation in Korea began on August 9, launching air raids on the ports of Rajin (Rason) and Unggi, followed by a landing at Wonsan, located at the east end of the peninsula's neck. On August 11 Soviet troops invaded the Japanese territory of southern Sakhalin and on the morning of August 15 received an order from Marshal Vasilevsky to occupy the northern parts of the Kurile Islands. By August 15 the Soviet military operation had reached the central region of Manchuria. On August 16 Stalin told Washington that the Soviet Union had the right to occupy not only the Kuriles and South Sakhalin, as stipulated by the Yalta Agreement, but also the northern part of Hokkaidō. Truman opposed allowing Soviet influence over any part of Japan proper.

By August 22, 1945, Stalin acquiesced, but Soviet forces had started shelling and invading the Kurile Islands, an unnecessary operation after Japan's surrender especially because the Allies' provisions had recognized Soviet control over the Kuriles and Sakhalin/Karafuto. The Soviet military advance in the Kuriles was met with Japanese resistance. Only on August 21 did the Japanese garrison on Shumushu surrender following orders from the Imperial General Headquarters. The Battle of Shumushu produced 1,018 Japanese and 1,567 Soviet casualties, the costliest battle for Soviet forces in the Far East, far exceeding the operations in Manchuria and Korea.[51] The Soviet military assault in the Kuriles and Sakhalin resulted in overall deaths of approximately 2,500 Japanese soldiers and 1,460 Japanese

51. Nakayama Takashi, *1945-nen natsu saigo no NiSso sen* (Summer 1945 the final Japanese-Soviet War) (Tokyo: Kokusho Kankō Kai, 1995), 199.

civilians.[52] By September 1, 1945, the last Japanese troops in the area surrendered, without resistance, to the Soviets on Kunashiri and Etorofu. The Soviet military operation in the Kuriles Islands continued after September 2, the day the Japanese government signed the formal surrender document on board the battleship USS *Missouri*. That very day Soviet troops received an order to occupy the Habomai Islands, not geographically part of the Kurile archipelago and therefore not recognized in the original Yalta agreement as part of the legitimate Soviet war spoils.[53]

Meanwhile the chaos and confusion in China and Korea rapidly evolved into a battle between communist and capitalist forces. Japan's surrender in China set off a new race among the players in China's civil war. Already in early August General Wedemeyer had been concerned that Japan's surrender, if it occurred in the near future, would create widespread confusion and disorder in China. The Joint Chiefs of Staff in Washington instructed him to assist the GMD as much as possible so that the GMD could rapidly deploy forces to strategic areas in China. Wedemeyer and Chiang agreed that once Japan surrendered, the GMD and American forces would swiftly occupy key ports of Shanghai, Dagu, Canton, Qingdao, and even Pusan in Korea.[54]

Mao was frustrated that shortly before the Potsdam Conference Stalin had met with T. V. Soong who was trying to negotiate a Soviet-GMD treaty, on behalf of Chiang Kai-shek. The Soviet declaration of war against Japan surprised Mao. He had counted on the war to continue into 1946 because the longer the war dragged on, the more he could push CCP forces to further expansion, even without foreign support. Mao nonetheless cabled Stalin on August 9, publicly welcomed the Soviet entry into the war, and expressed his desire to coordinate strategy with Soviet and other Allied forces against Japan. That same day Mao ordered CCP forces to move to "cooperate with the Soviet Red Army" in the final battle to liberate China from Japan.

Mao's troops were not yet well placed enough to move northwest, synchronize with the rapid Soviet military advance, and take advantage of the Soviet occupation of the region. At the same time, Mao thought that the Soviet entry into the war was a favorable development for the CCP in the civil war. The CCP leaders believed that, in spite of the Stalin-Soong meeting, the Soviet Union would not

52. Etō Jun, ed., *Senryō hishi* (The secret history of the US occupation of Japan), vol. 2, "Teisen to gaikō-ken teishi" (The war's conclusion and the suspension of diplomacy) (Tokyo: Kōdansha Gakujutsu Bunko, 1989), 40–41.

53. On February 2, 1946 the Soviet Union unilaterally declared the annexation of southern Sakhalin and all the islands of the Kurile archipelago including Etorofu and Kunashiri as well as Habomai and Shikotan, the southernmost islands.

54. Jonathan Spence, *The Search for Modern China* (New York: W.W. Norton, 1990), 484.

allow the emergence of an American-backed China and there would be a limit to Stalin's compromise with the GMD. Mao ordered CCP troops to take aggressive action in northern China. Even if Soviet forces were only to express a lukewarm cooperative attitude toward CCP forces in lieu of direct support, Mao was ready to take the opportunity to win Manchuria.[55]

The manner of Japanese surrender in China was confused. By early August, there were still 1.8 million Japanese troops and also 780,000 troops belonging to the Nanjing puppet regime. At midnight of August 10–11, Marshal Zhu De, as the commander-in-chief of the People's Liberation Army of the CCP, ordered all Chinese troops in the Soviet districts to instruct the Japanese armies to surrender their weapons and ammunition to them. Chiang Kai-shek, as the leader of China, ordered the CCP forces not to accept the surrender of Japanese troops or troops belonging to the Nanjing puppet regime as an immediate countermeasure.[56] The China Expeditionary Army of Japan at first questioned the authenticity of Japan's unconditional surrender in China. In a telegram to Foreign Minister Tōgō on August 14, Tani Masayuki, Japanese ambassador to the Nanjing puppet government, explained how General Okamura Yasuji, the commander-in-chief of the China Expeditionary Army, expressed hesitance, especially because they had not yet fought and won a decisive battle in China.[57]

Merely four days later on August 18, the China Expeditionary Army accepted Japan's surrender to the GMD, as the Allies had instructed, and issued to all Japanese troops in China "A General Outline on Japanese Surrender." This document cast Japanese surrender in China as a mutually beneficial truce and not a product of Japan's defeat at the hands of the GMD. The outline began with the following declaration:

> From now on, China begins a new path as the only remaining great power in East Asia [*TōA ni zanzon suru yui'itsu no taikoku*]. As China takes on the great challenge of building itself under pressure of the

---

55. Michael Hunt, *The Genesis of Chinese Communist Foreign Policy* (New York: Columbia University Press, 1996), 160–62; Chen Jian, *Mao's China and the Cold War* (Chapel Hill: University of North Carolina Press, 2001), 26–27. Hunt and Chen have presented differently nuanced interpretations concerning Mao's view of the Soviet entry into war against Japan. While Hunt downplays the impact of Soviet military presence in Manchuria on CCP's military options, Chen emphasizes Mao's readiness to maximize the opportunity provided by the Soviet operation in the Northeast. Chen argues that Stalin, not believing in the CCP's ability to win the Civil War against the GMD, did not want to risk directly confronting the United States by supporting the CCP.

56. Uno Shigeaki, "Chūgoku Tairiku ni okeru 'shūsen (haisen)' to KoKkyō Naisen (The "end of (defeat in)" the war in China and the CCP-GMD civil war), in Etō Jun, ed., *Senryō hishi*, vol. 2, "Teisen to gaikō-ken teishi," 17–19; Chen Jian, *Mao's China*, 27. Uno and Chen mention different dates for Chiang's first order: August 11 according to Uno and August 12 according to Chen.

57. "Shina Haken-gun Sō-Shirei-bu ikō" (Opinions of the General Headquarters of the China Expeditionary Army) (August 14, 1945), in Etō Jun, ed., *Senryō hishi*, vol. 2, 137–39.

> foreign powers, the Japanese empire will rid itself of bellicosity, return to pursue its original goal in China, and support and strengthen China as much as possible as a way to contribute to the future development of the Japanese empire as well as to the recovery of East Asia.

The outline did not refer to Japan's previous endorsement of the CCP. The relationship between the GMD and the CCP was now a domestic issue to be resolved by the Chinese. The outline instructed that the best way to strengthen and support China was to facilitate the GMD government's efforts to unify China as a way to speed China's recovery. If CCP forces continued to express anti-Japanese hostility, the outline added, Japan would not be tolerant.[58]

The developing situation did not turn out favorably for Chiang Kai-shek. In Inner Mongolia most Japanese troops surrendered to Soviet forces. In North China they surrendered to either Soviet or CCP forces. On August 20 the Japanese government sent a telegram conveying the hardships Japanese troops were confronting in China to General MacArthur. GMD and CCP forces were competing to occupy the regions previously under Japanese control, each demanding that Japanese troops disarm and surrender to them.[59] On August 24 the Post-Surrender Management Council (Shūsen Shori Kaigi), formerly the Supreme Council for the Direction of the War, decided to negotiate with the Allied nations so that Japanese troops who had difficulty surrendering to the GMD could be allowed to surrender to the CCP. On August 25 the Imperial General Headquarters in Tokyo subsequently telegraphed MacArthur to ask for his approval.[60]

The situation in Korea was equally chaotic. Uncertainties about the future of Korea diluted the Korean jubilation over the collapse of Japanese colonialism. As of August 10, one day after the Soviet advance into northern Korea, the Office of the Governor-General had not received any specific instructions from Tokyo. It learned from a short-wave foreign broadcast about the Japanese government's readiness to accept the Potsdam Proclamation conditional on the continuity of the emperor system. The Seventeenth Area Army's response to the Soviet assault

---

58. "Wahei chokugo no tai-Shi shori yōkō" (The outline of Chinese policy immediately after the truce) (August 18, 1945), in Etō Jun, ed., *Senryō hishi*, vol. 2, 148–51.

59. "Ōden dai-14-gō Shina jōsei ni kansuru ken" (Telegram #14, Concerning the Chinese situation) (August 20), in Etō Jun, ed., *Senryō hishi*, vol. 2, 43–44.

60. Shūsen Shori Kaigi kettei, "Tairiku hōmen no jōsei ni taisuru Teikoku no sochi ni kansuru ken" ("On the measurement to be taken by the Japanese Empire concerning the continental situation," Approved by the Post Surrender Management Council) (August 24, 1945); "Busō kaijo jisshi yōryō ni kansuru tai-teki kōshō no ken" (Negotiation with the enemy concerning the disarmament) (August 24, 1945) and "Ōden dai-44-gō" (Telegram #44) (August 25, 1945), in Etō Jun, ed., *Senryō hishi*, vol. 2, 55–59.

was greatly compromised because the heavy defense in southern Korea left the Seventeenth Area Army with insufficient troops at strategic locations in the north. Worse, the troops stationed in Rajin (Rason), the city in northern Korea that borders China and Russia, received an order not to resist Soviet forces but to wait for special instructions. The instructions, according to a Japanese captain, were to withdraw two *ri* (an old Japanese unit of distance) when the Soviets advanced one ri; withdraw three ri when the Soviets advanced two ri. Subsequently they began a complete withdrawal on August 10.[61] On August 11, the Soviet forces attempted to land at Chongjin, a port city in northern Korea near the East Korea Bay in the Sea of Japan. The Seventeenth Area Army decided to withdraw and halt the Soviets at Wonsan, more than 200 miles south of Chongjin.[62]

US forces never invaded southern Korea in parallel to the Soviet operation, as the Japanese military planners had anticipated. By the time of the Soviet advance to Korea, the US troops closest to Korea were still based in Okinawa. US troops could not move quickly enough to stop the Soviet forces that seemed on the verge of capturing all of Korea in a short period of time. The updated version of Operation Blacklist, issued on August 8, referred to the occupation of Korea as a largely vague plan with no set US-Soviet boundary. General Joseph Stilwell, former US commander in China and now the commander of the Tenth Army on Okinawa, had at least learned that, according to that plan, his forces would occupy the American zone in Korea.[63]

On the evening of August 10–11, the State-War-Navy Coordinating Committee in Washington, D.C., rushed to adopt a unilateral plan to divide Korea at the thirty-eighth parallel into American and Soviet occupation zones. Truman approved the plan on August 13. That same day Stilwell flew to Manila to confer with MacArthur. While he was there Blacklist was amended and Lieutenant General John R. Hodge was designated to command the Korean occupation. This change reflected Washington's speculation that Chiang Kai-shek still considered Korea a part of the "China coast" and worried about Stilwell exercising control over the peninsula after Japan's withdrawal. Both President Truman and MacArthur had

61. Morita Yoshio, *Chōsen shūsen no kiroku: Bei-So ryōgun no shinchū to Nihonjin no hikiage* (A record of the fall of colonial Korea: US-Soviet military advances and Japanese withdrawal) (Tokyo: Gen'nandō Shoten, 1964), 35.

62. Dai-17 Hōmen-gun, *Hondo sakusen kiroku* (Record of operation plan for the mainland), vol. 5, in SHKA, 245–47.

63. Gye-Dong Kim, *Foreign Intervention in Korea* (Aldershot, England; Brookfield, VT: Dartmouth Pub. Co., 1993), 41; U.S. Army Forces Pacific, "Basic Outline for Blacklist Operations to Occupy Japan Proper and Korea after Surrender or Collapse," August 8, 1945 (Combined Arms Research Library, U.S. Army Command and General Staff College, Fort Leavenworth, KS, Digital Library), available online at http://cgsc.contentdm.oclc.org/.

decided to remove Stilwell from the Korean occupation, assuring Chiang that Stilwell, his antagonist in the military partnership, would not command US troops to land on the "China coast."[64] On August 14 Stalin agreed to accept the American plan even though Soviet ground forces were preponderant in the Korean peninsula and could have expanded further southward. The Americans did not arrive in Korea until September 8.

The same day around 11:00 p.m., the Office of the Governor-General confirmed Japan's formal surrender, not directly with the Japanese government in Tokyo, but by way of the Keijō Bureau of the Dōmei News Agency, which had received the complete text of the Imperial Rescript accepting the Potsdam Proclamation. Tanemura Sakō, now chief of the Staff Operations Plans Division of the Seventeenth Area Army, dispatched surrender instructions to the Japanese troops in northern Korea and Manchuria, which convinced diehard generals and soldiers of the legitimacy of giving up their weapons to the Soviet forces.[65] Tanemura thus accommodated the Soviet arrival in the Far East and brought an end to the war in the peninsula.

In the early morning of August 15, at 3:00 a.m., the Governor-General's Office decided to release all Korean political prisoners. Around 6:00 a.m., the secretary-general for political affairs at the Governor-General's Office invited Yo Un-hyong, a well-regarded nationalist leader, to help in the aftermath of Japanese surrender. Yo Un-hyong was a moderate leftist with considerable international connections with people in the Soviet Union, China, India, and even Japan. He managed the newspaper *Chungang ilbo* (Central Daily). The secretary-general told Yo that Soviet forces would most likely arrive in Seoul by the morning of August 17, disarm the Japanese forces in Korea, and release all political criminals from prison. This timing was based on the calculation that a train trip from Chongjin to Seoul would take only twenty hours. Fearing pandemonium, the Japanese needed Korean leadership to maintain order.

In addition to Yo, the Governor-General's Office also approached Song Chin-u, a Christian nationalist and an alumnus of Meiji University in Japan. Song declined to work with the office. Nor did he prefer to work with Yo.[66] Yo alone agreed. On August 16, a day after the Koreans celebrated *haebang*, liberation from Japan, Yo established his own organization, the Committee for the Preparation of Korean Independence with himself as chairman. After Yō's enthusiastic radio broadcast

---

64. Donald W. Boose, Jr., "Portentous Sideshow: The Korean Occupation Decision," *Parameters*, vol. XXL (winter 1995–96): 112–29, available online at http://www.carlisle.army.mil/USAWC/Parameters/Articles/1995/boose.htm.

65. Morita Yoshio, *Chōsen shūsen no kiroku*, 95–100 and 159–60.

66. Morita Yoshio, *Chōsen shūsen no kiroku*, 67–71.

on *haebang*, the Korean people assumed that they had gained full independence, as one people and one nation.

From then until the end of August, the Committee for the Preparation of Korean Independence opened 145 branches throughout the Korean peninsula. The Korean people believed the Governor-General's Office to be defunct upon Japan's surrender and demanded immediate transfer of power and authority to the Committee for the Preparation of Korean Independence. In contrast, the Governor-General's Office believed that Allied forces, not the Korean people, would dismantle the colonial structure and requested that the committee limit its activities strictly to the maintenance of order, which it refused.[67] While Yo and his political allies advocated a coalition government that included revolutionary factions both inside and outside Korea, the rightist nationalists insisted on the legitimacy of the Korean Provisional Government at Chongqing, the capital of the GMD regime in China. Domestic consensus proved elusive. According to several postwar memoirs, some leftist nationalists urged Song Chin-u to form a united front with Yo Un-hyong so their coalition would become an invincible political force. It did not happen.[68]

In many parts of Korea, rumors of the impending arrival of Soviet liberation forces galvanized the Korean people. To welcome the arrival of Soviet force in the capital, crowds bedecked the Seoul train station with banners, the Red flag, and the Korean flag. The streets of Seoul were also dotted with billboards for the Korean Communist Party. On August 19 Soviet forces began landing at Wonsan and occupying the five northern provinces. Japanese troops duly surrendered to Soviet forces. The Japanese government and the Governor-General's Office still did not know who would dismantle the Japanese colony, or when, or how.

On August 22 the Governor-General's Office received a telegram from Tokyo concerning the prospect that Japanese troops stationed north of the thirty-eighth parallel would surrender to the Soviet Union and those stationed south of the parallel would surrender to the United States. Since landing, the Soviet authorities had established in the northern provinces People's Political Committees, the jurisdictions of which conflicted with Yo's committee and its local offices. Amid this confusion the Governor-General's Office requested specific instructions from Tokyo on the postsurrender nature of their power and authority.

On August 24, when 200,000 Soviet troops entered Pyongyang, the Post-Surrender Management Council (Shūsen Shori Kaigi) in Tokyo sent a telegram to the governor-general, clarifying its understanding of the situation. The council

---

67. Morita Yoshio, *Chōsen shūsen no kiroku*, 76–85.

68. Morita Yoshio, "Chōsen ni okeru Nihon tōchi no shūen," *Kokusai Seiji*, no. 2 (1962), 86–88; *Chōsen shūsen no kiroku*, 72 and 76–80; Gye-Dong Kim, *Foreign Intervention in Korea*, 46–48.

stated that regardless of what Yo Un-hyong demanded, sovereignty in the Korean Peninsula belonged to Japan until the ratification of a peace treaty with specific provision for Korean independence. Yet the council also conceded that the occupation of Korea by foreign troops might effectively end Japanese sovereignty and give de facto sovereignty to the occupying power even before the conclusion of a peace treaty. The council suggested a dual approach toward the question of Japanese sovereignty in Korea: its continuity vis-à-vis the Koreans and suspension vis-à-vis the US and Soviet occupation forces. To avoid further confusion about who ruled Korea, the council recommended not suppressing Yo's Committee for the Preparation of Korean Independence and called for discretion in securing order and avoiding stirring anti-Japanese sentiments among Koreans.[69] On August 28 the Headquarters of the Seventeenth Area Army formally announced Japan's surrender to the Soviet Union north of the thirty-eighth parallel and to the United States south of it. On the same day the Korean people learned about the division of their nation.[70]

Nothing had yet been settled regarding the future of Korea. About a week before the American arrival in Korea on September 8, the State-War-Navy Coordinating Committee of the United States had worked on a plan for the four-power administration of Korea by the United States, Britain, China and the Soviet Union. Since the four occupation forces should have "equal" rights in the administration of Korea, their forces would occupy specific zones of Korea: Hamgyeong-do and Gangwon-do for the Soviet Union; Gyeonggi-do, Chungcheong-namdo, and Jeolla-do for the United States; Pyeongan-do and Hwanghae-do for China; and Chungcheong-bukdo and Gyeongsang-do for Britain.[71] This plan never materialized.

Who gained most in Korea after Japan's demise? On the one hand, the United States captured half of Korea without bloody combat. Had Japan surrendered before the Soviet entry into the war, the United States could have obtained control over all of Korea. On the other hand, in spite of its extremely short engagement in the war in East Asia, the Soviet Union secured at least half of Korea with American approval, even though earlier it had preferred an independent Korea with little American influence.

Whereas Japanese leaders and strategists had astutely inferred the rise of the CCP as the ultimate unifier of China, they had difficulty forecasting Korea's fu-

---

69. "Shūsen Shori Kaigi ni okeru tai-Chōsen shori kettei no ken" (The Post-Surrender Management Council's decision concerning the disposition of Korea), in Etō Jun, ed., *Senryō hishi*, vol. 2, 120–22. Morita Yoshio, "Chōsen ni okeru Nihon tōchi no shūen," 95.

70. Morita Yoshio, *Chōsen shūsen no kiroku*, 154–55.

71. Gye-Dong Kim, *Foreign Intervention in Korea*, 41–45.

ture. They did not try enough to understand the nature and direction of Korean nationalism. Korea's nationalist movements remained too fragmented under the conflicting sponsorships of the Soviet Union, the CCP, the GMD, and the United States. By preoccupying themselves with the geopolitical transition from World War II to the cold war, the Japanese strategists who predicted the end of Japan's colonialism neglected the fate of Korean people and perpetuated colonial Japan's "moral" failing—one of the forgotten legacies of Japan's war.

Appendix

Telegram number 0649, "Concerning the Matter of Accepting the Three Nations Proclamation," from Foreign Minister Tōgō in Tokyo to Minister Kase in Switzerland, 9:00 a.m., August 10, 1945 [in the English original].

In obedience to the gracious command of His Majesty the Emperor who, ever anxious to enhance the cause of world peace, desires earnestly to bring about an early termination of hostilities with a view to saving mankind from the calamities to be imposed upon them by further continuation of the war, the Japanese Government asked several weeks ago the Soviet Government, with which neutral relations then prevailed, to render good offices in restoring peace vis-à-vis the enemy Powers. Unfortunately, these efforts in the interest in the peace having failed, the Japanese Government, in conformity with the august wish of His Majesty to restore the general peace and desiring to put an end to the untold suffering entailed by war as quickly as possible, have [*sic*] decided upon the followings [*sic*]:

The Japanese Government are [*sic*] ready to accept the terms enumerated in the Joint Declaration which was issued at Potsdam on July 26th, 1945, by the heads of the Governments of the United States, Great Britain and China, and later subscribed by the Soviet Government, with the understanding that the said Declaration does not comprise any demand which prejudices the prerogatives of His Majesty as a sovereign ruler.

The Japanese Government hope [*sic*] sincerely that this understanding is warranted and desire keenly that an explicit indication to that effect will be speedily forthcoming.

The Japanese Government have [*sic*] the honor to request the Government of Switzerland (the Royal Swedish Government) to be good enough to forward immediately the above communications to the Governments of the United States and China (Governments of the Soviet Union and Great Britain).[72]

72. JC, vol. 2, 817–18. Note that the usage of the plural verb for the word "government" is consistent with British English. Also see "Offer of Surrender from Japanese Government" in *the Department of State Bulletin*, vol. XIII, no. 320, August 12, 1945.

Part IV

INVENTING JAPAN'S WAR

Eurasian Eclipse

8

MEMORIES AND NARRATIVES OF JAPAN'S WAR

Once the war was over, the mythic emergence of the United States as the primary conqueror would almost entirely eclipse the role of the Soviet Union. In the months leading up to the war's end and shortly after the war, however, Japanese people continued to speculate about the motivations behind American, Soviet, and Japanese actions and, given those parameters, debated how Japan should best position itself to survive the war. Discussion of Japan's fate in world politics, with a strong focus on the Soviet Union and the United States, occupied the nation for some time even after the war. First under the US military occupation, and then under the US-Japanese military alliance, the Eurasian dimension of the war receded in the Japanese history and memory.

Views of the War's End and Beyond

On September 2, 1945, the Japanese government and the Imperial General Headquarters signed the formal Instrument of Surrender on board the USS *Missouri* and jointly declared that Japan accepted the surrender terms set forth by the United States, Britain, and China (under Chiang Kai-Shek) on July 26, 1945, at Potsdam and "*subsequently adhered to by*" the Soviet Union (emphasis added). However, no high-profile Soviet representative was in sight. As the supreme commander for the Allied Powers, Douglas MacArthur presided over the ceremony and accepted Japan's surrender for the United States, Republic of China, United Kingdom, and the Soviet Union, and also "in the interests of the other United

Nations at war with Japan." After the Japanese delegation signed the surrender documents and departed the scene, MacArthur broadcast a radio message to the world and announced that a great tragedy had ended. He mentioned the grim days of Bataan and Corregidor, a merciful God, a spiritual recrudescence and improvement of human character. He did not acknowledge the battlefields of China, the Eurasian dimension of Japan's war. The surrender ceremony projected a vision of Japan having surrendered exclusively to the United States.

The end of Japan's war and of the Japanese empire did not look to the Japanese people as simple as the American occupation's narrative portrayed it. After the surrender, even while under American occupation, the Japanese people did not necessarily abruptly turn pro-American and anti-Soviet. Socialists and communists regained influence and popularity for their wartime opposition to imperialism. In May 1947 Katayama Tetsu, chief secretary of the Japan Socialist Party, became the first socialist prime minister in Japanese history. After the surrender, many Japanese people continued their engagement with world politics insofar as this concerned Japan. Rather than coping with the trauma of Japan's absolute surrender to the United States, they found themselves baffled by Stalin's final conduct in the war and wondered what had happened with Japan's relationship with the Soviet Union.

The Special Higher Police (Tokkō) recorded the perspectives of ordinary Japanese people. From the time the morning newspapers on August 11 conveyed the news of Japan's readiness to accept the Potsdam Proclamation, the Japanese government carefully monitored Japanese citizens in the transition to this new phase of the nation's history. The Special High Police investigated people's reactions to the Soviet declaration of war and the American use of the "new type of weapon" (*shingata bakudan*) and their speculations about the reason for Japan's surrender. Quite understandably, the atomic bombs did *not* evoke in Japanese minds awe and respect for the United States. The final actions of Soviet forces were far from noble, but they did not make US nuclear bombs look any better either. The Japanese did not believe the bombings of Hiroshima and Nagasaki legitimized America as the sole winner of the war.

Regarding the "new type of weapon," or more specifically the atomic bombs (depending on the level of information people obtained), the immediate public response was similar to the finding of the US strategic bombing survey, a study commissioned by President Truman on August 15, 1945. This US study questioned 300 civilians, 350 officials, and 500 enlisted men in Japan in order to evaluate the effects of air attacks on Japan for the purposes of planning the future development of the US armed forces. According to the final report, issued in July 1946, the primary reaction of the populace to the atomic bombs was "fear, uncontrolled terror, strengthened by the sheer horror of the destruction."[1]

Findings of the Special Higher Police of Japan attest that these fears and terrors did not necessarily trigger awe and the urge to surrender instantly to the United States. In Fukuoka, the region equidistant from both Hiroshima and Nagasaki, one farmer uttered that with *fourteen or fifteen more* of this new weapon Japan would be completely wiped off the face of the earth. A regional manager of Japan Securities (Nippon Shōken) admitted that the people were now very frightened and upset by the nuclear weapon, but a Korean leader of Kōsē-kai, an official organization that supervised and promoted the proper Japanization of Korean immigrants in Japan, said it was only because the new weapon's efficiency was yet to be determined.[2] On August 11 the Special Higher Police found that the president of Kyūshū Imperial University, a director of the Mitsui Tagawa Mining Company, and a factory worker all saw in the absolute destruction the enemy's scientific dominance of the horrifying power to destroy the human race. Some people, lacking information about nuclear weapons, urged others not to be intimidated by the technology but to come up quickly with a scientific countermeasure and continue the fight. On August 9 and 11, in Tottori Prefecture, both a mayor of a town and a manager of a bank insisted that they were not convinced why Japan should be afraid of the atomic bombs. Several others in Tottori Prefecture shared this opinion.[3]

In stark contrast the Soviet declaration of war elicited a much more complex, and reflective, reaction. A large number of the Japanese people understood that the fate of Japan's war against the United States depended on Japan's diplomacy with Moscow. More critically, the success of Japan's pan-Asianism rested with

1. *The United States Strategic Bombing Survey, Summary Report (Pacific War)* (Washington, DC: U.S. Government Printing Office, 1946), 22–25.

2. Kōsē-kai was a national Japanese organization with local branch offices all over Japan. The leader's name is Higashida Toshio, which is his adopted Japanese name. In general Koreans were assigned to be Kōsē-kai supervisors (*shidōin*) who were responsible for the "proper" Japanization of the Korean residents in their region.

3. "Soren no tai-Nichi sensen fukoku narabi ni shingata bakudan ni taisuru minshin no dōkō ni kansuru ken" (Concerning popular attitudes toward the Soviet entry into the war against Japan and the new type of bombs) (Fukuoka Prefecture, August 11, 1945), in NRPP, vol. 7, 122–23, 125–26, 129–31; "Gen senkyoku ni taisuru minshin no dōkō ni kansuru ken" (Concerning popular attitudes toward the current Japanese situation in the war) (Fukuoka Prefecture, August 13, 1945), in NRPP, vol. 7, 135; "Soren no sensen nado ni tomonau kenmin no dōkō no ken" (Concerning popular attitudes toward the Soviet entry into the war and other new developments) (Ōita Prefecture, August 11, 1945), in NRPP, vol. 7, 234; "Haisen no shinsō kaimei ni taisuru hankyō naisa no ken (Concerning popular perceptions of the truth about Japan's defeat) (Tottori Prefecture, September 9, 1945), in "Japanese Army and Navy Archives," M 5041, Roll 220, Frames 91263–67 [Microfilm Collection], LOC.

Soviet neutrality, from Soviet ideological support for independence in Asia and Soviet racial and cultural compatibility with pan-Asianism, to its strategic capability to counterbalance Anglo-America in Asia. The Soviet entry into the war against Japan did not decimate the cities of mainland Japan as the two atomic bombs did, but it instantly incapacitated the strategic logic of Japan's war on the continent. Moreover, the Soviet forces put to rout more than a million Japanese settlers in Manchukuo and Korea and demolished Japan's continental empire amid their flight. The Soviet declaration of war administered a far deeper shock to the Japanese: this emotional, psychological, and intellectual shock compelled the people to confront the ultimate fate of Japan's colonial empire, Japan's defeat, and its future.

According to the Special Higher Police, there were those, though never the majority, who chanted that regardless of what had happened, be it the Soviet war or the atomic bomb, Japan should continue fighting and show its national spirit. One even said until the nation lost one-third of its population. More people expressed a measured appraisal of Japan's fighting capacity against the Soviet forces. On August 11, 1945, in Hyōgo Prefecture, a factory worker remarked that Moscow's refusal to renew the neutrality pact had convinced him long ago that the Soviets would attack Japan at the most crucial moment in the war. A farmer was caught arguing that now that the Soviets were coming in, Japan would not last for more than a month.[4]

While many people referred to the impacts of the Soviet and US attacks as synergistic, the Japanese people reacted to the respective Soviet and US final acts in strikingly different ways. Most people expressed disappointment that Japanese diplomacy with the Soviet Union never bore fruit and proved an utter failure. At the same time they wondered why Stalin chose to betray Japan. In Fukuoka on August 11, a politician and a colonel in the reserves each speculated that Stalin's motivation was political: when he predicted Japan's inevitable defeat at American hands, he decided to enter the war to obstruct American ascendancy and increase his political influence in postwar Asia. A director of the *Nishi Nippon* newspaper and a factory worker shared the opinion that Japan's plea for peace mediation had convinced Stalin of Japan's predicament and led him to believe that Japan was easy prey: at the last minute Stalin attacked Japan's colonies for additional war spoils. A president of the Kyūshū Aircraft Manufacturing Company said that the text of the Soviet declaration of war (which had been printed in the Japanese newspapers) revealed to the entire world that the Japanese government had attempted peace negotiations with the Soviet government,

4. NRPP, vol. 6, 275–77.

only to be betrayed by it. Both a professor at Kyūshū Imperial University and a director of the Fukuoka bureau of the Dōmei News Agency believed that the Soviet declaration of war had a political aim against Anglo-American control in East Asia.[5] In Ōita Prefecture on August 11, an individual described as belonging to the intellectual class argued that the Soviet entry into the war must have been some kind of reaction to the American use of the "new type of bomb"—that Stalin got so alarmed or enraged he had to demonstrate his own might in the Far East.[6]

The Special Higher Police discovered that many people raised questions about the peculiar behavior of the Japanese government upon the Soviet entry into the war. They were baffled that the Japanese government did not declare war against the Soviet Union but seemed to allow the Soviets to expand into the Japanese empire, from Manchukuo, northern Korea, and to the southern Sakhalin and beyond: did the Japanese government have a plan so that something positive might come from such passivity? A professor at the First Fukuoka Teacher's College (Fukoka Dai-ichi Shihan) wondered why neither the Japanese government nor the media criticized the Soviet Union and suspected Japanese leaders had some secret plan for coping with the crisis. Others shared this view, including an executive member of a right-wing organization, two politicians of the cities of Ōmuta and Fukuoka, the aforementioned director of the *Nishi Nippon* newspaper, as well as the Kyūshū Imperial University professor. Several people believed that because the Soviet Union wanted Manchuria, Japan should hand it over in exchange for a better peace. The professor at the First Fukuoka Teacher's College and the Fukuoka city politician said Japan could then settle for a separate peace treaty with the Soviet Union in lieu of an unconditional surrender to all Allied nations.[7]

The colonel in the reserves in Fukuoka who had speculated about Stalin's political motivations expressed a mild sense of confusion. As he understood it, the Japanese government must have anticipated the Soviet entry into the war upon conclusion of the war in Europe. Yet the Japanese military did not seem capable of launching an effective counteroffensive. He wondered if Japan's unpreparedness was related to the fact that the Japanese government knew the Soviet goal was to gain political influence in Asia and not to annihilate Japan as a nation and

---

5. "Soren no tai-Nichi sensen fukoku narabi ni shingata bakudan ni taisuru minshin no dōkō ni kansuru ken," 126–27, 128–30; "Gen senkyoku ni taisuru minshin no dōkō ni kansuru ken," 134, 138.

6. "Soren no sensen nado ni tomonau kenmin no dōkō ni kansuru ken" (Concerning popular attitudes toward the Soviet entry into the war and other new developments) (Ōita Prefecture, August 12, 1945), in NRPP, vol. 7, 240.

7. "Soren no tai-Nichi sensen fukoku narabi ni shingata bakudan ni taisuru minshin no dōkō ni kansuru ken," 125, 128–30; "Gen senkyoku ni taisuru minshin no dōkō ni kansuru ken," 134–35.

a people. A person in Tokushima Prefecture argued on August 16 that the Japanese government might have made some tacit arrangement with the Soviet government. Otherwise it was hard to explain why Japan, almost immediately after the Soviet declaration of war, called for a cease-fire without even fighting back.[8] Even ordinary Japanese speculated about Japan's strategic possibilities with the Soviet Union.

After Japan's surrender, public interest fixated on the impact of the Soviet-US rivalry on Japan, for better or worse. On August 27 a newspaper reporter in Saga Prefecture explained why Japan would be better off under Anglo-American occupation. If Japan were under Soviet occupation, the country would be attacked and invaded by the United States and Britain in the event of war between Anglo-America and the Soviet Union. The Japanese mainland would then be turned into a bloody battlefield. So let America keep Japan.[9] On October 1 a painter in Mie Prefecture with a record of leftist activities said that defeated Japan was destined to perish under US occupation. Once the US-Soviet war occurred within a few years, it would be fought on the Japanese mainland; then the United States would send Japanese soldiers to the front to fight against the Soviet Army. Japan would then perish for good.[10]

In Tokushima Prefecture, a person, with a record of leftist activism, expressed on August 16 a unique foresight. The two victors, the United States and the Soviet Union, would sooner or later experience a great political discomfort with each other's presence in the Far East and defer punishing vanquished Japan; this would be the moment for Japan to recover from defeat. Another said on August 16: now that Japan recedes into the back stage of world politics, we Japanese will sit and entertain ourselves by watching how the Soviets are going to outsmart the United States and frustrate its ambition in Asia. He intended to find solace in this prospect for the rest of his life. One individual said on a Tokyo street that, given the international political outlook in Asia at the end of this war, the United States would need Japan in the next war—in the event of a final showdown with the Soviet Union; therefore, it would not harshly treat Japan once it began its occupation. A staff member at a railway company said Japan could start adopting

8. "Taishō Kanpatsu ni tomonau sochi narabi ni hankyō nado naisa ni kansuru ken" (Concerning the measure accompanying the promulgation of the Imperial Rescript and the popular response to it) (Tokushima Prefecture, August 16, 1945), in "Japanese Army and Navy Archives," M 5041, Roll 220, Frames 90996–97 [Microfilm Collection], LOC.

9. "Shinjitaika ni okeru chian jōsei ni kansuru ken" (Concerning peace preservation under the latest development) (Saga Prefecture, August 27, 1945), in "Japanese Army and Navy Archives," M 5041, Roll 220, Frame 91759 [Microfilm Collection], LOC.

10. "Shūsengo ni okeru sayoku bunshi no dōkō ni kansuru ken,"(Concerning leftist attitudes after the war) (Mie Prefecture, October 1, 1945), in "Japanese Army and Navy Archives," M 5041, Roll 220, Frames 91825–26 [Microfilm Collection], LOC.

the best from each: the political system from the United States and ideological values from the Soviet Union.[11]

Leading Japanese politicians and strategists shared these views in their quest to secure the nation's survival and recovery. The search for survival in the balance between foreign powers prompted the postwar government to adopt an ecumenical approach to the United States and the Soviet Union. Japanese leaders attempted to emphasize Japan's surrender to *both* the United States and the Soviet Union, but not exclusively to either one of them, as a precautionary step toward the nation's recovery in an unstable world.

The postsurrender Japanese government reinterpreted the Potsdam Proclamation as if Stalin had been among the original signers. Shigemitsu Mamoru, one of the architects of the Yan'an recognition policy during the war, who was reappointed foreign minister in August–September 1945, defined his postwar mission as accepting the Potsdam Proclamation as a document of US-Soviet accord, and to carry out its terms as such, not as an exclusive commitment to the United States. Acting as if he had not noticed the growing US-Soviet discord, he remained cautious about Japan's future direction in the wake of growing rivalry between the United States and the Soviet Union.[12] Even Emperor Hirohito seemed to understand this point. He made two separate statements with two different reasons for his decision to surrender: one made on August 14 mentioned the atomic bombs and another made on August 17 mentioned the Soviet entry into the war. So technically he surrendered to *both* the United States and the Soviet Union and made that clear to all parties.[13]

A month after Japan's surrender, the Japanese Foreign Ministry issued a report analyzing how Japanese were divided between those who hoped to depend on the United States and Britain for reconstruction of Japan and those who wanted to check US power and influence in Asia through alliances with CCP-led China and the Soviet Union. It was unclear at the time which group of people—pro-US or pro-Soviet—would become predominant in postwar Japanese politics.[14]

Japanese political scientist Watanabe Akio explained how the pro-Anglo-American factions hoped that restoring friendship with the United States would be possible because of the latter's growing discomfort with the Soviet Union, the

11. "Taishō Kanpatsu ni tomonau sochi narabi ni hankyō nado naisa ni kansuru ken," (Tokushima Prefecture, August 16, 1945), Frames 90996–97; "Machi no koe" (Voices of the street) (August 15–31, 1945) (Keishi-cho Joho-ka), Frames 91154, 91758, in "Japanese Army and Navy Archives," M 5041, Roll 220 [Microfilm Collection], LOC.

12. Hatano Sumio, "Senji gaikō to sengo kōsō," in *Taiheiyō Sensō no shūketsu* (Tokyo: Kashiwa Shobō, 1997), 24.

13. Herbert Bix, *Hirohito and the Making of Modern Japan* (New York: Harper Collins, 2000), 529–30; "Chokugo" (Imperial rescript), *Asahi Shinbun* (August 18, 1945), 1.

14. Hatano Sumio, "Senji gaikō to sengo kōsō," 24.

very nation Japan had looked to as the key until the war's end. Watanabe's analysis of planners, such as Shidehara Kijūrō and Ugaki Kazushige as well as the Sengo Mondai Kenkyū-kai (the Association of Studies of Problems Confronting Postwar Japan), aptly demonstrates that scenarios of the postwar world drawn by the wartime strategists shaped the postwar principles of Japanese diplomacy.

On September 29, shortly before he was recalled to serve as prime minister in October, Shidehara Kijūrō, the foreign minister in the 1920s famous for his support of Wilsonianism, penned a memorandum "Shūsen zengo-saku" (A plan to make a good start out of the war's end). "The powers never keep the same friend or enemy for one hundred years," he wrote, referring to the fickle nature of international relations. "Even today, the Allied nations have conflicts of interest on numerous issues of critical importance; therefore, nations which once competed and fought against each other might well in due course face problems that require mutual cooperation and support. In order for Japan to pursue postwar politics, it should not be too difficult to turn yesterday's enemy into tomorrow's friend."

Watanabe examines a similar view expressed by General Ugaki Kazushige, known as a "political general" because of his career as governor-general of Korea between 1931 and 1936 and as also minister of Foreign and Colonial Affairs in 1938. Ugaki wrote in his diary on September 30, 1945, "It is imperative for us to start making the utmost effort to develop Japan as the most advanced pacifist nation [*heiwa kokka*]. In the near future, we can with ease predict a confrontation between the United States and Britain (for leadership in the capitalist world) as well as contention between the United States and the Soviet Union (for world leadership). What Japan should do is to mediate between these nations and save all of them from destruction so as to establish ourselves in a leadership position in creating true peace in the world." Ugaki believed that this was the chance to realize wartime Japan's unaccomplished dream of *Hakkō Ichiu* (the eight corners of the world under one roof). On October 8 shortly before the creation of the Shidehara cabinet, Ugaki added that it was Japan's unavoidable destiny in this dark age to adulate and keep in step with the United States (*ko-Bei-teki, Beikoku ni tsutomete chōshi o awashite iku*). In order for Japan to do so, he emphasized the importance of controlling people's anti-American sentiment.[15]

According to Watanabe, defeated Japan's awareness of being flanked by the United States and the Soviet Union prompted Japanese bureaucrats and technocrats to find the path of Japan's economic recovery in a confluence of US and

15. Watanabe Akio, "'Hitotsu no sekai' no yume to genjitsu" (A dream and reality of "One World"), in Watanabe Akio, ed., *Sengo Nihon no taigai seisaku* (The foreign policy of postwar Japan) (Tokyo: Yūhikaku, 1985), 10–11.

Soviet zones of influence. The Association of Studies of Problems Confronting Postwar Japan (Sengo Mondai Kenkyū-kai) spearheaded such thinking. Created by the foreign minister shortly before the war's end to prepare for the impending crisis in the nation's economy, the association's first meeting on August 16 drew young and aspiring scholars, bureaucrats, and technocrats. Its first report, "Nihon keizai saiken no kihon mondai" (Basic problems concerning a reconstruction of Japanese economy), issued in March 1946, demonstrated an awareness that Japan could not survive in isolation; people all over the world were going to be integrated on a global basis. In this emerging world economy, the report argued, the United States would exercise leadership through the Bretton Woods international monetary system. At the same time the report also predicted that, in spite of ideological differences, if the Soviet Union hoped to recover from the war's destruction, then its coexistence with the US-led economic system would be inevitable. Foreseeing the rise of the cold war, the report expressed the belief that the world would emerge as an integrated system. The report did not argue that either of the systems would establish world hegemony. Rather the report expressed belief in a harmonious fusion.

The most distinctive claim in this report was its view of Japan's place in such a world. "Geographically, Japan is located at a point of contact between the US bloc and the Soviet bloc," the report pointed out. Acknowledging Japan's current status within the US bloc, the report still predicted influences from both blocs. The waxing and the waning of the two blocs would greatly influence Japan's political and economic growth. The report urged Japan to avoid the risk of making an exclusive commitment to either one of the blocs and to maintain equal distance from both.[16] The US government wanted defeated Japan to reemerge as a Pacific nation with its Eurasian link severed. But for Japan, at least for some time after defeat, neutrality guided its postwar diplomacy in line with the principles of the United Nations, where there was no approved prerogative for a hegemonic power. Into the 1960s, in spite of the constraints of the US-Japan security alliance, "All-around equi-diplomacy" (of economy and culture) with communist nations became Japan's signature style.

What if Japan had surrendered upon the issuance of the Potsdam Proclamation? Even today nearly seventy years after the war, the Japanese public opinion holds strongly that Japan's early surrender could have spared Japanese lives. Japan's surrender in time to forestall Soviet entry into the war might have ceded the entire Korean peninsula to the United States. It might have also prevented Japanese troops from surrendering to CCP forces, which would have then been unable to expand easily into Manchuria. In this scenario a GMD victory, with strong backing

---

16. Watanabe Akio, "'Hitotsu no sekai' no yume to genjitsu," 11–15.

from the United States, might have been possible. It could have meant ultimate victory for the United States throughout East Asia, not just against Japan. What would China and Korea be like today if the United States had been the sole settler in the disposition of Japan's colonial empire? Moreover, what would have been the nature and direction of the US occupation of Japan?

The continuing focus on the Soviet-US rivalry into the cold war weakened Japanese recognition of their ultimate defeat by the peoples of Asia. By the beginning of the 1950s, the Soviet Union, the People's Republic of China, and even the two Koreas, had all receded from postwar Japan's "world," ensconced within the US defense perimeter. In China the Japanese felt they could dilute and obscure their defeat by their surrender to more than one party. As argued by Japanese critic Etō Jun, the vanguard of criticism of the US occupation of Japan in the 1980s, there was no "loser" in China, since the war's end came while the three parties—the GMD, the CCP, and Japanese forces—still competed against one another.[17]

The real situation was much more complex than Etō's claim, as reflected in stories hidden for decades after the war. One Kuwajima Setsurō, a former medic, reminisced how the Sixty-fourth Infantry Battalion of the Japanese Forty-third Army under the North China Area Army experienced the long and inexplicable aftermath of Japan's surrender in Shandong Province. During the war the North China Area Army had fought against the Eighth Route Army of the CCP and become familiar with the activities of the communist propagandists, particularly the activities of the Japanese Soldiers' Antiwar League. On the late night of August 15, 1945, an agent of the Japanese Soldiers' Antiwar League came near the camp of Kuwajima's Forty-third Army to address its mostly poorly trained and poorly equipped reservists. He praised their hard work thus far and invited them to promptly surrender to the Eighth Route Army so they could return to Japan quickly. On August 18, the Forty-third Army received a formal order to disarm and withdraw from China. Since there were no GMD armies in northern China by that time, they could not surrender and demobilize as stipulated by the Potsdam Proclamation. As a result, the Forty-third Army, along with other divisions, had no choice but continue fighting the Eighth Route Army. The Japanese soldiers noticed, however, that the Eighth Route Army no longer launched an all-out offensive against the already defeated.

Five months later, on January 16, 1946, GMD forces finally arrived in the Qingdao region in eastern Shandong Province and demobilized all remaining Japanese troops of the North China Area Army, some fifty thousand soldiers in

17. "Kaisetsu (Commentary)," in Etō Jun, ed., *Senryō hishi* (The secret history of the US occupation of Japan), vol. 2, "Teisen to gaikō-ken teishi" (The war's conclusion and the suspension of diplomacy) (Tokyo: Kōdansha Gakujutsu Bunko, 1989), 139.

total. Yet between April and December 1945, some thirty soldiers of the Sixty-fourth Infantry Division had surrendered to the Eighth Route Army, including one second lieutenant and two staff sergeants. Some voluntarily became hostages of the Eighth Route Army in order to fight with them against the GMD. On the evening of January 12, 1946, agents from the Japanese Soldiers' Antiwar League came near the Japanese camp again and repeatedly invited the Japanese soldiers to surrender to the Eighth Route Army, not to the GMD. Kuwajima's superior requested something to eat. The following morning, they delivered provisions such as pork, chicken, eggs, vegetables, and liquor, much to Japanese surprise as well as gratitude. Kuwajima later felt that unless the Japanese people learned about what the Eighth Route Army did for the remaining Japanese soldiers, they could not comprehend a larger and truer picture of Japan's war in China.[18]

For some twenty-six hundred soldiers of the China Expeditionary Army, the war's end did not come for four more years. Yan Xishan, a Chinese warlord who had controlled the province of Shanxi since the 1911 Revolution, successfully enticed these surrendered Japanese soldiers into staying in northwest Shanxi and to fight the CCP forces so he could keep the area surrounding Taiyuan under his control. Breaching the Potsdam Proclamation, he successfully hid the Japanese presence from the Allied inspections by posing them as disarmed soldiers or even plain laborers. Lieutenant General Sumida Raishirō, a commanding officer of the Japanese First Army, is said to have concluded a secret pact with Yan so the latter could command Japanese soldiers. Sumida did announce Japan's formal surrender to the GMD in August 1945. But he also made a false announcement to his subordinates that the Japanese Army had secretly decided to have them integrated into the GMD forces so that they might continue fighting the CCP. Sumita is believed to have done so with dual ambitions: to avoid being convicted as Class A war criminal and also to keep the Japanese armed forces in China for future operations.

Yan further recruited some 10,000 Japanese civilians into his service. At the peak, he had 15,000 Japanese troops under his control. Toward the end of the civil war in 1949, 1,600 remaining Japanese soldiers of the China Expeditionary Army were finally ready to repatriate. Some 550 had been killed in the battle against the CCP forces and more than 700 had been captured and still detained as hostages by the People's Liberation Army. The postwar Japanese government regarded those remaining troops as volunteers and refused to pay them military pensions and other benefits. The Japanese government refused to admit the Japanese Army's, or Sumida's, responsibility for keeping these soldiers armed against the CCP for four

18. Kuwajima Setsurō, *Kahoku senki—Chūgoku ni atta hontō no sensō* (The war chronicle in north China—a real story about a war in China) (Tokyo: Tosho Shuppan Sha, 1978).

years after Japan's formal surrender, because the military's failure to disarm all the Japanese soldiers amounted to a Japanese breach of the Potsdam Proclamation.[19]

In the obfuscated aftermath of the war's end, the Japanese never looked back at the split former colony of Korea. Had the Korean Peninsula remained one entity, would leftist Korean nationalists—including all these exiles in Manchuria, the Soviet Union and China—have readily collaborated with the US occupation of Korea, and vice versa? On July 19, 1947, Yo Un-hyong, the most probable choice to lead a provisional government in the event the United States and the Soviet Union succeeded in jointly forming one, was assassinated in South Korea. While Syngman Rhee and others on the right blamed communists for the death, the prevailing sense was that the right had done it. Yo Un-hyong's death inflicted a major blow to the right-left cooperative effort to build a unified Korea.[20]

The Japanese let the Soviet Union and the United States take charge of what Japan had left behind on the continent and also let Japan be governed by the cold war paradigm. The Japanese willingly and actively wiped traces of Japan's colonial empire from its national awareness and absolved themselves of further obligations, physical and moral, to their former colonies. Japan's postdefeat resurrection was destined to cost dearly in the long run.

Writing a History of Japan's War

After 1945, two narratives emerged to dominate the postwar historical reconstruction of the war. The US military government became the custodian of modern Japanese history and gave the Japanese people the so-called Pacific War narrative. That American-made war history propagated the orthodox interpretation of the war as Japan's reckless challenge to the United States, a war Japan never should have started. The Pacific War narrative was disseminated through public education, media, and popular culture. At the same time Japanese Marxists and liberals, who regained an intellectual foothold in the postwar era, dominated academic circles with a competing "War in Asia" narrative focused on Japan's culpability for its imperialism, invasions, and atrocities in China.

Although the two competing narratives share little common ground, both omit the Soviet Union, the hidden nexus in Japan's Eurasian-Pacific War. During

19. Ikeya Kaoru, *Ari no heitai—Nhion hei 2,600 nin Sansei shō zanryū no shinsō* (Army ants—a fact about the 2,600 Japanese soldiers who remained in the Shanxi Province) (Tokyo: Shinchō Sha, 2010); Donald Gillin, "Staying On: Japanese Soldiers and Civilians in China, 1945–1949," *Journal of Asian Studies* 42, no. 3 (May 1983): 497–518.

20. Yi Tong-Hwa, "Yŏ Un-hyŏng and the Preparation Committee for the Reconstruction of the Nation," *Korea Journal* 26, no. 11 (November 1986): 58; Hugh Deane, *The Korean War, 1945–1953* (San Francisco: China Books & Periodicals, 1999), 46–47.

the war, neither the Japanese public nor their leaders were so myopic as to see only either the United States or China on the postwar horizon. Yet the postwar rival narratives say very little about wartime Japan's manifold relationships with and understandings of the Soviet Union, much less about Japan's Soviet diplomacy and strategy.

As postwar Japan was gradually allowed to reenter the American-led club of Western industrialized nations less than a decade after the war's end, few people remembered how prewar Japan once had regarded Russia and the Soviet Union as a crossroads between the East and West and as central to pan-Asianism. Nor did they remember the Japanese government's pragmatic approach to communism: rapprochement with Moscow with an eye to the Soviet Union's ability to contain US ambitions juxtaposed with oppression of domestic communism and colonial communist-oriented nationalist movements. Memories rarely surfaced about wartime Japan's inclination to support the Chinese Communist Party (CCP) for its nationalism that could conceivably withstand the United States and the Soviet Union and thus aid Japan's effort to keep Asia for the Asians. Most problematically, the absence of the Soviet Union in the two postwar narratives effaced the final episode of Japan's war—the total collapse of Japan's colonial empire.

Depreciation of the Soviet's role in Japan's war occurred at the Tokyo War Crimes Trial, where the Allies indicted Japan for waging an unprovoked war against China, as well as aggressive wars against the United States, Britain, the Netherlands, France, and the Soviet Union. No nation—Japan, the United States, or the Soviet Union—wanted to bring to light that both Japan and the United States had had the Soviet Union as a "common" ally through the neutrality pact and the Grand Alliance.

The Japanese defendants did their part in presenting to the world a different version of the "facts" about their relations with the Soviets. When the Soviets joined the war against Japan, Japanese policymakers quickly destroyed long-term planning documents regarding critical players of Japan's Eurasian-Pacific War. They also engaged in notable self-censorship in the early postwar days. They may have done so fearing postwar retribution from the United States and the Soviet Union. After the war Japanese leaders emphasized their deplorably poor judgment, or desperate hope, that Moscow would keep its neutrality with Japan until the end and even mediate peace between Japan and the United States. In developing this narrative, they portrayed the Soviet entry into Japan's war in the last days of the war as a devastating surprise to, and an utter betrayal of, Japan.

The Japanese government authorized this version as part of the official narrative of Japan's war. As early as 1952, the Foreign Ministry edited and published *Nihon no sentaku—Dai-Niji Sekai Taisen shūsen shiroku* (Japan's choice—historical records on the conclusion of World War II), a three-volume anthology of primary and secondary sources concerning Japan's decision-making process inside and outside the government that eventually led to the acceptance of the Potsdam Proclamation. The leitmotif of the collection is that the Foreign Ministry misjudged the strength of the Grand Alliance between the United States and the Soviet Union and erred in holding on to the delusion that the Soviet Union would help Japan. Suppressing war planners' forecasts, the postwar Foreign Ministry even maintained that no signs indicated the cold war before the end of World War II. The Foreign Ministry expressed somber contrition for its tragic miscalculation of world politics in the war, which proved catastrophic for the nation. In the 1990 edition, the basic apologetic stance remains unchanged.[21] The Soviet-related diplomatic documents that escaped destruction and that are available for public viewing at the Diplomatic Record Office of the Ministry of Foreign Affairs in Tokyo still tell of the Foreign Ministry's misplaced trust in the Soviet Union as a peace mediator.

Soviet influence at the Tokyo War Crimes Trial contributed to the obscuring of its own role in wartime Japan's strategy. The Soviet Union was one of eleven nations that sent justices to the tribunal that held Japan guilty of conspiracy, aggression, and conventional war crimes. The tribunal found Japan guilty of aggression in two military engagements with the Soviet Union—the Changkufeng (1938) and Nomonhan (1939) incidents. The tribunal also found Japan guilty of conspiracy to wage aggressive war against the Soviet Union: Japan was unable to attack the Soviet Union and seize its eastern territories only because of its preoccupation with the war in China.[22] As evidence of Japan's aggressive designs on the Soviet Union, the judgment cited Japanese beliefs from the 1930s on about the inevitability of conflict with the Soviet Union.

At the Tokyo War Crimes Trial, the Soviet Union successfully presented the world with the narrative of Japan's deep-seated enmity against its northern neighbor as the backdrop of Soviet's war of defense against Japan. Neither the Japanese government nor the military challenged the tenet of Japan's conspiracy of preparing a war of aggression against the Soviet Union. Once a guilty verdict had been rendered, people came to take the verdict as a definitive history of events. Yet a verdict need not necessarily correlate with historical fact.

Lieutenant Colonel Sejima Ryūzō, a staff officer at the Imperial General Headquarters, bears much responsibility for burying what Japanese planners and

---

21. See Sumio Hatano's brief bibliographical essay on the Japanese sources on the Japanese role in terminating the Pacific War—"Sources in Japanese," in Tsuyoshi Hasegawa, ed., *The End of the Pacific War: Reappraisals* (Stanford, CA: Stanford University Press, 2007), 301–3. Note that Japanese scholars, too, largely rely on the official narrative of the Foreign Ministry.

22. Richard H. Minear, *Victor's Justice: The Tokyo War Crimes Trial* (Princeton, NJ: Princeton University Press, 1971), 134–38.

strategists conceived. At the tribunal he seemingly gave in to Soviet interests by admitting Japan's anti-Soviet conspiracy. His ulterior motive for doing so—along with the question of whether it was beneficial to the Soviet Union for him to take that course—remains to be investigated. Sejima, merely thirty-three years of age at the war's end, was among the key strategists who gathered intelligence about and devised plans to deal with both US and Soviet military operations. In fact Sejima's career delineates the evolution of Japan's strategic calculation about the two powers. In June 1941 Sejima helped formulate the Kantokuen Plan, the sudden large-scale reinforcement of the Kwantung Army when the Soviet Army was desperately fighting against German invasion. In February 1943 Sejima, then a central figure in strategic planning against the United States, decided on the withdrawal from Guadalcanal in the wake of Japan's defeat. In late 1944 Sejima went to Moscow in the guise of a diplomatic courier and, on returning to Japan, went to Kyūshū and Shikoku to estimate the points of US landing in the event of the latter's mainland invasion.

In July 1945 when the Soviet attack on Japan loomed, he was transferred to Kwantung Army headquarters in Manchuria, where he was in charge of arranging a cease-fire settlement with the Soviet forces. He was subsequently captured and sent to a Siberian labor camp. In September 1946 Sejima was brought to Tokyo as a Soviet witness. Kiyose Ichirō, defense counsel for former prime minister Tōjō Hideki, wanted to rebut the charge of Japanese aggression against the Soviet Union and instead condemn the Soviet Union for the attack on Japan in violation of the Neutrality Pact. Much to the frustration of Kiyose, Sejima's testimony neither denied nor confirmed the existence of the Japanese plan to invade the Soviet Union.

After his testimony Sejima was sent back to Siberia where he spent eleven years in a POW camp. According to the testimony of Japanese detained at the same camp, Sejima received privileged treatment; he was appointed their leader so he mostly avoided hard labor during those eleven years. He finally returned to Japan in 1956. Capitalizing on his experience as a military strategist, he began a new career in international business, eventually branching into oil and motor industry-related sectors. In the 1980s Sejima assisted Prime Minister Nakasone Yasuhiro in domestic reforms such as the privatization of public businesses. He also facilitated diplomacy with South Korea. Sejima helped Japan reach the pinnacle of unprecedented prosperity in the twentieth century. In his lifetime Sejima never revealed how Imperial General Headquarters staff made key decisions concerning the war. He never disclosed what happened between him and the Soviet authority after Japan's surrender, nor did he share how he spent those years in the Soviet Union.[23]

23. Hosaka Masayasu, *Sejima Ryūzō: Sanbō no Shōwa-shi* (Sejima Ryuzo: a staff officer's history of the Showa era) (Tokyo: Bunshun Bunko, 1991), chapters 1 and 2; Kyōdō Tsūshin Sha Shakai-bu,

The United States in occupied Japan erased not only the Soviet Union but also Asia from Japan's war scenario. As part of an educational campaign, the Office of the Supreme Commander for the Allied Powers (SCAP) launched the "War Guilt Information Program," which promoted the Pacific War narrative as the dominant lesson for the Japanese and obscured the Eurasian dimension of their history. The SCAP Civil Information and Education Section ordered leading Japanese newspapers to print a ten-part series on the history of the Pacific War. This series ran from December 8 to December 17, 1945. The Civil Information and Education Section simultaneously ordered NHK, Japan's national public broadcasting organization, to broadcast a similar program "Shinsō wa kouda" (This is the truth) from December 9 to February 10, 1946. The story began with Japan's aggression in Manchuria and resulting Anglo-American opposition then moved quickly to battle episodes in the Pacific, culminating in the two atomic bombs.[24] These stories emphasized America's unprecedented scientific and material supremacy. The most important message SCAP attempted to inculcate was Japan's complete surrender to the United States. From the perspective of SCAP, there was no need to instill in Japanese minds that Japan also surrendered to China and the Soviet Union.

That same month SCAP issued a directive prohibiting the Japanese from using the "ultra-nationalistic" and "racist" term "Greater East Asia War." The Allies argued that Japan's war goal had been primarily a racist one, Japan's crime an attempt to drive white man out of Asia. Thus at the Tokyo War Crimes Trial, Japan's aggression against Britain, the Netherlands, and France meant its invasion of their colonies in Southeast Asia: Hong Kong, Singapore, Malaysia, Indonesia, and French Indochina. SCAP was determined to stamp out consciousness about Japanese war aims in Asia altogether, particularly the propaganda "Asia for the Asians."[25]

The surge of new communist movements across Asia purportedly under Moscow's orchestration gave the US authority another reason to detach Eurasia from Japanese memories of the war. August and September 1948 saw the respective creation of the US-sponsored Republic of Korea (South Korea) and the Soviet-sponsored Democratic People's Republic of Korea (North Korea). In China the Nationalists suffered losses against the Communist forces in the continuing civil

---

ed., *Chinmoku no fairu—"Sejima Ryūzō" to wa nandattanoka* (A silent file—what was "Sejima Ryuzo") (Tokyo: Shinchō Bunko, 1999), chapters 2, 3, and 4.

24. See *Asahi, Yomiuri,* and other leading national papers, "Taiheiyō Sensō shi" (A history of the Pacific War), between December 8 and 17, 1945.

25. Yukiko Koshiro, *Trans-Pacific Racisms and the U.S. Occupation of Japan* (New York: Columbia University Press, 1999), 62, 65.

war, driving Chiang Kai-shek to resign as president of the Republic of China and eventually to flee to Taiwan in December 1949. Meanwhile in October 1949 the communist People's Republic of China was born with Mao Zedong as chairman. Subsequently the US-sponsored Republic of China transplanted itself to Taiwan, where Chiang resumed his duties as president. China, or "Red China," was now designated as a potential enemy within the frame of the US-Japanese security alliance.

The US authority needed to ensure that Japan would never be infected with communist fever from the continent. The US-sponsored Pacific War narrative dismissed wartime Japan's dealings with various communist entities in Asia and with their alleged motherland the Soviet Union, thereby removing the Eurasian dimension from accounts of Japan's war. By giving the Japanese a new identity as a quasi-member of a US-centered (capitalist) world, SCAP hoped that the Japanese would never develop any desire to join with other Asians in an anti-American movement. The Pacific War narrative, in which Japan was punished for the foolish arrogance it exhibited against the United States, was meant to cement Japan's allegiance to military alliance with the United States.

The US government was inclined to exonerate Japan for its past aggression in Asia and thus to alienate it further, psychologically and intellectually, from the continent. Criticism of Japanese colonialism in Korea was particularly inconvenient because SCAP did not want the Japanese to see the US military occupation of southern Korea as a replacement of one colonial master with another. When a SCAP-approved history textbook *Kuni no ayumi* (Our nation's progress) appeared in 1946, it euphemistically described Japan's colonialism in Korea as a cooperation between Japan and Korea. Articles advocating the rights of Korean people remaining in postwar Japan were routinely censored by SCAP.[26]

The manner in which the United States pardoned Japan for its war conduct and allowed it to join an American-centered international community further pushed Soviet Union, China, and Korea outside the memory of Japan's war. Under the San Francisco Peace Treaty of September 1951, the Allied powers agreed to terminate a state of war with Japan in exchange for Japan's agreement on the new territorial demarcation. The signatories—forty-eight nations, almost half from the Western Hemisphere—hardly represented Japan's primary adversaries in the war: Argentina, Australia, Belgium, Bolivia, Brazil, Cambodia, Canada, Ceylon, Chile, Colombia, Costa Rica, Cuba, the Dominican Republic, Ecuador, Egypt, El Salvador, Ethiopia, France, Greece, Guatemala, Haiti, Honduras,

26. Yukiko Koshiro, *Trans-Pacific Racisms*, 115–16; Monbu-shō (Ministry of Education), *Kuni no ayumi*, vol. 2 (Tokyo: Nihon Shoseki, 1946), 42–43.

Indonesia, Iran, Iraq, Laos, Lebanon, Liberia, Luxembourg, Mexico, the Netherlands, New Zealand, Nicaragua, Norway, Pakistan, Panama, Paraguay, Peru, the Republic of the Philippines, Saudi Arabia, Syria, Turkey, the Union of South Africa, Great Britain, the United States of America, Uruguay, Venezuela, and Vietnam.

The key players in Japan's Eurasian war—the Soviet Union and (now) the People's Republic of China—did not take part in that international agreement. The Soviet Union, regarding America's remaking of Japan as a direct challenge, considered the San Francisco Peace Treaty a breach of the Yalta Agreement because, among other reasons, it did not recognize Soviet sovereignty over south Sakhalin and the Kurile Islands. With the US-Japan Security Treaty signed on the same day as the peace treaty, the Soviets dismissed the latter as a political device that consolidated a US-Japanese military coalition against the Soviet Union. The Soviet Union refused to sign the treaty. The war with the Soviet Union continued until the two nations finally signed the Soviet-Japanese Joint Declaration on October 19, 1956, which normalized trade and cultural exchanges. Postwar Soviet's severance of ties with Japan further clouded its own role in Japan's war.

Japan's alienation from China and Korea deepened further. The day the San Francisco Peace Treaty went into effect, the Japanese government concluded a separate treaty with Taiwan (the Republic of China) as the official government of China, acquiescing to the one China policy of the United States. Only after the United States recognized the People's Republic of China and agreed to admit it to the United Nations did Japan sign a joint communiqué with Beijing in September 1972 that recognized the People's Republic of China as the "sole legal government of China." The legal end to the war did not arrive until August 12, 1978, when the China-Japan Peace and Friendship Treaty finally normalized relations. The two Koreas were not even at the San Francisco Peace Conference due to the Korean War. Japan's postwar policy toward the Korean Peninsula had thus been immobilized for some time. Only in June 1965 did Japan sign the Korea-Japan Treaty with South Korea and establish diplomatic relations on the basis of the recognition that the Republic of Korea was the only legitimate government on the peninsula. North Korea, condemned as the aggressor by the United States after the Korean War, stands without any formal diplomatic relations with Japan even today.

The Pacific War narrative matured with full academic apparatus when Edwin Reischauer published what soon became known as the Reischauer modernization theory. In 1961 when President Kennedy appointed him ambassador to Japan, one of his chief tasks was to subdue Japan's anti-Americanism and to nurture pro-American feeling among the Japanese public. Toward that end he praised Japan's singular Asian achievement in modernization. In interviews with the Japanese press as well as in his own publications, Reischauer assured the Japanese people that they had, in fact, been on the right track of modernization ever since Commodore Perry's expedition in 1853. While praising Japan's "indigenous democratic tradition" extant long before Perry's arrival, he added that behind Japan's successful modernization was the ever present friendly assistance of the United States. Reischauer comforted the Japanese public by asserting that Japan's fascism and militarism was merely a decade-long tragic detour. Anti-Americanism during the war (i.e., the Pacific War) was just a plot by a vicious military clique. Reischauer urged the Japanese to put the war behind them and to maintain good US-Japanese relations in the interests of a better world so that Japan could continue to serve as a shining beacon to Asia.[27]

The subtext of Reischauer's praise of Japan's modernization was the disparagement of communist-style modernization in China under Mao Zedong. More problematically, in Reischauer's terminology "the West" exclusively meant "the United States" and Japan's modernization meant its adoption of American-style modernity. This use was inconsistent with Japan's history: Japan had since the Meiji period an affinity for Russian culture and thought and had learned from Soviet- and other European-style modernizations.

Disregarding historical accuracy, Japan officially began reconstructing a new nation based exclusively on the lessons of the Pacific War. Peace feelers who had attempted to effect a truce with the United States, without regard to the colonies, attained critical positions in occupied Japan, collaborated with the US occupation authority, and expressed vocal sympathy for its anticommunist stance. They saw Japan's defeat as a forward step toward establishing democracy and capitalism in the image of the United States and Western Europe.[28] In their view Japan's most costly mistake before 1945 had been the war against the United States.

Scholars and intellectuals who agreed with them constructed a history of the war that began with the road to Pearl Harbor as an aberration from good US-Japanese relations. Japan's invasion of China and other Asian nations was outside their American-centric purview. Japan's expansion up until 1931 had been conducted in the name of "cooperative imperialism," with tacit approval from the United States. Had it not been for the tragic mistake of Pearl Harbor, Japan might have been able to persuade the United States of Japan's "righteous" intentions in Asia and the Pacific.

---

27. Edwin O. Reischauer and Nakayama Ichirō, "Nihon kindai-ka no rekishi-teki hyōka: taidan" (Discussion: historical evaluations of Japan's modernization), *Chūō Kōron* 76 (September 1961), 84–97; Edwin O. Reischauer, "Nihon rekishi kenkyū no igi" (Significance of studies of Japanese history), *Asahi Jānaru* (Asahi journal) 3 (November 5, 1961): 28–33.

28. Hidaka Rokurō, "Sengo shisō no shuppatsu" (Beginning of postwar thoughts), in *Sengo Nihon shisō taikei* (Great works on postwar Japanese thoughts), vol. 1 (Tokyo: Chikuma Shobō, 1968), 3–16.

The crowning achievement of the Japanese version of the Pacific War narrative was the compilation of a seven-volume study on the Pacific War, published in 1963, in which the Japanese contributors agreed to limit their analyses to the decision-making process of Japan's foreign relations and to not use any "jargon" such as imperialism, colonialism, subjugation, and other Marxist terms. In addition they avoided the phrase "Japanese invasion."[29] Most tellingly, the Soviet Union had no place in their narrative except for a brief interlude when it emerged as a potential peace mediator. The absence of the Soviet Union revealed their inability to resolve how to deal with the Grand Alliance during World War II. Even with their anticommunist stance, they were unsure whether it was proper to disparage and vilify the Soviet Union. To do so openly would be an indirect criticism of the United States for allying with the Soviet Union.

The Japanese public did not completely succumb to the American-led censorship of Japan's past in Asia because the Asian dimension of Japan's war was hard to forget. Coping with the influx of more than 6 million people repatriating from former Japanese colonies and battlefields, the Japanese could hardly accept that the war had occurred only in the Pacific against the United States. Regardless of Washington's intentions, many wished to learn about what the Japanese Army had done in Asia. They first satisfied this appetite through literary works. The novel *Ikiteiru heitai* (Living soldiers) by Ishikawa Tatsuzō, printed in a severely censored form in the March 1938 issue of *Chūō Kōron* (Central review), Japan's leading intellectual journal, was the first attempt to report the Nanjing Massacre. Although the issue was immediately recalled from bookstores across the nation, the novel itself reemerged in a complete version in December 1945, much to the excitement of those people who had been aware of the original version. Leading newspapers responded favorably to the publication: they commented how the bold exposure of heinous atrocities would compel the Japanese to confront their past and subsequently work toward the extinction of such acts.[30]

Tanuma Taijirō's novel *Shunpu-den* (A tale of a prostitute), published in 1947, chronicles the tragic love between a Japanese private and a Korean comfort woman catering to Japanese soldiers in China. Ending in the deaths of the two lovers, the novel was praised for its criticism of the inhumanity plaguing the Japanese military and was turned into a film twice, in 1950 and 1965, by major film studios. During the filming of the 1950 version of *Shunpu-den,* SCAP censors

---

29. Nihon Kokusai Seiji Gakkai (The Japanese Association of International Relations), ed., *Taiheiyō Sensō e no michi* (Road to the Pacific War), 7 vols. (Tokyo: Asahi Shinbun Sha, 1963). For criticism of such approach see Furuya Tetsuo's review in "1963-nen no rekishi gakkai" (Historical studies in Japan, 1963), *Shigaku Zasshi* (Journal of historical science) 73 (May 1964): 165–67.

30. Ishikawa Tatsuzō, *Ikite iru heitai* (Living soldiers) (Tokyo: Kawade Shobō, 1945). Also see *Yomiuri Shinbun* (March 9, 1946) for such review.

intervened and cut the character of the military prostitute because Japanese prostitutes catering to American G.I.s had become a serious social issue in occupied Japan. SCAP ordered the female protagonist to be changed into a singer; she became a character bereft of sexuality.[31] Gomikawa Junpei's six-volume masterpiece *Ningen no jōken* (Prerequisites for a human being), published between 1956 and 1958, exposed Japanese atrocities against Chinese prisoners of war kept as forced laborers at a mine in Manchuria. Tracing the moral quandary of the Japanese protagonist, who is eventually captured by the Soviet Union and sent to a labor camp in Siberia, the novel became a national sensation and sold 13 million copies. It was turned into a film in 1959 and into a graphic novel (*manga*) in the early 1980s.

Along with such popular explorations of the battlefield in China, Japanese Marxists and leftists presented rival accounts to the Pacific War narrative that sharply criticized Japan's aggression in Asia. Throughout the war Japan's political and intellectual Marxists formed the most prominent force against the war and government. Once the war was over, the Marxist/leftist liberals at first welcomed the US occupation forces as a liberation army in the spirit of the Grand Alliance between the United States and the Soviet Union in World War II. In October 1945 when SCAP liberated some three thousand Japanese political prisoners, most of them Marxist and communist intellectual and politicians, leftists thanked the American forces for their pacifist and democratic policies.[32] The Japanese Communist Party was subsequently legalized for the first time in Japanese history. Leftist politicians did well in the first post-war election in April 1946, in which women gained suffrage. In the 1947 general election, the first one held under the new Japanese constitution, the Japan Socialist Party won the majority vote and its party president, Katayama Tetsu, became Japan's prime minister between May 1947 and March 1948. In January 1949, the Japanese Communist Party gained thirty-five seats in the Lower House election.

Although the SCAP subsequently put into effect the so-called reverse course, purging communists and communist sympathizers and suppressing labor movements in Japan, the Japanese Communist Party was legalized again as soon as Japan gained independence and the leftists resumed their own democratization movements. They strove to make amends for the damage inflicted on the people in Asia by Japanese imperialism and colonialism. Under the US occupation, these

31. For the analysis of the SCAP censorship of its film version "Akatsuki no dassō" (Desertion at Dawn), see Kyoko Hirano, *Mr. Smith Goes to Tokyo: Japanese Cinema under the American Occupation, 1945–1952* (Washington, DC: Smithsonian Institution Press, 1992), 87–91. Also see http://www.eiga-kawaraban.com/98/98070903.html.

32. Hidaka Rokurō, "Sengo shisō no shuppatsu," 4–7, 23–25.

leftist narratives of Japan's war crimes in Asia had to tread a treacherous path of censorship. But now they vigorously promoted the War in Asia narrative.

Leftists defined the scope of Japan's war as long and expansive, a frame appropriate for a revolutionary theory. Contrary to the pro–Anglo-American liberals who saw nothing wrong with Japan's industrial and economic modernization—namely, imperialism—leftists saw Japan's fascism as rooted in the nature of Japanese modernization since the late nineteenth century. They cast Japan's war as the inevitable outcome of the perpetual rivalry among competing capitalist states, aggravated by worldwide depression. Japan's fascist government chose to galvanize the course of aggression overseas to address economic stagnation at home and also to divert growing public dissatisfaction with ever-widening inequities. At the end of World War II, with the overthrow of fascism, the world seemed ripe for socialism. These Marxists hoped that by learning from the aggressions committed in the name of Japanese imperialism, a new Japan could become a truly peaceful nation. The paperback *Shōwa-shi* (History of the Showa era), a Marxist interpretation of Japan's road to World War II published in 1955, became a bestseller read by generations of Japanese.[33]

With the prospect of hot wars across Asia, the War in Asia narrative gained popularity with opponents of the US-Japanese security alliance. As a satellite of the United States, postwar Japan risked military involvement in the cold war. The Japanese public increasingly criticized the Japanese government for focusing on capitalism, nationalism, and the security alliance with the United States as prerequisites for the nation's recovery, at the expense of worker's rights and public welfare. They attacked the Japanese government for refusing to show due contrition for war crimes and yet allowing the survival of, and even encouraging the growth of, the old systems of Japan, from militarism and the emperor system to zaibatsu monopoly.

Numerous popular books and college-level history textbooks featured the Marxist interpretation that the US occupation of Japan was a continuation of Japan's war. The five-volume series, *Taiheiyō Sensō shi* (A history of the Pacific War) extended the war period from the Manchurian Incident of 1931 to the conclusion of the San Francisco Peace Treaty and the US-Japan Security Treaty of 1951.[34] Only by overthrowing the conservative Japanese regime with ties to US capitalism and militarism, and joining the world peace movement, the authors argued, could Japan finally achieve true peace and assimilate the real lessons of the war.

---

33. Tōyama Shigeki, Imai Sei'ichi and Fujiwara Akira, *Shōwa-shi* (History of the Showa era) (Tokyo: Iwanami Shoten, 1955). The Showa era covered the reign of Emperor Hirohito from 1926 to 1989.

34. Rekishigaku Kenkyū-kai (The Historical Science Society of Japan), ed., *Taiheiyō Sensō-shi* (History of the Pacific War) (Tokyo: Tōyō Keizai Shinpō Sha, 1953–54).

By the 1960s the leftist intellectual current engendered a powerful protest movement against the Japanese government and the American war in Vietnam. The appeal of such histories suggests that the Japanese public, unconvinced by the Pacific War narrative that presented a definitive end to the war in Japan's complete surrender to the United States, wanted to know why the war seemed to be still going on.

Even in this leftist intellectual climate, however, attempts to understand the continuation of the war and imperialism did not examine the role of the Soviet Union. Like the pro-US, anti-Marxist scholars of the Pacific War school, Marxist historians had reason to avoid consideration of the Soviet Union as the crucial factor in Japan's war. These Marxist scholars had difficulties explaining the relationship between domestic communist influence during the war and Tokyo's dealings with Moscow. They did not want to confront the shameful wartime collaboration, legitimized by the neutrality pact, between the "heroic" Soviet Union and the "fascist-totalitarian-militarist" Japanese government. They also found Stalin's "betrayal" in entering the war against Japan and his subsequent "illegal" acts, from the internment of Japanese prisoners of war in labor camps in Siberia to the occupation of Japan's northern islands, inconvenient to their revolutionary narrative pitting communism against fascism. In the 1960s the Japanese Communist Party increasingly asserted independence from Moscow and tried to be "neutral" in the Sino-Soviet split.

To make matters more complex, Japanese Marxists, affected by the Sino-Soviet split over revolutionary theory, had difficulty evaluating the achievements of the Japanese Soldiers' Antiwar League because they could not differentiate between who had worked under Stalin's instruction and who had worked directly with Mao. As a result they expunged from their war narrative not just the presence of the Antiwar League but also those Japanese soldiers, ranging from eight thousand to ten thousand in number, who chose to stay with Mao's People's Liberation Army after the war.[35]

In the 1960s, the schism between pro-US liberals and Marxist intellectuals widened, as the cold war in Asia escalated and Japan became further embroiled in the Vietnam War through the provision of military bases, munitions, and other war materials to US forces. This ideological split, institutionalized by separate intellectual exchange programs run by the two camps, contributed to the further polarization of the understanding of Japan's war—with an exclusive focus on either the United States or China. In 1962 a group of historians investigated the nature of area studies of Japan, asking whether grants provided by American

35. Furukawa Mantarō, *Chūgoku zanryū Nihon-hei no kiroku* (Records of Japanese soldiers who remained in China) (Original edition, Sanseidō, 1984) (Tokyo: Iwanami Shoten, 1994), 64–65.

foundations to Japanese students of contemporary Chinese studies were attempting to train scholars who conformed to US policies in Asia. Despite concerns about a proliferation of US-centric area studies, Japanese scholarly works on US-Japanese relations remained scarce. Historical studies of Japan's foreign relations published in scholarly journals between 1955 and 1964 were strongly Marxist, especially those on Japan's relations with the communist states. In that period, fifty-one works were published on Sino-Japanese relations and thirty-six on Soviet-Japanese relations, while only thirteen works were published on US-Japanese relations.[36] Compared to sixteen works published on Korean-Japanese relations, the paucity of academic interest in the United States among Japanese historians was telling.

Violent protest movements against the US-Japanese security alliance and the Vietnam War as well as accelerating economic growth in the early 1970s provided the backdrop for the further polarization of war studies. While Marxist riots on university campuses upset the country and paralyzed research, non-Marxist Americanists approached war studies through American political science methodology. They studied decision making in the Imperial Cabinet, the foreign ministry, the military, and other political institutions. They sought to locate a historical juncture where the pull of positive US-Japanese relations lost momentum to be replaced by the push toward Pearl Harbor. In addition they started a new field of studies in search of conditions for a positive relationship with the United States. Comparative studies of American and Japanese cultures became a favorite topic. Through scholarly and popular books, leading Americanists in Japan promoted a vision of American influence on Japan from the late nineteenth century to the 1920s as a harbinger of Japan's Americanization.[37]

The scholarly call for a positive understanding of US-Japanese relations did not lead to public repentance for Pearl Harbor and the subsequent war against the United States. Nor did the growing popularity of American material culture cause the Japanese public, especially youth, to become critical of Japan's attack on Pearl Harbor. Popular journals printed heroic memoirs and narratives of military leaders to stoke anew national pride. In boys' magazines and comic books, stories glamorized gallant Japanese marines and pilots in the Pacific in the face of strong

---

36. "Genjiten ni okeru rekishigaku no arikata" (Raison d'être of historical studies in today's Japan), *Rekishi Hyōron* (Historical journal) 143 (July 1962): 1–26.

37. Early works include: Saitō Makoto, Honma Nagayo, Kamei Shunsuke, eds., *Nihon to Amerika—ishitsu bunka no shōgeki to hadō* (Japan and America—shocks and impacts from different cultures) (Tokyo: Nan'un Dō, 1973); Kamei Shunsuke, *Nihonjin no Amerika-ron* (Japanese views of America) (Tokyo: Kenkyū Sha, 1977); and idem., *Meriken kara Amerika e* (From "Meriken" to America) (Tokyo: Tokyo Daigaku Shuppan-kai, 1979).

opposition from educators and parents.[38] The masculine heroism of Japanese soldiers manifested only against the powerful US military; battlefields in Asia barely appealed to action-thirsty audiences. The Soviet Red Army, whose formidable presence across the Manchurian border was once on every Japanese mind, had almost no place in the postwar Japanese imagination of the late 1960s and 1970s.

As Japan's economy received further boosts from the Vietnam War, the Japanese regained confidence in their own long history of modernization and Japanese supporters of the Reischauer modernization theory defended Japan's war. The mass media published a plethora of articles and books legitimizing Japan's war as one to liberate Asia from the yoke of Western colonialism and to help Asian people modernize in a uniquely Japanese way. Ueyama Shunpei, professor of history at Kyoto University, and Hayashi Fusao, a former Marxist turned right-wing critic, wrote sensational defenses of Japan's casus belli.[39]

Disturbed by American aggression in Vietnam and Japan's contributions to the US military effort, Marxist-Asianist scholars called for brotherhood with other Asians in support of their anti-US independence movements. By doing so they unwittingly promoted a standpoint that resembled the distasteful wartime rhetoric of "Asia for Asians." Takeuchi Yoshimi (1910–77), a scholar of Chinese literature and culture and one of the foremost leftist thinkers in postwar Japan, questioned whether modern Japan's cultural identity should be caught between Asia and the West. As he exposed the inherent problems in Western imperialism and colonialism, he criticized modern Japan's uncritical acceptance of Western modernity, which he claimed had spurred Japan's expansionism culminating in the Fifteen Years War. He himself had witnessed the horrors of Japan's aggression during his service in that war. Impressed by the communist victory in China, Takeuchi hardened his position against the "American mode of civilization" and Japan's postwar military alliance with the United States. While fully recognizing the atrocious nature of Japan's expansion into Korea and China, Takeuchi nonetheless found solace in that during their seventy years in Korea and China the Japanese had cultivated a strong awareness that Japan could not live without

38. Yoshida Yutaka, *Nihonjin no sensō-kan: sengo-shi no naka no hen'yō* (Japanese view of the war: its transformation in postwar history) (Tokyo: Iwanami Shoten, 1995), 84–97, 112–15.

39. Ueyama Shunpei, "DaiTōA Sensō no shisō-shi-teki igi" (Significance of the Greater East Asia War in Japan's intellectual history), *Chūō Kōron* 76 (September 1961): 98–107. Note that this article appeared in the same issue that introduced the Reischauer modernization theory. He later published a book version, *DaiTōA Sensō no imi* (Significance of the Greater East Asia War) (Tokyo: Chūō Kōron Sha, 1964). For a much more aggressive defense of Japan's war, see Hayashi Fusao, *DaiTōA Sensō kōtei ron* (Defense argument on Japan's Greater East Asia War) (Tokyo: Banchō Shobō, 1964).

these Asian neighbors. He advocated unity between Japan and Asia in an "Oriental resistance" against the West, a theme curiously in consonance with Japan's wartime pan-Asianism that Takeuchi censured.[40]

In the 1970s and 1980s, scholars of Japan's war, weary of history defined by the superpowers' ideologies, gradually began detaching themselves from the cold war modes of thinking. As the economic growth of the decades accelerated Japan's globalization, the Japanese people finally began to see the war on a global scale. First a transnational concept of human rights emerged as a new tool of analysis. Scholars discovered the meaning of Japan's multilayered war crimes: how Japan as a nation and the Japanese people had violated the dignity of Asian peoples in their colonies and battlefields. These scholars indicted the Japanese people as both imperial subjects and modern (civil and educated) individuals. There were overt expositions of the Nanjing Massacre, Unit 731 (a top secret biological and chemical warfare research and development unit of the Kwantung Army), forced military prostitution, and other atrocities committed by the Japanese military. Morimura Seiichi's novel *Akuma no hōshoku* (Satan's delirious feast) exposed the Japanese Army's wartime experimentation with biological weapons on Chinese and Russian prisoners of war and became a best-seller in 1982.

Furthermore, in a new attempt to understand Japan's war, scholars and journalists delved into the lives of ordinary people and explored their mental landscapes under the influence of the French Annales School. Marxist historians welcomed the trend, though they conceded that the thesis of popular struggle against the system of class and imperialism still could not effectively explain the cause and significance of Japan's Fifteen Years War. Scholars of the people's history unearthed the popular front movement during World War II in villages and cities, analyzed fascism and its opposition at the grassroots level, and looked at how ordinary people actively executed and opposed the national projects of colonialism, imperialism, and total war. The nonpolitical Annales approach rekindled popular interest in wartime Japan, its society, and culture. Frequently supported by local governments, oral history and local history projects flourished. The underlying hope was that one might demonstrate that the drive to war would have been avoidable had people only known better.

Yet the methodology contained a critical shortcoming. Personalizing and humanizing the war could romanticize it as well as unintentionally idealize peoplehood and nationhood. Once "memories of the war" became a mainstream genre of the historical narrative, historians culled individuals' memories and experiences

---

40. The latest Japanese work on Takeuchi's view of Asia is Matsumoto Ken'ichi, *Takeuchi Yoshimi "Nihon no Ajia-shugi" seidoku* (A close reading of Takeuchi Yoshimi's "Japan's Asianism") (Tokyo: Iwanami Shoten, 2000).

of war in the Pacific, China, and elsewhere and placed them in the service of postwar reconstructions of Japan's war. Such an approach tended to place the juggernaut of the war machine into the background. These personal memories alone could never reconstitute the existence of the war planners' strategies, perceptions, and executions vis-à-vis the United States, Soviet Union, China, and Korea. In an effort to transcend the cold war frame, this "human approach" sidestepped the fundamental questions: which war, how, and why?[41]

Postwar Japan's recollection of the war and its studies thus became paralyzed by a binary between a solid alliance with the United States and reconciliation with China. The war had been portrayed either as Japan's all-out aggression under the banner of pan-Asianism against China, the imagined, unified nation-state; or, alternatively, as a black-and-white clash with the United States over culture, ideology, and sphere of influence, accelerated by bureaucratic malfunctioning on either or both sides. Different narratives added other Manichean views of Japan's war: fascist and imperialist Japan against revolutionary China, militarist Japan against the liberal-democratic-capitalist United States, or "yellow" Japan against "white" America. If postwar Japan had noticed how the war planners once regarded communism as a positive force for Asian nationalism, they would not have erred in claiming that "imperial Japan," or the "champion of the colored races," tried to liberate Asia from the shackle of western, or the white man's, imperialism. The oversimplified cold war paradigm has long precluded the expansion of perspective, but recognizing the roles Russia and the Soviet Union played in Japan's war can profitably widen the scope of investigation.

41. For general criticism of "people's history" as a "non-historical approach to history," see Yuge Tōru, "1978-nen no rekishi gakkai—sōsetsu" (Historical studies in Japan—general survey of the year 1978), *Shigaku Zasshi* (Journal of historical science) 88 (May 1979): 1–6; Kabayama Kōichi, "Rekishi riron" (Historical theory), *Shigaku Zasshi*, 7–11.

Epilogue

TOWARD A NEW UNDERSTANDING OF JAPAN'S EURASIAN-PACIFIC WAR

The 1990s was a decade fraught with a number of potentially dangerous anniversaries of World War II. More than half a century after the end of World War II, the Japanese people still have not arrived at a consensus about which nations Japan fought, about which nations Japan surrendered to, or the reasons for surrender. Despite the successes of Japan's physical reconstruction and reorientation of its diplomacy, the postwar generation lacks a clear understanding of the war, its goals, and the nature of its conclusion. The conflicting lessons offered by the US military government and diverse groups of Japanese scholars, journalists, and educators have only worsened the fuzziness surrounding Japan's Eurasian-Pacific War.

Japan celebrated the year 1991 as the fiftieth anniversary of Pearl Harbor rather than as the sixtieth anniversary of the Manchurian Incident. In 1995 Hiroshima and Nagasaki dominated the national scene. The general public did not pay attention to the fact that 1995 was also the fiftieth anniversary of the fall of their colonial empire. The ceremonies at Hiroshima and Nagasaki featured a solemn national message: "We shall never repeat the same mistake." No one was sure which mistakes and whose: the atrocities on the battlefields, Pearl Harbor, the Axis alliance, Manchukuo, colonialism, fascism, Japan's entire course of modernization, American racism toward the Japanese, the Manhattan Project, the postwar nuclear race, or the Soviet-Japanese Neutrality Act. In contrast, the United States exhibited a positive official stance on the use of the atomic bombs. When the National Air and Space Museum of the Smithsonian Institute planned to display the cockpit and nose section of the Enola Gay to commemorate the first aircraft to drop the atomic bomb on Hiroshima, critics charged that the planned exhibit focused too much on civilian casualties and maintained that the atomic bomb(s) had caused an obstinate Japan to surrender and had thus prevented massive casualties on both sides in the planned mainland invasion. After a long heated debate, the planned Smithsonian exhibit was canceled and the museum director dismissed. Throughout this process, the Japanese remained silent. They could not refute the pro–atomic bomb interpretation because they did not have the knowledge or memory of how the Japanese were *not* going to fight against the invading US forces in Kyūshū in the fall of 1945 and the Kanto metropolitan area in the spring of 1946, regardless of the two atomic bombs.

Instead young and old Japanese people held onto a victim mentality stemming from the nuclear destruction of Hiroshima and Nagasaki. This passive response to the American use of the atomic bomb further obstructed a proper understanding of their war. The new interest in Japan's violations of human rights in Asia never included American soldiers as victims of Japan's wartime crimes. Even pro-American scholars seemed reluctant to study Japanese "collective guilt and responsibility" toward the United States for Pearl Harbor to the Bataan Death March and other prisoner of war abuses.

Through the 1990s Rekishi Kyōiku-sha Kyōgi-kai (The Association for History Teachers and Educators) conducted annual surveys of a thousand to four thousand students, ages six to eighteen, on their views of modern Japanese history. They predominantly understood Japan's war as one in which Japan was a victim of the United States. In their popular conception, the atomic bombs were collectively one of the worst tragedies in the war.[1] The initial American effort to educate the Japanese people with an "appropriate" understanding of the war had proved successful in excluding the full scope of the war but was spectacularly unsuccessful with its account of Japanese culpability. As SCAP had intended, the students lacked a clear awareness that China had been the original battlefield of Japan's war; the Japanese mentality as "victims" in the Pacific War blocked the remembrance of the Nanjing Massacre and other atrocities in Asia. No one remembered that many Japanese had tried to let the Soviet Union thwart US ambitions in East Asia in the last phase of the war.

Even the so-called "narrative of Japan's culpability in Asia," which emerged in the 1990s, allowed only limited approaches to Japan's war. When the role of women in the war effort came under scrutiny as part of gender studies, the Japanese feminist scholar Ueno Chizuko wrote on the accountability of Japanese women in permitting the Japanese military to exploit other Asian women as military prosti-

---

1. Kon'no Hideharu, "Sogai sareru rekishi kyōiku" (Ever alienated historical education), *Rekishi Hyōron* (Historical journal) 582 (October 1998): 72–86.

tutes. Ueno maintained that in addition to their obligations as mothers and wives, Japanese women should bear responsibility as members of the nation of Japan, as citizens of a modern state, and as individual women. Their feminist consciousness should cross national boundaries.[2] This narrative contained an indictment of Japan for overwhelming Asia and as such only applied to the war in Asia. The Pacific War had to be omitted from this narrative for logical coherence.

The most unsettling syndrome in war studies of the 1990s was the emergence of the "liberal historical view" (*jiyū shugi shikan*) among right-wing Japanese at all levels, governmental, popular, journalistic, and academic. Much to the chagrin of those who tried to indict Japan's war conduct in the new arena of international justice, these right-wing Japanese revived the wartime rhetoric that Japan had sought to defend and liberate Asia from Western aggression. They attacked the "sado-masochistic" leftist approach to Japanese history and proposed instead to establish a "proud" narrative of the "people's" history, which would highlight positive (capitalist) accomplishments that overshadowed negative legacies in Japan's colonialism and war.[3] Supporters of this view seem not to know that Japan's wartime vision for an Asian future was never "Asia for Asians," because it foresaw both the United States and the Soviet Union in the region. Neither did they acknowledge that Japan "deserted" Korea.

Only after the demise of the Soviet Union in 1991 did Japanese scholars and journalists gradually begin to think about the role of the Soviet Union as they looked at Japan's war in a more global context. Akira Iriye's *Power and Culture: The Japanese-American War, 1941–1945* (1981) was the leading early attempt to synthesize the Pacific War with the battlefield in China against a background of World War II in Europe. More than a decade later, Michael A. Barnhart pointed out the need to examine roles of Britain, the Soviet Union, France, the Netherlands, and China, in search of the origin(s) of Pearl Harbor, and called for a new scholarly attempt to synthesize the two wars.[4] *Gunji Shigaku* (Journal of military history), edited by Gunji-shi Gakkai (The Military History Society of Japan) published a three-part special issue on Japan and World War II that presented a

---

2. Ueno Chizuko, *Nashonarizumu to jendā* (Nationalism and gender) (Tokyo: Seido Sha, 1998).

3. The group that promoted the "liberal historical view" edited and published a four-volume series: Fujioka Nobukatsu et al., eds., *Kyōkasho ga oshienai rekishi* (The Japanese history no textbook teaches) (Tokyo: Fusō Sha, 1996–97), which sold 1.2 million copies, according to the publisher. For a concise criticism of the liberal historical view within the academic circle, see Ishii Noric, "1998 nen no rekishi gakkai—rekishi riron" (Historical studies in Japan, 1998—theory of history), *Shigaku Zasshi* (Journal of historical science) 108 (May 1999): 7–12.

4. Michael A. Barnhart, "The Origins of the Second World War in Asia and the Pacific: Synthesis Impossible?" *Diplomatic History* 20 (April 1996): 241–60, also reprinted in Michael Hogan, ed., *Paths to Power: The Historiography of American Foreign Relations to 1941* (Cambridge: Cambridge University Press, 2000), 268–96.

comprehensive survey of international military, political, economic, and diplomatic aspects of Japan's war.[5] Two separate scholarly works followed—*Taiheiyō Sensō* (The Pacific War) and *Taiheiyō Sensō no shūketsu: Ajia Taiheiyō no sengo keisei* (The close of the Pacific War and the formation of postwar Asia and the Pacific)—both aiming to provide international approaches to Japan's war.[6] These anthologies, unfortunately, fail to present a theoretical framework that synthesizes the Pacific, Asian, and European dimensions of Japan's war even as they document global aspects of Japan's war.

When books on Japan's final war against the Soviet Union appeared in the 1990s, they captured considerable public attention.[7] The demise of the Soviet Union probably allowed the memory to be revived with fewer political, ideological, or psychological constraints. While shedding light on the Soviet importance in Japan's war, these works focused exclusively on military operations, ranging from the Soviet unilateral abrogation of the neutrality pact with Japan and attacks on Manchuria, Korea, Sakhalin, and the Kurile Islands to the capture of some 600,000 or more Japanese prisoners sent to labor camps across Siberia after the war. These new works did not delve into the complex layers of Soviet-Japanese relations during the war. Nor did they discuss that the Soviet Union was Japan's most critical ally in the war in China as well as in the war against the United States. Even with the inclusion of the Soviet Union, a comprehensive narrative of the Eurasian-Pacific War remained elusive.[8]

Japanese people today rarely question that the miracle of postwar Japan's rapid recovery and growth is a windfall amid the rise of communism in Asia. In the standard narrative of modern Japanese history, postwar Japan's economic growth is treated as a footnote to cold war history. Standard American books on the cold war explain how the United States *allowed* Japan to survive and recover because of the latter's strategic value as a bastion of capitalism and anticommunism in

---

5. See the following special issues of *Gunji Shigaku* (Journal of military history): "Kaisen e no kiseki" (Toward Pearl Harbor), 26 (September 1990); "Shinju-wan zengo" (On the eve of Pearl Harbor), 27 (December 1991); and "Shūsen" (Termination), 31 (September 1995).

6. Hosoya Chihiro, Honma Nagayo, Iriye Akira, and Hatano Sumio, eds., *Taiheiyō Sensō* (Tokyo: Tokyo Daigaku Shuppan-kai, 1993); Hosoya Chihiro, Iriye Akira, Gotō Ken'ichi, Hatano Sumio, eds., *Taiheiyō Sensō no shūketsu: Ajia Taiheiyō no sengo keisei* (Tokyo: Kashiwa Shobō, 1997).

7. Nakayama Takashi, *Manshū 1945.8.9: Soren-gun shinkō to Nihon-gun* (Manchuria August 9, 1945: the advancing Soviet Army and Japanese Army) (Tokyo: Kokusho Kankō Kai, 1990); idem, *1945-nen natsu saigo no NiSso sen* (Summer 1945 the final Japanese-Soviet War) (Tokyo: Kokusho Kankō Kai, 1995); Handō Kazutoshi, *Soren ga Manshū ni shinkō shita natsu* (The summer when the Soviets invaded Manchuria) (Tokyo: Bungei Shunjū, 1999).

8. For example, Tsuyoshi Hasegawa's *Racing the Enemy: Stalin, Truman, and the Surrender of Japan* (2005) usefully highlighted the US-Soviet endgame in Asia in the context of Japan's decision-making process, with less focus on the role of the China war and Japan's colonial empire in Korea and Manchuria. See Yukiko Koshiro, "Review of Tsuyoshi Hasegawa's *Racing the Enemy: Stalin, Truman, and the Surrender of Japan, Journal of Japanese Studies* 33, no. 1 (2007): 211–16.

the Far East. As long as Japanese today continue to believe that during and shortly after World War II they were utterly ignorant or naïve bystanders of the two superpowers' growing rivalry, the transitional period from World War II to the cold war can never become an integral part of Japanese history. Worse, these critical years of Japanese history might forever remain uncoupled from world history. Japanese people should begin to discuss the Soviet Union as a factor in their own war, particularly the strategic planning of the government and military in "dissolving" the colonial empire and ending the war. They must ask themselves to what extent Japanese strategists anticipated, perhaps even encouraged, the outcome of Japan's war to be the origins of the cold war in Asia.

Since Japan's actions in the final phase of the Eurasian-Pacific War catalyzed the nation's survival and prosperity after surrender, Japanese people today should address the ethics of the total disregard for the lives of their own people behind such planning. If Manchukuo really was strategically allowed to fall to the Soviets, to what extent did the war planners consider the residents of Manchukuo? Postwar Japan has seen passionate debates on the government's sheer disregard of the defense of civilian settlers in Manchuria and Korea. The Imperial General Headquarters War Operations Plans Division considered the early evacuation of Japanese civilian settlers "inappropriate," as it would have contradicted Japan's basic policy of preserving the status quo with the Soviet Union and aroused suspicions. As a result some 180,700 of the 1.5 million civilian settlers in Manchuria died attempting to evacuate from the Soviet attack and repatriate to Japan.[9]

The Japanese prisoners of war taken to the Siberian labor camps after Japan's surrender also remain a highly sensitive aspect of the strategists' motives. The key military strategists Sejima Ryūzō and Tanemura Sakō left Tokyo for Manchuria and Korea respectively a short time before the presumed Soviet attack, arranged for Soviet-Japanese cease-fire, and were themselves arrested and sent to the labor camps. According to one record, the Soviet Army captured some 563,000 Japanese soldiers and 11,700 officials and engineers in Manchukuo—other records claim the combined figures exceed 650,000—and detained them at labor camps across Siberia and elsewhere, some until 1956. Approximately 100,000 of them died in detention. Whether Sejima and other military strategists agreed to the arrest and detention of these soldiers as part of a secret deal with Moscow still cannot be answered due to the lack of conclusive archival evidence in both Japan or Russia.[10]

Vassili Molodiakov, a scholar of Japanese history and international relations, disclosed another secret deal Prince Konoe was planning to propose to Moscow

9. WHS-KA, 339–40, 353–55.

10. Hosaka Masayasu, *Sejima Ryūzō: Sanbō no Shōwa-shi* (Tokyo: Bunshun Bunko, 1991), chapter 1, especially 65–74.

during his peace mission scheduled in the summer of 1945. According to Molodiakov, Konoe was ready not only to acquiesce to Soviet claims over Japanese territory but also to extradite as prisoners of war Kwantung Army soldiers to the Soviet Union to be used as a labor force.[11] Strangely enough even after the "peace" mission failed and the Soviets entered the war, the Kwangtung Army Headquarters proposed the same offer to Marshal Vasilevsky on August 29, 1945. In 1993 the document detailing this transaction was discovered and its content publicized by Kyōdō Tsūshin Sha (Kyodo News), a nonprofit cooperative news agency. In December 2007 thirty former soldiers detained in Siberia sued the Japanese government for the abandonment of its people and soldiers.[12]

The ethics of Japan's wartime actions weigh particularly heavy in postwar Japan's responsibility for its colonial empire, especially Korea. Japanese strategists supported the CCP because they correctly saw that it would be in a better position to take back China for the Chinese. There was no similar concern for the future of Korea. A divided Korea as the outcome of Japan's defeat is in part the legacy of the scant regard Japan as the colonial ruler had for the Korean people.

The racial dimension of Japan's strategizing during the war also needs to be reconsidered. Had the postwar Japanese remembered how they once looked to the Soviet Union (Russia) to bridge East and West racially and culturally, they might have rediscovered that wartime Japan could not be so simplistically characterized as "anti-West," "antiwhite," or "pro-Asian." Japan's Eurasian-Pacific War was never a race war driven by hatred of whites. The racial dimension of the Eurasian-Pacific War provides a key to understanding a radical shift in Japanese racial identity after 1945. Prewar and wartime Japanese people had fluid conceptions of "whiteness" and "Westernness" particularly in relation to the Russian people. The rhetoric of pan-Asianism even endorsed a Russian presence in the Japanese empire. Postwar Japan's encounter with white America under the latter's military occupation radically changed the Japanese perception of race and culture such that they became bound by American norms. Postwar Japanese pursued the second phase of "Escape from Asia," racially and culturally: to detach themselves from Asia and to reposition themselves as "honorary whites" in the American-centered racial hierarchy. The US occupation authority encouraged this kind of

---

11. Vassili Molodiakov, "Yūrashia no senshi Rihyaruto Zoruge (Richard Sorge, the warrior of Eurasia), in Shirai Hisaya and Kobayashi Shun'ichi, eds., *Zoruge wa naze shikei ni saretaka: "kokusai supai jiken" no shinsō* (Why Sorge was executed: the depths of the "international espionage incident") (Tokyo: Shakai Hyōron Sha, 2000), 208.

12. "Kihei kimin no sekinin o tou: Shiberia yokuryū kokka baishō seikyū soshō (Pursuing responsibility for abandoning Japanese soldiers and civilians: lawsuit seeking Japanese government compensation for Siberian detention); the report of the lawsuit is available online at http://www.daiichi.gr.jp/publication/makieya/2008s/05.html.

racial identity for the Japanese as a way to strengthen the security alliance against the communist bloc on the continent.[13] It is doubtful whether as a result of such occupation policy postwar Japanese felt much closer to and more comfortable with "whiteness" than in the prewar period.

Japanese relations with the Russians living in Japan quickly deteriorated after the war. Toward the war's end, Russians in the Tokyo metropolitan area were forced to move to Karuizawa and live there under strict police surveillance. Celebrities such as the baseball hero Victor Starffin were no exception. Some who remained in Tokyo were brought to the Itabashi District, which was dubbed "Rosuke mura" (Russky ghetto).[14] They did not escape the great Tokyo air raid of March 1945. The record of the whereabouts of Russian émigrés after the war is thin. Many migrated to Australia and the United States, some even returned to the Soviet Union. Only a small number of them married into Japanese families, losing their Russian identity.[15] That the majority did not choose to remain in Japan suggests that postwar Japan no longer provided for them a place as comfortable as wartime Japan's propaganda had claimed. Postwar Japanese perceptions of whiteness and themselves became all the more distorted.

The reexamination of Japan's wartime thinking, especially in the final stage in the war, should lead the Japanese to scrutinize the flawed nature of postwar Japan's exclusive commitment to the United States and detachment from Eurasia. Such a lopsided attachment to the US sphere of influence was never what the war planners and strategists, as well as the ordinary citizens, imagined to be Japan's destiny after the defeat. Even after defeated Japan was incorporated into the new defense perimeter of what General MacArthur and Dean Acheson called the "Anglo Saxon lake," or the Pacific Ocean, this vast oceanic division never became as intimate to Japanese lives and hearts as when Japan owned the South Sea Mandate of Micronesia. The Pacific War narrative did not turn Japan into a vital player in the Pacific. Rather, it expelled vanquished Japan from the Pacific Ocean and contained it in what Dean Atcheson articulated as a "great crescent," a metaphor of America's anticommunist bloc stretching from Japan through Southeast Asia and India to the Persian Gulf—the vast region with no unified cultural and geographical identity. Even after the cold war when such containment presumably

13. Yukiko Koshiro, *Trans-Pacific Racisms and the U.S. Occupation of Japan* (New York: Columbia University Press, 1999).

14. "Lyubōfi Semyōnobuna Shūetsu san ni kiku" (Interview with Lyubov Semyonova Shvets, conducted by Shimizu Megumi), in Nakamura Yoshikazu, Naganawa Mitsuo and Nagayo Susumu, eds., *Ikyō ni ikiru*, vol. 2 (Yokohama: Seibun Sha, 2003), 19–21.

15. Petr E. Podalko, "Roshiyajin wa ikani shite rai-Nichi shitaka," in Nakamura, Naganawa, and Nagayo, eds., *Ikyō ni ikiru*, vol. 2, 43–44.

lifted, Japan remains unable to return to either the Pacific Ocean or Eurasia. Defeat in the war did not reorient Japan from the Eurasian continent toward the Pacific Ocean; it displaced Japan in both worlds.

Postwar Japanese have forgotten how wartime Japanese once grasped the trends of rapidly changing world and had been so eager to influence geopolitics. During the war the Japanese synthesized various players and factors in world politics and made them guiding principles for the nation's survival. In matters of culture and race, ideology and geopolitics, they tried to find equilibrium in the dichotomies of Asia versus the West, yellow versus white, communism versus capitalism, and Eurasia versus the Pacific. They attempted to situate the nation's identity and fate in the balance. By doing so they also sought to neutralize the bankruptcy of Japanese imperialism and colonialism. At irrevocable human and moral cost, they exited the Eurasian theater by letting the dynamics of the cold war guide the liquidation of their colonies. In the last phase of the war they observed the spatial and temporal origins of the cold war in East Asia and let the ensuing competition absorb the aftermath of their abandonment of Manchuria and Korea.

The Japanese began a long voyage into *sengo*, the postwar era, without refining their knowledge and understanding of their war. As they built a postwar "success" on their ensconced islands away from the rubbles of the colonial empire, they quickly and thoroughly obliterated their colonial responsibility for Asia and its peoples. Should the Japanese today bring back the memory of their dexterity in understanding the balance of power and be proud of their preoccupation with the geopolitics in the world, even when to do so would raise ethical questions? Soul searching should begin about whether Japan's manner of "concluding" its war in World War II proved right or tragic, a source of long-term benefit or damage, within the larger historical framework of the twentieth century and beyond. The Japanese people have to come to terms with the sins and virtues of Japan's strategic thinking and planning regarding the Soviet Union and the United States within the larger framework of the twentieth-century world history. Only in this way might they finally have a chance to overcome the long shadow of sengo and start a path toward reconciliation with Eurasia, the United States, and the wider world.

Index

STUDIES OF THE WEATHERHEAD EAST ASIAN INSTITUTE

COLUMBIA UNIVERSITY

Selected Titles

(Complete list at: http://www.columbia.edu/cu/weai/weatherhead-studies.html)

The Nature of the Beasts: Empire and Exhibition at the Tokyo Imperial Zoo, by Ian J. Miller. University of California Press, 2012

Redacted: The Archives of Censorship in Postwar Japan, by Jonathan E. Abel. University of California Press, 2012

Asia for the Asians: China in the Lives of Five Meiji Japanese, by Paula Harrell. MerwinAsia, 2012

The Art of Censorship in Postwar Japan, by Kirsten Cather. University of Hawai'i Press, 2012

Occupying Power: Sex Workers and Servicemen in Postwar Japan, by Sarah Kovner. Stanford University Press, 2012.

Empire of Dogs: Canines, Japan, and the Making of the Modern Imperial World, by Aaron Herald Skabelund. Cornell University Press, 2011.

Russo-Japanese Relations, 1905-17: From enemies to allies, by Peter Berton. Routledge, 2011.

Realms of Literacy: Early Japan and the History of Writing, by David Lurie. Harvard University Asia Series, 2011.

Planning for Empire: Reform Bureaucrats and the Japanese Wartime State, by Janis Mimura. Cornell University Press, 2011

Passage to Manhood: Youth Migration, Heroin, and AIDS in Southwest China, by Shao-hua Liu. Stanford University Press, 2010

Imperial Japan at its Zenith: The Wartime Celebration of the Empire's 2,600th Anniversary, by Kenneth J. Ruoff. Cornell University Press, 2010

Behind the Gate: Inventing Students in Beijing, by Fabio Lanza. Columbia University Press, 2010

Postwar History Education in Japan and the Germanys: Guilty Lessons, by Julian Dierkes. Routledge, 2010

The Aesthetics of Japanese Fascism, by Alan Tansman. University of California Press, 2009

The Growth Idea: Purpose and Prosperity in Postwar Japan, by Scott O'Bryan. University of Hawai'i Press, 2009

National History and the World of Nations: Capital, State, and the Rhetoric of History in Japan, France, and the United States, by Christopher Hill. Duke University Press, 2008

Leprosy in China: A History, by Angela Ki Che Leung. Columbia University Press, 2008

Kingdom of Beauty: Mingei and the Politics of Folk Art in Imperial Japan, by Kim Brandt. Duke University Press, 2007.

Mediasphere Shanghai: The Aesthetics of Cultural Production, by Alexander Des Forges. University of Hawai'i Press, 2007.

Modern Passings: Death Rites, Politics, and Social Change in Imperial Japan, by Andrew Bernstein. University of Hawai'i Press, 2006.

The Making of the "Rape of Nanjing": The History and Memory of the Nanjing Massacre in Japan, China, and the United States, by Takashi Yoshida. Oxford University Press, 2006.